A TEXT BOOK OF

OPTICAL & MICROWAVE COMMUNICATION

For

Semester - I

FINAL YEAR (BE) DEGREE COURSE IN ELECTRONICS / ELECTRONICS AND TELECOMMUNICATION / INDUSTRIAL ELECTRONICS AND ELECTRONICS AND COMMUNICATION ENGINEERING

Strictly As Per the New Revised Syllabus of
Dr. Babasaheb Ambedkar Marathwada University, Aurangabad
(2009-10)

Mrs. REKHA P. LABADE
M.E. (Electronics)
Asst. Professor and Head
Electronics and Telecommunication Deptt.,
Amrutvahini College of Engineering,
SANGAMNER (Dist. Ahmednagar)

Dr. SACHIN RUIKAR
M.E. (Microwave)
Asst. Professor,
Electronics and Telecommunication Deptt.,
Sinhgad Academy of Engineering,
Kondhwa (Bk.), **PUNE.**

NIRALI PRAKASHAN

N2668

OPTICAL & MICROWAVE COMM. (BE: E & TC / EC / IND. ELEC.)   ISBN: 978-93-83525-90-4

First Edition : October 2013

© : Authors

The text of this publication, or any part thereof, should not be reproduced or transmitted in any form or stored in any computer storage system or device for distribution including photocopy, recording, taping or information retrieval system or reproduced on any disc, tape, perforated media or other information storage device etc., without the written permission of Authors with whom the rights are reserved. Breach of this condition is liable for legal action.

Every effort has been made to avoid errors or omissions in this publication. In spite of this, errors may have crept in. Any mistake, error or discrepancy so noted and shall be brought to our notice shall be taken care of in the next edition. It is notified that neither the publisher nor the authors or seller shall be responsible for any damage or loss of action to any one, of any kind, in any manner, therefrom.

Published By :
NIRALI PRAKASHAN
Abhyudaya Pragati, 1312, Shivaji Nagar,
Off J.M. Road, PUNE – 411005
Tel - (020) 25512336/37/39, Fax - (020) 25511379
Email : niralipune@pragationline.com

Printed at
Repro Knowledgecast Limited
India

DISTRIBUTION CENTRES
PUNE

Nirali Prakashan
119, Budhwar Peth, Jogeshwari Mandir Lane
Pune 411002, Maharashtra
Tel : (020) 2445 2044, 66022708, Fax : (020) 2445 1538
Email : niralilocal@pragationline.com

Nirali Prakashan
S. No. 28/25, Dhyari,
Near Pari Company, Pune 411041
Tel : (022) 24690204 Fax : (020) 24690316
Email : bookorder@pragationline.com

MUMBAI
Nirali Prakashan
385, S.V.P. Road, Rasdhara Co-op. Hsg. Society Ltd.,
Girgaum, Mumbai 400004, Maharashtra
Tel : (022) 2385 6339 / 2386 9976, Fax : (022) 2386 9976
Email : niralimumbai@pragationline.com

DISTRIBUTION BRANCHES

NAGPUR
Pratibha Book Distributors
Above Maratha Mandir, Shop No. 3, First Floor,
Rani Jhanshi Square, Sitabuldi, Nagpur 440012,
Maharashtra, Tel : (0712) 254 7129

BENGALURU
Pragati Book House
House No. 1, Sanjeevappa Lane, Avenue Road Cross,
Opp. Rice Church, Bengaluru – 560002.
Tel : (080) 64513344, 64513355,
Mob : 9880582331, 9845021552
Email:bharatsavla@yahoo.com

JALGAON
Nirali Prakashan
34, V. V. Golani Market, Navi Peth, Jalgaon 425001,
Maharashtra, Tel : (0257) 222 0395
Mob : 94234 91860

KOLHAPUR
Nirali Prakashan
New Mahadvar Road,
Kedar Plaza, 1st Floor Opp. IDBI Bank
Kolhapur 416 012, Maharashtra. Mob : 9855046155

CHENNAI
Pragati Books
9/1, Montieth Road, Behind Taas Mahal, Egmore,
Chennai 600008 Tamil Nadu, Tel : (044) 6518 3535,
Mob : 94440 01782 / 98450 21552 / 98805 82331, Email : bharatsavla@yahoo.com

RETAIL OUTLETS
PUNE

Pragati Book Centre
157, Budhwar Peth, Opp. Ratan Talkies,
Pune 411002, Maharashtra
Tel : (020) 2445 8887 / 6602 2707, Fax : (020) 2445 8887

Pragati Book Centre
Amber Chamber, 28/A, Budhwar Peth,
Appa Balwant Chowk, Pune : 411002, Maharashtra,
Tel : (020) 20240335 / 66281669
Email : pbcpune@pragationline.com

Pragati Book Centre
676/B, Budhwar Peth, Opp. Jogeshwari Mandir,
Pune 411002, Maharashtra
Tel : (020) 6601 7784 / 6602 0855

PBC Book Sellers & Stationers
152, Budhwar Peth, Pune 411002, Maharashtra
Tel : (020) 2445 2254 / 6609 2463

MUMBAI
Pragati Book Corner
Indira Niwas, 111 - A, Bhavani Shankar Road, Dadar (W), Mumbai 400028, Maharashtra
Tel : (022) 2422 3526 / 6662 5254, Email : pbcmumbai@pragationline.com

www.pragationline.com   info@pragationline.com

Dedicated to

* *Hon'ble Dr. Sudhirji Tambe and Mrs. Durgatai Tambe*

— **Mrs. Rekha Labade**

* *My Daughter Ku. Sonal*

— **Sachin Ruikar**

Preface...

It gives us great pleasure for giving the book **'Optical and Microwave Communication'**. This book is written in accordance with the syllabus of BE (E & TC) and Electronics Group of Dr. Babasaheb Ambedkar Marathwada University, Aurangabad.

The book is the combination of two sections, viz. Fiber Optic Communication and Microwave Communication. Therefore, proper care has been taken to give indepth knowledge of both the sections. In order to give a clear idea and also to cover all six units, the chapters are assigned as per the units mentioned in the syllabus.

As the subject is more of descriptive in nature, care has been taken to include the required formulae in order to solve numericals. Every unit is included a large number of **Solved Problems, Important Points to Remember and Questions** in order to provide better learning process from the students perspective.

A set of **Oral Questions** listed at the end of the book will enhance the knowledge of the students in the subject and also to perform better in their practical and oral course also.

Nirali Prakashan put the book, what we thought of into reality. Our sincere thanks to Shri. Dineshbhai Furia, Shri. Jignesh Furia and Shri. M. P. Munde. The books could be completed in time, due to sincere and hard work of Nirali Prakashan's staff namely Mr. Malik Shaikh, Mrs. Prajakta, Mrs. Sonal and Miss Chaitali Takale. We thank them all.

Valuable suggestions from our esteemed readers to improve the text will be most welcome and highly appreciated.

8th October, Pune   **Authors**

Syllabus ...

1. **Introduction to OFC and its Components**

   Optical fiber communication system, Advantages over other communication systems. Ray theory, types of fibers, Fiber materials, Fiber fabrication (Double crucible method) and their Mechanical Properties, Fiber cable. Basics of light sources (LED and LASER), Light detectors (PIN and APD), Numericals based on above topics.

2. **Signal Degradation in Optical Fiber**

   Various degradation mechanisms: Attenuation, Dispersion-Intermodal and Intra modal, Pulse broadening in GI fibers, Mode coupling, Coupling losses, Fiber splicing, Connectorization, Coupling methods and their losses, Numericals based on above topics.

3. **FOC System**

   Analog: Overview of analog links.

   Digital: Point-to-point links, System consideration, Link power budget, Rise time budget, Wavelength division multiplexing, Optical networks: SONET/SDH, Photonic switching and sensor applications. OTDR (Principle, Concept and applications), Numericals based on above topics.

4. **Microwave Wave-guides and Components**

   Rectangular wave-guide, Wave equation, Modes (TE and TM), Excitation of modes, Power transmission and losses.

   Microwave cavity resonator, Wave guide Tees (E, H, Magic), Circulators, Isolators, Bends, Twists, Matched termination, Attenuators, Phase shifters, Co-axial to waveguide transitions, Microwave filters, Concept of Scattering parameters, S-matrix of above components, Numericals based on above topics.

5. **Microwave Tubes**

   High frequency limitations of conventional vacuum tubes (triode, Tetrode, Pentode), Klystrons (multicavity, reflex): velocity modulation, bunching process, applications, TWT: slow-wave structure, Wave modes, gain and Applications, Magnetron oscillator, Types, Numericals based on above topics.

6. **Solid-State Microwave Devices**

   Principle of operation, Construction, Characteristics, Parameters with analysis of Microwave transistor, Varactor Diode, Tunnel, PIN Diode, Gunn Diode.

***

Contents ...

1. **Introduction to OFC and its Components**   1.1 - 1.58

2. **Signal Degradation in Optical Fiber**   2.1 - 2.60

3. **FOC System**   3.1 - 3.60

4. **Microwave Wave-guides and Components**   4.1 - 4.86

5. **Microwave Tubes**   5.1 - 5.40

6. **Solid-State Microwave Devices**   6.1 - 6.24

- **Oral Questions**   O.1 - O.12

***

Unit I

INTRODUCTION TO OFC AND ITS COMPONENTS

1.1 Introduction

During the past 10 years, a phenomenal increase in voice, data, and video communications has caused a corresponding increase in the demand for more economical and larger capacity communications systems and hence caused a technical revolution in the electronic communications industry.

Communications systems that use light as the carrier of information-have recently received a great deal of attention. Communications systems that carry information through a *guided fiber cable* are called *fiber optic systems*. The *information-carrying capacity* of a communications system is directly proportional to its bandwidth; the wider the bandwidth, the greater its information-carrying capacity.

For comparison purposes, it is common to express the bandwidth of a system as a percentage of its carrier frequency. For instance, a VHP radio system operating at 100 MHz could have a bandwidth equal to 10 MHz (i.e., 10% of the carrier frequency). A microwave radio system operating at 6 GHz with a bandwidth equal to 10% of its carrier frequency would have a bandwidth equal to 600 MHz. Thus, the higher the carrier frequency, the wider the bandwidth possible and consequently, the greater the information-carrying capacity.

Light frequencies used in fiber optic systems are between 10^{14} and 4×10^{14} Hz (100,000 to 400,000 GHz). Ten percent of 100,000 GHz is 10,000 GHz. To meet today's communications needs or the needs of the foreseeable future, 10,000 GHz is an excessive bandwidth. However, it does illustrate the capabilities of optical fiber systems.

1.2 History of Fiber Optics

Actually, visual light was a primary means of communicating long before electronic communications came about. Smoke signals and mirrors were used ages ago to convey short, simple messages. Bell's contraption, however, was the first attempt at using a beam of light for carrying information. Transmission of light waves for any useful distance through Earth's atmosphere is impractical because water vapour, oxygen, and particulates in the air absorb and attenuate the signals at light frequencies. Consequently, the only practical type of optical communications system is one that uses a fiber guide.

In 1930, J. L. Baird, an English scientist, and C. W. Hansell, a scientist from the United States, were granted patents for scanning and transmitting television images through uncoated fiber cables. A few years later a German scientist named H. Lamm successfully transmitted images through a single glass fiber. At that time, most people considered fiber optics more of a toy or a laboratory stunt and, consequently, it was not until the early 1950's that any substantial breakthrough was made in the field of fiber optics. In 1951, A. C. S. Van Heel of Holland and H. H. Hopkins and N. S. Kapany of England experimented with light transmission through *bundles* of fibers. Their studies led to the development of the *flexible fiberscope*, which is used extensively in the medical field. It was Kapany who coined the term "fiber optics" in 1956.

In 1958, Charles H. Townes, an American, and Arthur L. Schawlow, a Canadian, wrote a paper describing how it was possible to use stimulated emission for amplifying light waves (laser) as well as microwaves (maser). Two years later, Theodore H. Maiman, a scientist with Hughes Aircraft Company, built the first optical maser. The laser (light amplification by stimulated emission of radiation) was invented in 1960. The laser's relatively high output power, high frequency of operation, and capability of carrying an extremely wide bandwidth signal make it ideally suited for high-capacity communications systems. The invention of the laser greatly accelerated research efforts in fiber optic communications, although it was not until 1967 that K. C. Kao and G. A. Bockham of the Standard Telecommunications Laboratory in England proposed a new communications medium using *cladded* fiber cables.

The fiber cables available in the 1960's were extremely lossy (more than 1000 dB/km), which limited optical transmissions to short distances. In 1970, Kapron, Keck, and Maurer of Corning Glass Works in Corning, New York, developed an optical fiber with losses less than 2 dB/km. That was the "big" breakthrough needed to permit practical fiber optics communications systems. Since 1970, fiber optics technology has grown exponentially. Recently, Bell Laboratories successfully transmitted 1 billion bps through a fiber cable for 600 mi without a regenerator. In the late 1970's and early 1980's, the refinement of optical cables and the development of high-quality, affordable light sources and detectors opened the door to the development of high-quality, high-capacity and efficient fiber optics communications systems. The branch of electronics that deals with light is called optoelectronics.

1.3 Optical Fibers Vs Metallic Cable Facilities

Communications through glass or plastic fiber cables has several overwhelming advantages over communications using conventional metallic or *co-axial* cable facilities.

1.3.1 Advantages of Fiber Systems

1. Fiber systems have a **greater capacity** due to the inherently larger bandwidths available with optical frequencies. Metallic cables exhibit capacitance between and inductance along their conductors. These properties cause them to act as low-pass filters, which limit their transmission frequencies and bandwidths.

2. Fiber systems are immune to **cross talk** between cables caused by magnetic induction. Glass or plastic fibers are non-conductors of electricity and therefore, do not have a magnetic field associated with them. In metallic cables, the primary cause of cross talk is magnetic induction between conductors located near each other.

3. Fiber cables are **immune to static interference** caused by lightning, electric motors, fluorescent lights and other electrical noise sources. This immunity is also attributable to the fact that optical fibers are non-conductors of electricity. Also, fiber cables do not radiate RF energy and therefore, cannot cause interference with other communications systems.

4. Fiber cables are **more resistive to environmental** extremes. They operate over a larger temperature variations than their metallic counterparts and fiber cables are affected less by corrosive liquids and gases.

5. Fiber cables are **safer and easier to install** and maintain. Because glass and plastic fibers are non-conductors, there are no electrical currents or voltages associated with them. Fibers can be used around volatile liquids and gases without worrying about their causing explosions or fires. Fibers are smaller and much more lightweight than their metallic counterparts. Consequently, they are easier to work with. Also, fiber cables require less storage space and are cheaper to transport.

6. Fiber cables are **more secure** than their copper counterparts. It is virtually impossible to tap into a fiber cable without the user knowing about it. This is another quality attractive for military applications.

7. Fiber systems will **last longer** than metallic facilities. This assumption is based on the higher tolerances that fiber cables have to change in the environment.

8. The long-term cost of a fiber optic system is projected to be less than that of metallic counterpart.

1.3.2 Disadvantages of Fiber Systems

1. The higher initial cost of installing a fiber system, although in the future it is believed that the cost of installing a fiber system will be reduced dramatically.

2. There are no systems that have been in operation for an extended period of time.
3. Maintenance and repair of fiber systems is also more difficult and expensive than metallic systems.

1.4 Ray Theory

The total electromagnetic frequency spectrum is shown in Fig. 1.1. It can be seen that the frequency spectrum extends from a few hertz to gamma rays (10^{18} Hz). The light frequency spectrum can be divided into three general bands:

(i) **Infrared:** Band of light wavelengths that are too long to be seen by the human eye.

(ii) **Visible light:** Band of light wavelengths that the human eye will respond to.

(iii) **Ultraviolet:** Band of light wavelengths that are too short to be seen by the human eye.

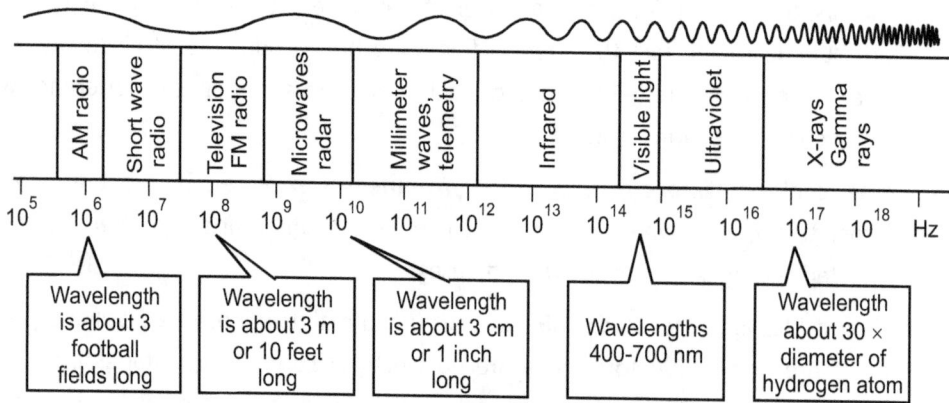

Fig. 1.1: Total Electromagnetic Frequency Spectrum

When dealing with higher-frequency electromagnetic waves, such as light, it is common to use units of *wavelength* rather than frequency. Wavelength is the length of the wave that one cycle of an electromagnetic wave occupies in space. The wavelength depends on the frequency of the wave and the velocity of light. Mathematically, wavelength is,

$$\lambda = \frac{c}{f} \quad \ldots (1.1)$$

where, λ = wavelength (m/cycle)
c = velocity of light (300,000,000 m/s)
f = frequency (Hz)

With light frequencies, wavelength is often stated in *microns* (1 micron = 1 micro-meter) or nanometers (1 nanometer = 10^{-9} meters or 0.001 micron). However, when describing the optical spectrum, the unit angstrom (Å) often has been used to express wavelength (1 Å = 10^{-10} meters or 0.0001 micron).

1.5 Optical Fiber Communications Systems

Fig. 1.2 shows a simplified block diagram of an optical fiber communications link. The three primary building blocks of the link are:
1. Transmitter   2. Receiver   3. Fiber

The transmitter consists of an analog or digital interface, a voltage-to-current converter, a light source, and a source-to-fiber light coupler. The fiber guide is either an ultra pure glass or plastic cable. The receiver includes a fiber-to-light detector coupling device, a photo detector, a current-to-voltage converter, an amplifier and an analog or digital interface.

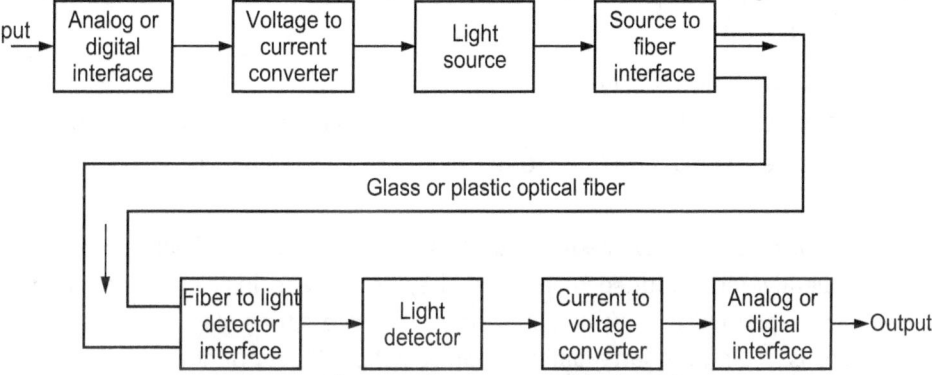

Fig. 1.2: Fiber Optic Communications Link

In an optical fiber transmitter, the light source can be modulated by a digital or an analog signal. For analog modulation, the input interface matches impedances and limits the input signal amplitude. For digital modulation, the original source may already be in digital form or, if in analog form, it must be converted to a digital pulse stream. For the latter case, an analog-to-digital converter must be included in the interface.

The voltage-to-current converter serves as an electrical interface between the input circuitry and the light source. The light source is either a light-emitting diode (LED) or an injection laser diode (ILD). The amount of light emitted by either an LED or an ILD is proportional to the amount of drive current. Thus, the voltage-to-current converter converts an input signal voltage to a current that is used to drive the light source.

The source-to-fiber coupler (such as a lens) is a mechanical interface. Its function is to couple the light emitted by the source into the optical fiber cable. The optical fiber consists of a glass or plastic fiber core, a cladding, and a protective jacket. The fiber-to-light detector coupling device is also a mechanical coupler. Its function is to couple as much light as possible from the fiber cable into the light detector.

The light detector is very often either a PIN (P-type-Intrinsic-N-type) diode or an APD (Avalanche Photo Diode). Both the APD and the PIN diode convert light energy to current. Consequently, a current-to-voltage converter is required. The current-to-voltage converter transforms changes in detector current to changes in output signal voltage. The analog or digital interface at the receiver output is also an electrical interface. If analog modulation is used, the interface matches impedances and signal levels to the output circuitry. If digital modulation is used, the interface must include a digital-to-analog converter.

1.6 Fiber Types

Essentially, there are three varieties of optical fibers available today. All three varieties are constructed of either glass, plastic or a combination of glass and plastic.

The three varieties are:
1. Plastic core and cladding (PCC).
2. Glass core with plastic cladding (often called PCS fiber, Plastic-Clad Silica).
3. Glass core and glass cladding (often called SCS, Silica-Clad Silica).

Plastic fibers have several advantages over glass fibers. First, plastic fibers are more flexible and, consequently, more rugged than glass. They are easy to install, can better withstand stress, are less expensive, and weigh approximately 60% less than glass. The disadvantage of plastic fibers is their high attenuation characteristics; they do not propagate light as efficiently as glass. Consequently, plastic fibers are limited to relatively short runs, such as within a single building or a building complex.

Fibers with glass cores exhibit low attenuation characteristics. However, PCS fibers are slightly better than SCS fibers. Also, PCS fibers are less affected by radiation and, therefore, are more attractive to military applications.

SCS fibers have the best propagation characteristics and they are easier to terminate than PCS fibers. Unfortunately, SCS cables are the least rugged and they are more susceptible to increase in attenuation when exposed to radiation. Therefore, the selection of a fiber for a particular application is a function of specific system requirements. There are always trade-offs based on the economics and logistics of a particular application.

1.7 Cable Construction

There are many different cable designs available today. Fig. 1.3 shows examples of several fiber optic cable configurations. Depending on the configuration, the cable may include a *core*, a *cladding*, a *protective tube*, *buffers*, *strength members*, and one or more *protective jackets*.

With the *loose* tube construction (shown in Fig. 1.3 (a)) each fiber is contained in a protective tube. Inside the protective tube, a polyurethane compound encapsulates the fiber and prevents the intrusion of water.

Fig. 1.3 (b) shows the construction of a constrained optical fiber cable. Surrounding the fiber cable are a primary and a secondary buffer. The buffer jackets provide protection for the fiber from external mechanical influences that could cause fiber breakage or excessive optical attenuation. Kevlar is a yarn-type material that increases the tensile strength of the cable. Again, an outer protective tube is filled with polyurethane, which prevents moisture from coming into contact with the fiber core.

Fig. 1.3 (c) shows a multiple-strand configuration. To increase the tensile strength, a steel central member and a layer of Mylar tape wrap are included in the package. Fig. 1.3 (d) shows a ribbon configuration, which is frequently seen in telephone systems using fiber optics. Fig. 1.3 (e) shows both the end and side views of a plastic-clad silica cable. The type of cable construction used depends on the performance requirements of the system and both the economic and environmental constraints.

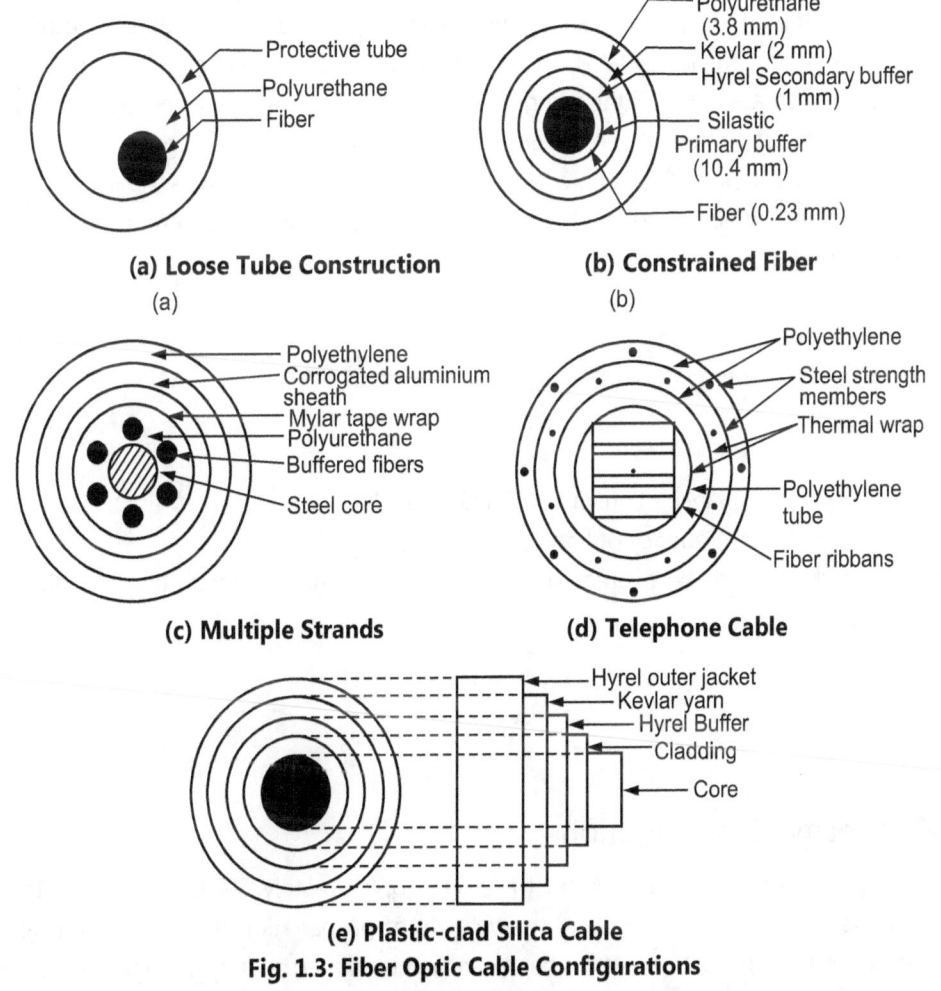

Fig. 1.3: Fiber Optic Cable Configurations

1.8 Light Propagation

1.8.1 The Physics of Light

Although the performance of optical fibers can be analyzed completely by application of Maxwell's equations, this is necessarily complex. For most practical applications, *geometric wave tracing* may be used instead of Maxwell's equations; ray tracing will yield sufficiently accurate results. An atom has several energy levels or states, the lowest of which is the ground state. Any energy level above the ground state is called an *excited state*. If an atom in one energy level decays to a lower energy level, the loss of energy (in electron volts) is emitted as a photon. The energy of the photon is equal to the difference between the energy of the two energy levels. The process of decay from one energy level to another energy level is called *spontaneous decay* or *spontaneous emission*.

Atoms can be irradiated by a light source whose energy is equal to the difference between the ground level and an energy level. This can cause an electron to change from one energy level to another by absorbing light energy. The process of moving from one energy level to another is called absorption. When making the transition from one energy level to another, the atom absorbs a packet of energy called a *photon*. This process is similar to that of emission. The energy absorbed or emitted (photon) is equal to the difference between the two energy levels.

Mathematically,

$$E_2 - E_1 = E_p \qquad \ldots (1.2)$$

where, E_p is the energy of the photon.

Also,

$$E_p = hf \qquad \ldots (1.3)$$

where,

h = Planck's constant = 6.625×10^{34} J-s

f = frequency of light emitted (Hz)

Photon energy may also be expressed in terms of wavelength. Substituting equation (1.1) into equation (1.3) yields,

$$E_p = hf$$
$$= \frac{h \cdot c}{\lambda} \qquad \ldots (1.4)$$

1.8.2 Velocity of Propagation

Electromagnetic energy, such as light, travels at approximately 300,000,000 m/s (186,000 miles per second) in free space. Also, the velocity of propagation is the same for all light frequencies in free space. However, it has been demonstrated that in materials more dense than free space, the velocity is reduced. When the velocity of an electromagnetic wave is reduced as it passes from one medium to another medium of a denser material, the light ray is *refracted* (bent) toward the normal. Also, in materials more dense than free space, all light frequencies do not propagate at the same velocity.

1.8.3 Refraction

Fig. 1.4 (a) shows how a light ray is refracted as it passes from a material of a given density into a less dense material. (Actually, the light ray is not bent, but rather, it changes direction at the interface). Fig. 1.4 (b) shows how sunlight, which contains all light frequencies, is affected as it passes through a material more dense than free space. Refraction occurs at both air/glass interfaces. The violet wavelengths are refracted the most, and the red wavelengths are refracted the least. The spectral separation of white light in this manner is called prismatic refraction. It is this phenomenon that causes rainbows; water droplets in the atmosphere act as small prisms that split the white sunlight into the various wavelengths, creating a visible spectrum of color.

1.8.4 Refractive Index

The amount of bending or refraction that occurs at the interface of two materials of different densities is quite predictable and depends on the *refractive index* (also called *index of refraction*) of the two materials. The refractive index is simply the ratio of the velocity of propagation of a light ray in free space to that of a light ray in a given material. Mathematically, the refractive index is,

$$n = \frac{c}{v}$$

where, c = Speed of light in free space (300,000,000 m/s)
         v = Speed of light in a given material

Although the refractive index is also a function of frequency, the variation in most applications is insignificant and, therefore, omitted. The indexes of refraction of several common materials are given in Table 1.1.

How a light ray reacts when it meets the interface of two transmissive materials that have different indexes of refraction can be explained with *Snell's law*. Snell's law simply states,

$$n_1 \sin \theta_1 = n_2 \sin \theta_2 \quad \ldots (1.5)$$

where,
n_1 = Refractive index of material 1 (unitless)
n_2 = Refractive index of material 2 (unitless)
θ_2 = Angle of incidence (degrees)
θ_2 = Angle of refraction (degrees)

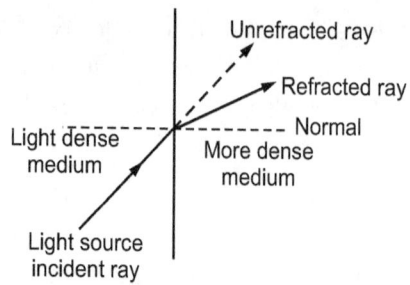

(a) Light Refraction

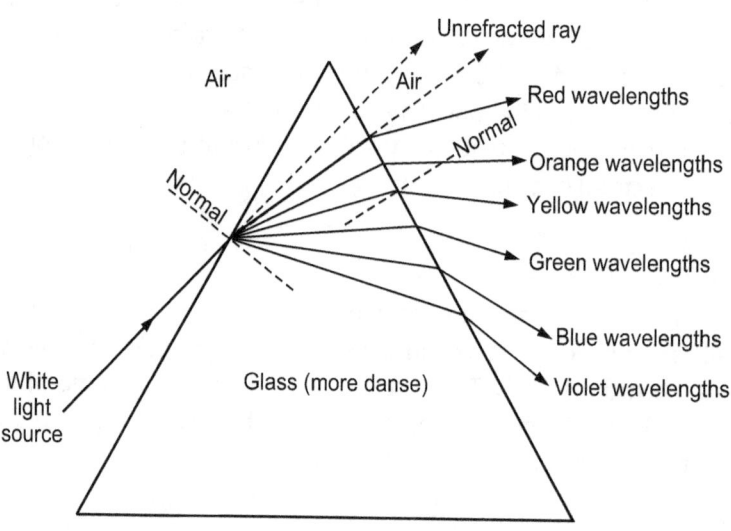

(b) Prismatic Refraction

Fig. 1.4: Refraction of Light

A refractive index model for Snell's law is shown in Fig. 1.5. At the interface, the incident ray may be refracted toward the normal or away from it, depending on whether n_1 is less than or greater than n_2. Fig. 1.6 shows how a light ray is refracted as it travels from a more dense (higher refractive index) material into a less dense (lower refractive index) material. It can be seen that the light ray changes direction at the interface and the angle of refraction is greater than the angle of incidence. Consequently, when a light ray enters a less dense material, the ray bends away from the normal. The normal is simply a line drawn perpendicular to the interface at the point where the incident ray strikes the interface. Similarly, when a light ray enters a more dense material, the ray bends toward the normal.

Table 1.1: Typical Indexes of Refraction

Medium	Index of refraction
Vacuum	1.0
Air	1.0003 (~1.0)
Water	1.33
Ethyl alcohol	1.36
Fused quartz	1.46
Glass fiber	1.5-1.9
Diamond	2.0-2.42
Silicon	34
Gallium-arsenide	3.6

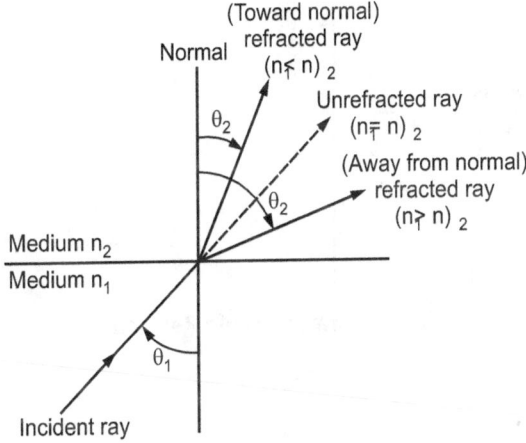

Fig. 1.5: Refractive Model for Snell's Law

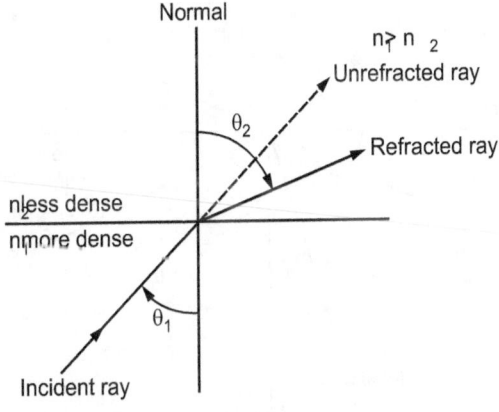

Fig. 1.6: Light ray refracted away from the normal

1.8.5 Critical Angle

Fig. 1.7 shows a condition in which an *incident ray* is at an angle such that the angle of refraction is 90° and the refracted ray is along the interface. (It is important to note that the light ray is travelling from a medium of higher refractive index to a medium with a lower refractive index). Again, using Snell's law,

$$\sin\theta_1 = [n_2/n_1] \cdot \sin\theta_2$$

where, $\theta_2 = 90°$

Therefore, $\sin\theta_1 = [n_2/n_1] \cdot (1)$ or $\sin\theta_1 = [n_2/n_1]$

and $\sin^{-1}[n_2/n_1] = \theta_1 = \theta_c$ ... (1.6)

where, θ_c = Critical angle

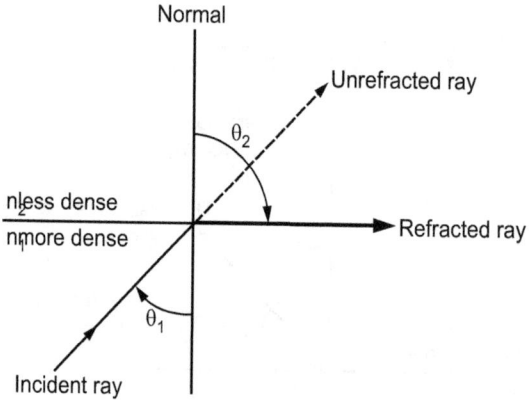

Fig. 1.7: Critical Angle Refraction

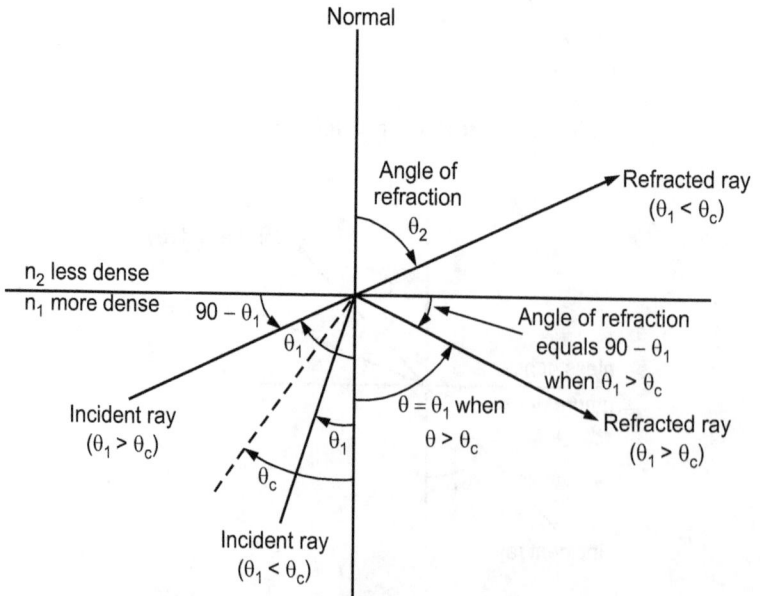

Fig. 1.8: Angle of Reflection and Refraction

The *critical angle* is defined as the minimum angle of incidence at which a light ray may strike the interface of two media and result in an angle of refraction of 90° or greater. (This definition pertains only when the light ray is travelling from a more dense medium into a less dense medium). If the angle of refraction is 90° or greater, the light ray is not allowed to penetrate the less dense material. Consequently, total internal reflection takes place at the interface, and the angle of reflection is equal to the angle of incidence. Fig. 1.8 shows a comparison of the angle of refraction and the angle of reflection when the angle of incidence is less than or more than the critical angle.

1.9 Propagation of Light through an Optical Fiber

Light can be propagated down an optical fiber cable by either **reflection** or **refraction** and how the light is propagated through the fiber depends on the **mode of propagation** and the **index profile** of the fiber.

1.9.1 Mode of Propagation

In fiber optics terminology, the word *mode* simply means path. If there is only one path for light to take down the cable, it is called *single mode*. If there is more than one path, it is called *multimode*. Fig. 1.9 shows single and multimode propagation of light down an optical fiber.

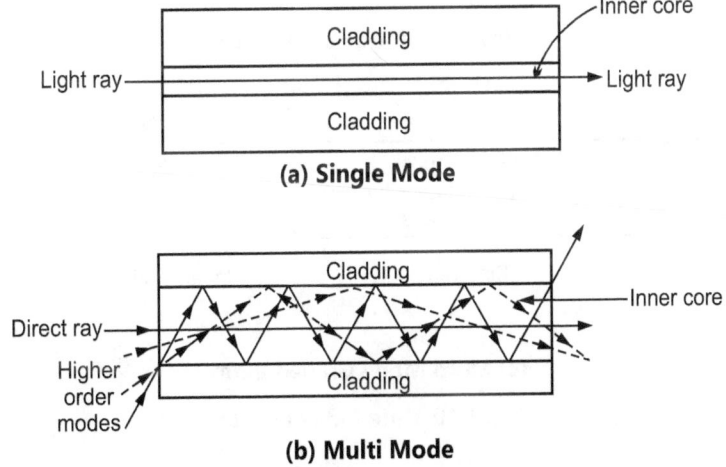

(a) Single Mode

(b) Multi Mode

Fig. 1.9: Modes of Propagation

1.9.2 Index Profile

The index profile of an optical fiber is a graphical representation of the value of the refractive index across the fiber. The refractive index is plotted on the horizontal axis and the radial distance from the core axis is plotted on the vertical axis. Fig. 1.10 shows the core index profiles of three types of fiber cables. There are two basic types of index profiles: step and graded.

A *step-index fiber* has a central core with a uniform refractive index. The core is surrounded by an outside cladding with a uniform refractive index less than, that of the central core. It can be seen that in a step-index fiber there is an abrupt change in the refractive index at the core/cladding interface.

In a graded-index fiber there is no cladding, and the refractive index of the core is non-uniform. It is highest at the center and decreases gradually with distance toward the outer edge.

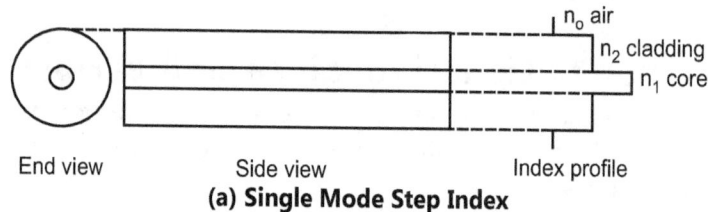
End view   Side view   Index profile
(a) Single Mode Step Index

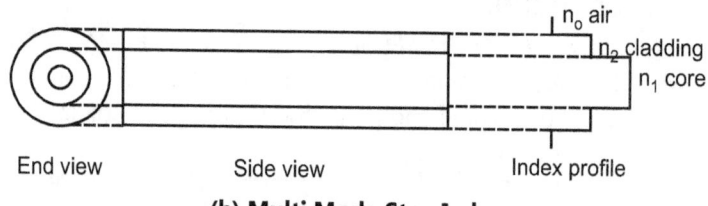
End view   Side view   Index profile
(b) Multi Mode Step Index

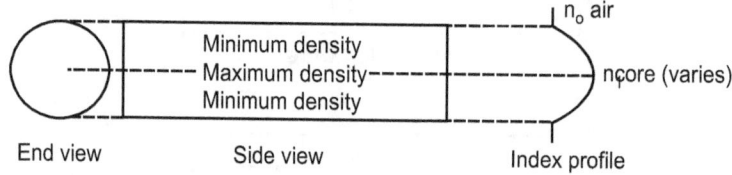
End view   Side view   Index profile
(c) Multi Mode Graded Index

Fig. 1.10: Core Index Profiles

1.10 Configurations of Optical Fiber

There are three types of optical fiber configurations, viz.:

1. Single Mode Step Index
2. Multi Mode Step Index
3. Multi Mode Graded Index

1.10.1 Single Mode Step Index Fiber

A *single mode step index fiber* has a central core that is sufficiently small so that there is essentially only one path that light may take as it propagates down the cable. In this form of single mode step index fiber, the outside cladding is simply air as shown in Fig. 1.11 (a). The refractive index of the glass core (n_1) is approximately 1.5 and the refractive index of the air cladding (n_0) is 1. The large difference in the refractive indexes results in a small critical angle (approximately 42°) at the glass/air interface. Consequently, the fiber will accept light from a wide aperture. This makes it relatively easy to couple light from a source into the cable. However, this type of fiber is typically very weak and of limited practical use.

Another type of single mode step index fiber is one that has a cladding other than air as shown in Fig. 1.11 (b). The refractive index of the cladding (n_2) is slightly less than that of the central core (n_1) and is uniform throughout the cladding. This type of cable is physically stronger than the air clad fiber, but the critical angle is also much higher (approximately 77°). This results in a smaller acceptance angle and a narrow source-to-fiber aperture, making it much more difficult to couple light into the fiber from a light source.

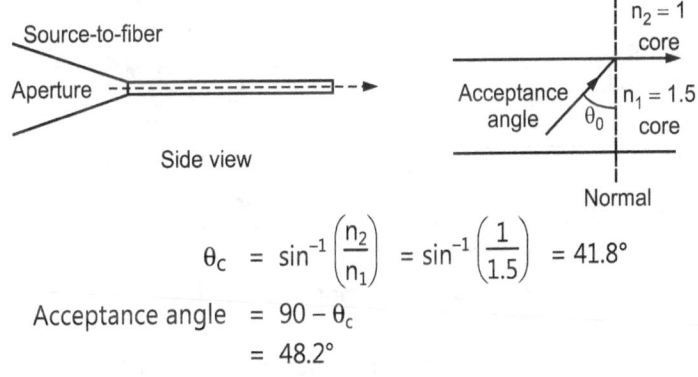

$$\theta_c = \sin^{-1}\left(\frac{n_2}{n_1}\right) = \sin^{-1}\left(\frac{1}{1.5}\right) = 41.8°$$

$$\text{Acceptance angle} = 90 - \theta_c$$
$$= 48.2°$$

(a) Air Cladding

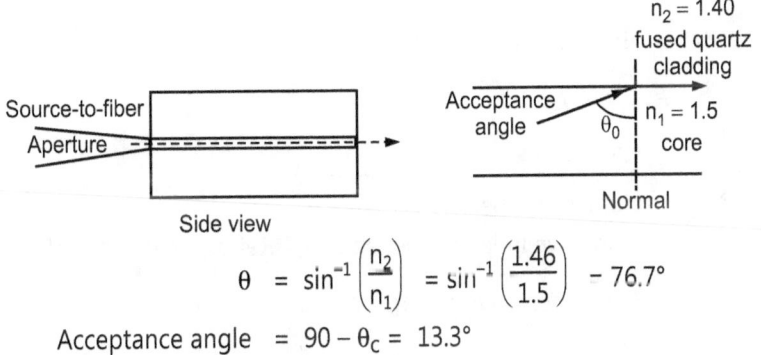

$$\theta = \sin^{-1}\left(\frac{n_2}{n_1}\right) = \sin^{-1}\left(\frac{1.46}{1.5}\right) = 76.7°$$

$$\text{Acceptance angle} = 90 - \theta_c = 13.3°$$

(b) Glass Cladding

Fig. 1.11: Single Mode Step Index

In both types of single mode step index fibers, light is propagated down the fiber through reflection. Light rays that enter the fiber propagate straight down the core or perhaps, are reflected once. Consequently, all light rays follow approximately the same path down the cable and take approximately the same amount of time to travel the length of the cable. This is one significant advantage of single mode step index fibers.

1.10.2 Multimode Step-Index Fiber

A multimode step index fiber is similar to the single mode configuration except that the center core is much larger as shown in Fig. 1.12. This type of fiber has a large light-to-fiber aperture and consequently allows more light to enter the cable. The light rays that strike the core/cladding interface at an angle greater than the critical angle (ray A) are propagated down the core in a zigzag fashion, continuously reflecting off the interface boundary. Light rays that strike the core/cladding interface at an angle less than the critical angle (ray B) enter the cladding and are lost. It can be seen that there are many paths that a light ray may follow as it propagates down the fiber. As a result, all light rays do not follow the same path and, consequently, do not take the same amount of time to travel the length of the fiber.

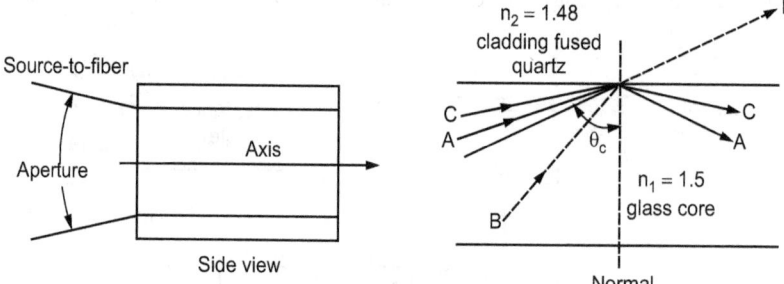

Fig. 1.12: Multi Mode Step Index

The total number of modes (M) in a multimode fiber may be given by,

$$M = \frac{V^2}{2}$$

where,   V = Normalized frequency

$$= \frac{2\pi a}{\lambda}(NA) = \frac{2\pi a n_1 (2\Delta)^{1/2}}{\lambda}$$

where,   a = Core radius

NA = Numerical Aperture = $\sqrt{n_1^2 - n_2^2}$

n_1 = Refractive Index of core and n_2 = Refractive index of cladding

λ = Free space wavelength = $\frac{c}{f}$

Δ = Refractive index difference = $\frac{n_1^2 - n_2^2}{2n_1^2} \simeq \frac{n_1 - n_2}{n_1}$

1.10.3 Multi Mode Graded Index Fiber

A *multimode graded index fiber* is shown in Fig. 1.13. A multimode graded-index fiber is characterized by a central core that has a refractive index that is non-uniform and it is maximum at the center and decreases gradually toward the outer edge. Light is propagated down this type of fiber through refraction. As a light ray propagates diagonally across the core toward the center it is continually intersecting a less-dense-to-more-dense interface. Consequently, the light rays are constantly being refracted, which results in a continuous bending of the light rays. Light enters the fiber at many different angles. As they propagate down the fiber, the light rays that travel in the outermost area of the fiber travel a greater distance than the rays travelling near the center. Because the refractive index decreases with distance from the center and the velocity is inversely proportional to the refractive index, the light rays travelling farthest from the center propagate at a higher velocity. Consequently, they take approximately the same amount of time to travel the length of the fiber.

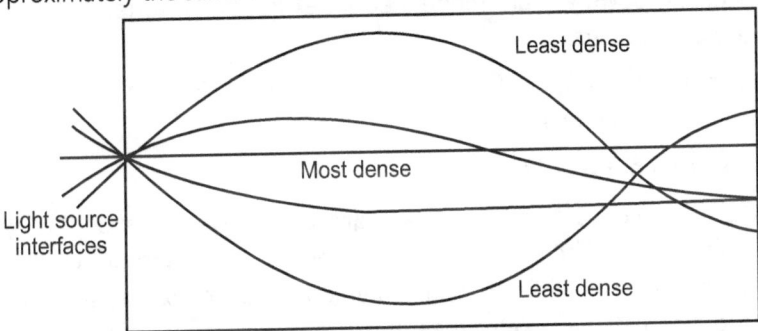

Fig. 1.13: Multimode graded index

1.10.4 Comparison of the Three Types of Optical Fibers

1. **Single mode step index fiber:**

Advantages:
   (i) There is minimum dispersion. Because all rays propagating down. The fiber take approximately the same path, they take approximately the same amount of time to travel down the cable. Consequently, a pulse of light entering the cable can be reproduced at the receiving end very accurately.
   (ii) Larger bandwidths and higher information transmission rates are possible with single mode step index fibers than with the other types of fibers, because of the high accuracy in reproducing transmitted pulses at the receiving end.

Disadvantages:
   (i) It is difficult to couple light into and out of this type of fiber, because the central core is very small. The source-to-fiber aperture is the smallest of all the fiber types.

(ii) A highly directive light source such as a LASER is required to couple light into a single mode step index fiber, because of the small central core.

(iii) Single-mode step-index fibers are expensive and difficult to manufacture.

2. Multimode step index fiber:

Advantages:

(i) Multi mode step index fibers are inexpensive and simple to manufacture.

(ii) It is easy to couple light into and out of multimode step index fibers; they have a relatively large source-to-fiber aperture.

Disadvantages:

(i) Light rays take many different paths down the fiber, which results in large differences in their propagation times. Because of this, rays travelling down this type of fiber have a tendency to spread out. Consequently, a pulse of light propagating down a multi mode step index fiber is distorted more than with the other types of fibers.

(ii) The bandwidth and rate of information transfer possible with this type of cable are less than the other types.

3. Multimode graded-index fiber:

Essentially, there are no outstanding advantages or disadvantages of this type of fiber. Multi-mode graded index fibers are easier to couple light into and out of as compared to step-index fibers but more difficult than multimode step index fibers. Distortion due to multiple propagation paths is greater than in single mode step index fibers but less than in multimode step index fibers. Graded index fibers are easier to manufacture than single mode step index fibers but more difficult than multimode step index fibers. The multimode graded index fiber is considered an intermediate fiber compared to the other types.

1.10.5 Acceptance Angle and Acceptance Cone

Fig. 1.14 shows the source end of a fiber cable, which helps to deal with the light-gathering ability of the fiber or the ability to couple light from the source into the fiber cable. When light rays enter the fiber, they strike the air/glass interface at normal A. The refractive index of air is 1 and the refractive index of the glass core is 1.5. Consequently, the light entering at the air/glass interface propagates from a less dense medium into a more dense medium. Under these conditions and according to Snell's law, the light rays will refract toward the normal. This causes the light rays to change direction and propagate diagonally down the core at an angle (θ_c) that is different than the external angle of incidence at the air/glass interface (θ_{in}). In order for a ray of light to propagate down the cable, it must strike the internal core/cladding interface at an angle that is greater than the critical angle (θ_c).

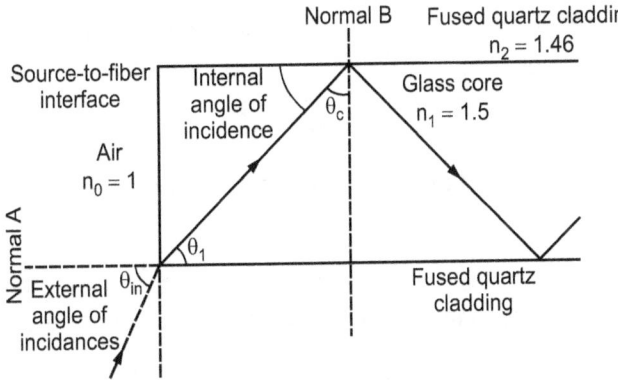

(a) Propagation of Light Ray into and down an Optical Fiber Cable

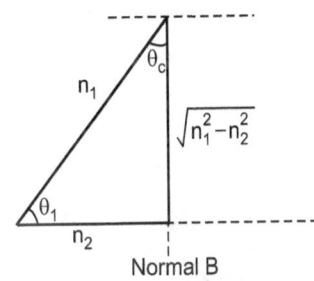

(b) Geometric Relationship
Fig. 1.14: Source End of a Fiber Cable

Applying Snell's law to the external angle of incidence yields the following expression:

$$n_0 \sin \theta_0 = n_1 \sin \theta_1 \qquad \ldots (1.7)$$

and
$$\theta_1 = 90 - \theta_c$$

Thus,
$$\sin \theta_1 = \sin(90 - \theta_c) = \cos \theta_c \qquad \ldots (1.8)$$

Substituting equation (1.8) into equation (1.7) yields the following expression, we get,

$$n_0 \sin \theta_{in} = n_1 \cos \theta_c$$

Rearranging and solving for $\sin \theta_{in}$ gives us,

$$\sin \theta_{in} = [n_1/n_0] \cos \theta_c \qquad \ldots (1.9)$$

The geometric relationship of equation (1.9) has been shown in Fig. 1.14 (b) and using the Pythagorean theorem, we get,

$$\cos \theta_c = \frac{\sqrt{n_1^2 - n_2^2}}{n_1} \qquad \ldots (1.10)$$

Substituting equation (1.10) into equation (1.9) yields,

$$\sin \theta_{in} = \frac{n_1}{n_0} \frac{\sqrt{n_1^2 - n_2^2}}{n_1} \qquad \ldots (1.11)$$

Because light rays generally enter the fiber from an air medium, n_0 is equal to 1. This reduces the equation and is given by,

$$\theta_{in}(max) = \sin^{-1}\sqrt{n_1^2 - n_2^2} \qquad \ldots (1.12)$$

where, θ_{in} is called the **acceptance angle** or **acceptance cone half-angle**.

Acceptance Angle: It is the maximum angle in which external light rays may strike the air/fiber interface and still propagate down the fiber with a response that is no greater than 10 dB down from the peak value.

Acceptance Cone: Rotating the acceptance angle around the fiber axis describes the acceptance cone of the fiber input and is shown in Fig. 1.15.

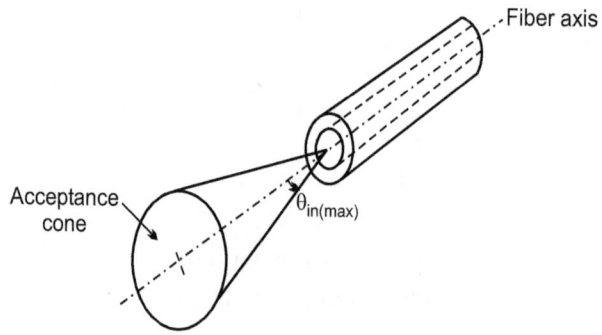

Fig. 1.15: Acceptance Cone

1.10.6 Numerical Aperture

Numerical Aperture (NA) is a figure of merit that is used to describe the light-gathering or light-collecting ability of an optical fiber. The larger the magnitude of NA, the greater the amount of light accepted by the fiber from the external light source. For a step index fiber, numerical aperture is mathematically defined as the sine of the acceptance half-angle.

Thus,
$$NA = \sin \theta_{in}$$

$$NA = \sqrt{n_1^2 - n_2^2} \qquad \ldots (1.13)$$

and also,
$$\sin^{-1} NA = \theta_{in} \qquad \ldots (1.14)$$

For a graded index, NA is simply the sine of the critical angle i.e,

$$NA = \sin \theta_c \qquad \ldots (1.15)$$

1.11 Light Sources

In fiber optic communications systems, there are two devices commonly used to generate light:

(i) Light Emitting Diodes (LEDs)

(ii) Injection Laser Diodes (ILDs).

Both devices have advantages and disadvantages and selection of one device over the other is determined by system economic and performance requirements.

1.11.1 Light Emitting Diodes

A Light Emitting Diode (LED) is simply a p-n junction diode. It is usually made from a semiconductor material such as aluminum gallium arsenide (AlGaAs) or gallium arsenide phosphide (GaAsP). LEDs emit light by spontaneous emission; light is emitted as a result of the recombination of electrons and holes. When forward biased, minority carriers are injected across the p-n junction. Once, across the junction, these minority carriers recombine with majority carriers and give up energy in the form of light. This process is essentially the same as in a conventional diode except that in LEDs certain semiconductor materials and dopants are choosen such that the process is radiative; a photon is produced.

A photon is a quantum of electromagnetic wave energy. Photons are particles that travel at the speed of light but at rest have no mass. In conventional semiconductor diodes (germanium and silicon, for example), the process is primarily non-radiative and no photons are generated. The energy gap of the material used to construct an LED determines whether the light emitted by it is invisible or visible and of what colour.

Classification of LED Structures:

1. **Homojunction LED:** This may be of epitaxially grown or single-diffused devices as shown in Fig. 1.16. Epitaxially grown LEDs are generally constructed of silicon-doped gallium arsenide (Fig. 1.16 (a)). A typical wavelength of light emitted from this construction is 940 nm, and a typical output power is approximately 3 mW at 100 mA of forward current. Planar diffused (homojunction) LEDs (Fig. 1.16 (b)) output approximately 500 µW at a wavelength of 900 nm. The primary disadvantage of homojunction LEDs is the non-directionality of their light emission, which makes them a poor choice as a light source for fiber optic systems.

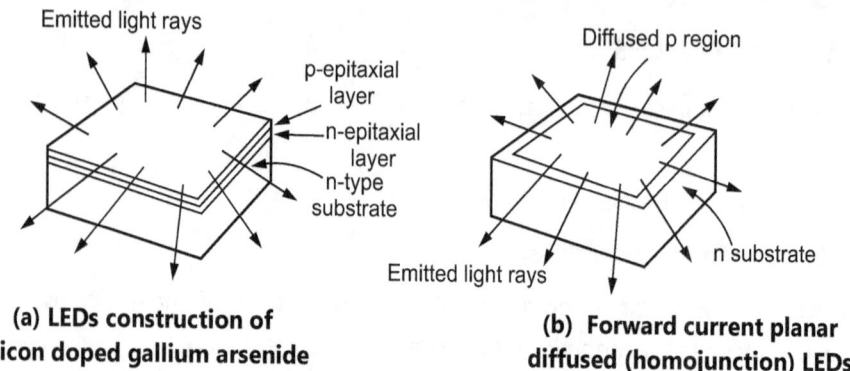

(a) LEDs construction of silicon doped gallium arsenide

(b) Forward current planar diffused (homojunction) LEDs

Fig. 1.16: Homojunction LED

2. Planar Heterojunction LED: This is quite similar to the epitaxially grown LED except that the geometry is designed such that the forward current is concentrated to a very small area of the active layer (Fig. 1.17). Because of this, the planar heterojunction LED has several advantages over the homojunction type. They are:

- The increase in current density generates a more brilliant light spot.
- The smaller emitting area makes it easier to couple its emitted light into a fiber.
- The small effective area has a smaller capacitance, which allows the planar heterojunction LED to be used at higher speeds.

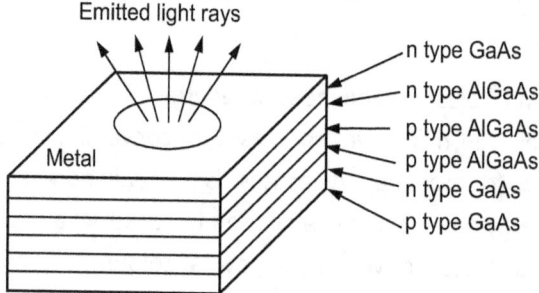

Fig. 1.17: Planar Heterojunction LED

3. Burrus etched-well surface-emitting LED: This used for more practical applications, such as telecommunications where the data rates in excess of 100 Mbps are required. This etched-well LED was developed. Burrus and Dawson of Bell Laboratories. It is a surface-emitting LED and is shown in Fig. 1.18. The Burrus etched-well LED emits light in many directions. The etched well helps concentrate the emitted light to a very small area. Also, domed lenses can be placed over the emitting surface to direct the light into a smaller area. These devices are more efficient than the standard surface emitters and they allow more power to be coupled into the optical fiber, but they are also more difficult and expensive to manufacture.

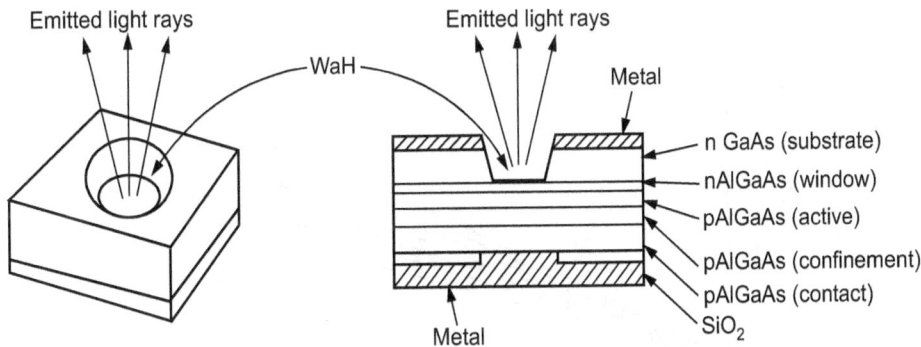

Fig. 1.18: Burrus etched-well surface-emitting LED

4. Edge-emitting LED: The edge-emitting LED, developed by RCA, is shown in Fig. 1.19. These LEDs emit a more directional light pattern than do the surface-emitting LEDs. The construction is similar to the planar and Burrus diodes except that the emitting surface is a stripe rather than a confined circular area. The light is emitted from an active stripe and forms an elliptical beam. Surface-emitting LEDs are more commonly used than edge emitters because they emit more light. However, the coupling losses with surface emitters are greater and they have narrower bandwidths.

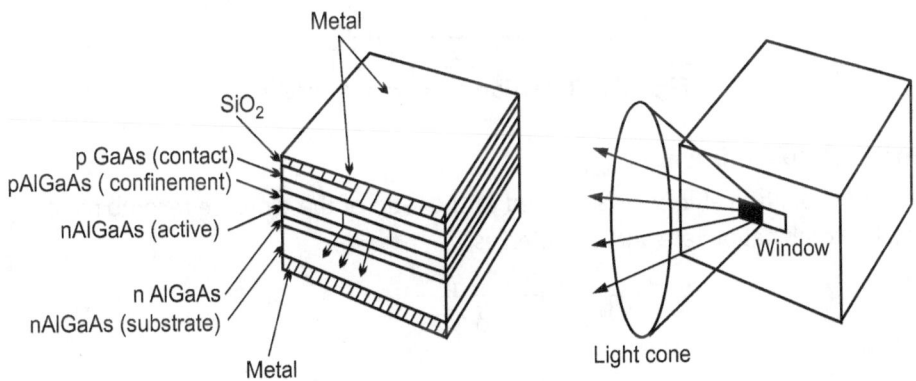

Fig. 1.19: Edge-emitting LED

The radiant light power emitted from an LED is a linear function of the forward current passing through the device as shown in Fig. 1.20. It can also be seen that the optical output power of an LED is in part, a function of the operating temperature. Fig. 1.21 shows the radiation pattern of typical LED.

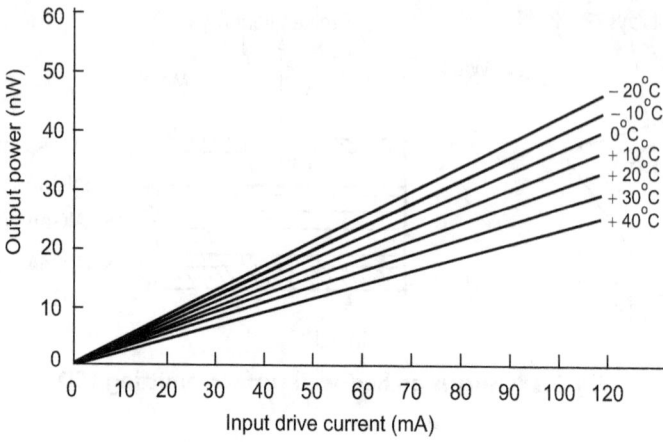

Fig. 1.20: Characteristics of typical LED

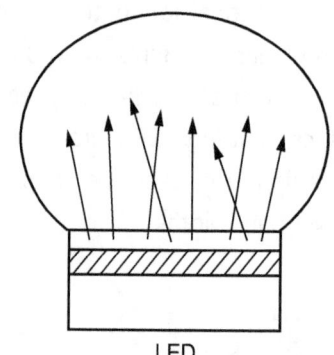

Fig. 1.21: Radiation pattern of typical LED

Internal Quantum Efficiency (η_{int}):

The internal quantum efficiency is defined as the ratio of the radiative recombination rate to the total recombination rate and is written as,

$$\eta_{int} = \frac{\gamma_r}{\gamma_t} = \frac{\gamma_r}{\gamma_r + \gamma_{nr}} \qquad \ldots (1.16)$$

where,

γ_r is the radiative recombination rate per unit volume.

γ_{nr} is the non-radiative recombination rate per unit volume.

By rearranging (1.16), we get,

$$\therefore \quad \gamma_r = \eta_{int} \cdot \gamma_t \qquad \ldots (1.17)$$

where,

γ_t = Total number of recombinations per second = $\frac{i}{e}$

i = Forward biased current into the device

e = Charge on an electron = 1.602×10^{-19} C

Therefore, from equation (1.17),

$$\therefore \quad \gamma_r = \eta_{int} \cdot \frac{i}{e} \quad \ldots (1.18)$$

Since, γ_r is also equivalent to the total number of photons generated per second and each photon has an energy equal to hf joules, the optical power generated internally by the LED,

$$\left. \begin{array}{l} P_{int} = \eta_{int} \cdot \dfrac{i}{e} \cdot hf \text{ (Watts)} \\ \\ = \eta_{int} \dfrac{i}{e} \cdot \dfrac{h \cdot c}{\lambda} \end{array} \right\} \quad \ldots (1.19)$$

where,

$$h = \text{Planck's constant}$$
$$= 6.625 \times 10^{-34} \text{ Js}$$

The above equation (1.19) displays a linear relationship between the optical power generated in the LED and the drive current into the device.

From equation (1.16), it can be re-written as,

$$\eta_{int} = \frac{1}{1 + \left(\dfrac{\gamma_{nr}}{\gamma_r}\right)} = \frac{1}{1 + \left(\dfrac{\tau_r}{\tau_{nr}}\right)} \quad \ldots (1.20)$$

where, τ_r is the radiative minority carrier life time $= \dfrac{\Delta n}{\gamma_r}$.

τ_{nr} is the non-radiative minority carrier life time $= \dfrac{\Delta n}{\gamma_{nr}}$.

Δn is the minority carrier density.

Further, the total recombination life time (τ) can be written as $\tau = \dfrac{\Delta n}{\gamma_t}$ and gives,

$$\frac{1}{\tau} = \frac{1}{\tau_r} + \frac{1}{\tau_{nr}} \quad \ldots (1.21)$$

OR

$$\tau = \frac{\tau_r \cdot \tau_{nr}}{\tau_r + \tau_{nr}}$$

$$\therefore \quad \eta_{int} = \frac{\tau}{\tau_i} \quad \ldots (1.22)$$

On the other side, the external power efficiency reduces to a few percent as most of the light generated within the device is trapped by the total internal reflection, when it is radiated at greater than the critical angle for a crystal – air interface. In the injection laser, the external power efficiency. η_{ep} is defined as the ratio of the optical power emitted externally (P_e) to the electrical power provided to the device (P) as given by,

$$\eta_{ep} = \frac{P_e}{P} \times 100\% \qquad \ldots (1.23)$$

Hence, the optical power emitted (P_e) into a medium of low refractive index (n) from the face of a planar LED fabricated from a material of refractive index (n_x) is given approximately by,

$$P_e = \frac{P_{int} \cdot Fn^2}{4n_x^2} \qquad \ldots(1.24)$$

where, P_{int} is the power generated internally
F is the transmission factor of the semiconductor-external interface.
Therefore, it is possible to estimate the percentage of optical power emitted.

1.11.2 Injection Laser Diode

Lasers [LASER: Light Amplification by Stimulated Emission of Radiation] are constructed from many different materials, including gases, liquids, and solids, although the type of laser used most often for fiber optic communications is the semiconductor laser. General concept and applications of Laser is covered in Section 1.14.

The *Injection Laser Diode* (ILD) is similar to the LED. In fact, below a certain threshold current, an ILD acts similarly to an LED. Above the threshold current, an ILD oscillates; lasing occurs. As current passes through a forward-biased p-n junction diode, light is emitted by spontaneous emission at a frequency determined by the energy gap of the semiconductor material. When a particular current level is reached, the number of minority carriers and photons produced on either side of the p-n junction reaches a level where they begin to collide with already excited minority carriers.

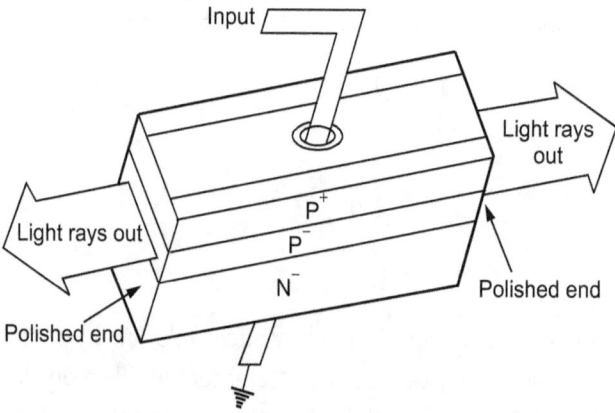

Fig. 1.22: Construction of ILD

This causes an increase in the ionization energy level and makes the carriers unstable. When this happens, a typical carrier recombines with an opposite type of carrier at an energy level that is above its normal before-collision value. In the process, two photons are created; one is stimulated by another. Essentially, a gain in the number of photons is realized. For this to happen, a large forward current that can provide many carriers (holes and electrons) is required.

Fig. 1.22 shows the construction of an ILD, which is similar to that of an LED except that the ends are highly polished. The mirror-like ends trap the photons in the active region and, as they reflect back and forth, stimulate free electrons to recombine with holes at a higher than normal energy level. This process is called losing.

The characteristics of a typical ILD is shown in Fig. 1.23. It can be seen that very little output power is realized until the threshold current is reached; then lasing occurs. After lasing begins, the optical output power increases dramatically, with small increase in drive current. It can also be seen that the magnitude of the optical output power of the ILD is more dependent on operating temperature than in the LED. Also, the Fig. 1.24 shows the radiation pattern of a typical ILD. As the light is radiated out the end of an ILD in a narrow concentrated beam, it has a more direct radiation pattern or narrow beam width.

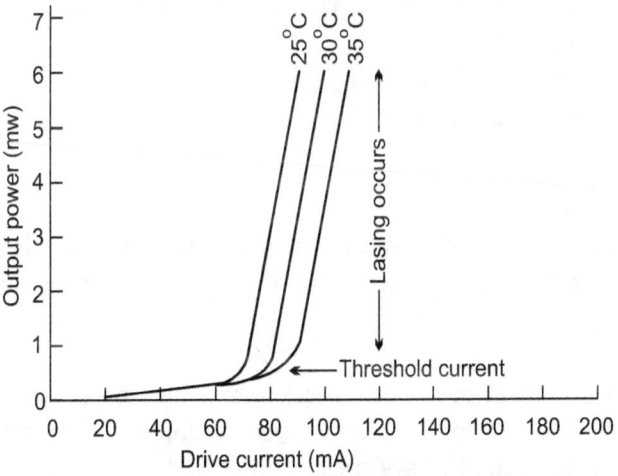

Fig. 1.23: Characteristics of typical ILD

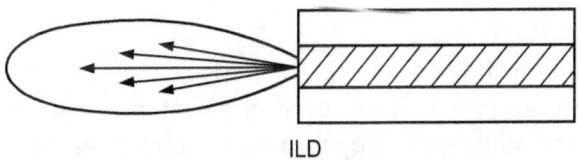

ILD
Fig. 1.24: Radiation pattern of a typical ILD

1.11.3 Comparison of Light Sources

Advantages of ILDs:
1. Because ILDs have a more direct radiation pattern, it is easier to couple their light into an optical fiber. This reduces the coupling losses and allows smaller fibers to be used.
2. The radiant output power from an ILD is greater than that for an LED. A typical output power for an ILD is 5 mW (7 dBm) and 0.5 mW (−3 dBm) for LEDs. This allows ILDs to provide a higher drive power and to be used for systems that operate over longer distances.
3. ILDs can be used at higher bit rates than LEDs.
4. ILDs generate monochromatic light, which reduces chromatic or wavelength dispersion.

Disadvantages of ILDs:
1. ILDs are typically on the order of 10 times more expensive than LEDs.
2. Because ILDs operate at higher powers, they typically have a much shorter lifetime than LEDs.
3. IDLs are more temperature dependent than LEDs.

1.12 Light Detectors

There are two devices that are commonly used to detect light energy in fiber optic communication receivers. They are,
1. PIN (P-type-Intrinsic-N-type) diodes
2. APD (Avalanche Photo Diodes)

1.12.1 PIN Diodes

A *PIN diode* is a *depletion-layer photodiode* and is the most common device used as a light detector in fiber optic communication systems. Fig. 1.25 shows the basic construction of a PIN diode.

A very lightly doped (almost pure or intrinsic) layer of n-type semiconductor material is sandwiched between the junctions of the two heavily doped n- and p-type contact areas. Light enters the device through a very small window and falls on the carrier-void intrinsic material. The intrinsic material is made thick enough so that most of the photons that enter the device are absorbed by this layer.

Essentially, the PIN photodiode operates just the opposite of an LED. Most of the photons are absorbed by electrons in the valence band of the intrinsic material. When the photons are absorbed, they add sufficient energy to generate carriers in the depletion region and allow current to flow through the device.

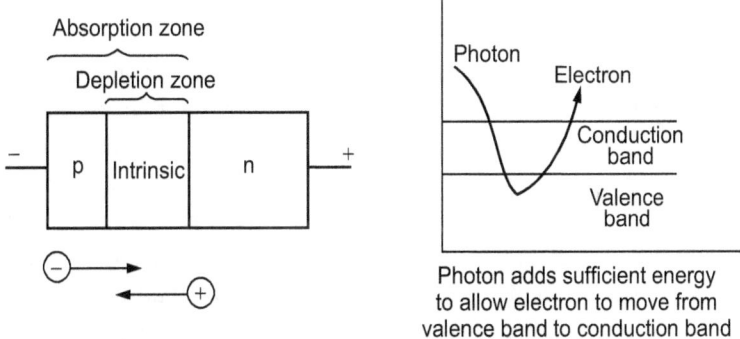

Fig. 1.25: Construction of PIN Diode

1.12.2 Photoelectric Effect in PIN Diode

Light entering through the window of a PIN diode is absorbed by the intrinsic material and adds enough energy to cause electrons to move from the valence band into the conduction band. The increase in the number of electrons that move into the conduction band is matched by an increase in the number of holes in the valence band. To cause current to flow in a photodiode, light of sufficient energy must be absorbed to give valence electrons enough energy to jump the energy gap. The energy gap for silicon is 1.12 eV (electron volts). Mathematically, the operation is as follows:

For silicon, the energy gap (E_g) equals 1.12 eV:

We know that, $1 \text{ eV} = 1.6 \times 10^{-19}$ J

Thus, the energy gap for silicon is,

$$E_g = (1.12 \text{ eV}) \cdot [1.6 \times 10^{-19} \text{ J/eV}] = 1.792 \times 10^{-19} \text{ J}$$

and Energy (E) = hf ... (1.25)

where, h = Planck's constant = 6.6256×10^{-34} J/Hz

f = Frequency (Hz)

Rearranging and solving for 'f' yields,

$$f = \frac{E}{h}$$

For Silicon photodiode, $f = \dfrac{1.792}{6.6256} = 2.705 \times 10^{14}$ Hz

Converting to wavelength yields λ = 1109 nm/cycle

Summary: Therefore, light wavelengths of 1109 nm or shorter or light frequencies of 2.705×10^{14} Hz or higher are required to cause enough electrons to jump the energy gap of a silicon photodiode.

1.12.3 Avalanche Photo Diode

The basic construction of an *Avalanche Photodiode* (APD) is shown in Fig. 1.26. An APD is a p-i-p-n structure. Light enters the diode and is absorbed by the thin, heavily doped n-layer. A high electric field intensity developed across the i-p-n junction by reverse-bias causes impact ionization to occur. During impact ionization, a carrier can gain sufficient energy to ionize other bound electrons. These ionized carriers, in turn, cause more ionization to occur. The process continues as in an avalanche and is, effectively, equivalent to an internal gain or carrier multiplication. Consequently, APDs are more sensitive than PIN diodes and require less additional amplification. The disadvantages of APDs are relatively long transit times and additional internally generated noise due to the avalanche multiplication factor.

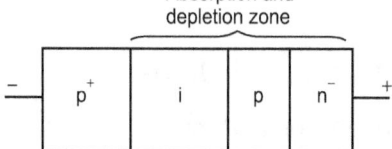

Fig. 1.26 (a): Construction of Avalanche Photo Diode

The avalanche photodiode (APD) has more sophisticated structure than the p-i-n photodiode which create an extremely high electric field region (approximately 3×10^5 V/cm), as may be seen in Fig. 1.26 (b). The depletion region is the region, where most of the photons are absorbed and the primary carrier pairs are generated and hence there is a high field region in which holes and electrons can acquire sufficient energy to excite new electron-hole pairs. This process is known as *impact ionization* and is the phenomenon that leads to avalanche breakdown in ordinary reverse biased diodes. It often requires high reverse bias voltages (50 to 400 V) in order that the new carriers created by impact ionization can themselves produce additional carriers by same mechanism as shown in Fig. 1.26 (c). However, it should be noted that these devices will operate, at much lower bias voltages (15 to 25 V).

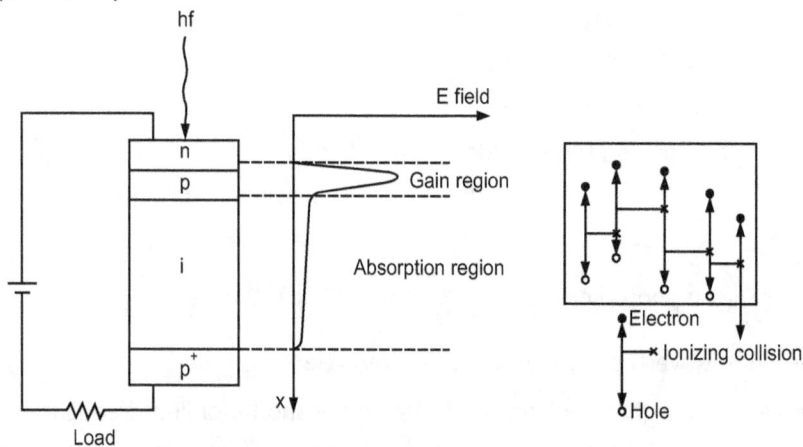

(b) APD showing high electric field region   **(c) Carrier pair multiplication in the region**

Fig. 1.26

Silicon Reach through Avalanche Photo Diodes (RAPD):

In order to ensure carrier multiplication without excess noise for a specific thickness of multiplication region within the APD, it is necessary to reduce the ratio of the ionization coefficients for electrons and holes. In silicon this ratio is a strong function of the electric field varying from around 0.1 at 3×10^5 V/m to 0.5 at 6×10^5 V/m. Hence, for minimum noise, the electric field at avalanche breakdown must be as low as possible and the impact ionization should be initiated by electrons. To this end a 'reach through' structure has been implemented with the silicon avalanche photodiode. The silicon 'reach through' APD (RAPD) consists of p^+-π-p-n^+ layers as shown in Fig. 1.26 (d). As may be seen from the corresponding field plot in Fig. 1.26 (e), the high field region where the avalanche multiplication takes place in relatively narrow and centered on the p-n^+ junction. Thus, under low reverse bias most of the voltage is dropped across the p-n^+ junction.

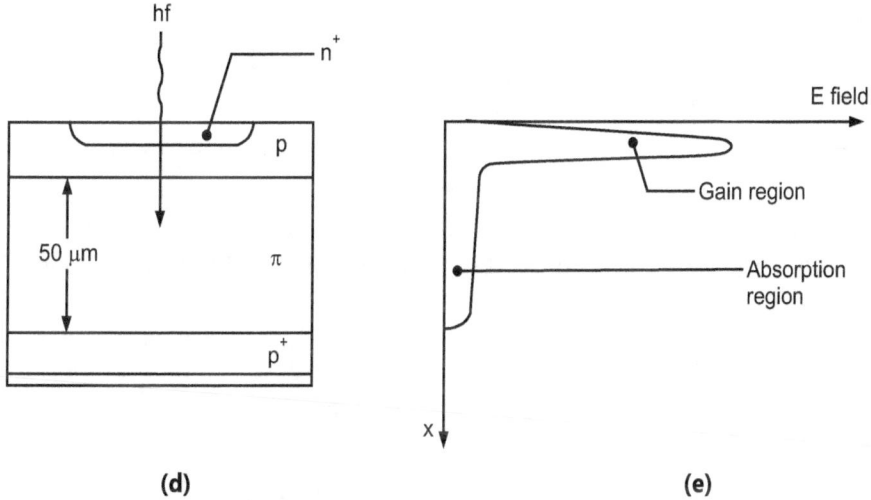

Fig. 1.26 (d): Structure of Si-RAPD and (e) Field distribution across the p-n+ junction

When the reverse bias voltage is increased the depletion layer widens across the p-region until it 'reaches through' to the nearly intrinsic (lightly doped) π-region. Since the π-region is much wider than the p-region the field in the π-region is much lower than that at the p-n^+ junction. This has the effect of removing some of the excess applied voltage from the multiplication region to the π-region giving a relatively slow increase in multiplication factor with applied voltage. Although the filed in the π-region is lower than in the multiplication region it is high enough (2×10^4 V/m) when the photodiode is operating to sweep the carriers through to the multiplication region at their scattering limited velocity (10^7 cm/s). This limits the transit time and ensures a fast response (as short as 0.5 ns).

Measurements for a silicon RAPD for optical fiber communication applications at a wavelength of 0.825 μm have shown a quantum efficiency (without avalanche gain) of nearly 100% in the working region. The dark currents for this photodiode are also low and depend only slightly on bias voltage.

1.12.4 Characteristics of Light Detectors

The most important characteristics of light detectors are:

1. Responsivity:

It is a measure of the conversion efficiency of a photo detector. It is the ratio of the output current of a photodiode to the input optical power and has the unit of amperes/watt. Responsivity is generally given for a particular wavelength or frequency.

Responsivity (R) is often useful when characterizing performance of a photodetector and is defined as,

$$R = \frac{I_p}{P_o} (AW^{-1}) \qquad \ldots (1.26)$$

where,
I_p = Output photo current in Amperes
P_o = Incident optical power in Watts

The ideal responsivity against wavelength characteristic for a silicon photodiode with unit quantum efficiency is illustrated in Fig. 126 (f). Also shown in the typical responsivity of a practical 'Si' device.

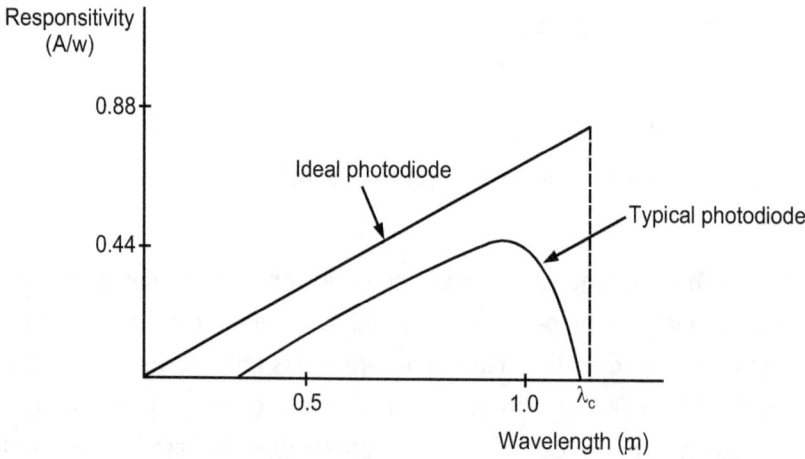

Fig. 1.26 (f)

2. Dark Current:

Dark current is the leakage current that flows through a photodiode with no light input. Dark current is caused by thermally generated carriers in the diode.

3. Transit time:

Transit time is the time it takes a light-induced carrier to travel across the depletion region. This parameter determines the maximum bit rate possible with a particular photodiode.

4. Spectral response:

Spectral response is the range of wavelength values that can be used for a given photodiode. Generally, relative spectral response is graphed as a function of wavelength or frequency. Fig. 1.26 (g) is an illustrative example of a spectral response curve of a typical light detector. It can be seen that this particular photodiode more efficiently absorbs energy in the range 800 nm to 820 nm.

5. Quantum efficiency:

The quantum efficiency 'η' is defined as the fraction of incident photons which are absorbed by the photodetector and generated electrons which are collected at the detector terminals as,

$$\eta = \frac{\text{Number of electrons collected}}{\text{Number of incident photons}} \quad \ldots (1.27)$$

Hence,
$$\eta = \frac{\gamma_e}{\gamma_p} \quad \ldots (1.28)$$

where, γ_p is the incident photon rate (photons/sec.)

γ_e is the corresponding electron rate (electrons/sec.)

The quantum efficiency is determined by the absorption co-efficient of the semiconductor material used within the photodetector. Generally, the quantum efficiency is less than unity as not all of the incident photons are absorbed to create electron-hole pairs. It is often quoted as percentage.

For example, η = 75% is equivalent to 75 electrons collected per 100 incident photons.

The quantum efficiency is related to responsivity (R) as,

$$R = \eta \cdot \frac{e \cdot \lambda}{hc} \quad \ldots (1.29)$$

Fig. 1.26 (g): Spectral Response a typical light detector

1.13 Laser

For understanding of the light-generating mechanisms within the major optical sources used in optical fiber communications it is necessary to consider both the fundamental atomic concepts and the device structure. In this context, the requirements for the laser source are far more stringent than those for the LED. Unlike the LED, strictly speaking, the laser is a device which amplifies light. Hence, the derivation of the term LASER as an acronym for Light Amplification by Stimulated Emission of Radiation. Lasers, however, are seldom used as amplifiers since there are practical difficulties in relation to the achievement of high gain whilst avoiding oscillation from the required energy feedback. Thus, the practical realization of the laser is an optical oscillator. The operation of the device may be described by the formation of an electromagnetic standing wave within a cavity (or optical resonator) which provides an output of monochromatic highly coherent radiation. By contrast the LED provides optical emission without an inherent gain mechanism. This results in incoherent light output.

Absorption and Emission of Radiation:

The interaction of light with matter takes place in discrete packets of energy or quanta called photons. Furthermore, the quantum theory suggests that atom exists only in certain discrete energy states such that absorption and emission of light causes them to make a transition from one discrete energy state to another. The frequency of the absorbed or emitted radiation/is related to the difference in energy E between the higher energy state E_2 and the lower energy state E_1 by the expression:

$$E_2 = E_2 - E_1 = hf \qquad \ldots (1.30)$$

where, $h = 6.626 \times 10^{-34}$ Js is Planck's constant. These discrete energy states for the atom may be considered to correspond to electrons occurring in particular energy levels relative to the nucleus. Hence, different energy states for the atom correspond to different electron configurations, and a single electron transition between two energy levels within the atom will provide a change in energy suitable for the absorption or emission of a photon. It must be noted, however, that modern quantum theory gives a probabilistic description which specifies the energy levels in which electrons are most likely to be found. Nevertheless, the concept of stable atomic energy states and electron transitions between energy levels is still valid.

Fig. 1.27 (a) illustrates a two energy state or level atomic system where an atom is initially in the lower energy state E_1. When a photon with energy $E_2 - E_1$ is incident on the atom it may be excited into the higher energy state E_2 through absorption of the photon. This process is sometimes referred to as **stimulated absorption**. Alternatively, when the atom is initially in the higher state E_2, it can make a transition to the lower energy state E_1 providing the emission of a photon at a frequency corresponding to equation (1.30). This emission process can occur in two ways.

(a) by spontaneous emission in which the atom returns to the lower energy state in an entirely random manner;
(b) by stimulated emission when a photon having an energy equal to the energy difference between the two states ($E_2 - E_1$) interacts with the atom in the upper energy state causing it to return to the lower state with the creation of a second photon.

These two emission processes are illustrated in Fig. 1.27 (b) and (c) respectively. The random nature of the spontaneous emission process where light is emitted by electronic transitions from a large number of atoms gives incoherent radiation. A similar emission process in semiconductors provides the basic mechanisms for light generation within the LED.

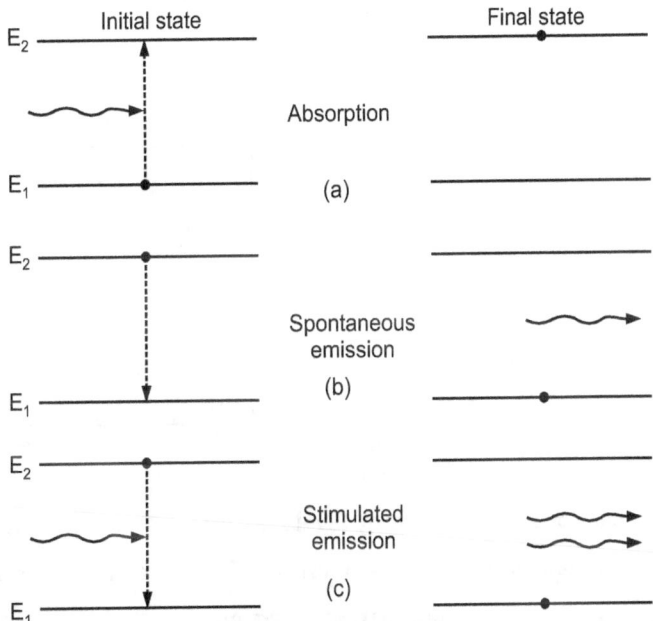

Fig. 1.27: Energy state diagram showing: (a) absorption, (b) spontaneous emission, (c) stimulated emission. The black dot indicates the state of the atom before and after a transition takes place

It is the stimulated emission process, however, which gives the laser its special properties as an optical source. Firstly, the photon produced by stimulated emission is generally of an identical energy to the one which caused it and hence the light associated with them is of the same frequency. Secondly, the light associated with the stimulating and stimulated photon is in phase and has the same polarization. Therefore, in contrast to spontaneous emission, coherent radiation is obtained. Furthermore, this means that when an atom is stimulated to emit light energy by an incident wave, the liberated energy can add to the wave in a constructive manner, providing amplification.

Population Inversion:

Under the conditions of thermal equilibrium given by the Boltzmann distribution, the lower energy level E_1 of the two level atomic system contains more atoms than the upper energy level E_2. This situation, which is normal for structures at room temperature, is illustrated in Fig. 1.27 (A) (a). However, to achieve optical amplification, it is necessary to create a non-equilibrium distribution of atoms such that the population of the upper energy level is greater than that of the lower energy level (i.e. $N_2 > N_1$). This condition which is known as population inversion, is illustrated in Fig. 1.28 (A) (b).

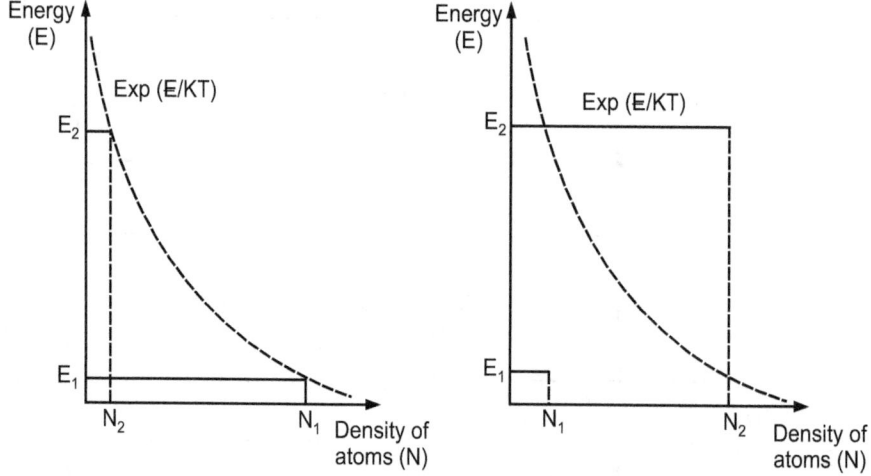

Fig. 1.28 (A): Populations in a two energy level system: (a) Boltzmann distribution for a system in thermal equilibrium, (b) a non-equilibrium distribution showing population inversion

In order to achieve population inversion, it is necessary to excite atoms into the upper energy level E_2 and hence obtain a non-equilibrium distribution. This process is achieved using an external energy source and is referred to as 'pumping'. A common method used for pumping involves the application of intense radiation (e.g. from an optical flash tube or high frequency radio field). In the former case atoms are excited into the higher energy state through stimulated absorption. However, the two level system discussed above does not lend itself to suitable population inversion and when the two levels are equally degenerate (or not degenerate), then $B_{12} = B_{21}$. Thus, the probabilities of absorption and stimulated emission are equal, providing at best equal populations in the two levels.

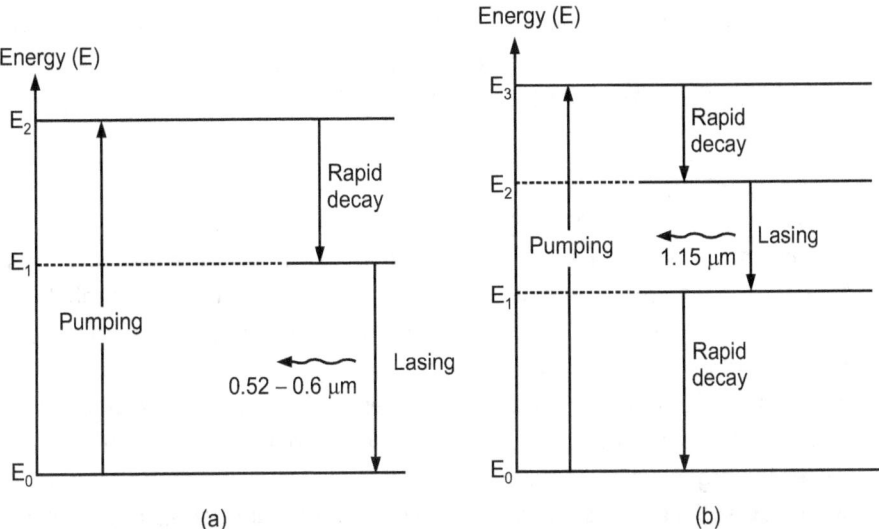

Fig. 1.28 (B): Energy level diagrams showing population inversion and lasing for two non-semiconductor lasers: (a) three level system – ruby (crystal) laser; (b) four level system – He-Ne (gas) laser

Population inversion, however, may be obtained in systems with three or four energy levels. The energy level diagrams for two such systems, which correspond to two non-semiconductor lasers, are illustrated in Fig. 1.27 (B). To aid attainment of population inversion both systems display a central metastable state in which the atoms spend an usually long time. It is from this metastable level that the stimulated emission or lasing takes place. The three level system as shown in Fig. 1.27 (B) (a) consists of a ground level E_0, a metastable level E_1 and a third level above the metastable level E_2. Initially, the atomic distribution will follow Boltzmann's law. However, with suitable pumping the electrons in some of the atoms may be excited from the ground state into the higher level E_2. Since E_2 is a normal level the electrons will rapidly decay by non-radiative processes to either E_1 or directly to E_0. Hence, empty states will always be provided in E_2. The metastable level E_1 exhibits a much longer lifetime than E_2 which allows a large number of atoms to accumulate at E_1. Over a period the density of atoms in the metastable state N_1 increases above those in the ground state. No and a population inversion is obtained between these two levels. Stimulated emission and hence lasing can then occur creating radiative electron transitions between levels E_1 and E_0. A drawback with the three level system such as the ruby laser is that it generally requires very high pump powers because the terminal state of the laser transition is the ground state. Hence, more than half the ground state atoms must be pumped into the metastable state to achieve population inversion.

By contrast, a four level system such as the He-Ne laser illustrated in Fig. 1.27 (B) (b) is characterized by much lower pumping requirements. In this case the pumping excites the atoms from the ground state into energy level E_3 and they decay rapidly to the metastable level E_2. However, since the populations of E_3 and E_1 remain essentially unchanged and hence a small increase in the number of atoms in energy level E_2 creates population inversion and lasing takes place between this level and level E_1.

1.13.1 Laser Types
Basically, there are four types of lasers: gas, liquid, solid, and semiconductor.
1. **Gas lasers:** Gas lasers use a mixture of helium and neon enclosed in a glass tube. A flow of coherent (one frequency) light waves is emitted through the output coupler when an electric current is discharged into the gas. The continuous light-wave output is monochromatic (one colour).
2. **Liquid lasers:** Liquid lasers use organic dyes enclosed in a glass tube for an active medium. Dye is circulated into the tube with a pump. A powerful pulse of light excites the organic dye.
3. **Solid lasers:** Solid lasers use a solid, cylindrical crystal, such as ruby, for the active medium. Each end of the ruby is polished and parallel. The ruby is excited by a tungsten lamp tied to an alternating-current power supply. The output from the laser is a continuous wave.
4. **Semiconductor lasers:** Semiconductor lasers are made from semiconductor p-n junctions and are commonly called injection laser diodes (ILDs). The excitation mechanism is a direct-current power supply that controls the amount of current to the active medium. The output light from an ILD is easily modulated, making it very useful in many electronic communication applications.

1.13.2 Characteristics of Lasers
Lasers have several common characteristics:
1. They all use an active material to convert energy into laser light.
2. A pumping source to provide power or energy.
3. Optics to direct the beam through the active material to be amplified.
4. Optics to direct the beam into a narrow powerful cone of divergence.
5. A feedback mechanism to provide continuous operation.
6. An output coupler to transmit power out of the laser.

The radiation of a laser is extremely intense and directional. When focused into a fine hair like beam, it can concentrate all its power into the narrow beam. If the beam of light were allowed to diverge, it would lose most of its power.

1.13.3 Construction of Laser
The construction of a basic laser is shown in Fig. 1.29. A power source is connected to a flashtube that is coiled around a glass tube that holds the active medium. One end of the glass tube is a polished mirror face for 100% internal reflection. The flashtube is energized by a trigger pulse and produces a high level burst of light (similar to a flashbulb). The flash

causes the chromium atoms within the active crystalline structure to become excited. The process of pumping raises the level of the chromium atoms from ground state to an excited energy state. The ions then decay, falling to an intermediate energy level.

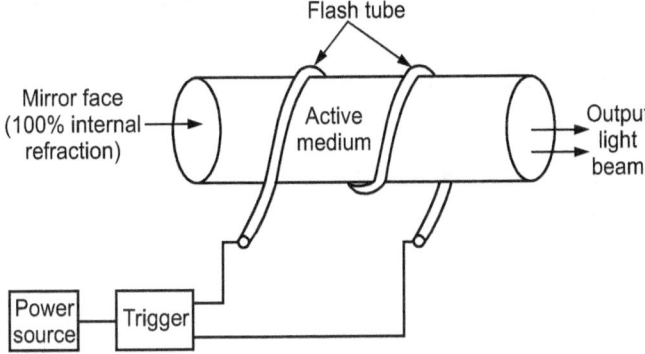

Fig. 1.29: Construction of a LASER

When the population of ions in the intermediate level is greater than the ground state, a population inversion occurs. The population inversion causes laser action (lasing) to occur. After a period of time, the excited chromium atoms will fall to the ground energy level. At this time, photons are emitted. A photon is a packet of radiant energy. The emitted photons strike atoms and two other photons are emitted (hence, the term "stimulated emission"). The frequency of the energy determines the strength of the photons; higher frequencies cause greater strength photons.

1.13.4 Applications of Laser

1. Lasers have become commonly used devices for both commercial and industrial applications.
2. Lasers are used in electronics communications, holography, medicine, direction finding, and manufacturing.
3. In electronics communications, lasers are used in audio, radio, and television transmission.
4. Laser beams have a very narrow bandwidth and they are also highly directional. Modulated light is a necessity for optical fiber applications.
5. In medicine, ruby lasers are used for precise applications such as eye surgery. Argon ion lasers are replacing scalpels.
6. The military uses lasers for distance measuring and surveying.
7. In manufacturing, the laser is used for holography to detect stains and measure irregular objects.
8. High-power lasers are used to cut reams of cloth and drill fine holes.
9. Because of its narrow beam width, laser can be used to cut fabric within the accuracy of a single thread.

1.14 Overview of Losses in Optical Fiber Cables

Transmission losses in optical fiber cables are one of the most important characteristics of the fiber. Losses in the fiber result in a reduction in the light power and, thus, reduce the system bandwidth, information transmission rate, efficiency and overall system capacity. The predominant fiber losses are as follows.

1. Absorption losses
2. Material or Rayleigh scattering losses
3. Chromatic or wavelength dispersion
4. Radiation losses
5. Modal dispersion
6. Coupling losses

1.14.1 Absorption Losses

Absorption loss in optical fibers is analogous to power dissipation in copper cables; impurities in the fiber absorb the light and convert it to heat. The ultra pure glass used to manufacture optical fibers is approximately 99.9999% pure. Still, absorption losses between 1 dB/km and 1000 dB/km are typical. Essentially, there are three factors that contribute to the absorption losses in optical fibers: ultraviolet absorption, infrared absorption, and ion resonance absorption.

Ultraviolet absorption: Ultraviolet absorption is caused by valence electrons in the silica material from which fibers are manufactured. Light ionizes the valence electrons into conduction. The ionization is equivalent to a loss in the total light field and, consequently, contributes to the transmission losses of the fiber.

Infrared absorption: Infrared absorption is a result of *photons* of light that are absorbed by the atoms of the glass core molecules. The absorbed photons are converted to random mechanical vibrations typical of heating.

Ion resonance absorption: Ion resonance absorption is caused by OH^- ions in the material. The source of the OHT ions is water molecules that have been trapped in the glass during the manufacturing process. Ion absorption is also caused by iron, copper, and chromium molecules.

Fig. 1.29 shows typical losses in optical fiber cables due to ultraviolet, infrared, and ion resonance absorption.

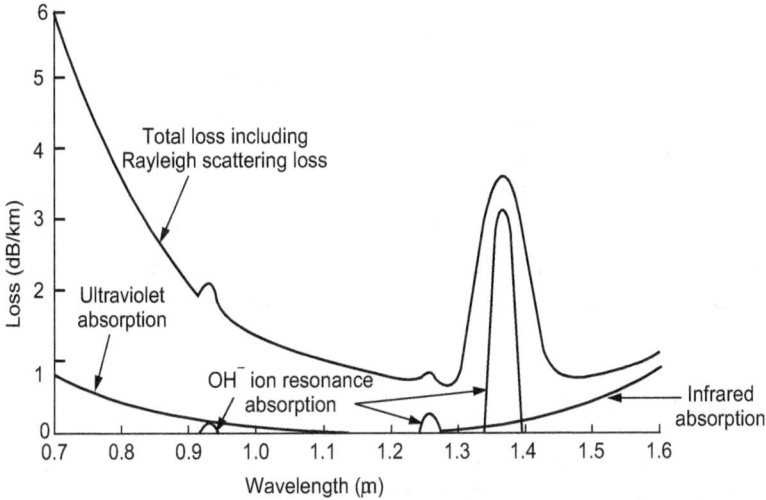

Fig. 1.30: Absorption losses in optical fiber cables

1.14.2 Material or Rayleigh Scattering Losses

During the manufacturing process, glass is drawn into long fibers of very small diameter. During this process, the glass is in a plastic state (not liquid and not solid). The tension applied to the glass during this process causes the cooling glass to develop submicroscopic irregularities that are permanently formed in the fiber. When light rays that are propagating down a fiber strike one of these impurities they are *diffracted*. Diffraction causes the light to disperse or spread out in many directions. Some of the diffracted light continues down the fiber and some of it escapes through the cladding. The light rays that escape represent a loss in light power. This is called *Rayleigh scattering loss*. Fig. 1.31 graphically shows the relationship between wavelength and Rayleigh scattering loss.

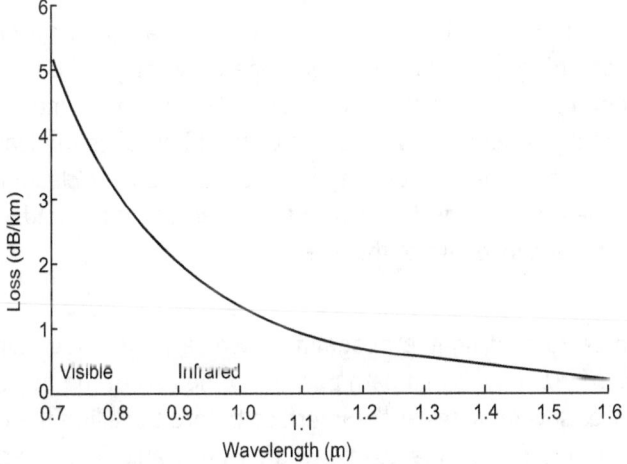

Fig. 1.31: Rayleigh scattering loss

1.14.3 Chromatic or Wavelength Dispersion

As stated previously, the refractive index of a material is wavelength dependent. Light-emitting diodes (LEDs) emit light that contains a combination of wavelengths. Each wavelength within the composite light signal travels at a different velocity. Consequently, light rays that are simultaneously emitted from an LED and propagated down an optical fiber do not arrive at the far end of the fiber at the same time. This result in a distorted receive signal; the distortion is called *chromatic distortion*. Chromatic distortion can be eliminated by using a monochromatic source such as an injection laser diode (ILD).

1.14.4 Radiation Losses

Radiation losses are caused by small bends and kinks in the fiber. Essentially, there are two types of bends: micro bends and constant radius bends.

Micro bending: It occurs as a result of differences in the thermal contraction rates between the core and cladding material. A micro bend represents a discontinuity in the fiber where Rayleigh scattering can occur.

Constant radius bends: It occurs when fibers are bent during handling or installation.

1.14.5 Modal Dispersion

Modal dispersion or *pulse spreading* is caused by the difference in the propagation times of light rays that take different paths down a fiber. Obviously, modal dispersion can occur only in multimode fibers. It can be reduced considerably by using graded index fibers and almost entirely eliminated by using single mode step index fibers.

Modal dispersion can cause a pulse of light energy to spread out as it propagates down a fiber. If the pulse spreading is sufficiently severe, one pulse may fall back on top of the next pulse (this is an example of inter-symbol interference: ISI). In a multi mode step index fiber, a light ray that propagates straight down the axis of the fiber takes the least amount of time to travel the length of the fiber. A light ray that strikes the core/cladding interface at the critical angle will undergo the largest number of internal reflections and, consequently, take the longest time to travel the length of the fiber.

Fig. 1.32 shows three rays of light propagating down a multimode step index fiber. The lowest order mode (ray-1) travels in a path parallel to the axis of the fiber. The middle order mode (ray-2) bounces several times at the interface before travelling the length of the fiber. The highest order mode (ray-3) makes many trips back and forth across the fiber as it propagates the entire length. It can be seen that ray-3 travels a considerably longer distance than ray-1 as it propagates down the fiber. Consequently, if the three rays of light were emitted into the fiber at the same time and represented a pulse of light energy, the three rays would reach the far end of the fiber at different times and result in a spreading out of the light energy with respect to time. This is called modal dispersion and results in a stretched pulse that is also reduced in amplitude at the output of the fiber. All three rays of light propagate through the same material at the same velocity, but ray-3 must travel a longer distance and, consequently, takes a longer period of time to propagate down the fiber.

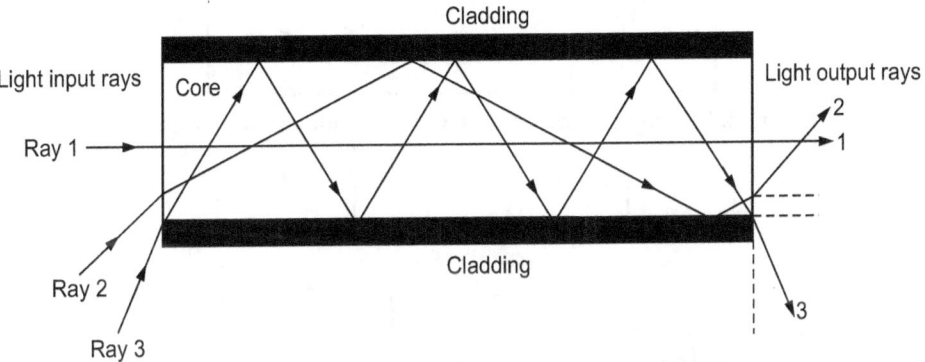

Fig. 1.32: Propagation of light in a multimode step index fiber

Fig. 1.33 shows light rays propagating down a single mode step index fiber. Because the radial dimension of the fiber is sufficiently small, there is only a single path for each of the rays to follow, as they propagate down the length of the fiber. Consequently, each ray of light travels the same distance in a given period of time and the light rays have exactly the same time relationship at the far end of the fiber as they had when they entered the cable. The result is no *modal dispersion or pulse stretching*.

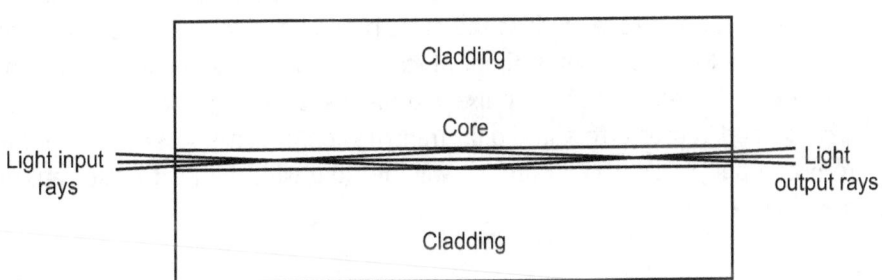

Fig. 1.33: Propagation of light in a single mode step index fiber

Fig. 1.33 shows light propagating down a multi-mode graded index fiber. Three rays are shown travelling in three different modes. Each ray travels a different path but they all take approximately the same amount of time to propagate the length of fiber. This is because the refractive index of the fiber decreases with distance from the center and the velocity at which a ray travels is inversely proportional to the refractive index. Consequently, the farther ray-2 and ray-3 travel from the center of the fiber, the faster they propagate.

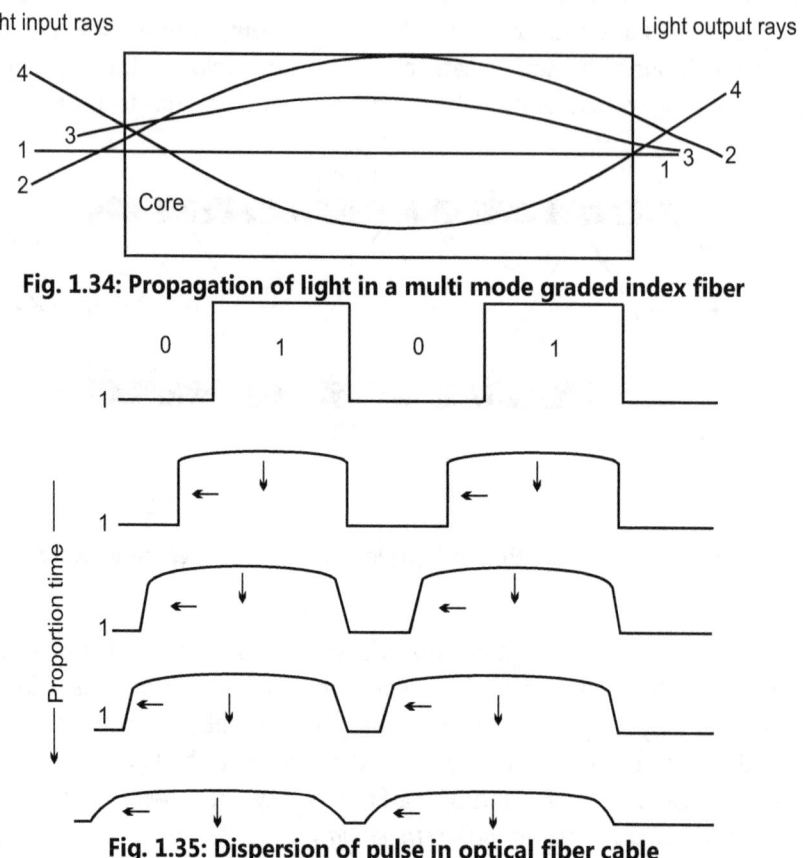

Fig. 1.34: Propagation of light in a multi mode graded index fiber

Fig. 1.35: Dispersion of pulse in optical fiber cable

Fig. 1.35 shows the relative time/energy relationship of a pulse of light as it propagates down a fiber cable. It can be seen that as the pulse propagates down the fiber, the light rays that make up the pulse spread out in time, which causes a corresponding reduction in the pulse amplitude and stretching of the pulse width. This is called pulse spreading or *pulse-width dispersion* and causes errors in digital transmission. It can also be seen that as light energy from one pulse falls back in time, it will interfere with the next pulse causing inter symbol interference.

1.14.6 Coupling Losses

Coupling losses are predominant in fiber cables and can occur at any of the following three types of optical junctions:
1. Light source-to-fiber connections
2. Fiber-to-fiber connections
3. Fiber-to-photo detector connections

These junction losses or coupling losses, as shown in Fig. 1.36 are caused by one of the following alignment problems:
1. Lateral misalignment
2. Gap misalignment
3. Angular misalignment
4. Imperfect surface finishes

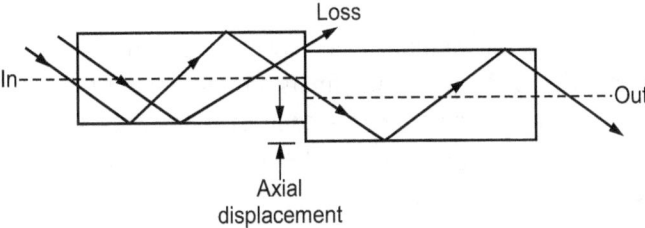

(a) Lateral misalignment

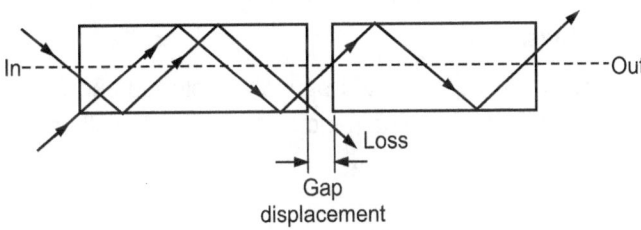

(b) Gap misalignment

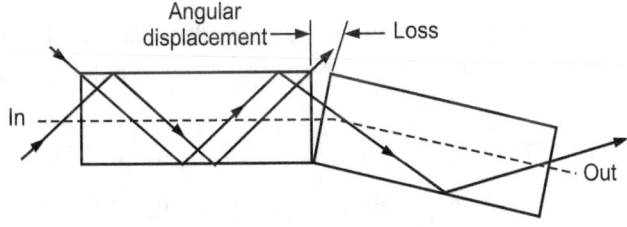

(c) Angular misalignment

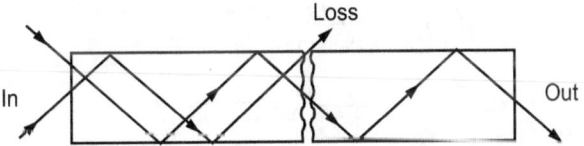

(d) Imperfect surface finishes

Fig. 1.36: Coupling losses

1. Lateral misalignment:

This is the lateral or axial displacement between two pieces of adjoining fiber cables as shown in Fig. 1.35 (a). The amount of loss can be from a couple of tenths of a decibel to several decibels. This loss is generally negligible if the fiber axes are aligned to within 5% of the smaller fiber's diameter.

2. Gap misalignment:

This is sometimes called end separation. When splices are made in optical fibers, the fibers should actually touch. The farther apart the fibers are the greater the loss of light as shown in Fig. 1.35 (b). If two fibers are joined with a connector, the ends should not touch. This is because the two ends rubbing against each other in the connector could cause damage to either or both fibers.

3. Angular misalignment:

This is sometimes called angular displacement. If the angular displacement is less than 2°, the loss will be less than 0.5 dB. This is shown in Fig. 1.36 (c).

4. Imperfect surface finish:

The ends of the two adjoining fibers should be highly polished and fit together squarely. If the fiber ends are less than 3° off from perpendicular, the losses will be less than 0.5 dB. This is shown in Fig. 1.35 (d).

SOLVED PROBLEMS

Problem 1.1:

Determine the angle of refraction of light, when its incident medium is glass with refractive index of 1.5 and its refraction medium is water with refractive index of 1.33 for an angle of incidence of 30°.

Solution:

Given: $n_1 = 1.5$, $\theta_1 = 30°$, $n_2 = 1.33$, $\theta_2 = ?$

As we know, the 'Snell's law',

$$n_1 \sin \theta_1 = n_2 \sin \theta_2$$

$$\sin \theta_2 = \frac{n_1}{n_2 \sin \theta_1}$$

$$= \frac{1.5}{1.33} \sin(30°)$$

$$= 0.5639$$

Refraction angle $\theta_2 = \sin^{-1}(0.5639)$

$$= 34.33° \qquad \text{... Ans.}$$

Problem 1.2:

An optical fiber cable made from silica material has refractive index of its core as 1.5. If the refractive index of cladding is made 10% less than that of the core, calculate its numerical aperture.

Solution:

Given: $n_1 = 1.5$ and $n_2 = 0.9(n_1) = 1.35$

As we know,

$$\text{Numerical Aperture, (NA)} = \sqrt{n_1^2 - n_2^2}$$
$$= \sqrt{(1.5)^2 - (1.35)^2}$$
$$\text{NA} = 0.65 \quad \ldots \text{Ans.}$$

Problem 1.3:

If the refractive indices of incident medium (n_1) and refracted medium (n_2) are 1.6 and 1.4 respectively, calculate the angle of refraction (θ_2) for an angle of incidence (θ_1) of 40°.

Solution:

Given:
$n_1 = 1.6$
$n_2 = 1.4$
$\theta_1 = 40°$

and $\theta_2 = ?$

According to Snell's Law,

$$n_1 \sin\theta_1 = n_2 \sin\theta_2$$

$\therefore$
$$\sin\theta_2 = \frac{n_1}{n_2} \cdot \sin\theta_1$$

$$\sin\theta_2 = \left[\left(\frac{n_1}{n_2}\right) \cdot \sin\theta_1\right]$$

$$= \frac{1.6}{1.4} \sin 40°$$

$$= 0.7346 \quad \ldots \text{Ans.}$$

$\therefore$ Angle of refraction, $\theta_2 = \sin^{-1}(0.7346)$
$$= 47.27° \quad \ldots \text{Ans.}$$

Problem 1.4:

Calculate the critical angle (θ_c) when a light ray is incident from medium 1 to medium 2 having refractive indices 1.48 and 1.36 respectively.

Solution:

Given:
$n_1 = 1.48$
$n_2 = 1.36$

As we know,

$$n_1 \sin\theta_1 = n_2 \sin\theta_2$$

From definition of critical angle,

$$\theta_2 = 90°$$

and $\quad \theta_1 = \theta_c$

$\therefore \quad \sin \theta_c = \dfrac{n_2}{n_1} \sin 90°$

$$= \dfrac{1.36}{1.48} \sin 90°$$

$$= 0.9189 \quad \text{... Ans.}$$

$\therefore \quad$ Critical angle, $\theta_c = \sin^{-1} [0.9189]$

$$= 66.77° \quad \text{... Ans.}$$

Problem 1.5:
For a multimode step index fiber with a glass core ($n_1 = 1.5$) and a fused quartz cladding ($n_2 = 1.46$) determine the critical angle (θ_c) will this result in total internal reflection if the angle of incidence is 80°?

Solution:

Given:
$$n_2 = 1.46$$
$$n_1 = 1.5$$
and $\quad \theta_1 = 80°$

We know,
$$\theta_c = \sin^{-1}\left(\dfrac{n_2}{n_1}\right) = \sin^{-1}\left(\dfrac{1.46}{1.5}\right)$$

$$= 76.7° \quad \text{... Ans.}$$

Since critical angle $\theta_c = 76.7°$ is less than angle of incidence of 80°, the total internal reflection will take place and the light will propagate down the fibers, as $\theta_1 > \theta_c$ which is the necessary condition.

Problem 1.6:
Calculate the Numerical Aperature of a step index fiber having $n_1 = 1.48$ and $n_2 = 1.46$. What is the maximum entrance angle of this fiber, if the outer medium is air with $n_0 = 1.00$?

Solution: $n_1 = 1.48$, $n_2 = 1.46$, $n_0 = 1.00$

$$\text{Numerical Aperture (NA)} = \sqrt{n_1^2 - n_2^2}$$

$$= \sqrt{(1.48)^2 - (1.46)^2} = \mathbf{0.242}$$

We know, $\quad N = n_0 \sin \theta_{a\,max}$

$\therefore \quad \sin \theta_{a\,max} = \left(\dfrac{NA}{n_0}\right)\left(\dfrac{0.242}{1.00}\right) = \mathbf{0.242}$

$\quad$ Entrance Angle $(\theta_a) = \sin^{-1}(0.242)$

$$= \mathbf{14.0°} \textbf{ degrees} \quad \text{... Ans.}$$

Problem 1.7:

For a multimode step index fiber, with glass core ($n_1 = 1.6$) and fused quartz cladding ($n_2 = 1.46$), determine the critical angle (θ_c), acceptance angle (θ_a) and numerical aperture (NA). The source to fiber media is air.

For the above data, what would be the NA, if it is a graded index fiber.

Solution:

Given: $n_1 = 1.6$, $n_2 = 1.46$, $n_0 = 1$.

(i) Critical Angle (θ_c) $= \sin^{-1}\left(\dfrac{n_2}{n_1}\right)$

$\qquad\qquad\qquad\qquad\quad = 65.85°$ ... Ans.

(ii) Acceptance Angle (θ_a) $= \sin^{-1}\sqrt{n_1^2 - n_2^2}$

$\qquad\qquad\qquad\qquad\quad = 40.88°$ ... Ans.

(iii) NA for Step index fiber,

$\quad$ NA $= \sin\theta_a \qquad = \sin(40.88)$

$\qquad\qquad\qquad\qquad = 0.6545$ ... Ans.

(iv) NA for Graded index fiber,

$\quad$ NA $= \sin\theta_c \qquad = \sin(65.85)$

$\qquad\qquad\qquad\qquad = 0.9125$ ... Ans.

Problem 1.8

While connecting two fibers, it is noticed that there is an unintended differences of diameter between them. Calculate the loss in dB.

(i) When transmitting from a fiber whose core and radius is 50 micrometer to the one having the core radius of 30 micrometer.

(ii) When transmitting from a fiber whose NA is 0.8 to the one having the NA of 0.6.

(iii) When it is reversed in the case (i) and (ii)?

Solution:

Given: $\qquad a_2 = 30\ \mu m$

$\qquad\qquad\quad a_1 = 50\ \mu m$

(i) $\qquad$ Loss (dB) $= -10\log\left(\dfrac{a_2}{a_1}\right)^2$

$\qquad\qquad\qquad\qquad = -10\log\left(\dfrac{30}{50}\right)$

$\qquad\qquad\qquad\qquad = -4.437\ \text{dB}$ ... Ans.

(ii)   Loss (dB) $= -10 \log \left(\dfrac{NA_2}{NA_1}\right)^2$

$= -10 \log \left(\dfrac{0.6}{0.8}\right)$

$= -2.499$ dB   ... Ans.

(iii)   There is no loss when reversed in case (i) and (ii).

Problem 1.9:

If a multimode step index fiber having the core refractive index of 1.5, cladding refractive index of 1.38, core radius of 25 μm operates at the wavelength of 1300 nanometer. Calculate –

 (i)   Numerical aperture
 (ii) Normalized frequency
 (iii) Solic acceptance angle
 (iv) Total number of modes entering the fiber.

Solution:

Given: $n_1 = 1.5$
        $n_2 = 1.38$
        $a = 25$ μm
and $\lambda = 1300$ nm

(i) Numerical Aperture, (NA) $= \sqrt{n_1^2 - n_2^2}$

$= \sqrt{(1.5)^2 - (1.38)^2}$

$= 0.5878$ ... Ans.

(ii) Normalized frequency (v) $= \dfrac{2\pi a}{\lambda} \cdot NA$

$= \dfrac{2\pi (25 \times 10^{-6})}{1300} \times 0.5878$

$= 71.033$ ... Ans.

(iii) Solid acceptance angle

$\theta_a = \sin^{-1}(NA)$

$= \sin^{-1}(0.5878) = 36°$ ... Ans.

(iv) The total number of modes entering the fiber

$M = \dfrac{v^2}{2}$

$= \dfrac{(71.033)^2}{2} = 2522.84$ ... Ans.

Problem 1.10:

What must be the –

(i) cross sectional area of the core

(ii) refractive index of the cladding

(iii) critical angle

(iv) maximum entrance angle of a step index fiber used at 840 nm with v-number of 60, refractive index of the core of 1.55 and numerical aperture of 0.45. Also calculate the NA if it were a graded index fiber.

Solution:

Given:
$$NA = 0.45$$
$$v = 60$$
$$\lambda = 840 \text{ nm}$$
$$n_1 = 1.55$$

(i) Cross sectional area if the core

$$v = \frac{2\pi a}{\lambda}(NA)$$

$$\therefore \quad a = \frac{v \cdot \lambda}{2\pi (NA)} = \frac{60 \times 840 \times 10^{-9}}{2\pi (0.45)}$$

$$= 17.825 \text{ µm} \quad \text{... Ans.}$$

(ii) Refractive indx of the cladding:

$$NA = \sqrt{n_1^2 - n_2^2}$$
$$NA^2 = n_1^2 - n_2^2$$

$$\therefore \quad n_2^2 = n_1^2 - NA^2$$

$$n_2 = \sqrt{n_1^2 - NA^2}$$

$$= \sqrt{(1.55)^2 - (0.45)^2}$$

$$= 1.4832 \quad \text{... Ans.}$$

(iii)

$$\text{Critical angle, } \theta_c = \sin^{-1}\left(\frac{n_2}{n_1}\right)$$

$$= \sin^{-1}\left(\frac{1.4832}{1.55}\right)$$

$$= 73.12° \quad \text{... Ans.}$$

(iv) Max entrance angle of the S.I. fiber:

$$\theta_{in\ max} = \sin^{-1}\left(\frac{NA}{n_o}\right)$$

$$= \sin^{-1}\left(\frac{0.45}{1.0}\right)$$

$$= 26.74° \qquad \text{... Ans.}$$

NA if it were GIF $= \sin\theta_c$

$$= \sin 73.12°$$

$$= \mathbf{0.9569} \qquad \text{... Ans.}$$

Problem 1.11:

Compute the critical angle, numerical aperture, maximum entrance angle and number of modes for a give step index fiber, whose core diameter is 50 μm and having refractive index of core and cladding of 1.5 and 1.46 respectively. The outer medium is air. Let $\lambda = 0.82$ μm.

Solution:

Given:
$$n_1 = 1.5$$
$$n_2 = 1.46$$
$$n_o = 1 \text{ (air)}$$
$$\text{Diameter} = 50 \text{ μm}$$
$$\therefore \quad a = 25 \text{ μm}$$
$$\lambda = 0.82 \text{ μm}$$

(i) Critical angle, $\theta_c = \sin^{-1}\dfrac{n_2}{n_1}$

$$= \sin^{-1}\left[\frac{1.46}{1.5}\right]$$

$$= \mathbf{76.74°} \qquad \text{... Ans.}$$

(ii) NA $= \sqrt{n_1^2 - n_2^2}$

$$= \sqrt{(1.5)^2 - (1.46)^2}$$

$$= \mathbf{0.344} \qquad \text{... Ans.}$$

(iii) Maximum entrance angle, $\theta_{o\ max} = \sin^{-1}\left(\dfrac{NA}{n_o}\right)$

$$= \sin^{-1}\left[\frac{0.344}{1.0}\right]$$

$$= \mathbf{20.12°} \qquad \text{... Ans.}$$

(iv) Number of modes (v) = $\dfrac{2\pi a}{\lambda}$ [NA]

$$= \dfrac{2\pi \times 25 \times 10^{-6}}{0.82 \times 10^{-6}} [0.344]$$

$$= 65.9° \qquad \text{... Ans.}$$

Problem 1.12:

A double heterojunction InGaAsP LED emitting at a peak wavelength of 1310 nm has radiative and non-radiative recombination times of 30 nsec. and 100 nsec. respectively. The drive current is 40 mA. Determine the total recombination life time, internal quantum efficiency and internal power level of the source.

Solution:

Given:
$$\lambda = 1310 \text{ nm}$$
$$\tau_r = 30 \text{ nsec.}$$
$$\tau_{nr} = 100 \text{ nsec}$$
$$i = 40 \text{ mA}$$

(i) Total recombination life time (τ):

$$= \dfrac{\tau_r \cdot \tau_{nr}}{\tau_r + \tau_{nr}} = \dfrac{30 \times 100}{30 + 100} = 23.1 \text{ nsec.} \qquad \text{... Ans.}$$

(ii) Internal quantum efficiency:

$$\eta_{int} = \dfrac{\tau}{\tau_r} = \dfrac{23.1 \text{ n sec}}{30 \text{ n sec}} = 0.77 = 77\% \qquad \text{... Ans.}$$

(iii) Internal power level:

$$P_{int} = \eta_{int} \cdot \dfrac{i}{e} \times \dfrac{hc}{\lambda}$$

$$= \dfrac{0.77 \times 40 \times 10^{-3} \times 6.626 \times 10^{-34} \times 3 \times 10^{8}}{1.602 \times 10^{-19} \times 1310 \times 10^{-9}}$$

$$= 29.2 \text{ mW} \qquad \text{... Ans.}$$

Problem 1.13:

Determine the normalized frequency at 850 nm for a step index fiber has a core radius of 25 μm, core refractive index of 1.48 and cladding refractive index of 1.46. How many modes propagate in this fiber at 1320 nm and 1550 nm?

Solution:

Given: Step Index Fiber (SIF)

$$\lambda = 850 \text{ nm} = 850 \times 10^{-9} \text{ m}$$
$$a = 25 \text{ μm}$$
$$n_1 = 1.48 \text{ and } n_2 = 1.46$$

(i) Normalized frequency at λ = 850 nm

$$V = \frac{2\pi a}{\lambda}(NA)$$

where,

$$NA = \sqrt{n_1^2 - n_2^2} = \sqrt{(1.48)^2 - (1.46)^2}$$
$$= 0.24 \qquad \text{... Ans.}$$

$$\therefore \quad V = \frac{2 \times \pi \times 25 \times 10^{-6} \times 0.24}{850 \times 10^{-9}} = 44.35 \qquad \text{... Ans.}$$

(ii) Number of modes propagate at λ = 1320 nm.

$$N = \frac{V^2}{2} \text{ for SIF}$$

where,

$$V = \frac{2 \times \pi \times 25 \times 10^{-6} \times 0.24}{1320 \times 10^{-9}}$$
$$= 28.56$$

$$\therefore \quad N = \frac{V^2}{2} = \frac{(28.56)^2}{2} = 407.83$$

(or) $\boxed{N \cong 408}$ ... Ans.

(iii) Number of modes propagate at λ = 1550 m

$$V = \frac{2\pi \times 25 \times 10^{-6} \times 0.24}{1550 \times 10^{-9}} = 24.32$$

$$\therefore \quad N = \frac{V^2}{2} = \frac{(24.32)^2}{2} = 295.73$$

(or) $\boxed{N \cong 296}$ ... Ans.

Problem 1.14:

Estimate the external power efficiency of a GaAs planar LED when the transmission factor of the GaAs – air interface is 0.68 and the internally generated optical power is 30% of the electrical power supplied. The refractive index of GaAs may be taken as 3.6.

Solution:

Given: $F = 0.68$, $P_{int} = 0.3\, P$. $\therefore P = 3.33\, P_{int}$, $n_x = 3.6$ and $n_{air} = 1$ (assumed)

External power efficiency $\eta_{ep} = \dfrac{P_e}{P} \times 100\%$

where,

$$P_e = \frac{P_{int} \cdot F \cdot n^2}{4(n_x)^2} = \frac{P_{int} \times 0.68 \times (1)^2}{4(3.6)^2}$$

$$= 0.013\, P_{int}$$

Therefore,

$$\eta_{ep} = \frac{P_e}{P} = \frac{0.013\, P_{int}}{3.33\, P_{int}} = 0.0039 \times 100$$

$$\eta_{ep} = \mathbf{0.39\%} \quad \text{... Ans.}$$

Problem 1.15:

A multimode step index fiber has a relative refractive index difference of 1% and a core refractive index of 1.5. The number of modes propagating at a wavelength of 1.3 µm is 1100. Estimate the diameter of the fiber core.

Solution:

Given: $\Delta = 0.01$, $n_1 = 1.5$, $M = 1100$, $\lambda = 1.3$ µm.

We know that,

$$V = \frac{2\pi a n_1 (2\Delta)^{1/2}}{\lambda}$$

Given that,

$$M = \frac{V^2}{2} = 1100$$

∴

$$V^2 = 2200$$

and

$$V = \sqrt{2200} = \mathbf{46.9}$$

Therefore,

$$a = \frac{V \cdot \lambda}{2\pi n_1 (2\Delta)^{1/2}} = \frac{46.9 \times 1.3 \times 10^{-6}}{2 \times \pi \times 1.5 \times (2 \times 0.01)^{1/2}}$$

$$= \mathbf{45.77\ \mu m} \quad \text{... Ans.}$$

SUMMARY

- A fiber optic cable is essentially a light pipe that is used to carry a light beam from one place to another.
- Light is an electromagnetic signal like a radio wave. It can be modulated by information and sent over the fiber optic cable. As the light frequency is extremely light, it can accommodate very wide bandwidth of information and extremely high data rates can be achieved with excellent reliability. The primary application of fiber optic communication is in long distance telephone systems.

- The visible light spectrum is from 700 nm (red) to 400 nm (violet).
- The optical spectrum is made up of visible light, infra red at lower frequencies and ultraviolet at higher frequencies.
- Light waves also travel in a straight line, like microwaves in its medium or guide called optical fiber.
- A popular operating frequency is 1.3 µm because FOC has an attenuation null at this wavelength.

POINTS TO REMEMBER

- The principle of OFC is 'total internal reflection'.
- Refractive index is the ratio of "velocity of propagation in free space to the velocity of light in a given material".
- Snell's law : $n_1 \sin \theta_1 = n_2 \sin \theta_2$
- Critical angle is the minimum angle of incidence at which a light ray may strike the interface of two media and result in an angle of refraction of 90° or greater.

$$\theta_c = \sin^{-1}\left(\frac{n_2}{n_1}\right)$$

- Index profile is a graphical representation of the value of refractive index across the fiber. Types : Step index and graded index.
- Mode of propagation simply means path. Types : Single mode and multimode.
- Numerical Aperture (NA) is a figure of merit that is used to describe the light gathering or light collecting ability of the optical fibers.

$$NA = \sqrt{n_1^2 - n_2^2} \quad \text{– for step index}$$
$$NA = \sin \theta_c \quad \text{– for graded index}$$

- Single mode cable is very small in diameter whereas multimode cables are large.
- Fiber cables are made from glass and plastic. Glass has the lowest loss but is brittle. Plastic is cheaper and more flexible, but has high attenuation.
- Modal dispersion does not occur in single mode fibers.
- Cable attenuation is proportional to its length. Typical losses range from 1 dB/km in glass single mode step index fiber to 100 dB/km for plastic multimode step index cable.

- LEDs and ILDs emit light in the invisible near infra red range.
- LEDs are used in short distance, low speed systems and ILDs are used in long distance, high-speed systems.
- PIN diodes are faster and more sensitive than conventional photodiodes.
- APDs are faster and most sensitive light detectors.
- The predominant fiber losses are absorption losses, material or Rayleigh scattering losses, chromatic or wavelength dispersion, radiation losses, model dispersion and coupling losses.
- Characteristics of light detectors are responsivity, dark current, transit time, spectral response.
- Laser diodes emit monochromatic and coherent light whereas LEDs emit chromatic and non-coherent light.

QUESTIONS

1. Contrast the advantages and disadvantages of fiber optic cables and metallic cables.
2. Draw and explain the primary building blocks of a fiber optic system.
3. Compare: Glass fibers Vs. Plastic fibers.
4. Describe the construction of fiber optic cables in brief.
5. State, 'Snell's law' for refraction and also outline its significance.
6. Define and explain following terms:
   - (i) Velocity of propagation
   - (ii) Refractive index
   - (iii) Critical angle
   - (iv) Numerical aperture
   - (v) Index profile
   - (vi) Pulse spreading
7. Compare (i) Step index fiber Vs. Graded index fiber, (ii) Single mode Vs. Multimode propagation.
8. What is single mode propagation impossible with GIF?
9. What are acceptance angle and acceptance cone for a fiber cable?
10. List and briefly describe the losses associated with fiber cables.
11. What are various coupling losses in OFC? List and explain.

12. Explain the operation of LED and list its types.
13. Briefly explain the operation of ILD.
14. Compare LED Vs. ILD.
15. Describe the function of photodiode. Also explain the photoelectric effect.
16. Explain the difference between PIN diode and APD.
17. List and describe the primary characteristics of light detector.

Unit II

SIGNAL DEGRADATION IN OPTICAL FIBER

2.1 Introduction

The principles behind the transfer of light along an optical fiber were discussed earlier. You learned that propagation of light depended on the nature of light and the structure of the optical fiber. However, our discussion did not describe how optical fibers affect system performance.
In this case, system performance deals with signal loss and bandwidth.

Signal loss and system bandwidth describe the amount of data transmitted over a specified length of fiber. Many optical fiber properties increase signal loss and reduce system bandwidth. The most important properties that affect system performance are fiber attenuation and dispersion.

Attenuation reduces the amount of optical power transmitted by the fiber. Attenuation controls the distance an optical signal (pulse) can travel as shown in Fig. 2.1. Once the power of an optical pulse is reduced to a point where the receiver is unable to detect the pulse, an error occurs. Attenuation is mainly a result of **light absorption, scattering,** and **bending losses**. Dispersion spreads the optical pulse as it travels along the fiber. This spreading of the signal pulse reduces the system bandwidth or the information-carrying capacity of the fiber. Dispersion limits how fast information is transferred as shown in Fig. 2.1. An error occurs when the receiver is unable to distinguish between input pulses caused by the spreading of each pulse. The effects of attenuation and dispersion increase as the pulse travels the length of the fiber as shown in Fig. 2.2.

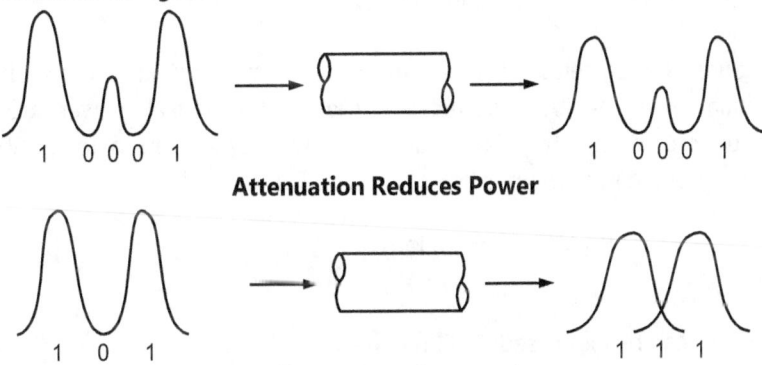

Attenuation Reduces Power

Dispersion Spreads the Pulse

Fig. 2.1: Fiber Transmission Properties

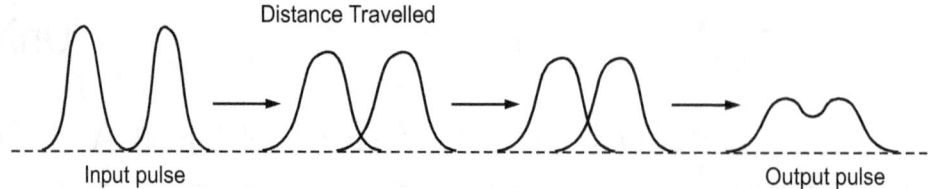

Fig. 2.2: Pulse Spreading and Power Loss along an Optical Fiber

In addition to fiber attenuation and dispersion, other optical fiber properties affect system performance. Fiber properties, such as modal noise, pulse broadening, and polarization, can reduce system performance.

Modal noise, pulse broadening, and polarization are too complex to discuss as introductory level material. However, you should be aware at attenuation and dispersion are not the only fiber properties that affect performance.

2.2 Attenuation

Attenuation in an optical fiber is caused by absorption, scattering, and bending losses. **Attenuation** is the loss of optical power as light travels along the fiber. Signal attenuation is defined as the ratio of optical input power (P_i) to the optical output power (P_o). Optical input power is the power injected into the fiber from an optical source. Optical output power is the power received at the fiber end or optical detector. The following equation defines signal attenuation as a unit of length:

$$\text{Attenuation} = \left(\frac{10}{L}\right) \log_{10}\left(\frac{P_i}{P_o}\right) \qquad \ldots (2.1)$$

i.e.
$$\alpha \text{ (dB/km)} = \left(\frac{10}{L}\right) \cdot \log_{10}\left(\frac{P_i}{P_o}\right) \qquad \ldots (2.2)$$

where, α = Fiber loss or fiber attenuation.

Signal attenuation is a log relationship. Length (L) is expressed in kilometers. Therefore, the unit of attenuation is decibels/kilometer (dB/km). The optical power are commonly expressed in units of dBm, which is the decibel power level referred to 1 mW. The input power can be expressed in dBm units as,

$$P_{in} \text{ (dBm)} = 10 \log_{10}\left[\frac{P_{in}(W)}{1 \text{ mW}}\right] \qquad \ldots (2.3)$$

The output power can be expressed in dBm units as,

$$P_{out} \text{ (dBm)} = 10 \log_{10}\left[\frac{P_{in}(W)}{1 \text{ mW}}\right] \qquad \ldots (2.4)$$

As previously stated, attenuation is caused by absorption, scattering and bending losses. Each mechanism of loss is influenced by fiber-material properties and fiber structure. However, loss is also present at fiber connections. Fiber connector, splice, and coupler losses are discussed in next topic. The present discussion remains relative to optical fiber attenuation properties.

Problem 2.1:

Find out the limitations in transmission length caused by fiber loss for P_{in} = 0.033 mW, P_{out} = 0.002 mW and the fiber attenuation, α = 0.4 dB/km.

Solution:

We have,
$$P_{in} = 0.033 \text{ mW}$$
$$P_{out} = 0.002 \text{ mW}$$
$$\alpha = 0.4 \text{ dB/Km}$$
$$L = ?$$

We know that the attenuation can be expressed as,
$$\alpha = \frac{10}{L} \cdot \log_{10}\left[\frac{P_{in}}{P_{out}}\right]$$

i.e.
$$L = \frac{10}{\alpha} \cdot \log_{10}\left[\frac{P_{in}}{P_{out}}\right]$$

$$L = \frac{10}{0.4} \cdot \log_{10}\left[\frac{0.033}{0.002}\right]$$

$$L = 30.437 \text{ km} \quad \text{... Ans.}$$

The typical distance between the two amplifiers should be around 40 to 45 km.

2.3 Absorption

Absorption is a major cause of signal loss in an optical fiber. Absorption is defined as the portion of attenuation resulting from the conversion of optical power into another energy form, such as heat. Absorption in optical fibers is explained by three factors:

- Imperfections in the atomic structure of the fiber material.
- The intrinsic or basic fiber-material properties.
- The extrinsic (presence of impurities) fiber-material properties.

Imperfections in the atomic structure induce absorption by the presence of missing molecules or oxygen defects. Absorption is also induced by the diffusion of hydrogen molecules into the glass fiber. Since intrinsic and extrinsic material properties are the main cause of absorption, they are discussed further.

2.3.1 Intrinsic Absorption

Intrinsic absorption is caused by basic fiber material properties. If an optical fiber were absolutely pure, with no imperfections or impurities, then all absorption would be intrinsic. Intrinsic absorption sets the minimal level of absorption.

In fiber optics, silica (pure glass) fibers are used predominately. Silica fibers are used because of their low intrinsic material absorption at the wavelengths of operation.

In silica glass, the wavelengths of operation range from 700 nanometers (nm) to 1600 nm. Fig. 2.3 shows the level of attenuation at the wavelengths of operation. This wavelength of operation is between two intrinsic absorption regions. The first region is the **ultraviolet** region (below 400 nm wavelength). The second region is the **infrared** region (above 200 nm wavelength).

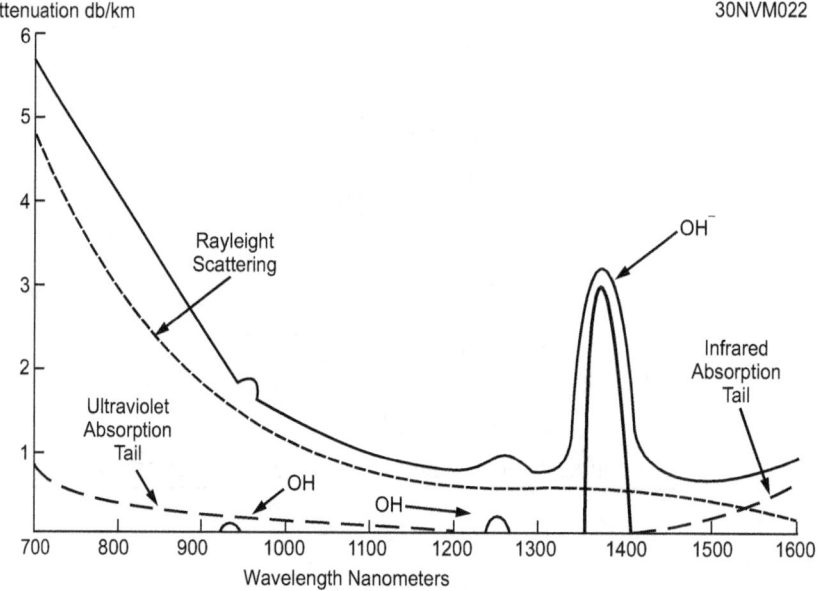

Fig. 2.3: Fiber Losses

Intrinsic absorption in the ultraviolet region is caused by electronic absorption bands. Basically, absorption occurs when a light particle (photon) interacts with an electron and excites it to a higher energy level. The tail of the ultraviolet absorption band is shown in Fig. 2.3.

The main cause of intrinsic absorption in the infrared region is the characteristic vibration frequency of atomic bonds. In silica glass, absorption is caused by the vibration of silicon-oxygen (Si-O) bonds. The interaction between the vibrating bond and the electromagnetic field of the optical signal causes intrinsic absorption. Light energy is transferred from the electromagnetic field to the bond. The tail of the infrared absorption band is shown in Fig. 2.3.

2.3.2 Extrinsic Absorption

Extrinsic absorption is caused by impurities introduced into the fiber material. Trace metal impurities, such as iron, nickel, and chromium, are introduced into the fiber during fabrication. **Extrinsic absorption** is caused by the electronic transition of these metal ions from one energy level to another.

Extrinsic absorption also occurs when hydroxyl ions (OH^-) are introduced into the fiber. Water in silica glass forms a silicon-hydroxyl (Si-OH) bond. This bond has a fundamental absorption at 2700 nm. However, the harmonics or overtones of the fundamental absorption occur in the region of operation. These harmonics increase extrinsic absorption at 1383 nm, 1250 nm, and 950 nm. Fig. 2.3 shows the presence of the three OH^- harmonics. The level of the OH^- harmonic absorption is also indicated.

These absorption peaks define three regions or windows of preferred operation. The first window is centered at **850** nm. The second window is centered at **1300** nm. The third window is centered at **1550** nm. Fiber optic systems operate at wavelengths defined by one of these windows.

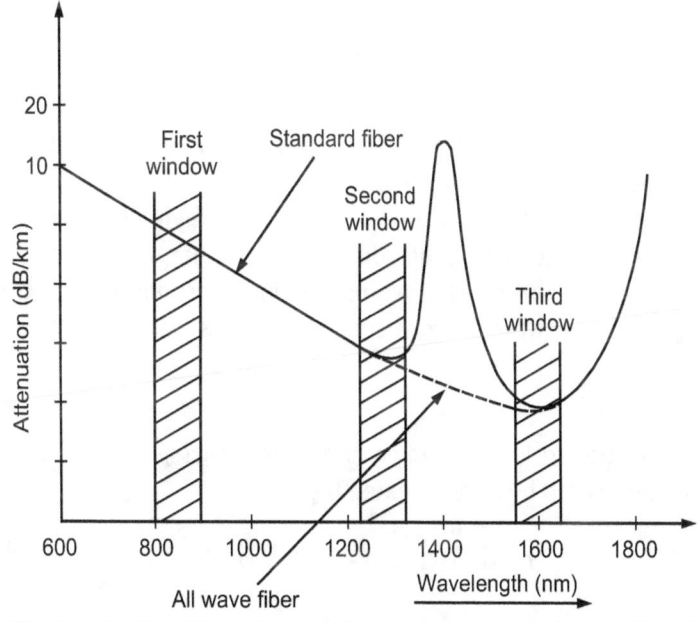

Fig. 2.4: Optical Fiber Attenuation as a Function of Wavelength

The amount of water (OH^-) impurities present in a fiber should be less than a few parts per billion. Fiber attenuation caused by extrinsic absorption is affected by the level of impurities (OH^-) present in the fiber. If the amount of impurities in a fiber is reduced, then fiber attenuation is reduced.

2.4 Scattering

Basically, scattering losses are caused by the interaction of light with density fluctuations within a fiber. Density changes are produced when optical fibers are manufactured.

During manufacturing, regions of higher and lower molecular density areas, relative to the average density of the fiber, are created. Light travelling through the fiber interacts with the density areas as shown in Fig. 2.5. Light is then partially scattered in all directions.

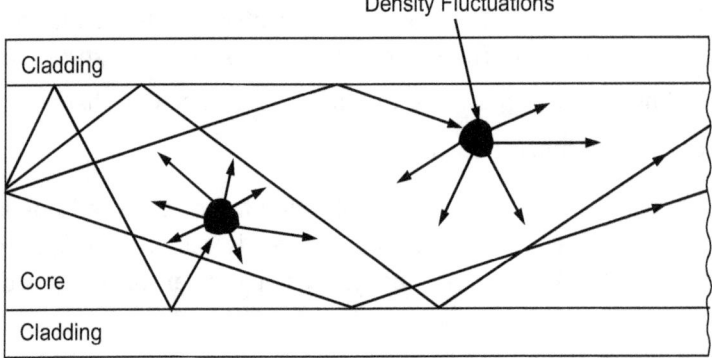

Fig. 2.5: Light Scattering

In commercial fibers operating between 700 nm and 1600 nm wavelength, the main source of loss is called Rayleigh scattering. Rayleigh scattering is the main loss mechanism between the ultraviolet and infrared regions as shown in (Fig. 2.5). **Rayleigh scattering** occurs when the size of the density fluctuation (fiber defect) is less than one-tenth of the operating wavelength of light. Loss caused by Rayleigh scattering is proportional to the fourth power of the wavelength. As the wavelength increases, the loss caused by Rayleigh scattering decreases.

The expression of scattering loss for single component glass, at a wavelength λ resulting from density fluctuations can be approximated by,

$$\alpha_{scat} = \frac{8\pi^3}{3\lambda^4}(n^2-1)^2 \, k_B \cdot T_F \cdot \beta_T \qquad \ldots (2.5)$$

where,

n = Refractive index

k_B = Boltzmann's constant

β_T = The isothermal compressibility of the material

T_F = Fictive temperature

For multicomponent glasses the scattering loss is given by,

$$\alpha = \frac{8\pi^3}{3\lambda^4} (\delta n^2)^2 \, \delta v \qquad \ldots (2.6)$$

where, $(\delta n^2)^2$ = The square of the mean square refractive index fluctuation over a volume of δv.

$$\therefore \quad (\delta n^2) = \left(\frac{\delta n}{\delta p}\right)^2 (\delta p)^2 + \sum_{i=1}^{m} \left(\frac{\delta n^2}{\delta c_i}\right)^2 (\delta c_i)^2 \qquad \ldots (2.7)$$

where, δp = Density fluctuation

δc_i = Concentration fluctuation of the ith glass

If the size of the defect is greater than one-tenth of the wavelength of light, the scattering mechanism is called **Mie scattering**. Mie scattering, caused by these large defects in the fiber core, scatters light out of the fiber core. However, in commercial fibers, the effects of Mie scattering are insignificant. Optical fibers are manufactured with very few large defects.

2.5 Bending Loss

Bending the fiber also causes attenuation. Bending loss is classified according to the bend radius of curvature microbend loss or macrobend loss.

2.5.1 Microbends

Microbends are small microscopic bends of the fiber axis that occur mainly when a fiber is cabled. **Macrobends** are bends having a large radius of curvature relative to the fiber diameter. Microbend and macrobend losses are very important loss mechanisms. Fiber loss caused by microbending can still occur even if the fiber is cabled correctly. During installation, if fibers are bent too sharply, macrobend losses will occur.

Microbend losses are caused by small discontinuities or imperfections in the fiber. Uneven coating applications and improper cabling procedures increase microbend loss. External forces are also a source of microbends. An external force deforms the cabled jacket surrounding the fiber but causes only a small bend in the fiber. Microbends change the path that propagating modes take, as shown in Fig. 2.6.

Microbend loss increases attenuation because low-order modes become coupled with high-order modes that are naturally lossy.

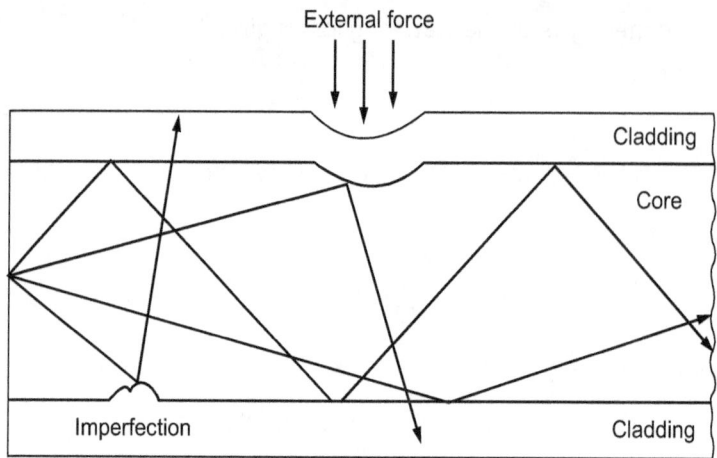

Fig. 2.6: Microbend Loss

2.5.2 Macrobend Losses

Macrobend losses are observed when a fiber bend's radius of curvature is large compared to the fiber diameter.

These bends become a great source of loss when the radius of curvature is less than several centimeters. Light propagating at the inner side of the bend travels a shorter distance than that on the outer side. To maintain the phase of the light wave, the mode phase velocity must increase. When the fiber bend is less than some critical radius, the mode phase velocity must increase to a speed greater than the speed of light. However, it is impossible to exceed the speed of light. This condition causes some of the light within the fiber to be converted to high-order modes. These high-order modes are then lost or radiated out of the fiber.

Fiber sensitivity to bending losses can be reduced. If the refractive index of the core is increased, then fiber sensitivity decreases. Sensitivity also decreases as the diameter of the overall fiber increases. However, increases in the fiber core diameter increase fiber sensitivity. Fibers with larger core size propagate more modes. These additional modes tend to be more lossy.

The amount of optical radiations from a bent fiber depends on the radius of curvature R. The higher order modes are bound less tightly to the fiber, core than lower order modes. The higher order modes will radiate out of the fiber first. Therefore, the total number of modes that can be supported by a curved fiber is less than in a straight fiber. The effective number of modes N_{eff} that are guided by a curved multimode fiber of radius a is,

$$N_{eff} = N_{\infty}\left\{1 - \frac{\alpha+2}{2\alpha\Delta} \cdot \left[\frac{2a}{k} + \left(\frac{3}{2n_2 k}\right)^{2/3}\right]\right\} \quad \ldots (2.8)$$

where, α = The graded index profile
Δ = The core-cladding index difference
n_2 = The cladding refractive index
$k = \dfrac{2\pi}{\lambda}$ the wave propagation constant

$$N_\infty = \dfrac{\alpha}{\alpha + 2} (n_1 \cdot ka)^2 \cdot \Delta$$

N_∞ = The total number of modes in a straight line.

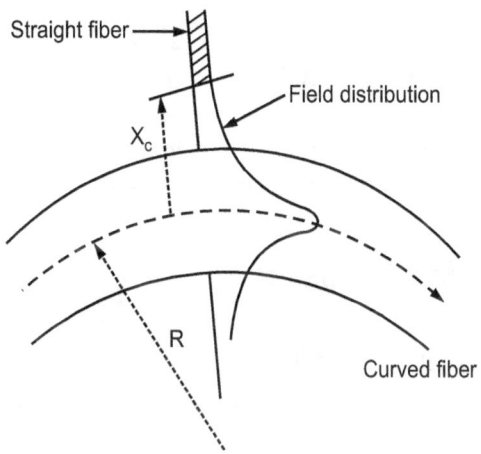

Fig. 2.7: A Curved Optical Fiber

Microbends are repetitive small scale fluctuations in the radius of curvature of the fiber axis as shown in Fig. 2.8.

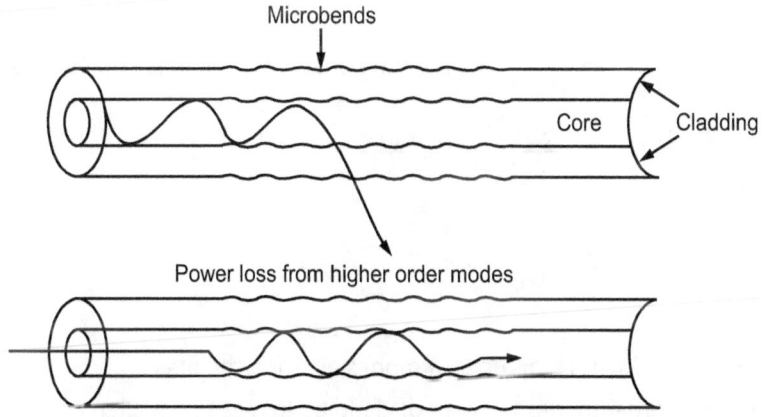

Fig. 2.8: Small Scale Fluctuation in the Radius of Curvature of the Fiber Axis

These losses are caused by non-uniformities in the manufacturing of the fiber or by non-uniform lateral pressure created during the cabling of fiber, or packaging of fiber. Microbends increases attenuation in fiber because the fiber curvature causes repetitive coupling of energy between the guided mode and the leaky or non-guided modes in the fiber. To minimize microbending losses use a compressible jacket over the fiber as shown in Fig. 2.9.

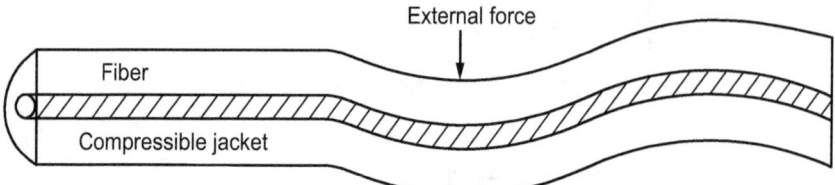

Fig. 2.9: A Compressible Jacket Extruded Over a Fiber

When external forces are applied to the above configuration shown in Fig. 2.9, the jacket will be deformed but the fiber will tend to stay relatively straight.

2.6 Core and Cladding Losses

The core and cladding have different refractive indices and therefore, differ in composition, the core of cladding generally have different attenuation coefficients, denoted α_1 and α_2 respectively. The loss for a mode of order (ϑ, m). For a step index waveguide is,

$$\alpha_{\vartheta m} = \alpha_1 \frac{P_{core}}{P} + \alpha_2 \cdot \frac{P_{clad}}{P} \quad \ldots (2.9)$$

where,

P = Total power in mode
P_{core} = The power in the core
P_{clad} = The power in the clad

$$\frac{P_{core}}{P} = \frac{P_{clad}}{P} = \text{The fractional power various LP}_{jm} \text{ modes}$$

i.e.
$$\frac{P_{clad}}{P} = 1 - \frac{P_{core}}{P} \quad \ldots (2.10)$$

$$\left(\frac{P_{clad}}{P}\right)_{total} = \frac{4}{3} M^{-1/2} \quad \ldots (2.11)$$

where,

M = The total number of modes entering the fiber

For several low order modes the core of cladding loss can be written as,

$$\alpha_{\vartheta m} = \alpha_1 + (\alpha_2 - \alpha_1) \cdot \frac{P_{clad}}{P} \quad \ldots (2.12)$$

The total loss of the fiber can be found by adding over all modes weighted by the fractional power in that mode.

In a graded index fiber the attenuation coefficient and the modal power tend to be functions of the radial co-ordinate. The loss at a distance r from the core axis is given by,

$$\alpha(r) = \alpha_1 + (\alpha_2 - \alpha_1) \cdot \frac{n^2(0) - n^2(r)}{n^2(0) - n_2^2} \quad \ldots (2.13)$$

where,

α_1 = Axial attenuation coefficients
α_2 = Cladding attenuation coefficients
n_2 = Refractive index of cladding

The loss encountered by a given mode is then,

$$\alpha_{gi} = \frac{\int_0^\infty \alpha(r) P(r) r \, dr}{\int_0^\infty P(r) \cdot r \cdot dr} \quad \ldots (2.14)$$

where,

$P(r)$ = The power density of that mode at r

In general the loss increases with increasing mode numbering

2.7 Dispersion

There are two different types of dispersion in optical fibers.

The types are intramodal and intermodal dispersion. Intramodal, or chromatic, dispersion occurs in all types of fibers. Intermodal, or modal, dispersion occurs only in multimode fibers. Each type of dispersion mechanism leads to pulse spreading. As a pulse spreads energy is overlapped. This condition is shown in Fig. 2.10. The spreading of the optical pulse as it travels along the fibe limits the information capacity of the fiber.

The information carrying capacity can be determined by examining the deformation of short light pulses, propagation along the fiber. Consider a signal that modulates an optical source. The modulated optical signal excites all modes equally at the input end of the fiber. Therefore, each mode carries equal amount of energy through the fiber. Each mode contains all the spectral components in the wavelength band over which the source emits.

The signal may be propagate along the fiber, each spectral component can be assumed to travel independently, and to undergo a time delay or group delay per unit length in the direction of propagation given by,

$$\frac{\tau_g}{L} = \frac{1}{v_g} = \frac{1}{c}\frac{d\beta}{dk} = -\frac{\lambda^2}{2\pi c}\cdot\frac{d\beta}{d\lambda} \qquad \ldots (2.15)$$

where,

L = The distance travelled by the pulse

β = The propagation constant along the fiber axis

$k = \frac{2\pi}{\lambda}$

τ_g = Group velocity

$$v_g = c\left(\frac{d\beta}{dk}\right)^{-1} = \left(\frac{\partial\beta}{\partial\omega}\right)^{-1} \qquad \ldots (2.16)$$

v_g = The velocity at which the energy in a pulse travels along the fiber.

From above equations (2.15), (21.6), the group delay depends on the wavelength. Each spectral component of any particular mode takes a different amount of time to travel a certain distance. Due to the difference in time delays, the optical signal pulse spread out with time during transmission.

If the spectral width of $\delta\lambda$ of an optical source is characterised by its r.m.s. value, then the pulse spreading can be denoted by the r.m.s. pulse width.

$$\sigma_g \approx \left|\frac{d\tau_g}{d\lambda}\right|\sigma_\lambda = \frac{L\sigma_\lambda}{2\pi c}\left|2\lambda\cdot\frac{d\beta}{d\lambda} + \lambda^2\cdot\frac{d^2\beta}{d\lambda^2}\right| \qquad \ldots (2.17)$$

The factor,

$$D = \frac{1}{L}\frac{d\tau_g}{d\lambda} = \frac{d}{d\lambda}\left(\frac{1}{v_g}\right) \qquad \ldots (2.18)$$

$$= -\frac{2\pi c}{\lambda^2}\cdot\beta_2$$

D = Dispersion

σ_λ = Spectral width

σ_g = Pulse spread

The dispersion is defined as the pulse spread as a function of wavelength and is measured in picoseconds per kilometer per nanometer (Ps/mm·km).

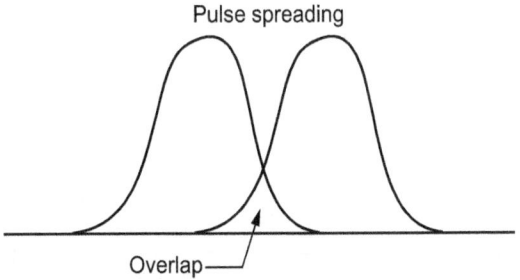

Fig. 2.10: Pulse Overlap

2.7.1 Intramodal Dispersion

Intramodal, or chromatic, dispersion depends primarily on fiber materials. There are two types of intramodal dispersion. The first type is material dispersion. The second type is waveguide dispersion.

Intramodal dispersion occurs because different colors of light travel through different materials and different waveguide structures at different speeds.

1. **Material Dispersion:** It occurs because the spreading of a light pulse is dependent on the wavelength's interaction with the refractive index of the fiber core. Different wavelengths travel at different speeds in the fiber material. Different wavelengths of a light pulse that enter a fiber at one time exit the fiber at different times. Material dispersion is a function of the source spectral width. The spectral width specifies the range of wavelengths that can propagate in the fiber. Material dispersion is less at longer wavelengths.

Let us consider a plane wave propagating in an infinitely extended electric medium that has a refractive index $n(\lambda)$ equal to that of the fiber core. The propagation constant β is given by,

$$\beta = \frac{2\pi \, n(\lambda)}{\lambda} \quad \ldots (2.19)$$

Substitute the β into the equation (2.15) with $k = \frac{2\pi}{\lambda}$. We get the group delay τ_{mat} resulting from the material dispersion.

$$\tau_{mat} = \frac{L}{c}\left(n - \lambda \frac{dn}{d\lambda}\right) \quad \ldots (2.20)$$

By using equation (2.17), the pulse spread σ_{mat} for a source of spectral width σ_λ is found by differentiating this group delay with respect to wavelength and multiplying by σ_λ,

$$\sigma_{mat} \approx \left|\frac{d\tau_{mat}}{d\lambda}\right| \sigma_\lambda$$

$$= \frac{\sigma_\lambda L}{c}\left|\lambda \cdot \frac{d^2 n}{d\lambda^2}\right|$$

$$\sigma_{mat} = \sigma_\lambda L \left|D_{mat}(\lambda)\right| \quad \ldots (2.21)$$

where,

$$D_{mat}(\lambda) = \text{Material dispersion}$$

A plot of material dispersion for unit length L and unit optical source spectral width σ_λ is shown in Fig. 2.11.

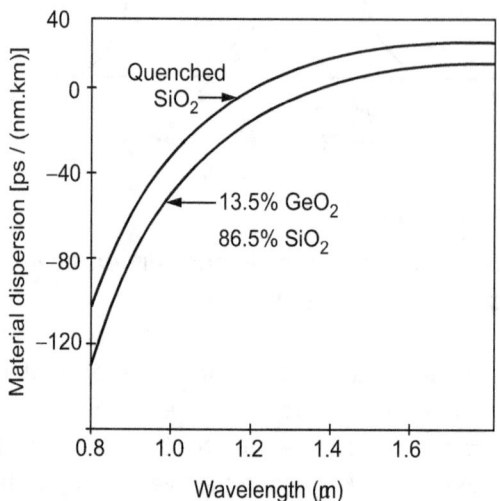

Fig. 2.11: Material Dispersion Versus Optical Wavelength

2. Waveguide dispersion: It occurs because the mode propagation constant (β) is a function of the size of the fiber's core relative to the wavelength of operation. Waveguide dispersion also occurs because light propagates differently in the core than in the cladding.

In multimode fibers, waveguide dispersion and material dispersion are basically separate properties. Multimode waveguide dispersion is generally small compared to material dispersion. Waveguide dispersion usually neglected.
However, in single mode fibers, material and waveguide dispersion are interrelated.

The total dispersion present in single mode fibers may be minimized by trading material and waveguide properties depending on the wavelength of operation.

Consider the group delay which is the time required for a mode to travel along a fiber of length L. The group delay can be expressed in terms of the normalized propagation constant 'b' as,

$$b = 1 - \left(\frac{\mu a}{v}\right)^2$$

$$b = \frac{\left(\frac{\beta^2}{k^2}\right) - n_2^2}{n_1^2 - n_2^2} \quad \ldots (2.22)$$

If index difference is small, i.e.
$$\Delta = \frac{(n_1 - n_2)}{n_1}$$

$$\therefore \quad b \simeq \frac{\left(\frac{\beta}{k}\right) - n_2}{n_1 - n_2} \qquad \ldots (2.23)$$

Solving above equations (2.22), (2.23) for β, we have,
$$\beta \simeq n_k k (b\Delta + 1) \qquad \ldots (2.24)$$

By considering the equation of β and assume that n_2 is not a function of wavelength, the group delay τ_{wg} existing from waveguide dispersion is written as,

$$\tau_{\omega g} = \frac{L}{c} \cdot \frac{d\beta}{dk} = \frac{L}{c}\left[n_2 + n_2\Delta \frac{d(kb)}{dk}\right] \qquad \ldots (2.25)$$

We can express the above equation (2.25) in terms of normalized frequency v,
$$v = ka(n_1^2 - n_2^2)^{1/2} \qquad \ldots (2.26)$$
$$v \simeq ka\, n_2 \sqrt{2\Delta} \qquad \ldots (2.27)$$

which is valid for small values of Δ, therefore,
$$\tau_{\omega g} = \frac{L}{c}\left[n_2 + n_2\Delta \frac{d(vb)}{dv}\right] \qquad \ldots (2.28)$$

When a light pulse is induced into a fiber, it is distributed among many guided modes. These various modes arrive at the fiber end at different times depending on their group delay therefore, a pulse spreading is produced. In multimode fibers, the waveguide dispersion is very small compared with material dispersion and hence it may be neglected.

3. Signal Distortion in Single Mode Fiber:

It is observed that for single mode fiber, the waveguide dispersion is approximately same order of magnitude as material dispersion. To observe this fact, let us compare the two dispersion factors. The pulse spread $\sigma_{\omega g}$ which takes place over a distribution of wavelength σ_λ is obtained from the derivative of the group delay with respect to wavelength.

$$\sigma_{\omega g} \simeq \left|\frac{d\tau_{\omega g}}{d\lambda}\right| \sigma_\lambda$$

$$= L\,|D_{\omega g}(\lambda)|\,\sigma_\lambda$$

$$= \frac{v}{\lambda}\left|\frac{d\tau_{\omega g}}{d\lambda}\right| \sigma_\lambda$$

$$\sigma_{\omega g} = \frac{n_2 L \Delta \sigma_\lambda}{c\lambda} \cdot v \cdot \frac{d^2(vb)}{dv^2} \qquad \ldots (2.29)$$

where,

$D_{\omega g}(\lambda)$ = Waveguide dispersion

To find the behaviour of the waveguide dispersion, the factor μa for the lowest order mode (i.e. LP_{01} mode) in the normalized propagation constant is considered. Therefore,

$$\mu a = \frac{(1 + \sqrt{2})\, v}{1 + (4 + v^4)^{1/4}} \qquad \ldots (2.30)$$

For lowest order mode $1 + E_{11}$, mode, substitute above equation (2.30) into the equation of "b", we get,

$$b(v) = 1 - \frac{(1 + \sqrt{2})^2}{[1 + (4 + v^4)^{1/4}]^2} \qquad \ldots (2.31)$$

The expression for b and its derivatives $d(v_b)/dv$ and $vd^2(v_b)/dv^2$ as a function of v have been plotted and as shown in Fig. 2.12.

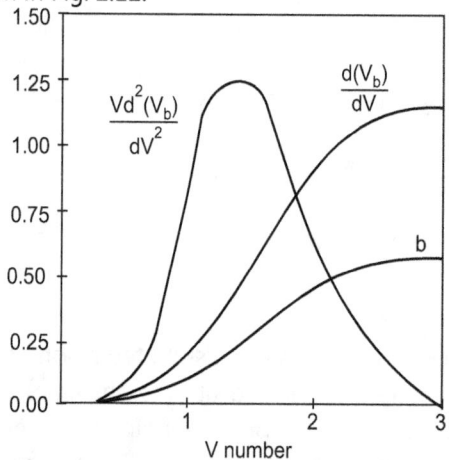

Fig. 2.12: Plot of Waveguide Parameter b and its Derivatives

The examples of the magnitude of material and waveguide dispersion for a fused-silica-core single mode fiber for v = 2.4 is shown in Fig. 2.13.

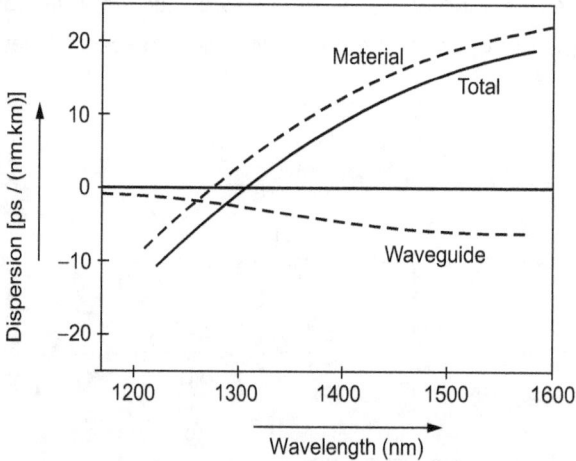

Fig. 2.13: Magnitude of Material and Waveguide Dispersion

To compare the waveguide dispersion with the material dispersion, it is observed that for non-dispersion shifted fiber, waveguide dispersion is of important around 1320 nm. At this wavelength the two dispersion factors cancel to give a zero total dispersion. At a shorter and longer wavelength the material dispersion dominates waveguide dispersion.

4. Polarization – Mode Dispersion:

Birefrigence can produce from intrinsic factors such as geometric irregularities of fiber core or internal stress on it. The fiber birefringence effects on the polarization states of an optical signal will results pulse broadening. The external factors such as bending, twisting or pinching of fiber, can also lead to birefringence. The polarization state is the fundamental property of an optical signal. The polarization means, the electric field orientation of a light signal, which can be very significantly along the length of a fiber as shown in Fig. 2.14. A varying birefringence along its length will result each polarization mode to travel at a slightly different velocity and the polarization orientation will rotate with distance. The signal energy occupies two orthogonal polarization. The propagation delay between two orthogonal polarization mode will result in pulse spreading. This is called as Polarization Mode Dispersion (PMD). Let us consider the group velocity of the two orthogonal polarization modes are ϑ_{gx} and ϑ_{gy}, then the differential time delay $\Delta\tau_{pol}$ between the two polarization components at propagation of the pulse over a distance L is,

$$\Delta\tau_{pol} = \left| \frac{L}{\vartheta_{gx}} - \frac{L}{\vartheta_{gy}} \right| \qquad \text{... (2.32)}$$

For long fiber length, the PMD in terms of the mean value of the differential group delay can be calculated according to the relationship,

$$\infty \Delta\tau_{pol} \approx D_{PMD} \sqrt{L} \qquad \text{... (2.33)}$$

where,

D_{PMD} = The average PMD parameter (Ps/$\sqrt{km}$)

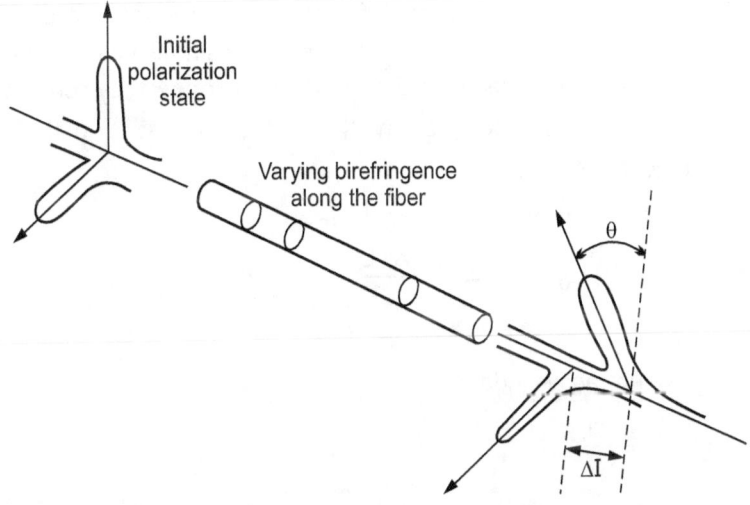

Fig. 2.14: Polarization Mode Dispersion

2.7.2 Intermodal Dispersion

Intermodal or modal dispersion causes the input light pulse to spread. The input light pulse is made up of a group of modes. As the modes propagate along the fiber, light energy distributed among the modes is delayed by different amounts. The pulse spreads because each mode propagates along the fiber at different speeds. Since modes travel in different directions, some modes travel longer distances. **Modal dispersion** occurs because each mode travels a different distance over the same time span, as shown in Fig. 2.15. The modes of a light pulse that enter the fiber at one time exit the fiber a different times. This condition causes the light pulse to spread. As the length of the fiber increases, modal dispersion increases.

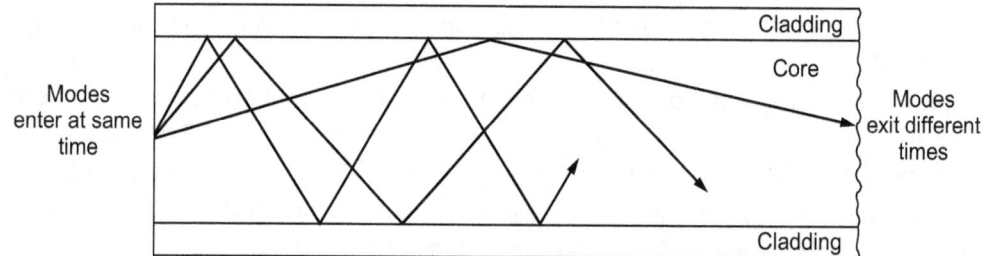

Fig. 2.15: Distance Travelled by Each Mode Over The Same Time Span

Modal dispersion is the dominant source of dispersion in multimode fibers. Modal dispersion does not exist in single mode fibers. Single mode fibers propagate only the fundamental mode. Therefore, single mode fibers exhibit the lowest amount of total dispersion. Single mode fibers also exhibit the highest possible bandwidth.

The variation in the group velocities of the different modes produces a group delay spread of intermodal distortion. The maximum pulse broadening arising from intermodal dispersion is the difference between the propagating time T_{max} of the longest ray congruence path for higher order modes and the propagating time t_{min} of the shortest ray path. For zero order mode or the fundamental mode i.e.

$$\delta T_{mod} = T_{max} - T_{min}$$

$$\delta T_{mod} = \frac{n_1 \cdot \Delta \cdot L}{c} \qquad \ldots (2.34)$$

where,

n_1 = Refractive index

$D = \dfrac{n_1 \cdot n_2}{n_2}$

L = Length of link

Above equation (2.34) is considered only for pulse broadening owing to meridonal rays and does not take into account skews rays.

2.7.3 Pulse Broadening in Graded Index Fiber

The analysis of the pulse broadening in graded index waveguide is more complicated since the refractive index of core varies radially. The feature of this grading of the refractive index profile is that it offers multimode propagation in a relatively large core. It has very low distortion as well. Therefore, this combination allows the transmission of high data rates over along distances while still maintaining a reasonable degree of light launching and coupling ease. In graded index waveguide, since the index of refraction is lower at the outer edges of the core, light ray will travel faster in this region than in the centre of the core where the refractive index is higher. It is clear from the relationship $v = \frac{c}{\eta}$, where v is the speed of light, η is refractive index.

Hence, the ray congruence characterising the higher order mode will tend to travel further than the fundamental ray congruence. This will lead to reduction in spread modal delay. To overcome the delay in two rays, we can design the core with different refractive indexes, so that beam travelling the shortest distance travels at slowest speed and the beam travelling the longer distances travels at highest speed. Such type of fiber are called graded index fiber. The root mean square (r.m.s.) pulse broadening σ in a graded index fiber can be obtained from the sum, is given as,

$$\sigma = (\sigma_{intermodal}^2 + \sigma_{intramodal}^2)^{1/2} \quad \ldots (2.35)$$

where,

$\sigma_{intermodal}$ = r.m.s. pulse width resulting from intermodal delay distortion

$\sigma_{intramodal}$ = r.m.s. pulse width resulting from pulse broadening with each mode

2.8 Mode Coupling

It has been observed that the pulse distortion will increase less rapidly after a certain initial length of fiber because of mode coupling and differential mode loss. The coupling of energy from one mode to another mode arised due to structure and imperfection, fiber diameter and refractive index profile variation and cabling induced microbends. The mode coupling tends to average out the propagation delays associated with the modes, thereby reducing intermodal dispersion. The coupling added loss, which is designed by h which has units of dB/km. Therefore, due to this phenomena, after a certain coupling length L_c, the pulse distortion will change from an L dependence to a $(L_c \cdot L)^{1/2}$ dependence. The improvement in pulse spreading due to mode coupling over the distance $z < L_c$ is related to the excess loss hz incurred over this distance is given by,

$$hz \left(\frac{\sigma_c}{\sigma_0} \right) = C \qquad \ldots (2.36)$$

where,

C = Constant which is independent of all dimensional quantities and refractive indices.

σ_0 = Pulse broadening in the presence of strong mode coupling.

hz = Excess attenuation resulting from mode coupling.

The constant C depends only on the fiber profile shape, the mode coupling strength and the modal attenuation.

As the length of fiber is significantly larger, effect of mode coupling on distortion is also significant as shown in Fig. 2.16. For various coupling losses in a graded index fiber. The different parameters for this fiber are $\Delta = 1$ percent, $\alpha = 4$ and $C = 1.1$. The coupling loss h must be determined experimentally. A value of L_c ranging from about 100 to 550 m has been obtained by measuring bandwidth as a function of distance.

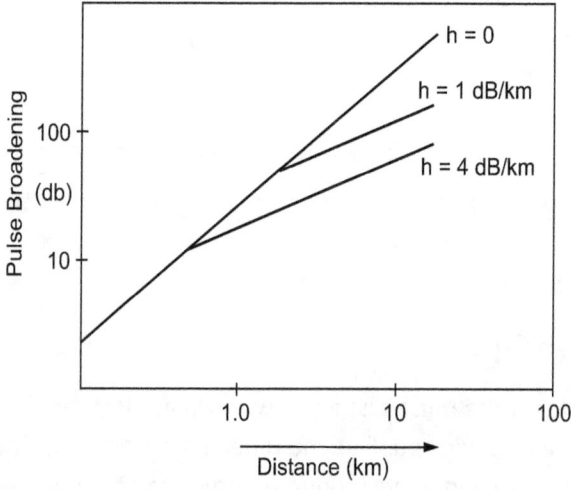

Fig. 2.16: Mode Coupling Effects on Pulse Distortion in Long Fibers

2.9 Fiber Optic Connections

A fiber optic data link performs three basic functions. First, the data link transmitter converts an electrical input signal to an optical signal. Then, the optical fiber transmits this optical signal. Finally, the data link receiver converts the optical signal back to an electrical signal identical to the original input.

This topic describes how optical power is transferred from one fiber optic component to another. It describes how an optical source launches optical power into a fiber as well as how one optical fiber couples light into another fiber. In fiber optic system design, this launching or coupling of optical power from one component to the next is important.

Fiber optic connections permit the transfer of optical power from one component to another. Fiber optic connections also permit fiber optic systems to be more than just point-to-point data communication links. In fact, fiber optic data links are often of a more complex design than point-to-point data links.

A system connection may require either a fiber optic splice, connector, or coupler. One type of system connection is a permanent connection made by splicing optical fibers together. A fiber optic **splice** makes a permanent joint between two fibers or two groups of fibers. There are two types of fiber optic splices - mechanical splices and fusion splices. Even though removal of some mechanical splices is possible, they are intended to be permanent. Another type of connection that allows for system reconfiguration is a fiber optic **connector**. Fiber optic connectors permit easy coupling and uncoupling of optical fibers. Fiber optic connectors sometimes resemble familiar electrical plugs and sockets. Systems may also divide or combine optical signals between fibers. Fiber optic **couplers** distribute or combine optical signals between fibers. Couplers can distribute an optical signal from a single fiber into several fibers. Couplers may also combine optical signals from several fibers into one fiber.

Fiber optic connection losses may affect system performance. **Poor fiber end preparation** and **poor fiber alignment** are the main causes of coupling loss. Another source of coupling loss is differences in optical properties between the connected fibers. If the connected fibers have different optical properties, such as different numerical apertures, core and cladding diameters, and refractive index profiles, then coupling losses may increase.

2.9.1 Optical Fiber Coupling Loss

Ideally, optical signals coupled between fiber optic components are transmitted with no loss of light. However, there is always some type of imperfection present at fiber optic connections that causes some loss of light. It is the amount of optical power lost at fiber optic connections that is a concern of system designers.

The design of fiber optic systems depends on how much light is launched into an optical fiber from an optical source and how much light is coupled between fiber optic components, such as from one fiber to another. The amount of power launched from a source into a fiber depends on the optical properties of both the source and the fiber. The amount of optical power launched into an optical fiber depends on the radiance of the optical source. An optical source's **radiance**, or brightness, is a measure of its optical power launching capability. Radiance is the amount of optical power emitted in a specific direction per unit time by a unit area of emitting surface. For most types of optical sources, only a fraction of the power emitted by the source is launched into the optical fiber.

The loss in optical power through a connection is defined similarly to that of signal attenuation through a fiber. Optical loss is also a log relationship. The loss in optical power through a connection is defined as,

$$\text{Loss} = 10 \log_{10} \frac{P_i}{P_o} \qquad \ldots (2.37)$$

For example, P_o is the power emitted from the source fiber in a fiber connection. P_i is the power accepted by the connected fiber. In optic connection, P_o and P_i are the optical power levels measured before and after the joint, respectively.

Fiber-to-fiber connection loss is affected by intrinsic and extrinsic coupling losses. **Intrinsic coupling** losses are caused by inherent fiber characteristics. **Extrinsic coupling losses** are caused by jointing techniques. Fiber-to-fiber connection loss is increased by the following sources of intrinsic and extrinsic coupling loss:
- Reflection losses
- Fiber separation
- Lateral misalignment
- Angular misalignment
- Core and cladding diameter mismatch
- Numerical aperture (NA) mismatch
- Refractive index profile difference
- Poor fiber end preparation.

Intrinsic coupling losses are limited by reducing fiber mismatches between the connected fibers. This is done by procuring only fibers that meet stringent geometrical and optical specifications. Extrinsic coupling losses are limited by following proper connection procedures.

Some fiber optic components are modular devices that are designed to reduce coupling losses between components. Modular components can be easily inserted or removed from any system. For example, fiber optic transmitters and receivers are modular components.

Fiber optic transmitters and receivers are devices that are generally manufactured with fiber pigtails or fiber optic connectors as shown in Fig. 2.17. A **fiber pigtail** is a short length of optical fiber (usually 1 meter or less) permanently fixed to the optical source or detector. Manufacturers supply transmitters and receivers with pigtails and connectors because fiber coupling to sources and detectors must be completed during fabrication. Reduced coupling loss results when source-to-fiber and fiber-to-detector coupling is done in a controlled manufacturing environment. Since optical sources and detectors are pigtailed or connectorized, launching optical power is reduced to coupling light from one fiber to another. In fact, most fiber optic connections can be considered fiber-to-fiber.

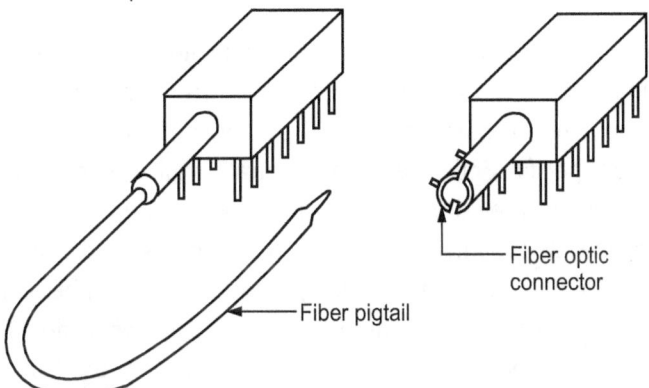

Fig. 2.17: Pigtailed and Connectorized Fiber Optic Devices

2.9.2 Reflection Losses

When optical fibers are connected, optical power may be reflected back into the source fiber. Light that is reflected back into the source fiber is lost. This reflection loss, called Fresnel reflection, occurs at every fiber interface. **Fresnel reflection** is caused by a step change in the refractive index that occurs at the fiber joint. In most cases, the step change in refractive index is caused by the ends of each fiber being separated by a small gap. This small gap is usually an air gap. In Fresnel reflection, a small portion of the incident light is reflected back into the source fiber at the fiber interface. The ratio (R), shown below, approximates the portion of incident light (light of normal incidence) that is reflected back into the source fiber.

$$R = \left(\frac{n_1 - n_0}{n_1 + n_0}\right)^2 \qquad \ldots (2.38)$$

R is the fraction of the incident light reflected at the fiber n_1 is the refractive index of the fiber core. n_0 is the refractive index of the medium between the two fibers.

Fresnel refraction occurs twice in a fiber-to-fiber connection.

A portion of the optical power is reflected when the light first exits the source fiber. Light is then reflected as the optical signal enters the receiving fiber. Fresnel reflection at each interface must be taken into account when calculating the total fiber-to-fiber coupling loss. Loss from Fresnel reflection may be significant. To reduce the amount of loss from Fresnel reflection, the air gap can be filled with an index matching gel. The refractive index of the index matching gel should match the refractive index of the fiber core. **Index matching gel** reduces the step change in the refractive index at the fiber interface, reducing Fresnel reflection.

In any system, index matching gels can be used to eliminate or reduce reflection. The choice of index matching gels is important. Fiber-to-fiber connections are designed to be permanent and require no maintenance. Over the lifetime of the fiber connection, the index material must meet specific optical and mechanical requirements. Index matching gels should remain transparent. They should also resist flowing or dripping by remaining viscous. Some index matching gels darken over time while others settle or leak out of fiber connections. If these requirements are not met, then the fiber-to-fiber connection loss will increase over time. In Navy applications, this variation in connection loss over time is unacceptable. In Navy systems, index matching gels are only used in fiber optic splice interfaces.

2.9.3 Fiber Alignment

A main source of extrinsic coupling loss in fiber-to-fiber connections is poor fiber alignment. The three basic coupling errors that occur during fiber alignment are fiber separation (longitudinal misalignment); lateral misalignment, and angular misalignment. Most alignment errors are the result of mechanical imperfections introduced by fiber jointing techniques. However, alignment errors do result from installers not following proper connection procedures.

With **fiber separation**, a small gap remains between fiber-end faces after completing the fiber connection. Fig. 2.18 illustrates this separation of the fiber-end faces.

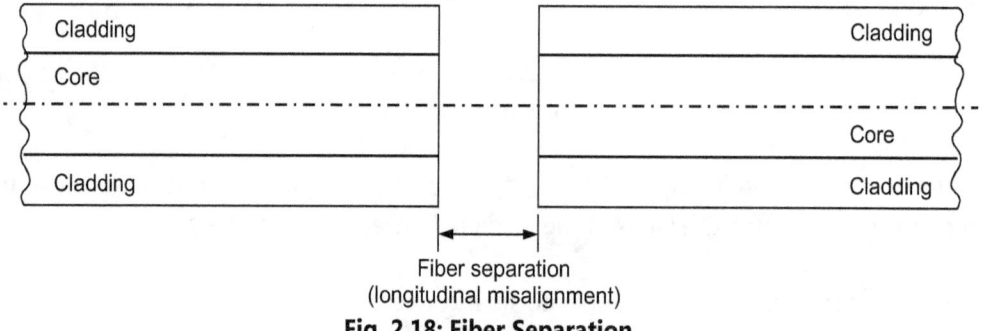

Fiber separation
(longitudinal misalignment)

Fig. 2.18: Fiber Separation

Lateral, or **axial**, **misalignment** occurs when the axes of the two fibers are offset in a perpendicular direction. Fig. 2.19 shows this perpendicular offset of the axes of two connecting fibers.

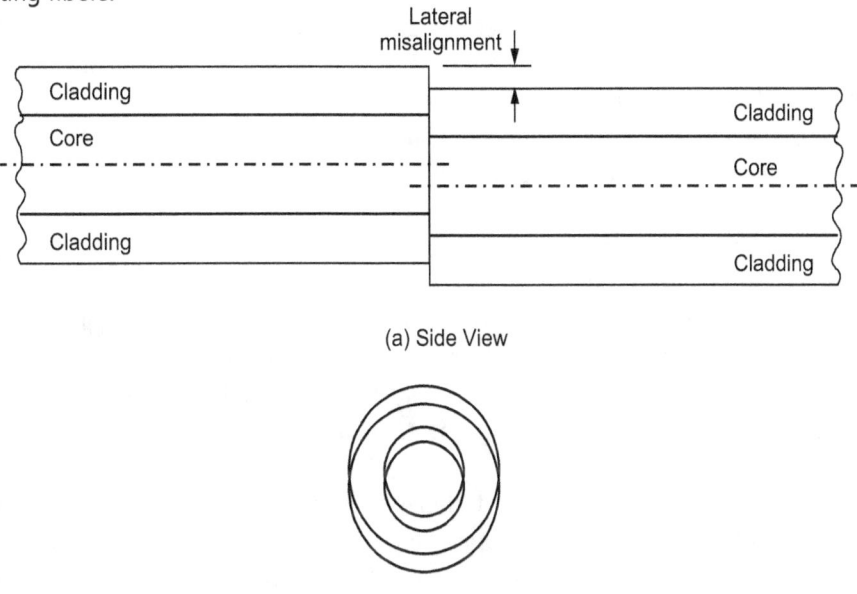

Fig. 2.19: Lateral Misalignment

Angular Misalignment occurs when the axes of two connected fibers are no longer parallel. The axes of each fiber intersect at some angle (Θ). Fig. 2.20 illustrates the angular misalignment between the core axes.

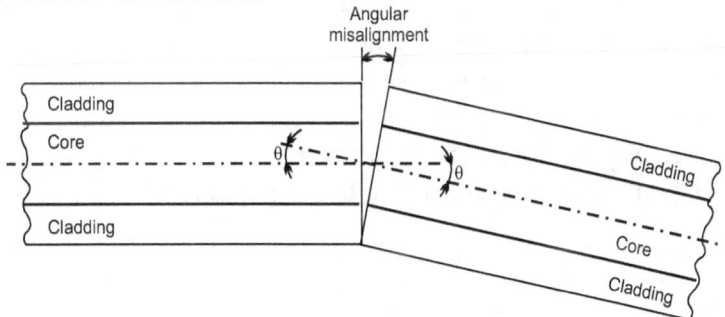

Fig. 2.20: Angular Misalignment

Coupling loss caused by lateral and angular misalignment typically is greater than the loss caused by fiber separation. Loss, caused by fiber separation, is less critical because of the relative ease in limiting the distance of fiber separation. However, in some cases, fiber optic connectors prevent fibers from actual contact. These fiber optic connectors separate the fibers by a small gap. This gap eliminates damage to fiber-end faces during connection. For connectors with an air gap, the use of index matching gel reduces the coupling loss.

Most newer connectors are designed so that the connector ferrule end faces contact when the connector is mated. The connector can be assembled onto the fiber so that the fibers also contact when mated. However, they also can be assembled so that the fibers do not. Whether or not the fibers contact is determined by whether the fiber sticks out slightly from the ferrule or is recessed inside the ferrule. The fiber position can be controlled by the connector polishing technique. The Physical Contact (PC) polish technique was developed for most connectors so that the fibers would touch when mated. In these types of connectors, index gel is not needed to reduce reflections.

While index matching gel reduces coupling loss from fiber separation, it does not affect loss in lateral misalignment. Additionally, index matching gel usually increases the fiber's coupling loss sensitivity to angular misalignment. Although angular misalignment involves fiber separation, index matching gel reduces the angle at which light is launched from the source fiber. Index matching gel causes less light to be coupled into the receiving fiber. To reduce coupling loss from angular misalignment, the angle Θ should be less than 1°.

Coupling losses due to fiber alignment depend on fiber type, core diameter, and the distribution of optical power among propagating modes. Fibers with large NAs reduce loss from angular misalignment and increase loss from fiber separation. Single mode fibers are more sensitive to alignment errors than multimode fibers because of their small core size. However, alignment errors in multimode fiber connections may disturb the distribution of optical power in the propagating modes, increasing coupling loss.

2.9.4 Fiber End Preparation

In fiber-to-fiber connections, a source of extrinsic coupling loss is poor fiber end preparation. An optical fiber-end face must be flat, smooth, and perpendicular to the fiber's axis to ensure proper fiber connection. Light is reflected or scattered at the connection interface unless the connecting fiber end faces are properly prepared. Fig. 2.21 shows some common examples of poor fiber ends. It illustrates a fiber end face **tilt**, **lip**, and **hackle**. Quality fiber-end preparation is essential for proper system operation.

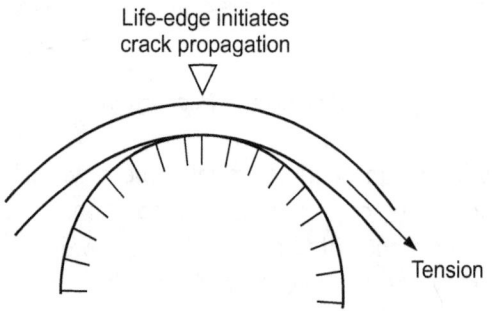

Fig. 2.21: Poor Fiber-End Preparation

Fiber-end preparation begins by removing the fiber buffer and coating material from the end of the optical fiber. Removal of these materials involves the use of mechanical strippers or chemical solvents. When using chemical solvents, the removal process must be performed in a well-ventilated area. For this reason mechanical strippers are used for buffer and coating removal in the shipboard environment. After removing the buffer and coating material, the surface of the bare fiber is wiped clean using a wiping tissue. The wiping tissue must be wet with isopropyl alcohol before wiping.

The next step in fiber-end preparation involves cleaving the fiber end to produce a smooth, flat fiber-end face. The **score-end-break**, or scribe-and-break, method is the basic fiber cleaving technique for preparing optical fibers for coupling. The score-and-break method consists of lightly scoring (nicking) the outer surface of the optical fiber and then placing it under tension until it breaks. A heavy metal or diamond blade is used to score the fiber. Once the scoring process is complete, fiber tension is increased until the fiber breaks. The fiber is placed under tension either by pulling on the fiber or by bending the fiber over a curved surface.

Fig. 2.22 shows the setup for the score-and-break procedure for fiber cleaving. Under constant tension, the score-and-break method for cleaving fibers produces a quality fiber end. This fiber end is good enough to use for some splicing techniques. However, additional fiber-end preparation is necessary to produce reliable low-loss connections when using fiber optic connectors.

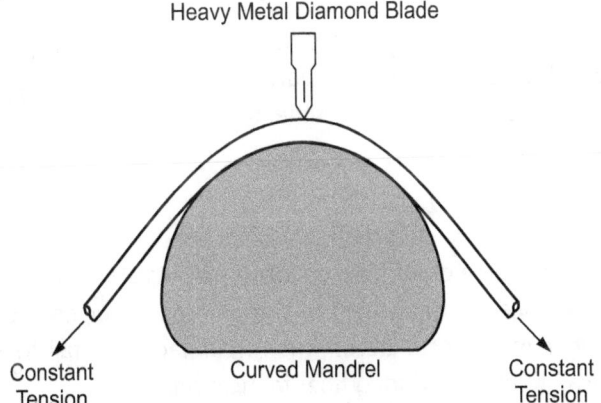

Fig. 2.22: Score-and-Break Procedure for Fiber Cleaving

Polishing the fiber ends removes most surface imperfections introduced by the fiber cleaving process. Fiber polishing begins by inserting the cleaved fiber into the ferrule of a connector assembly. A ferrule is a mixture, generally a rigid tube, used to hold the stripped end of an optical fiber in a fiber optic connector. An individual fiber is epoxied within the ferrule. The connector with the optical fiber cemented within the ferrule can then be mounted into a special polishing tool for polishing.

Fig. 2.23 shows one type of fiber polishing tool for finishing optical fibers in a connector assembly. Various types of connector assemblies are discussed later in this chapter. In this type of polishing tool, the connector assembly is threaded onto the polishing tool. The connector ferrule passes through the center of the tool allowing the fiber-end face to extend below the tool's circular, flat bottom. The optical fiber is now ready for polishing.

Fiber polishing involves a step-down approach. The first step is to give the surface of the fiber end a rough polish. **Rough-polishing** occurs when the fiber, mounted to the polishing tool, moves over a 5 μ to 15 μ grit abrasive paper. The mounted fiber moves over the abrasive paper in a figure-eight motion. The next step involves giving the surface of the fiber end a fine polish. **Fine-polishing** occurs when the mounted fiber moves over a 0.3μ to 1μ grit abrasive paper in the same Fig. 2.24 motion. Fiber inspection and cleanliness are important during each step of fiber polishing. Fiber inspection is done visually by the use of a standard microscope at 200 to 400 times magnification.

A standard microscope can be used to determine if the fiber-end face is flat, concave, or convex. If different parts of the fiber-end face have different focus points, the end face is not flat. If all parts of the fiber-end face are in focus at the same time, the end face is flat.

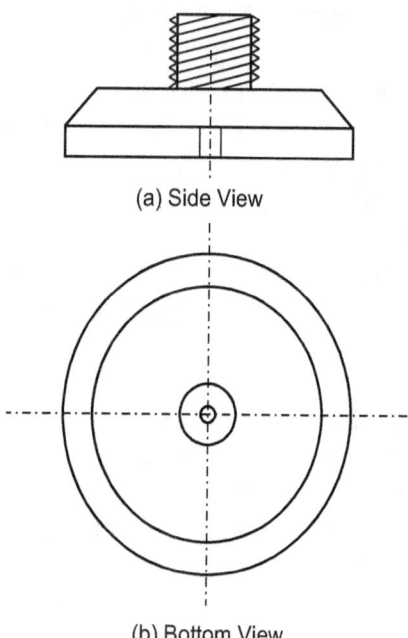

Fig. 2.23: Fiber Polishing Tool

2.9.5 Fiber Mismatches

Fiber mismatches are a source of intrinsic coupling loss. As stated before, intrinsic coupling loss results from differences (mismatches) in the inherent fiber characteristics of the two connecting fibers. Fiber mismatches occur when manufacturers fail to maintain optical or structural (geometrical) tolerances during fiber fabrication.

Fiber mismatches are the result of inherent fiber characteristics and are independent of the fiber jointing techniques. Types of fiber mismatches include fiber geometry mismatches, NA mismatch, and refractive index profile difference. Fiber geometry mismatches include core diameter, cladding diameter core ellipticity, and core-cladding concentricity differences. Fig. 2.24 illustrates each type of optical and geometrical fiber mismatch. Navy fiber specifications tightly specify these parameters to minimize coupling losses from fiber mismatches.

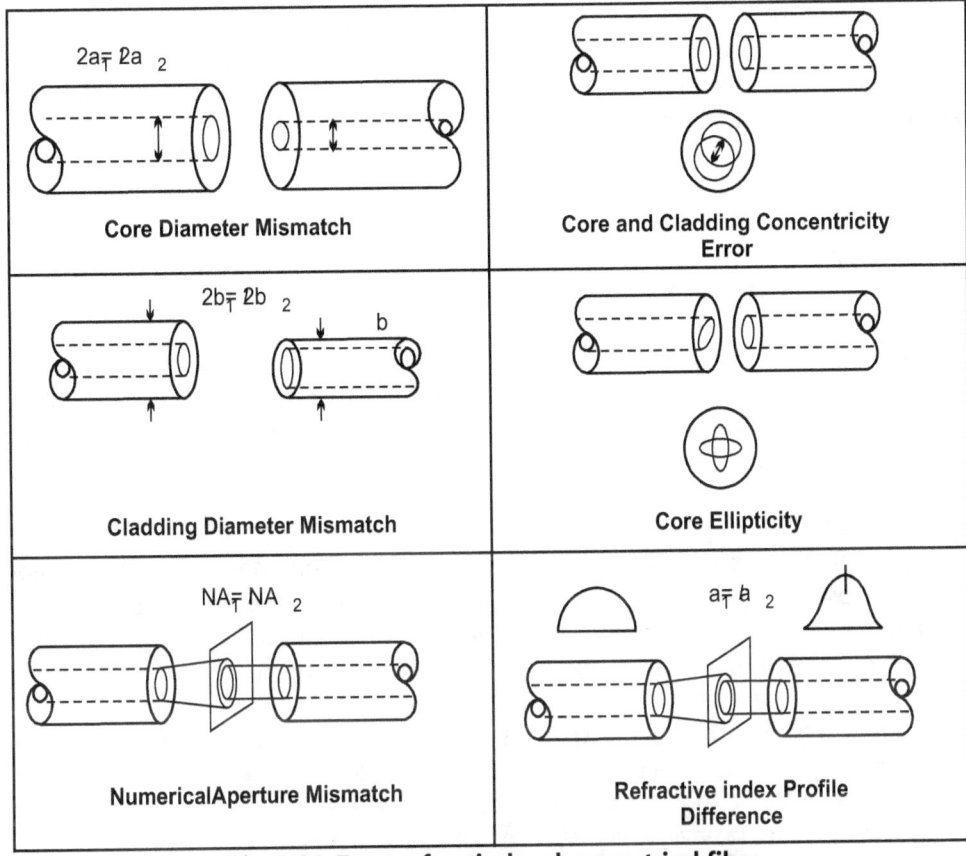

Fig. 2.24: Types of optical and geometrical fiber mismatches that cause intrinsic coupling loss

Core diameter and NA mismatch have a greater effect on intrinsic coupling loss than the other types of fiber mismatches. In multimode fiber connections, the coupling loss resulting from core diameter mismatch NA mismatch, and refractive index profile difference depends on the characteristics of the launching fiber. Coupling loss from **core diameter mismatch** results only if the launching fiber has a larger core radius (a) than the receiving fiber. Coupling loss from **NA mismatch** results only if the launching fiber has a higher NA than the receiving fiber. Coupling loss from **refractive index profile difference** results only if the launching fiber has a larger profile parameter (α) than the receiving fiber.

2.10 Fiber Optic Splices

A **fiber optic splice** is a permanent fiber joint whose purpose is to establish an optical connection between two individual optical fibers. System design may require that fiber connections have specific optical properties (low loss) that are met only by fiber-splicing. Fiber optic splices also permit repair of optical fibers damaged during installation, accident, or stress. System designers generally require fiber splicing whenever repeated connection or disconnection is unnecessary or unwanted.

Mechanical and fusion splicing are two broad categories that describe the techniques used for fiber splicing. A **mechanical splice** is a fiber splice where mechanical fixtures and materials perform fiber alignment and connection. A **fusion splice** is a fiber splice where localized heat fuses or melts the ends of two optical fibers together. Each splicing technique seeks to optimize splice performance and reduce splice loss. Low-loss fiber splicing results from proper fiber end preparation and alignment.

Fiber splice alignment can involve passive or active fiber core alignment. Passive alignment relies on precision reference surfaces, either grooves or cylindrical holes, to align fiber cores during splicing. Active alignment involves the use of light for accurate fiber alignment. Active alignment may consist of either monitoring the loss the splice during splice alignment or by using a microscope to accurately align the fiber cores for splicing. To monitor loss either an optical source and optical power meter or an optical time domain reflectometer (OTDR) are used. Active alignment procedures produce low-loss fiber splices.

2.10.1 Mechanical Splices

Mechanical splicing involves using mechanical fixtures to align and connect optical fibers. Mechanical splicing methods may involve either passive or active core alignment. Active core alignment produces a lower loss splice than passive alignment. However, passive core alignment methods can produce mechanical splices with acceptable loss measurements even with single mode fibers.

In the strictest sense, a mechanical splice is a permanent connection made between two optical fibers. Mechanical splices hold the two optical fibers in alignment for an indefinite period of time without movement. The amount of splice loss is stable over time and unaffected by changes in environmental or mechanical conditions.

If high splice loss results from assembling some mechanical splices, the splice can be reopened and the fibers realigned. Realignment includes wiping the fiber or ferrule end with a soft wipe, reinserting the fiber or ferrule in a new arrangement, and adding new refractive index material. Once producing an acceptable mechanical splice, splice realignment should be unnecessary because most mechanical splices are environmentally and mechanically stable within their intended application.

The types of mechanical splices that exist for mechanical splicing include glass, plastic, metal, and ceramic tubes; and V-groove and rotary devices. Materials that assist mechanical splices in splicing fibers include transparent adhesives and index matching gels. **Transparent adhesives** are epoxy resins that seal mechanical splices and provide index matching between the connected fibers.

2.10.2 Mechanical or Ceramic Alignment Tube Splices

Mechanical splicing may involve the use of a glass or ceramic alignment tube, or capillary. The inner diameter of this glass or ceramic tube is only slightly larger than the outer diameter of the fiber. A transparent adhesive, injected into the tube, bonds the two fibers together. The adhesive also provides index matching between the optical fibers. Fig. 2.25 illustrates fiber alignment using a glass or ceramic tube. This splicing technique relies on the inner diameter of the alignment tube. If the inner diameter is too large, splice loss will increase because of fiber misalignment. If the inner diameter is too small, it is impossible to insert the fiber into the tube.

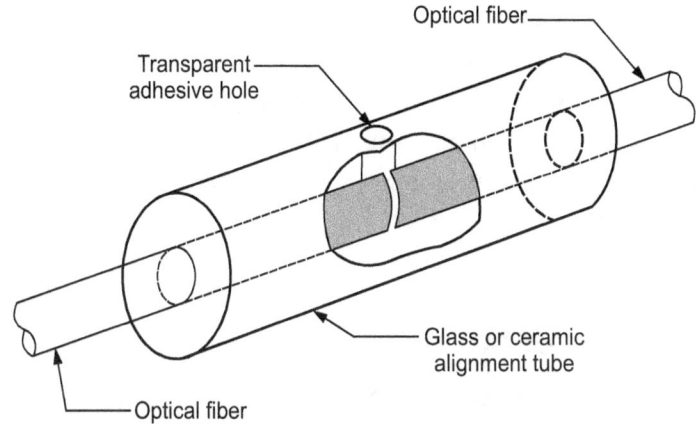

Fig. 2.25: A Glass or Ceramic Alignment Tube for Mechanical Splicing

2.10.3 V-Grooved Splices

Mechanical splices may also use either a grooved substrate or positioning rods to form suitable V-grooves for mechanical splicing. The basic V-grooved device relies on an open grooved substrate to perform fiber alignment. when inserting the fibers into the grooved substrate, the V-groove aligns the cladding surface of each fiber end. A transparent adhesive makes the splice permanent by securing the fiber ends to the grooved substrate. Fig. 2.26 illustrates this type of open V-grooved splice.

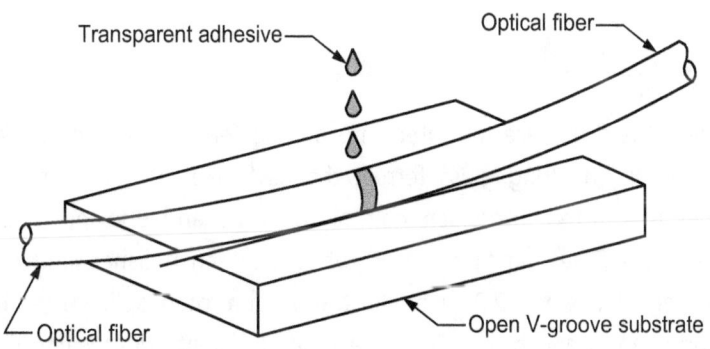

Fig. 2.26: Open V-grooved Spice

V-grooved splices may involve sandwiching the butted ends of two prepared fibers between a V-grooved substrate and a flat glass plate. Additional V-grooved devices use two or three positioning rods to form a suitable V-groove for splicing. The V-grooved device that uses two positioning rods is the spring V-grooved splice. This splice uses a groove formed by two rods positioned in a bracket to align the fiber ends. The diameter of the positioning rods permits the outer surface of each fiber end to extend above the groove formed by the rods. A flat spring presses the fiber ends into the groove maintaining fiber alignment. Transparent adhesive completes the assembly process by bonding the fiber ends and providing index matching. Fig. 2.27 is an illustration of the spring V-grooved splice. A variation of this splice uses a third positioning rod instead of a flat spring. The rods are held in place by a heat-shrinkable band, or tube.

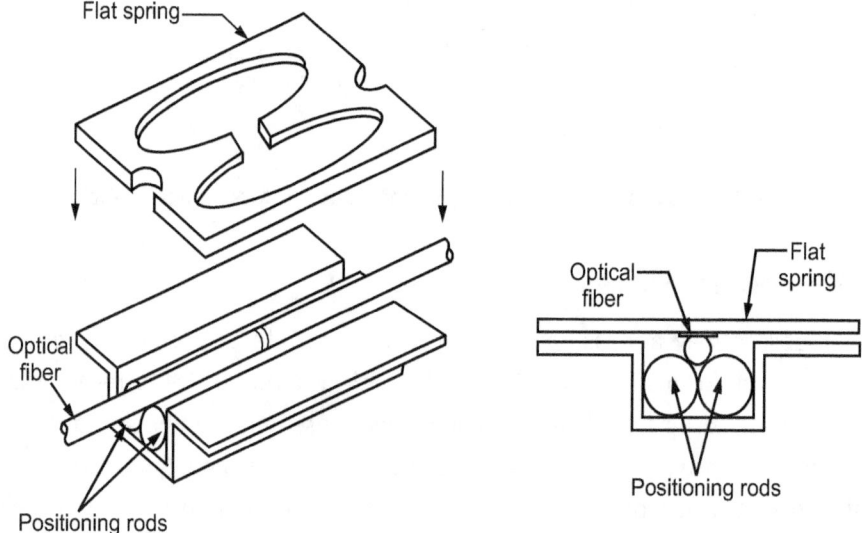

Fig. 2.27: Spring V-grooved Mechanical Splice

2.10.4 Rotary Splices

In a rotary splice, the fibers are mounted into a glass ferrule and secured with adhesives. The splice begins as one long glass ferrule that is broken in half during the assembly process. A fiber is inserted into each half of the tube and epoxied in place using an ultraviolet cure epoxy. The end face of the tubes are then polished and placed together using the alignment sleeve. Fig. 2.28 is an illustration of a rotary splice. The fiber ends retain their original orientation and have added mechanical stability since each fiber is mounted into a glass ferrule and alignment sleeve. The rotary splice may use index matching gel within the alignment sleeve to produce low-loss splices.

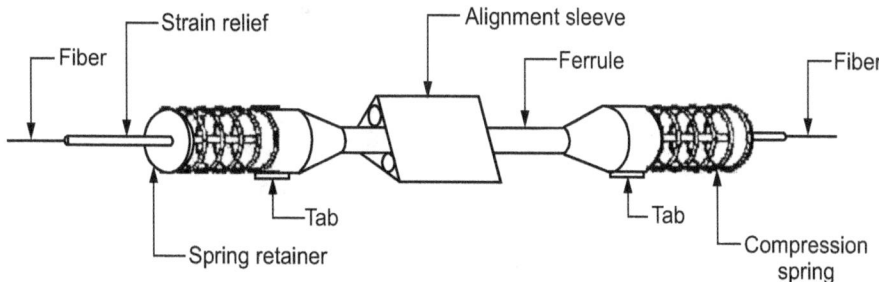

Fig. 2.28: Rotary Mechanical Splice

In shipboard applications, the Navy recommends using the rotary splice. The rotary splice is a low-loss mechanical splice that provides stable environmental and mechanical performance in the Navy environment.

Stable performance means that splice loss does not vary significantly with changes in temperature or other environmental or mechanical conditions. Completing a rotary splice also requires only a small amount of training, or expertise. This shorter training time is another reason why the Navy recommends using the rotary splice over other mechanical or fusion splicing techniques.

2.10.5 Fusion Splices

The process of fusion splicing involves using localized heat to melt or fuse the ends of two optical fibers together. The splicing process begins by preparing each fiber end for fusion. Fusion splicing requires that all protective coatings be removed from the ends of each fiber. The fiber is then cleaved using the score-and-break method. The quality of each fiber end is inspected using a microscope. In fusion splicing, splice loss is a direct function of the angles and quality of the two fiber-end faces.

The basic fusion splicing apparatus consists of two fixtures on which the fibers are mounted and two electrodes. Fig. 2.29 shows a basic zusion-splicing apparatus. An inspection microscope assists in the placement of the prepared fiber ends into a fusion-splicing apparatus. The fibers are placed into the apparatus, aligned, and then fused together. Initially, fusion splicing used nichrome wire as the heating element to melt or fuse fibers together. New fusion-splicing techniques have replaced the nichrome wire with carbon dioxide (CO_2) lasers, electric arcs, or gas flames to heat the fiber ends, causing them to fuse together. The small size of the fusion splice and the development of automated fusion-splicing machines have made **electric arc fusion** (arc fusion) one of the most popular splicing techniques in commercial applications.

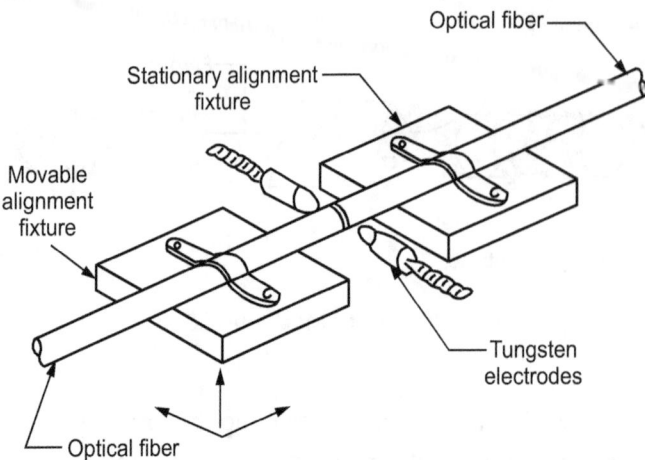

Fig. 2.29: A Basic Fusion Splicing Apparatus

Arc fusion involves the discharge of electric current across a gap between two electrodes. By placing the fiber ends between the electrodes the electric discharge melts or fuses the ends of each fiber. Fig. 2.29 shows the placement of the fiber ends between tungsten electrodes during arc fusion. Initially, a small gap is present between the fiber ends. A short discharge of electric current is used to prepare the fiber ends for fusion. During this short discharge, known as **prefusion**, the fiber ends are cleaned and rounded to eliminate any surface defects that remain from fiber cleaving. Surface defects can cause core distortions or bubble formations during fiber fusion. A fusion splice results when the fiber ends are pressed together, actively aligned, and fused using a longer and stronger electric discharge. Automated fusion splicers typically use built-in local optical power launch/detection schemes for aligning the fibers.

During fusion, the surface tension of molten glass tends to realign the fibers on their outside diameters, changing the initial alignment. When the fusion process is complete, a small core distortion may be present. Small core distortions have negligible effects on light propagating through multimode fibers. However, a small core distortion can significantly affect single mode fiber splice loss. The core distortion, and the splice loss, can be reduced by limiting the arc discharge and decreasing the gap distance between the two electrodes. This limits the region of molten glass. However, limiting the region of molten glass reduces the tensile strength of the splice.

Fusion splicing yields typically vary between 25 and 75 percent depending on the strength and loss requirements for the splice and other factors. Other factors affecting splice yields include the condition of the splicing machine, the experience of the splice personnel, and environmental conditions. Since fusion splicing is inherently permanent, an unacceptable fusion splice requires breakage and refabrication of the splice.

In general, fusion splicing takes a longer time to complete than mechanical splicing. Also, yields are typically lower making the total time per successful splice much longer for fusion splicing. Both the yield and splice time are determined to a large degree by the expertise of the fusion splice operator. Fusion splice operators must be highly trained to consistently make low-loss reliable fusion splices. For these reasons the fusion splice is not recommended for use in Navy shipboard applications.

2.10.6 Multifiber Splicing

Normally, multifiber splices are only installed on ribbon type fiber optic cables. Multifiber splicing techniques can use arc fusion to restore connection, but most splicing techniques use mechanical splicing methods. The most common mechanical splice is the ribbon splice.

A ribbon splice uses an etched silicon chip, or grooved substrate, to splice the multiple fibers within a flat ribbon. The spacing between the etched grooves of the silicon chip is equal to the spacing between the fibers in the flat ribbon. Before placing each ribbon on the etched silicon chip, each fiber within the ribbon cable is cleaved. All of the fibers are placed into the grooves and held in place with a flat cover. Typically, an index matching gel is used to reduce the splice loss. Fig. 2.30 shows the placement of the fiber ribbon on the etched silicon chip.

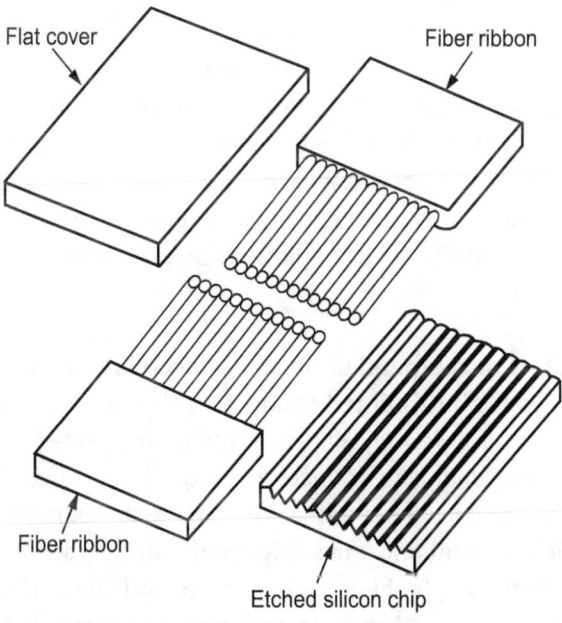

Fig. 2.30: Ribbon Splice on Etched Silicon Chip

2.11 Fiber Optic Connectors

A fiber optic connector is a demateable device that permits the coupling of optical power between two optical fibers or two groups of fibers. Designing a device that allows for repeated fiber coupling without significant loss of light is difficult. Fiber optic connectors must maintain fiber alignment and provide repeatable loss measurements during numerous connections. Fiber optic connectors should be easy to assemble (in a laboratory or field environment) and should be cost effective. They should also be reliable. Fiber optic connections using connectors should be insensitive to environmental conditions, such as temperature, dust, and moisture. Fiber optic connector designs attempt to optimize connector performance by meeting each of these conditions.

Fiber optic connector coupling loss results from the same loss mechanisms described earlier in this chapter. Coupling loss results from poor fiber alignment and end preparation (extrinsic losses), fiber mismatches (intrinsic loss), and Fresnel reflection. The total amount of insertion loss for fiber optic connectors should remain below 1 dB. Fiber alignment is the critical parameter in maintaining the total insertion loss below the required level. There is only a small amount of control over coupling loss resulting from fiber mismatches, because the loss results from inherent fiber properties. Index matching gels cannot be used to reduce Fresnel losses, since the index matching gels attract dust and dirt to the connection.

Fiber optic connectors can also reduce system performance by introducing modal and reflection noise. The cause of modal noise in fiber optic connectors is the interfering of the different wavefronts of different modes within the fiber at the connector interface. Modal noise is eliminated by using only single mode fiber with laser sources and only low-coherence sources such as light-emitting diodes with multimode fiber. Fiber optic connectors can introduce reflection noise is reflecting light back into the optical source. Reflection noise is reduced by index matching gels, physical contact polishes, or antireflection coatings. Generally, reflection noise is only a problem in high data rate single mode systems using lasers.

Butt-jointed connectors and **expanded-beam connectors** are the two basic types fiber optic connectors. Fiber optic **butt-jointed connectors** align and bring the prepared ends of two fibers into close contact. The end-faces of some butt-jointed connectors touch, but others do not depending upon the connector design. Types of butt-jointed connectors include cylindrical ferrule and biconical connectors. Fiber optic **expanded-beam connectors use two lenses to first expand and then refocus the light from the transmitting fiber into the receiving fiber. Single fiber butt-jointed and expanded beam connectors normally consist of two plugs and an adapter (coupling device). Fig. 2.31 shows how to configure each plug and adapter when making the connection between two optical fibers.**

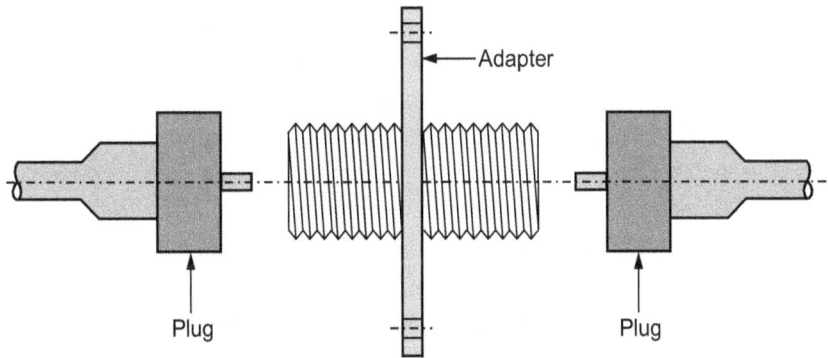

Fig. 2.31: Plug-Adapter-Plug Configuration

2.11.1 Ferrule Connectors

Ferrule connectors use two cylindrical plugs (referred to as ferrules), an alignment sleeve, and sometimes axial springs to perform fiber alignment. Fig. 2.32 provides an illustration of this basic ferrule connector design. Precision holes drilled or molded through the center of each ferrule allow for fiber insertion and alignment. Precise fiber alignment depends on the accuracy of the central hole of each ferrule. When the fiber ends are inserted, an adhesive (normally an epoxy resin) bonds the fiber inside the ferrule. The fiber-end faces are polished until they are flush with the end of the ferrule to achieve a low-loss fiber connection. Fiber alignment occurs when the ferrules are inserted into the alignment sleeve. The inside diameter of the alignment sleeve aligns the ferrules, which in turn align the fibers. Ferrule connectors lock the ferrules in the alignment sleeve using a threaded outer shell or some other type of coupling mechanism.

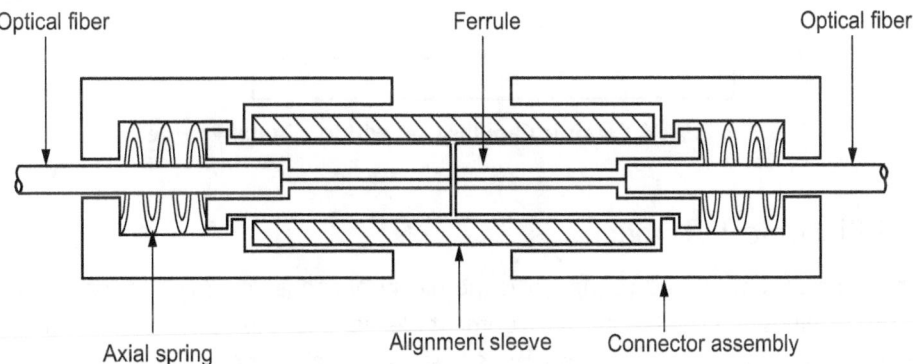

Fig. 2.32: Basic Ferrule Connector Design

As stated before, fiber alignment depends on an accurate hole through the center of the ferrule. Normally, ferrule connectors use ceramic or metal ferrules. The center hole is generally drilled in a metal ferrule. Drilling an accurate hole through the entire metal ferrule can be difficult. To improve fiber alignment, some metal ferrule connectors use precision watch-jeweled centering. In precision watch-jeweled centering, a watch jewel with a precision centered hole is placed in the tip of the ferrule. The central hole of the watch jewel centers the fiber with respect to the axis of the cylindrical ferrule. The watch jewel provides for better fiber alignment, because regulating the hole tolerance of the watch jewel is easier than maintaining a precise hole diameter when drilling through an entire ferrule.

The center hole in a ceramic ferrule is created by forming the ferrule around a precision wire, which is then removed. This method produces holes accurately centered in the ferrule. Most cylindrical ferrule connectors now use ceramic ferrules. The Straight Tip connector is an example of a ceramic ferrule connector.

Other cylindrical ferrule connectors have a ferrule that contains both metal and ceramic. For these connectors a ceramic capillary is placed within the tip of a metal ferrule to provide for precision fiber alignment. The ceramic capillary is a ceramic tube with a small inner diameter that is just larger than the diameter of the fiber. Fig. 2.33 shows the placement of the ceramic capillary within the metal ferrule.

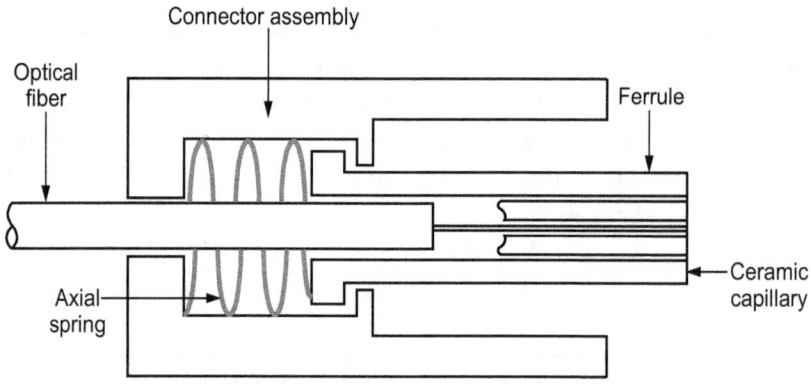

Fig. 2.33: A Ceramic Capillary Set within a Metal Ferrule

2.11.2 Biconical Connector

Another type of butt-jointed connector is the biconical connector. Biconical connectors use two conical plugs, a double conical alignment sleeve, and axial springs to perform fiber alignment. Fig. 2.34 is an illustration of this basic biconical connector design. Formation of the plugs and alignment sleeve involves transfer molding. Transfer molding uses silica-filled epoxy resin to mold the conical plug directly to the fiber or around a cast (precision wire). After connecting the conical plugs to the optical fibers, the fiber-end faces are polished before the plugs are inserted into the molded alignment sleeve. During fiber insertion, the inside surface of the double conical sleeve performs fiber alignment, while the axial springs push the fiber ends into close contact. If the alignment sleeve permits the fibers to actually become in contact, then the axial spring provides enough force to maintain fiber contact but prevent damage to the fiber-end faces. Normally, biconical connectors lock the fibers in alignment using a threaded outer shell.

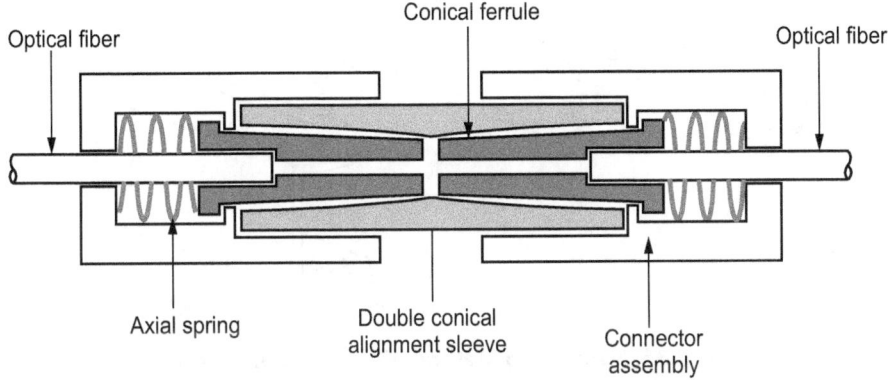

Fig. 2.34: Biconical Connector Design

2.11.3 Multifiber Connectors

Multifiber connectors join and align multifiber cables to reduce the time it takes to connect multiple fibers. One type of multifiber connector is the array connector.

The array connector is used to connect individual ribbons of ribbon-type cables. The array connector is similar to the ribbon splice. In the array connector, the fibers of each ribbon are epoxied into grooves of a silicon chip so that the fiber ends protrude from the end of the chip. The chip and the protruding fibers are polished flat for connection.

Each half of the connector is prepared separately before being butt-jointed. A spring clip and two grooved metal-backed plates are used to align and connect the stacked ribbons of the two ribbon cables.

Array connectors may also use an alignment sleeve with V-grooved silicon chips and metal springs to align and connect stacked ribbons. Fig. 2.35 shows the spring clip method of array connector alignment. The multifiber array connector is only one example of a multiple connector. Many types of multiple connectors exist that connect different types of multifiber cables.

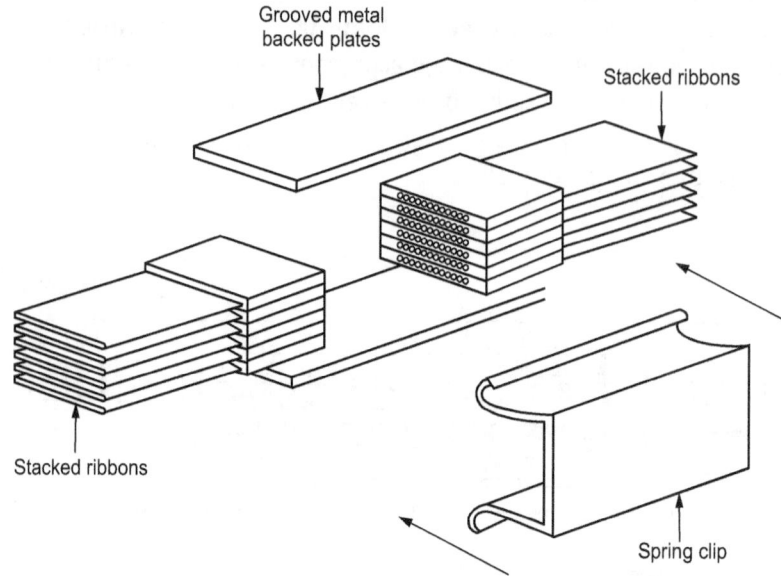

Fig. 2.35: Spring Clip Method of Ribbon Connection

2.11.4 Expanded Beam Connector

Fig. 2.35 shows how an expanded-beam connector uses two lenses to expand and then refocus the light from the transmitting fiber into the receiving fiber. Expanded-beam connectors are normally plug-adapter plug type connections. Fiber separation and lateral misalignment are less critical in expanded-beam coupling than in butt-jointing. The same amount of fiber separation and lateral misalignment in expanded beam coupling produces a lower coupling loss than in butt-jointing. However, angular misalignment is more critical. The same amount of angular misalignment in expanded-beam coupling produces a higher loss than in butt-jointing. Expanded-beam connectors are also much harder to produce. Present applications for expanded-beam connectors include multifiber connections, edge connections for printed circuit boards, and other applications.

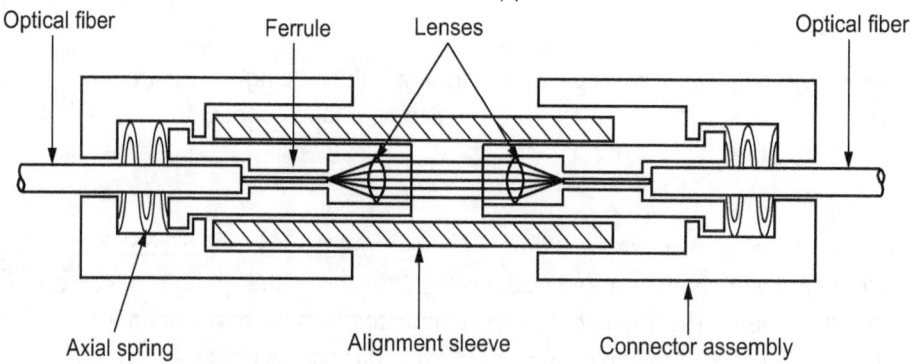

Fig. 2.36: Expanded-Beam Connector Operation

2.11.5 Military Connectors

Light-duty connectors and heavy-duty connectors are two ways that the Navy classifies fiber optic connectors. Light-duty connector shipboard applications include locations that protect the connectors from the environment, such as in a junction box or equipment enclosure. Heavy duty applications require a very rugged, stand-alone, sealed connector. A heavy-duty connector must also withstand pulls and tugs on the fiber cable without disrupting system operation. Light-duty connectors can be of the ferrule, biconical, or expanded-beam designs. Ferrule-type ST® connectors are becoming the commercial connector of choice for local area network (LAN) and data transfer links and are the standard connector for Navy light duty applications. This connector is described in specification sheets 16, 17, and 18 of MIL-C-83522. Fig. 2.37 shows the ST® type of light-duty connector.

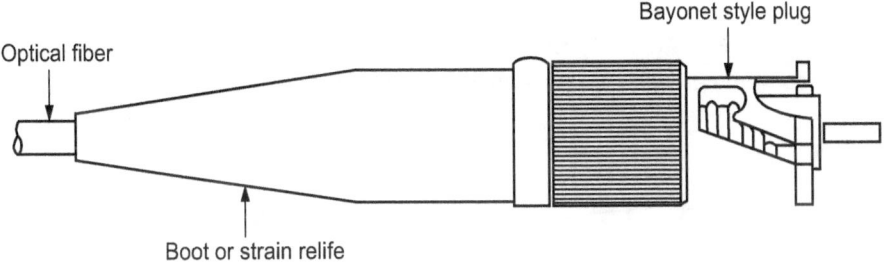

Fig. 2.37: ST® Light-Duty Connector

Fig. 2.38 shows one type of heavy-duty connector designed for use in harsh Navy environments. This connector is described by the military specification MIL-C-28876. This connector comes in various sizes capable of terminating 2, 4, 6, or 8 fibers. Each fiber termination, called a terminus, is of the cylindrical ferrule type. Two slightly different termini are used to form a connection; a pin terminus and a socket terminus. The pin terminus consists of a terminus body, which holds the terminus within the connector shell and a ceramic ferrule. The socket terminus consists of a terminus body, a ceramic ferrule, and an alignment sleeve, which attaches to the ceramic ferrule. Fiber alignment occurs when the pin terminus slides into the alignment sleeve of the socket terminus. The termini are held within an insert in the connector shell. When the connector halves are mated, the connector inserts align the mating termini, which then align the mating fibers. The connector shell and backshell protect the termini from the surrounding environment and provide strain relief for the multifiber cable.

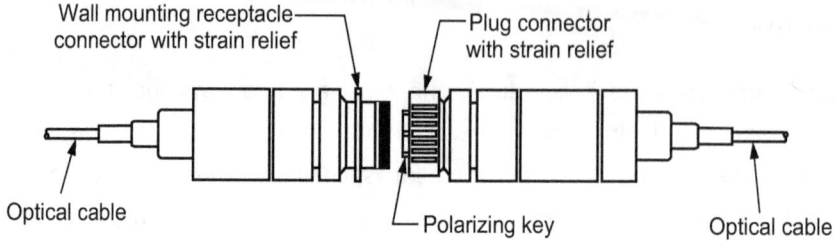

Fig. 2.38: MIL-C-28876 Heavy-Duty Connector

2.12 Fiber Optic Couplers

Some fiber optic data links require more than simple point-to-point connections. These data links may be of a much more complex design that requires multi-port or other types of connections. Fig. 2.39 shows some example system architectures that use more complex link designs. In many cases these types of systems require fiber optic components that can redistribute (combine or split) optical signals throughout the system.

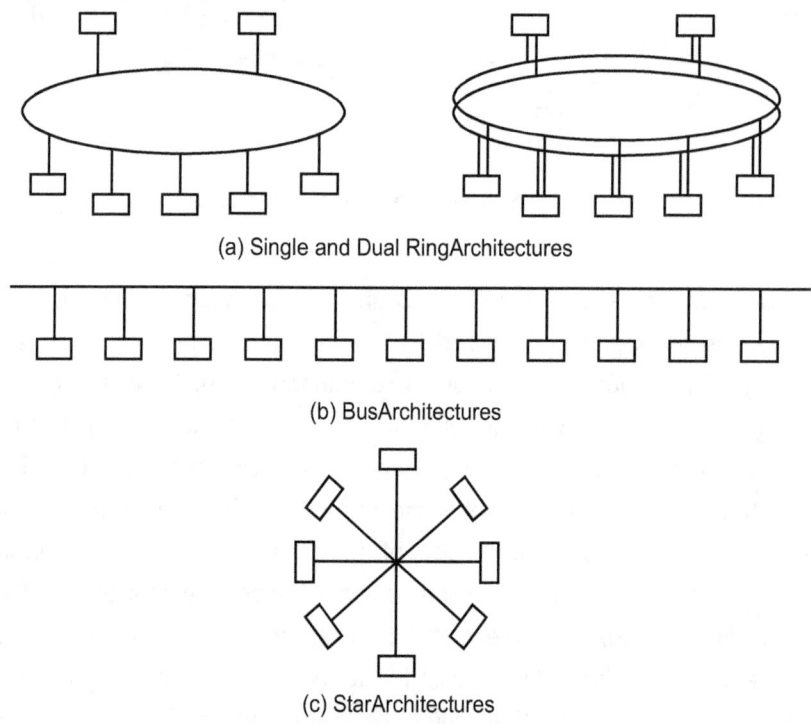

(a) Single and Dual RingArchitectures

(b) BusArchitectures

(c) StarArchitectures

Fig. 2.39: Examples of Complex System Architectures

One type of fiber optic component that allows for the redistribution of optical signals is a fiber optic coupler. A fiber optic coupler is a device that can distribute the optical signal (power) from one fiber among two or more fibers. A fiber optic coupler can also combine the optical signal from two or more fibers into a single fiber. Fiber optic couplers attenuate the signal much more than a connector or splice because the input signal is divided among the output ports. For example, with a 1×2 fiber optic coupler, each output is less than one-half the power of the input signal (over a 3 dB loss).

Fiber optic couplers can be either active or passive devices. The difference between active and passive couplers is that a **passive coupler** redistributes the optical signal without optical-to-electrical conversion. Active couplers are electronic devices that split or combine the signal electrically and use fiber optic detectors and sources for input and output.

Fig. 2.40 illustrates the design of a basic fiber optic coupler. A basic fiber optic coupler has N input ports and M output ports. N and M typically range from 1 to 64. The number of input ports and output ports vary depending on the intended application for the coupler. Types of fiber optic couplers include optical splitters, optical combiners, X couplers, star couplers, and tree couplers.

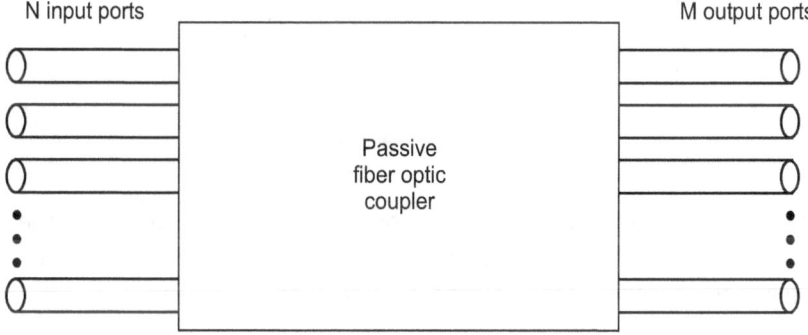

Fig. 2.40: Basic Passive Fiber Optic Coupler Design

2.12.1 Optical Splitter

An **optical splitter** is a passive device that splits the optical power carried by a single input fiber into two output fibers. Fig. 2.41 illustrates the transfer of optical power in an optical splitter. The input optical power is normally split evenly between the two output fibers. This type of optical splitter is known as a **Y-coupler**. However, an optical splitter may distribute the optical power carried by input power in an uneven manner. An optical splitter may split most of the power from the input fiber to one of the output fibers. Only a small amount of the power is coupled into the secondary output fiber. This type of optical splitter is known as a T-coupler, or an optical tap.

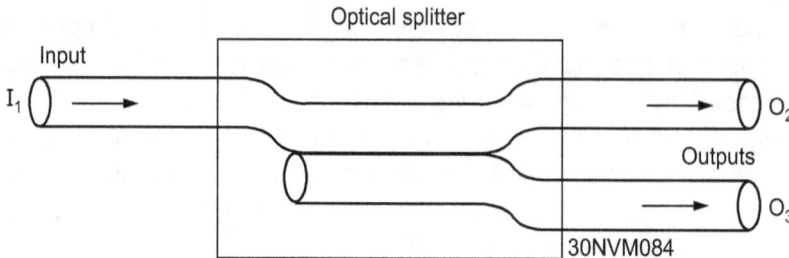

Fig. 2.41: Optical Splitter

2.12.2 Optical Combiner

An optical combiner is a passive device that combines the optical power carried by two input fibers into a single output fiber. Fig. 2.42 illustrates the transfer of optical power in an optical combiner.

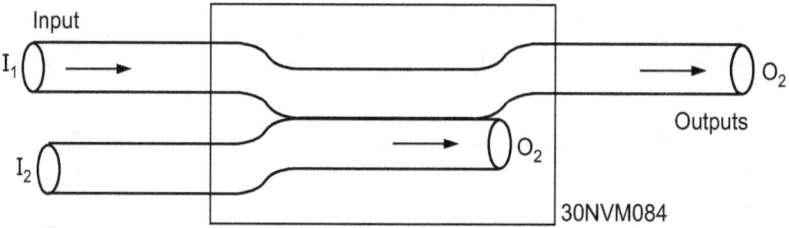

Fig. 2.42: Optical Combiner

An **X coupler** combines the functions of the optical splitter and combiner. The X coupler combines and divides the optical power from the two input fibers between the two output fibers. Another name for the X coupler is the 2×2 coupler.

SOLVED PROBLEMS

Problem 2.1:
A optical fiber has an attenuation of 0.9 dB/km at 1300 nm wavelength. If the optical power launched into a 30 km long optical fiber is 150 µW, find the optical output power.

Solution:

    Given data:

$$
\begin{aligned}
\alpha &= \text{Attenuation} &&= 0.9 \text{ dB/km} \\
\lambda &= \text{Wavelength} &&= 1300 \text{ nm} \\
P_{in} &= \text{Input power} &&= 150 \text{ µW} \\
L &= \text{Length of fiber} &&= 30 \text{ km} \\
P_{out} &= \text{Output power} &&= ?
\end{aligned}
$$

$$P_{in} \text{ (dBm)} = 10 \log \frac{P_{in} \text{ (W)}}{1 \text{ mW}}$$

$$= 10 \log \left[\frac{150 \times 10^{-6}}{1 \times 10^{-3}}\right]$$

$$= 10 \times (-0.824)$$

$$P_{in} \text{ (dBm)} = \mathbf{-8.24 \text{ dBm}}$$

The output power at length L = 30 km is,

$$P_{out} \text{ (dBm)} = 10 \log \left[\frac{P_{out} \text{ (W)}}{1 \text{ mW}}\right]$$

$$= 10 \log \left[\frac{P_{in} \text{ (W)}}{1 \text{ mW}}\right] - L \cdot \alpha$$

$$= 10 \log \left[\frac{150 \times 10^{-6}}{1 \times 10^{-3}}\right] - [30 \times 10^3 \times 0.9 \times 10^{-3}]$$

$$= -8.24 - 27$$

$$P_{out} \text{ (dBm)} = \mathbf{-35.24 \text{ dBm}}$$

In units of watts, the output power can be written as,

$$P_{out} \text{ (dBm)} = 10 \log \left[\frac{P_{out} \text{ (W)}}{1 \text{ mW}}\right]$$

$$P_{out} \text{ (W)} = \left[10^{P_{out} \text{ (dBm)}/10}\right] (1 \text{ mW})$$

$$P_{out} \text{ (W)} = 10^{(-35.24/10)} \times (1 \text{ mW})$$

$$= 0.2992 \times 10^{-3} \times 10^{-3} \text{ W}$$

$$= 0.2992 \times 10^{-6} \text{ W}$$

$$P_{out} \text{ (W)} = \mathbf{0.2992 \text{ μW}}$$

Alternative Method:

Attenuation optical fiber is given by,

$$\alpha = \frac{10}{L} \cdot \log \left[\frac{P_{in}}{P_{out}}\right]$$

$$0.9 = \frac{10}{30} \log \left[\frac{150 \text{ μW}}{P_{out}}\right]$$

$$2.7 = \log \left[\frac{150 \text{ μW}}{P_{out}}\right]$$

$$\frac{150 \times 10^{-6} \text{ (W)}}{P_{out}} = 10^{2.7}$$

$$P_{out} = \frac{150 \times 10^{-6}}{10^{2.7}}$$

$$P_{out} = \frac{150 \times 10^{-6}}{501.187}$$

$$P_{out} = 0.2992 \times 10^{-6} \text{ W}$$

P_{out} = 0.2992 μW ... Ans.

Problem 2.2:

An optical signal has lost 50% of its power after traversing 3.5 km of a fiber. What is the attenuation in dB/km of this fiber at an 1300 nm?

Solution:

Given data:

Length of fiber = L = 3.5 km

$$\frac{P_{in}}{P_{out}} = 50\%$$

$$= 0.5$$

$$\alpha = ?$$

$$\alpha = \frac{10}{L} \cdot \log\left[\frac{P_{in}}{P_{out}}\right]$$

$$= \frac{10}{3.5} \cdot \log[0.5]$$

$$\alpha = 2.85 \times (-0.3010)$$

α = –0.86 dB/km ... Ans.

Problem 2.3:

An optical fiber has an attenuation of 0.8 dB/km at 1300 nm. Determine the length of fiber at –

(a) Power decrease by 50%
(b) Power decrease by 60%.

Solution:

Given data:

$$\alpha = 0.8 \text{ dB/km}$$

$$L = ?$$

$$\alpha = \frac{10}{L} \cdot \log\left[\frac{P_{in}}{P_{out}}\right]$$

(a) At 50% decrease of power

i.e. $\dfrac{P_{in}}{P_{out}} = 50\%$

$= 0.5$

$\alpha = \dfrac{10}{L} \cdot \log\left[\dfrac{P_{in}}{P_{out}}\right]$

$0.8 = \dfrac{10}{L} \cdot \log[0.5]$

$L = \dfrac{10}{0.8} \log[0.5]$

$L = 3.763 \text{ km}$

Length of fiber, L = **3.763 km** ... Ans.

(b) At 60% of decrease of power

$\dfrac{P_{in}}{P_{out}} = 60\%$

$= 0.6$

$\alpha = \dfrac{10}{L} \cdot \log\left[\dfrac{P_{in}}{P_{out}}\right]$

$0.8 = \dfrac{10}{L} \cdot \log[0.6]$

$L = \dfrac{10}{0.8} \cdot \log[0.6]$

$L = 2.773 \text{ km}$

Length of fiber, L = 2.773 km ... Ans.

Problem 2.4:

A LED has a spectral width of 40 nm at 800 nm peak output. Determine total percentage of spectral width per peak wavelength. Also, determine the pulse spread. When material dispersion of 800 nm wavelength is 120 Ps/(nm · km).

Solution:

Given data:

Spectral width = σ_λ = 40 nm

Wavelength = λ = 40 nm

Material dispersion $D_{mat}(\lambda) = -120$ Ps/(nm·km)

Percentage spectral width $= \dfrac{\sigma_\lambda}{\lambda} = ?$

Pulse spread $= \sigma_{mat} = ?$

$$\dfrac{\sigma_\lambda}{\lambda} = \dfrac{40}{800}$$

$$\dfrac{1}{20} = 0.05$$

$$\dfrac{\sigma_\lambda}{\lambda} = 5\%$$

The pulse spread due to material dispersion can be written as,

$$\sigma_{mat} = \sigma_\lambda \cdot L \cdot |D_{mat}(\lambda)|$$

$$\dfrac{\sigma_{mat}}{L} = \sigma_\lambda \cdot |D_{mat}(\lambda)|$$

$$\dfrac{\sigma_{mat}}{L} \text{ (per km)} = 40 \times 120 \times 10^{-12}$$

$$\sigma_{mat} = 4.8 \text{ ns/km}$$

∴ **Total percentage spread per km = 4.8 ns/km** ... Ans.

Problem 2.5:

Determine the waveguide dispersion for a fiber system having $n_1 = 1.48$, index difference $\Delta = 0.2\%$ and V number = 2.4 at operating wavelength to be 1300 nm.

Solution:

Given data:

Core refractive index, $n_1 = 1.48$

Index difference, $\Delta = 0.2\%$

v number = 2.4

Operating wavelength, $\lambda = 1300$ nm

Waveguide dispersion $D_{\omega g}(\lambda) = ?$

$$D_{\omega g}(\lambda) = -\dfrac{n_2 \Delta}{C} \cdot \dfrac{1}{\lambda} \cdot \left[v \dfrac{d^2(v_b)}{dv^2} \right]$$

at v number 2.4, the square bracket $\left[v \cdot \dfrac{d^2 v_b}{dv^2} \right] = 0.26$

and
$$n_2 = n_1(1-\Delta)$$
$$n_2 = 1.48(1-0.02)$$
$$n_2 = 1.45 = \text{Cladding Index}$$

$$\therefore \quad D_{\omega g}(\lambda) = -\frac{1.45 \times 2}{3 \times 10^8 \times 1300}[0.26]$$
$$= -1.933 \times 10^{-14}$$
$$|D_{\omega g}(\lambda)| = 1.933 \times 10^{-12}$$

Waveguide dispersion = 1.933 Ps/nm · km ... Ans.

Problem 2.6:
Determine the limitation of transmission length caused by fiber loss for P_{in} = 0.028 mW, P_{out} = 0.002 mW and the fiber attenuation α = 0.3 dB/km.

Solution:

Given data:
$$P_{in} = 0.028 \text{ mW}$$
$$P_{out} = 0.002 \text{ mW}$$
$$\alpha = 0.3 \text{ dB/km}$$
$$L = ?$$

The attenuation can be written as,
$$\alpha = \frac{10}{L} \cdot \log\left(\frac{P_{in}}{P_{out}}\right)$$
$$L = \frac{10}{\alpha} \cdot \log\left(\frac{P_{in}}{P_{out}}\right)$$
$$L = \frac{10}{0.3} \cdot \log\left(\frac{0.028}{0.002}\right)$$
$$L = 38.2043 \text{ km}$$

The typical distance between two amplifier should be around 30 to **40 km**. ... Ans.

Problem 2.7:
A light source with a spectral width of 15 nm is used as an optical source. The optical fiber is of 30 km length. Due to material dispersion, the pulse spreads at the output due to material dispersion is 22 ns/km. Calculate the amount of material dispersion.

Solution:

Given Data:
$$\text{Length of fiber, } L = 30 \text{ km}$$
$$\text{Spectral width, } \sigma_\lambda = 15 \text{ nm}$$
$$\text{Pulse spread } \sigma_m = 22 \text{ ns/km}$$

$$\text{Material dispersion } D_m = \frac{\sigma_m}{\sigma_\lambda \cdot L}$$

$$D_m = \frac{22 \times 10^{-9}}{1.5 \times 10^{-9} \times 30}$$

$$= 48 \times 10^{-3} \text{ s/km}$$

Material dispersion $= 48 \times 10^{-3}$ s/km ... **Ans.**

Problem 2.8:

A single mode fiber operating at the wavelength of 1.8 μm is found to have a total material dispersion of 3.50 ns and a total waveguide dispersion of 0.5 ns. Determine the received pulse width and approximate bit rate of the fiber if the transmitted pulse has a width of 0.6 ns.

Solution: Given data:

Wavelength, λ = 1.8 μm
Transmitted pulse width = 0.6 ns
Material dispersion, τ_m = 3.50 ns
Waveguide dispersion, $\tau_{\omega g}$ = 0.5 ns
Received pulse width = ?
Bit rate = ?

$$\text{Total dispersion} = \Delta\tau = \sqrt{\tau_m^2 + \tau_{\omega g}^2}$$

$$= \sqrt{(3.50)^2 + (0.5)^2}$$

$$= \sqrt{12.5}$$

Total dispersion $(\Delta\tau)$ = 3.5355

Received pulse width = Transmitted pulse width + Total dispersion
$$= 0.6 + 3.5355$$

Received pulse width = **4.1355 ns** ... **Ans.**

$$\text{Maximum bit rate} = \frac{1}{5\Delta\tau}$$

$$= \frac{1}{5 \times 3.5355}$$

$$= 0.056 \times 10^{-9}$$

Maximum bit rate = **56.56 Mb/sec.** ... **Ans.**

Problem 2.9:

Determine the insertion loss of the connector when the power in the fiber is 150 μW and the output power after the connector is 90 μW.

Solution:

Given data:

Output power = 90 μW = P_{out}
Input power = 150 μW = P_{in}
Insertion Loss (α) = ?

$$\text{Insertion loss} = -10 \log_{10}\left(\frac{P_{out}}{P_{in}}\right) \text{ dB}$$

$$= -10 \log\left(\frac{90}{150}\right) \text{ dB}$$

Insertion loss = 2.2184 dB ... Ans.

Problem 2.10:

When the optical power launched into a 10 km length, fiber is 100 µW, the optical power at fiber output is 5 µW.

Calculate:

(i) Overall signal attenuation in dB.

(ii) Signal attenuation per km.

(iii) The overall signal attenuation for a 12 km optical link using same fiber splices at 1 km interval, each giving attenuation of 0.5 dB.

Solution:

Given data:
P_{in} = 100 µW
P_{out} = 5 µW
L = 10 km

(i) Signal attenuation:

$$\alpha = 10 \log_{10}\left(\frac{P_{in}}{P_{out}}\right) \text{ dB}$$

$$= 10 \log_{10}\left(\frac{100}{5}\right)$$

α = 13.0103 dB

Signal attenuation in dB = **13.0103 dB** ... Ans.

(ii) Signal attenuation per km:

$$\alpha = \frac{\alpha \text{ (dB)}}{L} \text{ dB/km}$$

$$= \frac{13.0103}{10}$$

α = 1.30103 dB/km

∴ Signal attenuation in dB per km = **1.30103 dB/km** ... Ans.

(iii) Overall signal attenuation for a 12 km optical link:

Here, L = 12 km

Loss along 12 km of the fiber = 1.30103 dB/km × 12 km
= 15.6124 dB

The link has splices at 1 km interval therefore there are total 11 splices each of 0.5 dB attenuation.

∴ The loss due to splices = 11 × 0.5 dB
= 5.5 dB

The overall signal attenuation = 5.5 dB + 15.6124 dB
= 21.11236 dB

The overall signal attenuation = **21.11236 dB** ... Ans.

Problem 2.11:

A multimode graded index fiber exhibits total pulse broadening of 0.1 μsec over a distance of 12 km.

Calculate:

(i) The maximum possible bandwidth on the link assuming no intersymbol interference.

(ii) The pulse broadening per unit length.

(iii) The bandwidth length product of the fiber.

Solution:

Given data:

Total pulse broadening, $\Delta\tau$ = 0.1 μsec.

Fiber length, L = 12 km

(i) The maximum possible bandwidth, B

$$B = \frac{1}{\Delta\tau}$$

$$= \frac{1}{0.1 \times 10^{-6}}$$

$$= 10 \times 10^6$$

∴ Maximum possible bandwidth B = **10 MHz** ... Ans.

(ii) Pulse broadening per unit length = $\frac{\Delta\tau}{L}$

$$= \frac{0.1 \times 10^{-6}}{12 \times 10^3}$$

$$= 8.33 \times 10^{-12}$$

∴ Pulse broadening per unit length = **8.33 Ps/km** ... Ans.

(iii) The bandwidth length product of the fiber:

$$= B \times L$$
$$= 10 \times 10^6 \times 12 \times 10^3$$
$$= 120 \text{ MHz} \cdot \text{km}$$

∴ The bandwidth length product = **120 MHz · km** ... **Ans.**

Problem 2.12:

A multimode graded index fiber exhibits total pulse broadening of 0.1 µs over a distance of 10 km. Assuming RZ format.

Calculate:

(i) The maximum possible bandwidth on the link assuming no intersymbol interference.

(ii) The pulse dispersion per unit length.

(iii) The bandwidth-length product for the fiber.

Solution:

Given data:

Pulse broadening, $\Delta\tau$ = 0.1 µs

Fiber length, L = 10 km

(i) Maximum possible bandwidth (B) = $\dfrac{0.35}{\Delta\tau}$

$$B = \dfrac{0.35}{0.1 \times 10^{-6}}$$

$$B = \mathbf{3.5 \text{ MHz}} \quad \ldots \textbf{Ans.}$$

(ii) Pulse dispersion per unit length = $\dfrac{\Delta\tau}{L}$

$$= \dfrac{0.1 \times 10^{-6}}{10 \times 10^3}$$

Pulse dispersion per unit length = 10×10^{-12}

Pulse dispersion per unit length = 10 Ps/km

(iii) Bandwidth length product = B × L

$$= 3.5 \text{ MHz} \times 10 \text{ km}$$

$$= \mathbf{35 \text{ MHz} \cdot \text{km}}$$

∴ Bandwidth length product = **35 MHz · km** ... **Ans.**

Problem 2.13:

Determine the maximum bit rate for RZ and NRZ encoding for the following pulse spreading constants and cable lengths.

   (i) $\Delta t = 10$ ns/m,   L = 100 m

   (ii) $\Delta t = 20$ ns/m,   L = 1000 m

   (iii) $\Delta t = 2000$ ns/m, L = 2 km

Solution:

$$\text{For RZ, maximum bit rate} = \frac{0.35}{\Delta \tau}$$

$$\text{For NRZ, maximum bit rate} = \frac{0.7}{\Delta t}$$

(i) $\Delta t = 10$ ns/m, L = 100 m

$$\Delta \tau = \left(\frac{10 \text{ ns}}{\text{m}}\right) \times 100 = 1 \text{ μsec.}$$

$$\text{Maximum bit rate (RZ)} = \frac{0.35}{\Delta \tau}$$

$$= \frac{0.35}{0.1 \text{ μsec}}$$

Maximum bit rate for RZ = 3.5 Mb/sec.

$$\text{Maximum bit rate for NRZ} = \frac{0.7}{\Delta \tau} = \frac{0.7}{0.1 \text{ μsec}}$$

Maximum bit rate for NRZ = **7 Mb/sec.**   … Ans.

(ii) $\Delta t = 20$ ns/m, L = 1000 m

$\Delta \tau = 20$ ns/m × 1000 m

$\Delta \tau = 20$ μsec.

$$\text{Maximum bit rate for RZ} = \frac{0.35}{\Delta \tau}$$

$$= \frac{\mathbf{0.35}}{\mathbf{20\ \mu sec}}$$

Maximum bit rate for RZ = 17.5 kb/sec.

$$\text{Maximum bit rate for NRZ} = \frac{0.7}{\Delta \tau}$$

$$= \frac{0.7}{20 \text{ μsec}}$$

Maximum bit rate for NRZ = **35 kb/sec.**   … Ans.

(iii) $\Delta t = 2000$ ns/m

    L = 2000 m

    $\Delta \tau = 2000$ ns/m × 2000 m = 4×10^{-3}

Maximum bit rate for RZ $= \dfrac{0.35}{\Delta\tau}$

$= \dfrac{0.35}{4 \times 10^{-3}}$

Maximum bit rate for RZ = 87.5 bit/sec.

Maximum bit rate for NRZ $= \dfrac{0.7}{\Delta\tau}$

$= \dfrac{0.7}{4 \times 10^{-3}}$

Maximum bit rate for NRZ = **175 bit/sec.** ... Ans.

SUMMARY

- Attenuation is the loss of optical power as light travels along an optical fiber, Attenuation in an optical fiber is caused by absorption, scattering and bending losses.
- Dispersion spreads the optical pulses as it travels along the fiber. Dispersion limits how fast information is transferred.
- Absorption is the conversion of optical power into another energy form such as heat.
- Intrinsic Absorption is caused by basic fiber-material properties.
- Extrinsic Absorption is caused by impurities introduced into the fiber material.
- Scattering losses are caused by the interaction of light with density fluctuation within a fiber. Rayleigh scattering is the main source of loss in commercial fibers operating between 700 nm and 1600 nm.
- Microbends are small microscopic bends of the fiber axis that occurs mainly when a fiber is cabled.
- Macrobends are bends having a large radius of curvature relative to the fiber diameter.
- Intramodal or chromatic dispersion occurs because light travels through different and different waveguide structures at different speeds.
- Material dispersion is dependent on the light wavelengths interaction with the refractive index of the core.
- Waveguide dispersion is a function of the size of the fiber's core relative to the wavelength of operation.
- Intermodal or modal dispersion occurs because each mode travels a different distance over the same time span.
- The coupling of energy from one mode to another mode arises due to structual imperfection, fiber diameter, refractive index profile variation and cabling induced microbends.
- Fiber optic connections transfer optical power from one component to another. Fiber optic connections also permit fiber optic systems to be more than just a point to point data link.

- A fiber optic splice is a permanent joint between two fibers or two groups of fibers.
- Fiber optic connectors permit easy coupling and un-coupling of optical fibers.
- Fiber optic couplers distribute or combine optical signals between fibers.
- Poor fiber end propagation and poor fiber alignment are the main causes of coupling loss.
- Radiance is the amount of optical power emitted by a unit area of emitting surface per unit time in a specified direction. An optical sources radiance, or brightness is a measure of its optical power launching capability.
- Fiber to fiber coupling loss is affected by intrinsic and extrinsic coupling losses. Intrinsic coupling losses are caused by inherent fiber characteristic. Extrinsic coupling losses are caused by jointing techniques.
- A fiber pigtail is a short length of optical fiber (usually 1 meter or less) permanently fixed to a fiber optic component, such as an optical source or detectors.
- Fresenel reflections occurs twice in a fiber to fiber connections. A portion of the optical power is reflected when the light first exists the source fiber. Light is then reflected as the optical signal enters the receiving fiber.
- Index matching GEL eliminates or reduces the step change in the refractive index at the fiber interface, reducing Fresnel reflection.
- Poor fiber alignment is a main source of coupling loss in fiber to fiber connections. The three basic coupling errors that occur during fiber alignment are fiber separation (longitudinal misalignment), lateral misalignment and angular misalignment.
- In fiber separation a small gap remains between fiber end faces after completing the fiber connections. Lateral or axial misalignment is when the axes of the two fibers are offset in a perpendicular direction. Angular displacement is when the axes of the two fibers are no longer parallel.
- Single mode fibers are more sensitive to alignment errors than multimode fibers because of their small core diameters and low numerical aperture.
- The Mode Power Distribution (MPD) is the distribution of radiant power among the various modes propagating along the optical fiber.
- Poor fiber end preparation is another sources of extrinsic coupling loss. An optical fiber end faces must be flat, smooth and perpendicular to the fibers axis to ensure proper fiber connection.
- The score and break method is the basic fiber cleaving techniques for preparing optical fibers for coupling.
- Polishing the fiber ends removes most surface imperfections introduced by the fiber cleaving or cutting process. Fiber polishing involves a step down approach. The first step is to give the surface of the fiber end to a rough polish. The next step involves giving the surface of the fiber end a fine polish.
- Fiber mismatches are a source of intrinsic coupling loss. Types of fiber mismatches include fiber geometry mismatches, NA mismatch, and refractive index profile difference.

- Fiber geometry mismatches include core diameter, cladding diameter, core ellipticity and core cladding concentricity differences.
- Core diameter mismatch causes coupling loss only if the launching fiber has a larger core radius than the receiving fiber.
- NA match causes coupling less only if the launching fiber has a higher NA than the receiving fiber.
- A refractive index profile differences causes coupling loss only if the launching fiber has a larger profile parameter than the receiving fiber.
- Mechanical and fusion splicing are two broad categories that describes the techniques used for fiber splicing. A mechanical splice is a fiber splice where mechanical fixtures perform fiber alignment and connection. A fusion splice is a fiber splice where localized heat fuses or melts the ends of the two lengths of optical fiber together.
- In mechanical splicing, mechanical fixtures hold the two optical fibers in alignment for an indefinite period of time without movement. The amount of splice loss is stable over time and unaffected by changes in environmental or mechanical conditions.
- ARC fusion involves the discharge and electric current across a gap between the two electrodes. By placing the fiber end between the two electrodes, the electric discharge melts or fuses the ends of the fiber.
- A fiber optic connector is a demeteable device that permits the coupling of optical power between the two optical fibers or two groups of fibers.
- Fiber alignment in a fiber optic connector is the critical parameter in maintaining total insertion loss below the required level.
- Fiber optic connectors can affect system performance by increasing modal and reflection noise.
- Modal noise is eliminated by using only single mode fiber with large sources and only low-coherence sources such as light emitting diodes with multimode fiber.
- Reflection noise is reduced by index matching gels, physical contact polishes or antireflection coatings.
- Butt jointed and expanded beams connectors are two ways to classify fiber optic connectors. Butt jointed connectors bring the prepared ends of two fibers into close contact. Expanded beam connectors use two lenses to first expand and then refocus the light from the transmitting fiber into the receiving fiber.
- An optical splitter is a passive device that splits the optical power carried by a single input fiber into two output fiber
- An optical combiner is a passive device that distributes optical power from more than two input ports among several output ports.

POINTS TO REMEMBER

- Attenuation is the loss of optical power as light travels along an optical fiber, Attenuation in an optical fiber is caused by absorption, scattering and bending losses.

- Dispersion spreads the optical pulses as it travels along the fiber. Dispersion limits how fast information is transferred.
- Absorption is the conversion of optical power into another energy form such as heat.
- Intrinsic Absorption is caused by basic fiber-material properties.
- Extrinsic Absorption is caused by impurities introduced into the fiber material.
- Scattering losses are caused by the interaction of light with density fluctuation within a fiber. Rayleigh scattering is the main source of loss in commercial fibers operating between 700 nm and 1600 nm.
- Microbends are small microscopic bends of the fiber axis that occurs mainly when a fiber is cabled.
- Macrobends are bends having a large radius of curvature relative to the fiber diameter.
- Intramodal or chromatic dispersion occurs because light travels through different and different waveguide structures at different speeds.
- Material dispersion is dependent on the light wavelengths interaction with the refractive index of the core.
- Waveguide dispersion is a function of the size of the fiber's core relative to the wavelength of operation.
- Intermodal or modal dispersion occurs because each mode travels a different distance over the same time span.
- The coupling of energy from one mode to another mode arises due to structural imperfection, fiber diameter, refractive index profile variation and cabling induced microbends.
- Fiber optic connections transfer optical power from one component to another. Fiber optic connections also permit fiber optic systems to be more than just a point to point data link.
- A fiber optic splice is a permanent joint between two fibers or two groups of fibers.
- Fiber optic connectors permit easy coupling and un-coupling of optical fibers.
- Fiber optic couplers distribute or combine optical signals between fibers.
- Poor fiber end propagation and poor fiber alignment are the main causes of coupling loss.
- Radiance is the amount of optical power emitted by a unit area of emitting surface per unit time in a specified direction. An optical sources radiance, or brightness is a measure of its optical power launching capability.
- Fiber to fiber coupling loss is affected by intrinsic and extrinsic coupling losses. Intrinsic coupling losses are caused by inherent fiber characteristic. Extrinsic coupling losses are caused by jointing techniques.
- A fiber pigtail is a short length of optical fiber (usually 1 meter or less) permanently fixed to a fiber optic component, such as an optical source or detectors.
- Fresenel reflections occurs twice in a fiber to fiber connections. A portion of the optical power is reflected when the light first exists the source fiber. Light is then reflected as the optical signal enters the receiving fiber.

- Index matching GEL eliminates or reduces the step change in the refractive index at the fiber interface, reducing Fresnel reflection.
- Poor fiber alignment is a main source of coupling loss in fiber to fiber connections. The three basic coupling errors that occur during fiber alignment are fiber separation (longitudinal misalignment), lateral misalignment and angular misalignment.
- In fiber separation a small gap remains between fiber end faces after completing the fiber connections. Lateral or axial misalignment is when the axes of the two fibers are offset in a perpendicular direction. Angular displacement is when the axes of the two fibers are no longer parallel.
- Single mode fibers are more sensitive to alignment errors than multimode fibers because of their small core diameters and low numerical aperture.
- The Mode Power Distribution (MPD) is the distribution of radiant power among the various modes propagating along the optical fiber.
- Poor fiber end preparation is another sources of extrinsic coupling loss. An optical fiber end faces must be flat, smooth and perpendicular to the fibers axis to ensure proper fiber connection.
- The score and break method is the basic fiber cleaving techniques for preparing optical fibers for coupling.
- Polishing the fiber ends removes most surface imperfections introduced by the fiber cleaving or cutting process. Fiber polishing involves a step down approach. The first step is to give the surface of the fiber end to a rough polish. The next step involves giving the surface of the fiber end a fine polish.
- Fiber mismatches are a source of intrinsic coupling loss. Types of fiber mismatches include fiber geometry mismatches, NA mismatch, and refractive index profile difference.
- Fiber geometry mismatches include core diameer, cladding diameter, core ellipticity and core cladding concentricity differences.
- Core diameter mismatch causes coupling loss only if the launching fiber has a larger core radius than the receiving fiber.
- NA match causes coupling less only if the launching fiber has a higher NA than the receiving fiber.
- A refractive index profile differences causes coupling loss only if the launching fiber has a larger profile parameter than the receiving fiber.
- Mechanical and fusion splicing are two broad categories that describes the techniques used for fiber splicing. A mechanical splice is a fiber splice where mechanical fixtures perform fiber alignment and connection. A fusion splice is a fiber splice where localized heat fuses or melts the ends of the two lengths of optical fiber together.
- In mechanical splicing, mechanical fixtures hold the two optical fibers in alignment for an indefinite period of time without movement. The amount of splice loss is stable over time and unaffected by changes in environmental or mechanical conditions.

- ARC fusion involves the dicharge and electric current across a gap between the two electrodes. By placing the fiber end between the two electrodes, the electric discharge melts or fuses the ends of the fiber.
- A fiber optic connector is a demeteable device that permits the coupling of optical power between the two optical fibers or two groups of fibers.
- Fiber aligment in a fiber optic connector is the critical parameter in maintaining total insertion loss below the required level.
- Fiber optic connectors can affect system performance by increasing modal and reflection noise.
- Modal noise is eliminated by using only single mode fiber with large sources and only low-coherence sources such as light emitting diodes with multimode fiber.
- Reflection noise is reduced by index matching gels, physical contact polishes or antireflection coatings.
- Butt jointed and expanded beams connectors are two ways to classify fiber optic connectors. Butt jointed connectors bring the prepared ends of two fibers into close contact. Expanded beam connectors use two lenses to first expand and then refocus the light from the transmitting fiber into the receiving fiber.
- An optical splitter is a passive device that splits the optical power carried by a single input fiber into two output fiber
- An optical combiner is a passive device that distributes optical power from more than two input ports among several output ports.
- An OTDR measures the fraction of light that is reflected back because of Rayleigh scattering and Fresenel reflection.

QUESTIONS

1. What do you mean by attenuation?
2. What are the types of dispersion and explain each?
3. Which type of dispersion does not exist in a single mode fiber and why?
4. What are the factors responsible for loss in optical fiber?
5. Discuss and illustrate the various types of mismatch and the resulting loss that can occur when two fibers are connected or spliced.
6. Describe the factors responsible for the loss while source to fiber and fiber to fiber coupling is considered.
7. Discuss the parameters on which the dispersion in an optical fiber depends?
8. What is the difference between a connector and a splice? When is a connector used instead of a splice?
9. Explain in brief OTDR.
10. Explain pulse broadening in GI fibers.

✱✱✱

Unit III

FOC SYSTEM

3.1 Introduction

There are several ways to classify fiber optic links, according to modulation type. There are two types, analog or digital. Modulation is the process of varying one or more characteristics of an optical signal to encode and convey information. Generally, the intensity of the optical signal is modulated in fiber optic communication systems. Digital modulation implies that the optical signal consists of discrete levels. Analog modulation implies that the intensity of the optical signal is proportional to a continuously varying electrical input. Most fiber optic systems are digital because digital transmission system generally provide superior performance over analog transmission systems.

3.2 Analog Systems

An analog signal is a continuous signal whose amplitude, phase or some other property varies in a direct proportion to the instantaneous values of a physical variable. An example of an analog signal is the output power of an optical source whose intensity is a function of a continuous electrical input signal. Most analog fiber optic communication system intensity modulate the optical source. In intensity modulation, the intensity of the optical sources output signal is directly modulated by the incoming electrical analog baseband signal. A baseband signal is a signal that is in its original form and has not been changed by a modulation technique.

In some cases, the optical source may be directly modulated by a incoming electrical signal that is not a baseband signal. In these cases, the original electrical signal generally modulates an electrical subcarrier frequency. The most common form of analog subcarrier modulation in fiber optic system is frequency modulation. The optical source is intensity modulated by the electrical subcarrier.

3.2.1 Overview of Analog Links

The basic elements of an fiber optic analog link is shown in Fig. 3.1.

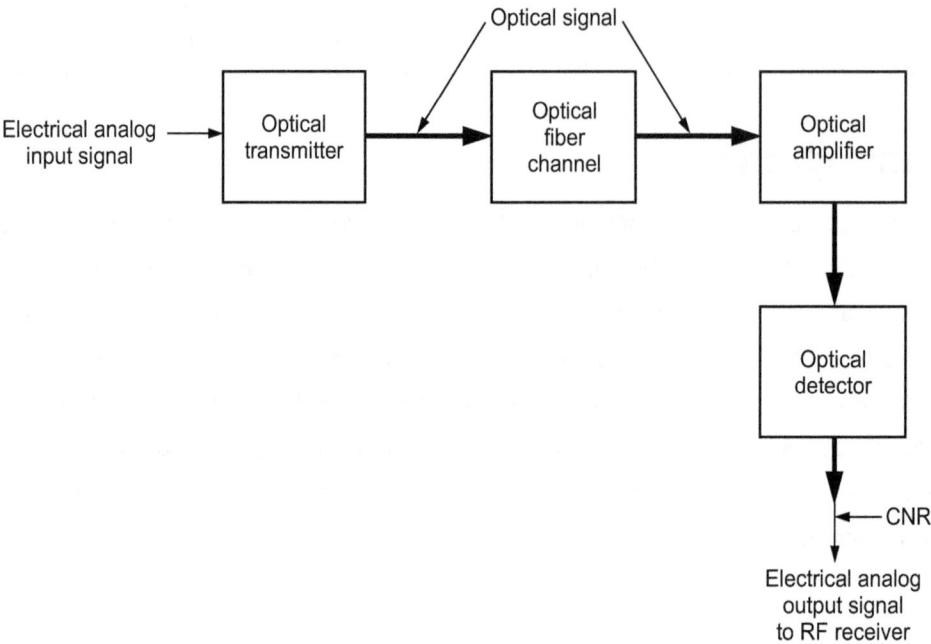

Fig. 3.1: Basic Elements of an Analog Link

In an optical transmitter LED or LASER diode is used as an optical source. There is need to set a bias point on the source approximately at the mid point of the linear output region. Therefore, the analog signal can be sent using one of several modulation techniques. The simplest form of modulation technique used for optical fiber link is direct intensity modulation. In this method, the optical output from the source is modulated simply by varying the current around the bias point in proportion to the message signal level. Therefore, the information signal is transmitted directly in the baseband.

The efficient method is to translate the baseband signal onto an electrical subcarrier prior to intensity modulation of the source, using Amplitude Modulation (AM), Frequency Modulation (FM) or Phase Modulation (PM) techniques. The signal impairments in the optical source are harmonic distortions, intermodulation products, relative intensity noise (RIN) in the LASER and laser clipping.

The major factors in the fiber optic elements are the frequency dependence of amplitude, phase and group delay in the fiber. Due to this, the fiber should have a flat amplitude and group delay response within the passband required to send the signal free of linear distortion. The modal distortion limited bandwidth is difficult to equalize, therefore, it is better to choose a single mode fiber. In accordance, the fiber attenuation is also important, because the carrier to noise performance of the system will change as a function of the received optical power.

The optical amplifier in the link introduces an additional noise, known as Amplified Spontaneous Emission (ASE). This noise is originates from the spontaneous recombination of electron and holes in the amplifier medium. This spontaneous recombination gives rise to a broad spectral background of photons that get amplified along with the optical signal. In optical receiver, the principal impairments are quantum or shot noise, APD gain noise and thermal noise.

3.2.2 Carrier to Noise Ratio

In the performance analysis of analog system, the Carrier to Noise Ratio (CNR) is considered. It can be calculated as the ratio of rms carrier power to rms noise power at the input of the RF receiver. Consider CNR_i represents the carrier to noise ratio related to a particular signal contaminant, then for N signal-impairment factors the total CNR is given by,

$$\frac{1}{CNR} = \sum_{i=1}^{N} \frac{1}{CNR_i}$$

When a single information channel is transmitted, the important signal impairments include laser intensity noise fluctuations, laser clipping, photo detector noise and optical amplifier noise. IF multiple message channels operating at different carrier frequencies are sent simultaneously over the same fiber then harmonic and intermodulation distortion arise.

3.2.3 Carrier Power

The carrier power can be found by considering the signal generated at the transmitter. The biasing conditions of a laser diode and its response is shown in Fig. 3.2. The drive current through the optical source is the sum of fixed bias current and a time varying sinusoid. The laser source acts as a square law device. Therefore, the envelope of the output optical power

P(t) has the same form as the input drive current. For the time varying analog drive signal S(t), the optical power can be written as,

$$P(t) = P_t [1 + m \cdot S(t)]$$

where, P_t = Optical output power at the bias current level
m = Modulation index

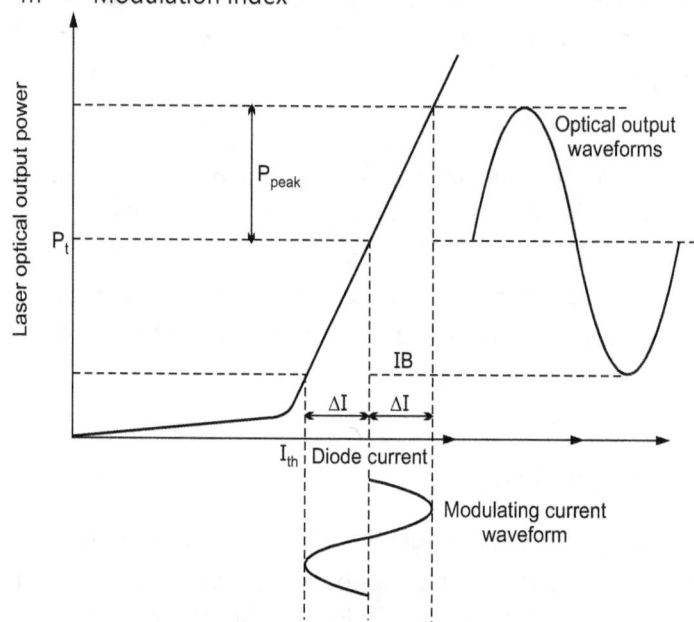

Fig. 3.2: Biasing Conditions of a Laser Diode

The modulation index can be expressed in terms of optical power as,

$$m = \frac{P_{peak}}{P_t}$$

where, P_{peak} = Maximum power

The values of modulation index or modulation depth for analog applications ranges from 0.25 to 0.50.

Let us consider a sinusoidal received signal, the carrier power 'C' at the output of a receiver is,

$$C = \frac{1}{2} (m \cdot \leftarrow_0 \cdot M \cdot \overline{P})^2$$

where,

C = Carrier power in units of A^2
$\leftarrow_0$ = Unit gain responsivity of the photodetector
M = Photodetector gain
  (M = 1 for PIN photodiodes)
$\overline{P}$ = Average received optical power

3.2.4 Photodetector and Preamplifier Noise

The photodiode noise can be written as,

$$\langle i_N^2 \rangle = \sigma_N^2 \approx 2q(I_P + I_D)M^2 F(M) B$$

where,

$\langle I_N^2 \rangle$ = The mean square photodetector noise
$I_P = \Re_0 \overline{P}$ = Primary photocurrent
I_D = Detector bulk dark current
M = Photodiode gain
$F(M)$ = Associated noise figure
B = Receiver bandwidth
q = Electron charge
σ_N = Variance

Therefore, the carrier to noise ratio for photodetector is,

$$CNR_{det} = \frac{C}{\sigma_N^2}$$

The preamplifier noise can be written as,

$$\langle i_T^2 \rangle = \sigma_T^2 = \frac{4 k_B T}{R_{eq}} B F_t$$

where,

R_{eq} = Equivalent resistance of the photodetector load and the preamplifier
F_t = Noise factor of the preamplifier
$\langle i_T^2 \rangle$ = Mean square thermal noise current
k_B = Boltzmann's constant
T = Absolute temperature

Therefore, the carrier to noise ratio for preamplifier can be written as,

$$CNR_{preamp} = \frac{C}{\sigma_T^2}$$

3.2.5 Relative Intensity Noise

In a semiconductor laser, fluctuations in the amplitude or intensity of the output produce optical intensity noise. These fluctuation can occur from temperature variations or from spontaneous emission contained in the laser output. The noise obtained from the random intensity fluctuation is called Relative Intensity Noise (RIN). The RIN can be defined in terms of the mean square intensity variation. Therefore,

$$\langle i_{RIN}^2 \rangle = \sigma_{RIN}^2 = RIN (\Re_0 \overline{P}) B$$

where, $\langle i_{RIN}^2 \rangle$ = Mean square current

The CNR due to laser amplitude fluctuations can be written as,

$$CNR_{RIN} = \frac{C}{\sigma_{RIN}^2}$$

The RIN, which is measured in dB/Hz, and defined by the noise to signal power ratio,

$$RIN = \frac{\langle (\Delta P_L)^2 \rangle}{\bar{P}_L^2}$$

where,

$\langle (\Delta P_L)^2 \rangle$ = The mean square intensity fluctuation of the laser output

$\bar{P}_L$ = The average laser light intensity

The relative intensity noise can be decreased as the injection current lever increases according to the relationship.

$$RIN \propto \left(\frac{I_B}{I_{th}} - 1\right)^{-3}$$

where,

I_B = Bias current

I_{th} = Lasing the threshold current

Therefore, the carrier to noise ratio for a single channel AM system can be written as,

$$\frac{C}{N} = \frac{\frac{1}{2}(m \leftarrow_o M\bar{P})^2}{RIN(\leftarrow_o \bar{P})^2 B + 2q(I_p + I_D)M^2 F(M) B + (4K_B T/R_{eq}) B F_t}$$

3.2.6 Limiting Conditions

If the optical power level at the receiver is low, the preamplifier circuit noise dominates the system noise. Therefore,

$$\left(\frac{C}{N}\right)_{limit_1} = \frac{\frac{1}{2}(M \leftarrow_o M \bar{P})^2}{(4 k_B T/R_{eq}) B F_t}$$

The carrier to noise ratio is directly proportional to the square of the received optical power, therefore, for each 1 dB variation in received optical power, C/N will change by 2 dB.

In photodiodes, the bulk and surface dark current are small compared with shot (quantum) noise for intermediate optical signal levels at the receiver. At the intermediate power levels the quantum-noise term of the photodiode will dominate the system noise. Thus,

$$\left(\frac{C}{N}\right)_{limit_2} = \frac{\frac{1}{2}m^2 \leftarrow_0 \bar{P}}{2q\, F(M)\, B}$$

Therefore, the carrier to noise ratio will vary by 1 dB for every 1 dB change in the received optical power.

When the LASER has a high RIN values, the reflection noise dominated over other noise terms, therefore, the carrier to noise ratio becomes constant,

$$\left(\frac{C}{N}\right)_{limit_3} = \frac{\frac{1}{2}(mM)^2}{RIN\, B}$$

The performance can be improved by increasing modulation index.

3.2.7 Multichannel Transmission Technique

In broadband analog applications there is need to send multiple analog signals over the same fiber. Thus, we need multiplexing technique where a number of baseband signals are superimposed on a set of N subcarriers that have different frequencies $f_1, f_2, \ldots, f_N$. These modulated sub-carriers are combined electrically through frequency division multiplexing (FDM) to form a composite signal that directly modulates a signal optical source. These can be achieved by Vestigial Sideband Amplitude Modulation (VSB-AM), Frequency Modulation (FM) and Subcarrier Multiplexing (SCM) methods.

The AM is simple and cost effective but its signal is very sensitive to noise and non-linear distortion. FM requires a larger bandwidth than AM and it provides a higher signal to noise ratio and is less sensitive to source non-linearities. Microwave SCM operates at higher frequencies than AM or FM and is used for broadband distribution of both analog and digital signal.

3.2.7.1 Multichannel Amplitude Modulation

The cable television (CATV) networks primarily use the AM-VSB method. The technique for combining N independent message shown in Fig. 3.3. An information-bearing signal on channel i amplitude-modulates a carrier wave which has frequency f_i, where i = 1, 2, ... , N. An RF power combiners sums these N amplitude modulate carriers to produce a composite Frequency Division Multiplexed (FDM) signal which intensity modulates a laser diode. Then, the optical receiver which has a bank of parallel bandpass filters separates the combined carriers back into individual channels. Then, the individual message signals are recovered from the carriers by standard RF techniques. In a large numbers of FDM carriers with random phrases, the carriers ad on a power basis. Therefore, the N-channels optical modulation index is related to per channel modulation index and denoted as m_i.

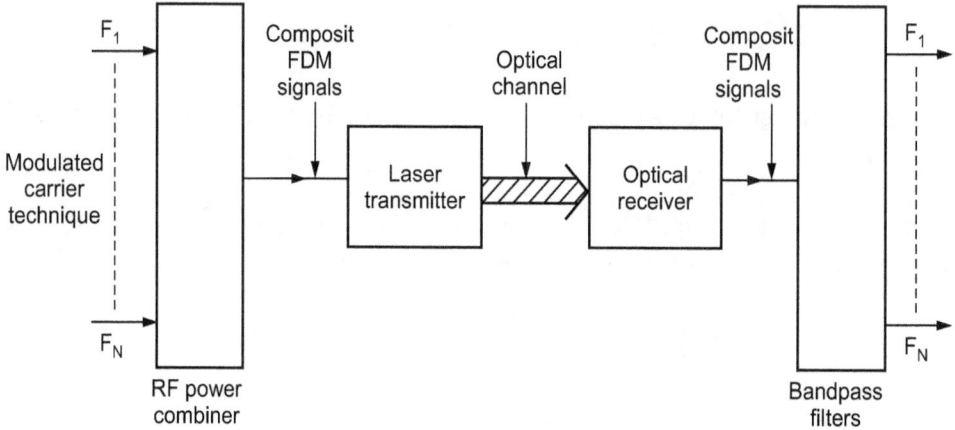

Fig. 3.3: Frequency Division Multiplexing

$$m = \left(\sum_{i=1}^{N} m_i^2 \right)^{1/2}$$

For each channel modulation index m_i has the same value m_c, then

$$m = m_c \cdot N^{0.5}$$

If N signals are frequency multiplexed and used to modulate a single optical source then the carrier to noise ratio of a single channel is degraded by 10 log N. If a few channels are combined, the signals will add in voltage rather than the power, therefore, the degradation will have a 20 log N characteristics.

If multiple carriers frequencies pass through a non-linear device such as a laser diode then the signal products other than the original frequencies can be produced. These undesirable signals are called intermodulation products. It causes serious interference in both in band and outband frequencies. From the intermodulation products, generally only the second order and third order terms are considered because higher order products tend to be significantly smaller. Third order intermodulation (IM) distortion products at frequencies $f_i + f_j - f_k$ and $2f_i - f_j$ are the most dominant. The $f_i + f_j - f_k$ are commonly referred as triple-beat IM products, and $2f_i - f_j$ are commonly referred as two tone third order IM products. The amplitude of the triple beat products are 3 dB higher than the two tone third order IM products. When a signal passband contains a large number of equally spaced carrier, several

IM terms will exist at or near the same frequency, this so called as beak stacking is additive on a power basis. The two tone third order terms are evenly spread through the operating passband. The triple products are concentrated in the middle of the channel passband. Therefore, the center carriers receive the most intermodulation interference.

The term beat stacking are commonly referred to as composite second order (CSO) and Composite Triple Beat (CTB). These are used to describe the performance of multichannel AM links which are defined as,

$$CSO = \frac{\text{Peak carrier power}}{\text{Peak power in composite second order IM tone}}$$

and

$$CTB = \frac{\text{Peak carrier power}}{\text{Peak power in composite third order IM tone}}$$

3.2.7.2 Multichannel Frequency Modulation

The use of AM-VSB signal for transmitting multiple analog channels are simple, it has a C/N requirement of atleast 40 dB for each AM channel, which places very stringent requirement on laser and receiver linearity. The frequency modulation (FM) is an alternative technique in which each subcarrier is frequency modulated by a message signal. It requires a wider bandwidth than AM, but it gives a signal to noise ratio improvement over the carrier to noise ratio. The S/N ratio at the output of FM detector is much larger than the ratio of C/N at the input of the detector. This can be written as,

$$\left(\frac{S}{N}\right)_{out} = \left(\frac{C}{N}\right)_{in} + 10 \log\left[\frac{3B}{2f_v}\left(\frac{\Delta f_{pp}}{f_v}\right)^2\right] + W$$

where, B = Bandwidth required
Δf_{pp} = Peak to peak frequency deviation of the modulator
f_v = Highest video frequency
W = Weighting factor

The weighing factor is used for the non-uniform response of the eye pattern to white noise in the video bandwidth. The ratio S/N improvement depends on the system design, which is generally in the range of 36-44 dB. The reduced C/N ratio requirement makes an FM system much less susceptible to laser and receiver noise than an AM system.

3.2.7.3 Subcarrier Multiplexing

The subcarrier multiplexing CSCM is used to describe the capability of multiplexing both multichannel analog of digital signal within the light wave system. The basic concept of SCM system shown in Fig. 3.4.

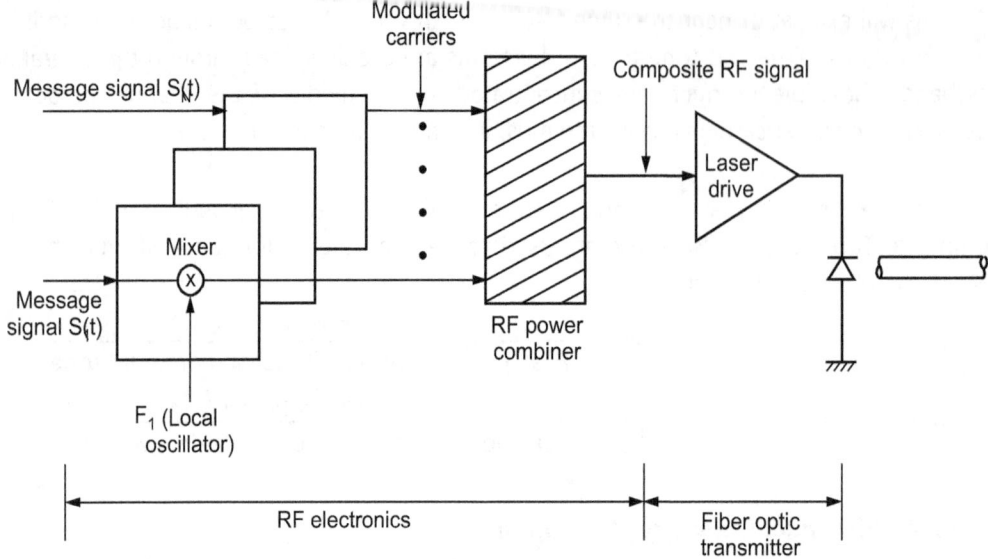

Fig. 3.4: Basic Concept of SCM

The input of the transmitter consists of a mixture of N independent analog and digital baseband signals. These band signals can carry either voice, data, video, digital audio, high definition video or any other or digital information. Each incoming signal $S_i(t)$ is mixed with a local oscillator of frequency f_i of range 2 to 8 GHz. This local oscillator frequency are called as the subcarriers. The transmitter combines the modulated multiplexed signal which is used to drive a LASER diode.

In receiver section, the optical signal is directly detected with a high speed wideband in G_aA_s PIN photodiode and reconverted to a microwave signals. For a long distance link a wideband in G_aA_s avalanch photodiode with a 50-80 GHz gain bandwidth product can be used or use an optical preamplifier. A wideband low noise amplifier or PIN FET receiver can be used for amplifying the received microwave signals.

3.3 Digital System

A digital system is a discontinuous signal that changes from one state to another in discrete steps. A popular form of digital modulation is binary or two level, digital modulation. In binary modulation the optical signal is switched from a low power level (usually off) to a high power level.

3.3.1 Point-to-Point Links

A point-to-point link is simplest transmission link. It has transmitter at one end and receiver on the other end as shown in Fig. 3.5. In an optical link design there are many inter-related variables among the fiber, source and photodetector operating characteristics. The performance and cost constraints are very important factors in fiber optic communication links, the designer must carefully choose the components to ensure that the desired performance level can be maintained over the expected system lifetime without over specifying the component characteristics.

To analyze a link the following key system requirements are needed.
1. The desired (or possible) transmission distance.
2. The data rate or channel bandwidth.
3. The bit error rate.

The designer has a choice of the following components and their associated characteristics to fulfill the above requirements.
1. **Multimode or Single Mode Optical Fiber:**
    (i) Core size.
    (ii) Core refractive index profile.
    (iii) Bandwidth or dispersion.
    (iv) Attenuation.
    (v) Numerical aperture or mode field diameter.

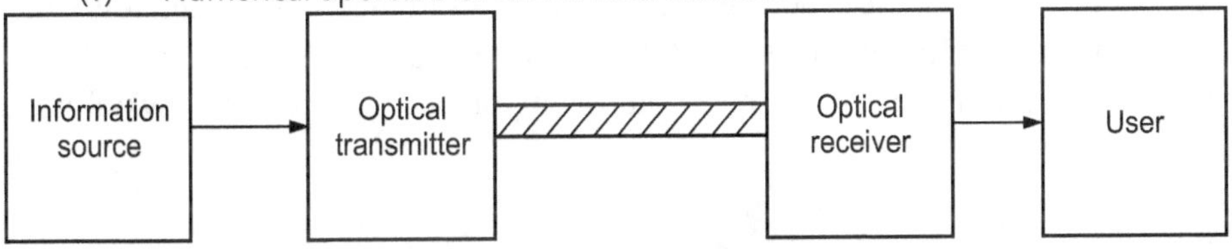

Fig. 3.5: Point-to-Point links

2. LED or LASER Diode Optical Source:
    (i) Emission wavelength.
    (ii) Spectral line width.
    (iii) Output power.
    (iv) Effective radiating area.
    (v) Emission pattern.
    (vi) Number of emitting modes.
3. **PIN or Avalanche Photodiode:**
    (i) Responsivity.
    (ii) Operating wavelength.
    (iii) Speed.
    (iv) Sensitivity.

The link power budget and the system rise time budget analyzes are carried out for the performance of desired system.

3.3.2 System Consideration

In the system performance, the link power budget and the system rise time budget analysis are considered. Fiber optic system design is a complicated process that involves link definition and analysis. The design process begins by providing a complete description of the communication requirements. This information is used to develop the link architecture and define the communication links. System designers must decide on the operational wavelength and types of components to use in the system. This decision affects numerous system and link design parameters, such as launched power, connection losses, bandwidth, cost and reliability.

The major optical link building blocks are receiver, transmitter and optical fiber. In general, designer chooses the characteristic of two of these elements and then computes those of the third. In designing, we first select the photodetector and then choose an optical source and so how far data can be transmitted over a particular fiber before an amplifier is needed in the line to boost up the power level of the optical signal. To choose a particular photodetector, we need to determine the minimum optical power that must fall on the photodetector to satisfy the bit error rate (BER) requirement at the specified data rate. A PIN photodiode receiver is simpler, more stable with changes in temperature and less expensive than an avalanche photodiode receiver. A PIN photodiodes bias voltage are normally less than 5 V, whereas those of avalanche photodiodes range from 40 V to several hundreds volts.

The system consideration for deciding the use of an LED and a laser diode are signal dispersion, data rate, transmission distance and cost. The spectral width of the laser output is much narrower than that of an LED. In the region of 800 to 900 nm the spectral width of an LED and the dispersion characteristics of silica fibers limit the data rate distance product to around 150 (Mb/s) · km. For higher data rate distance product [2500 (mb/s) · km] a laser must be used at wavelengths.

In the optical fiber consideration there are two choices between single mode and multimode fiber, either of which could have a step or a graded-index core. The choice of fiber depends on the type of light sources used and on the amount of dispersion that can be tolerated. Light emitting diodes tends to be used with multimode fibers. The optical power that can be coupled into a fiber from an LED depends on the core cladding index difference. As Δ increases, the fiber coupled power increases correspondingly. The dispersion also becomes greater with increasing Δ. The fiber attenuation also considered while designing. These include connector and splice losses as well as environmental induced losses that could arise from temperature variation, radiation effects and dust and moisture on the connectors.

3.3.3 Link Power Budget

The optical power loss model for a point-to-point link is shown in Fig. 3.6. The photodetector received optical power which is dependeds on the amount of light coupled into the fiber and the losses occuring in the fiber and at the connectors and splices. The link loss budget is obtained from the sequential loss contributions of each element in the link which is expressed in decibels (dB) as,

$$\text{Loss} = 10 \log \frac{P_{out}}{P_{in}}$$

where,

P_{in} = Optical powers emanating into the loss element

P_{out} = Optical power emanating out of the loss element

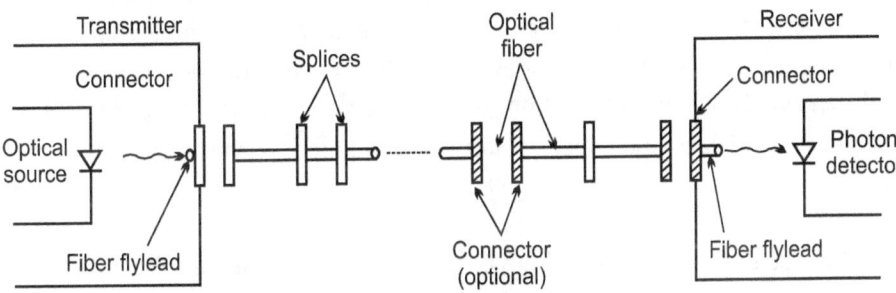

Fig. 3.6: Optical Power Loss Model for a Point-to-Point Link

In addition to link loss, a link power margin is normally provided in the analysis to allow for component aging, temperature fluctuations and losses arising from components. A link margin of 6-8 dB is generally used for systems. The link loss budget obtained from the total optical power loss P_T. The total optical power loss obtained from the light source and the photodetector and allocates this loss to attenuation, connector loss, splice loss and system margin.

$$P_T = P_S - P_R \qquad \ldots (3.1)$$

where,

P_S = The optical power emerging from the end of a fiber flylead attached to the light source

P_R = Receiver sensitivity

$$P_T = 2l_C + \alpha_f L + \text{System margin}$$

where,

l_C = Connector loss

α_f = Fiber attenuation (dB/km)

L = Transmission distance

3.3.4 Rise Time Budget

The rise time budget involves calculating rise time of the link transmitter and the optical fiber. The composite optical transmitter/fiber rise time is referred to as the fiber exit rise time. If the fiber exist rise time is less than the maximum input rise time specified for the link receiver, then the link design is viable. A rise time budget analysis is used for determining the dispersion limitation of an optical fiber link. In digital system the total rise time (t_{sys}) of the link is the root sum square of the rise times from each contributor t_i to the pulse rise time degradation.

$$t_{sys} = \left(\sum_{i=1}^{N} t_i^2 \right)^{1/2}$$

The system speed depends on the transmitter rise time (t_{tx}), the group velocity dispersion (GVD) rise time (t_{GVD}) of the fiber the modal dispersion rise time (t_{mod}) of the fiber, and the receiver rise time (t_{rx}). The transmitter rise time depends on the light source and its drive circuitry. The receiver rise time depends on the photodetector response and the 3 dB electrical bandwidth of the receiver front end. If the 3 dB electrical bandwidth (B_{rx}) of the receiver is given in MHz then the receiver front-end rise time is nanosecond is,

$$t_{rx} = \frac{350}{B_{rx}}$$

The fiber rise time t_{GVD} resulting from GVD over a length L can be written as,

$$t_{GVD} \approx |D| L \sigma_\lambda$$

where,

σ_λ = Half power spectral width of the source
D = Dispersion

The bandwidth B_m in a link length 'L' can be expressed using the empirical expression for modal dispersion as,

$$B_m(L) = \frac{B_0}{L^q}$$

where, the parameter q ranges from 0.5 to 1 and the B_0 is the bandwidth of a 1 km length of cable. The 3 dB electrical bandwidth B_{3dB} is defined as the modulation frequency f_{3dB} at which the received optical power has fallen to 0.5 of the zero frequency value. Therefore, the

$$F_{3dB} = B_{3dB} = \frac{0.44}{t_{FWHM}}$$

where, t_{FWHM} = The full width of the pulse at its half maximum value.
If the t_{FWHM} is the rise time obtained from modal dispersion.

$$t_{mod} = \frac{0.44}{B_M} = \frac{0.44 \, L^q}{B_0}$$

It t_{mod} is expressed in nanoseconds and B_M is given in MHz, then,

$$t_{mod} = \frac{440}{B_M} = \frac{440\, L^q}{B_o}$$

Therefore, the total system rise time can be written as,

$$t_{sys} = [t_{tx}^2 + t_{mod}^2 + t_{GVD}^2 + t_{rx}^2]^{1/2}$$

$$t_{sys} = \left[t_{tx}^2 + \left(\frac{440\, L^q}{B_o}\right)^2 + D^2\, \sigma_\lambda^2\, L^2 + \left(\frac{350}{B_{rx}}\right)^2\right]^{1/2}$$

where the all the times are in nanoseconds and the dispersion D is in ns/(nm·km).

3.4 Wavelength Division Multiplexing (WDM)

Wavelength division multiplexing is one of the best method of multiplexing as it uses optical power very efficiently. In this technique a number of wavelengths are combined and transmitted on single optical fiber. WDM enables the utilization of a significant portion of the available fiber bandwidth by allowing many independent signals to be transmitted simultaneously on one fiber, with each signals are located at a different wavelength. The features of WDM system are as follows:

1. **Capacity upgrade:** WDM is used to upgrade the capacity of existing point-to-point fiber optic transmission links.
2. **Transparency:** In WDM system each optical channel can carry any transmission format.
3. **Wavelength routing:** Wavelength routed networks use the actual wavelength of a signal as a final address.
4. **Wavelength switching:** Wavelength switched architectures are used in optical system.

To obtain the optical bandwidth corresponding to a particular spectral width in these regions, consider the relationship

$$C = \lambda \vartheta$$

where, λ = Wavelength
ϑ = Carrier frequency
C = Speed of light

Differentiate the above equation, we have,

$$|\Delta v| = \left(\frac{C}{\lambda^2}\right) |\Delta \lambda|$$

where, Δv = Deviation in frequency
$\Delta \lambda$ = Wavelength deviation
Δv = Optical bandwidth

In a simple WDM system, each laser must emit light at a different wavelength, with all laser wavelengths light are multiplexed together onto a single optical fiber. A typical WDM system contains various types of optical amplifier as shown in Fig. 3.7. After being transmitted through a high bandwidth optical fiber, the combined optical signals must be demultiplexed at the receiving end by distributing the total optical power to each output port and then requiring that each receiver selectivity recover only one wavelength by using a tunable optical fiber. Each laser is modulated at a given speed and the total aggregate capacity being transmitted along the high bandwidth fiber is the sum total of the bit rates of the individual. The demultiplexer should provide law lass path from each optical source to the multiplexer output. In demultiplexer, photodetectors are sensitive over a broad range of wavelengths. The demultiplexer must exhibit narrow spectral operation. The interchannel crosstalks levels can vary widely depending on the applications. In general the tolerable noise level of –10 dB is not satisfactory, whereas a level of –30 dB is acceptable.

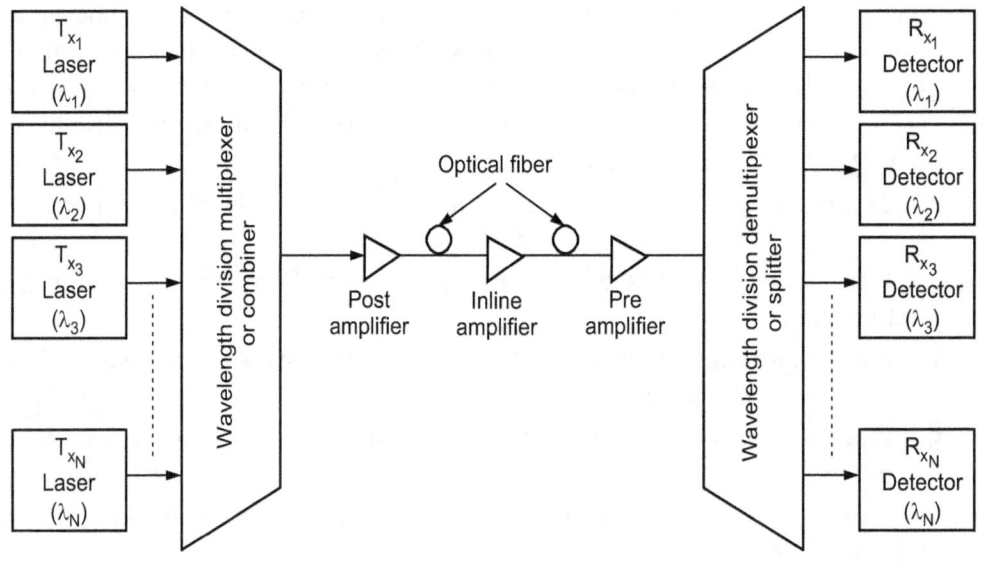

Fig. 3.7: WDM System

3.5 Passive Components

A device in which there is no control phenomenon such as electro or acousto-optic control and there is no scope of generation, amplification or switching of light called as passive devices. Optical (N × N) couplers, power splitter, power taps and star coupler. Passive components can be fabricated either from optical fibers or by means of planar optical waveguides using material such a lithium niobate ($LiNbO_3$) or I_nP. An active devices are basic functional devices such as modulators, switches or amplifiers.

3.5.1 2 × 2 Fiber Coupler

The 2 × 2 coupler is the fused fiber coupler. It has two inputs and two outputs. It is fabricated by twisting together, melting and pulling two single mode fibers so they get fused together over a uniform section of length W. Each input and output fiber has a long tapered section of L as shown in Fig. 3.8. This device is also known as a fused bioconical tapered coupler. It is observed from the Fig. 3.8 that P_0 is the input power P_1 is the throughout power, P_2 is the power coupled into the second fiber and P_3 and P_4 are extremely low signal levels resulting from backward reflections and scattering due to bending in and packaging of the device. Fiber optic couplers attenuate the signal much more than a connector or splice because the input signal is divided among the output ports. The power coupled to another fiber is depended on the axial length of the coupling region, the size of the reduced radius 'r' is the coupling region and the difference in the radii of the two fibers in the coupling region.

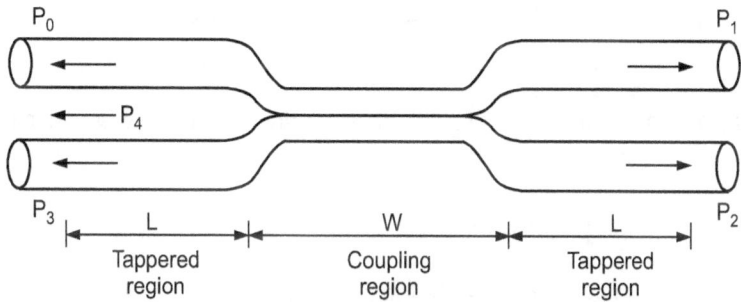

Fig. 3.8: Fused Fiber Coupler

The performance of an optical coupler are explained by the following parameter.

1. **Splitting Ratio:** The splitting ratio or coupling ratio is defined as the output power to the total output power.

$$\text{Splitting Ratio} = \left(\frac{P_2}{P_1 + P_2}\right) \times 100\%$$

2. **Excess Loss:** The excess loss is the ratio of the input power to the total output power.

$$\text{Excess Loss} = 10 \log \left(\frac{P_0}{P_1 + P_2}\right)$$

3. **Insertion Loss:** The insertion loss is the ratio of input port to the output port.

$$\text{Insertion Loss} = 10 \log \left(\frac{P_i}{P_j}\right)$$

where, P_i = Input power at port i

P_j = Output power at port j

4. Crosstalk: Crosstalk measures the degree of isolation between the input at one port and the optical power scattered or reflected back into the other input port.

$$\text{Crosstalk} = 10 \log \left(\frac{P_3}{P_0}\right)$$

3.5.2 Star Coupler

A star coupler is a passive device that distributes optical power from more than two input ports among several output ports equally. The star coupler are constructed by fusion fibers, micro-optic technologies and integrated optic schemes. Fig. 3.9 shows the fiber fusion method of star coupler.

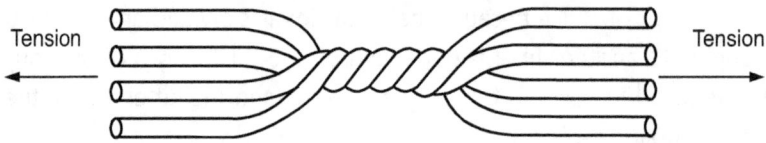

Fig. 3.9: 4 × 4 Fused Fiber Star Coupler

The total loss of star coupler consists of its splitting loss and excess in each path. The insertion loss and crosstalk are same.

1. $\quad\quad$ Splitting loss $= -10 \log \left(\frac{1}{N}\right)$

$\quad\quad\quad\quad$ Splitting loss $= 10 \log N$

2. $\quad\quad$ Excess loss $= 10 \log \left(\dfrac{P_{in}}{\sum\limits_{j=1}^{N} P_{out,\,i}}\right)$

$\quad\quad\quad\quad P_{in} = $ For single input power

$\quad\quad\quad\quad P_{out,\,i} = $ For N output power

3. $\quad\quad$ Insertion logs $= 10 \log \left(\dfrac{P_i}{P_j}\right)$

It gives the insertion loss for the path from input port i to output port j.

4. $\quad\quad$ Crosstalks $= 10 \log \left(\dfrac{P_3}{P_0}\right)$

There is another method to construct the star coupler by cascading 3 dB couplers. Fig. 3.10 shows an example for an 8 × 8 device formed by using twelve 2 × 2 couplers.

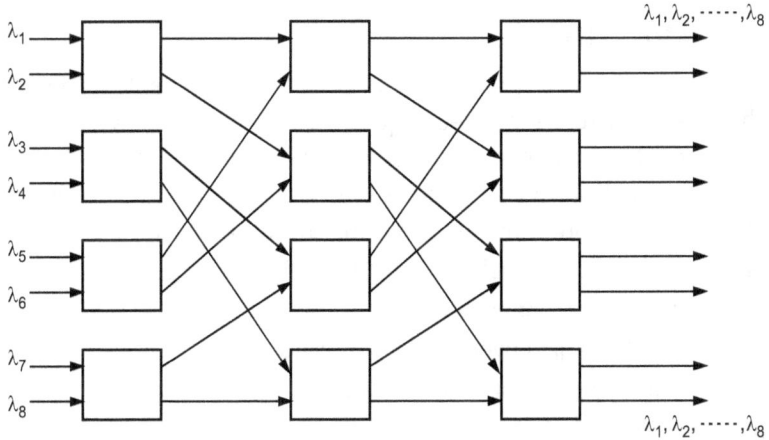

Fig. 3.10: 8 × 8 Star Coupler Formed by Using Twelve 2 × 2 Coupler

This star coupler is constructed from either fused fiber or integrated optic components. It is seen that from Fig. 3.10, a fraction 1/N of the launched power from each input port appears at all output ports, where N should be multiple of 2. That is $N = 2^n$ with the integer $n \geq 1$. The number of 3 dB couplers needed to construct an N × N star coupler is,

$$N_C = \frac{N}{2} \cdot \log_2 N$$

$$N_C = \frac{N}{2} \cdot \frac{\log N}{\log 2}$$

Therefore, there are N/2 elements in vertical direction and (log N/log 2) elements in the horizontal direction. The excess loss in decibels is written as,

$$\text{Excess loss} = -10 \log (F_T \log_2 N)$$

F_T = Fraction of power transversing each 3 dB coupler element

The splitting loss for this coupler is given by,

$$\text{Splitting loss} = 10 \log N$$

Therefore, the total loss is the sum of the splitting loss and excess loss. This total loss is found by a signal as it passes through the $\log_2 N$ stages of the N × N star and gets divided by N outputs. This total loss is decibels can be written as,

$$\text{Total loss} = \text{Splitting loss} + \text{Excess loss}$$

$$\text{Total loss} = -10 \log \left(\frac{F_T \log_2 N}{N} \right)$$

It shows that the loss increases logarithmically with N.

3.6 Optical Amplifier

When the optical power in the link reaches to the minimum detectable power, then we need to increase the power. There are two techniques used to increase power such as repeaters and optical amplifier. Repeaters consists of an optical detector, signal recovery circuits and an optical source. The optical amplifier amplify the optical signal without ever performing an electronic equivalent. There are some properties of optical amplifier:
1. It provides a high power gain in the order of 30 dB or more.
2. It has a wide spectral bandwidth.
3. It provides uniform gain over amplifier spectral width.
4. It adds minimum noise from the amplifier.
5. It has low insertion loss.
6. Good conversion efficiency.
7. It uses an optical pump source that is small and compact.

In general, there are three classes of optical amplifiers:
(i) Inline amplifiers.
(ii) Preamplifier.
(iii) Power amplifier.

There are two types of optical amplifier such as semiconductor optical amplifier and doped fiber amplifiers. Optical amplifier increase the power level of incident light through stimulated emission process. The structure of amplifier is similar to that of laser in which stimulated emission occurs. The basic operation of a generic optic amplifier is shown in Fig. 3.11.

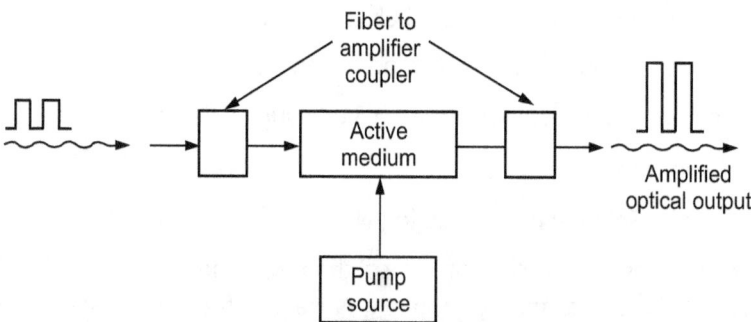

Fig. 3.11: Basic Block of Optical Amplifier

The pump source absorbs energy supplied from an external source. The pump power requirement is easily met by semiconductor laser diodes. The pump supplies energy to electronics, an incoming signal photon will trigger these excited electrons to drop to lower level through a stimulated emission process, therefore, amplification takes place.

3.6.1 Eribium – Doped Fiber Amplifiers

An optical fiber doped with eribium ions and this doped fiber used as an amplifying medium called as erbium doped fiber amplifier. It operates in the 1520 to 1550 nm window of the fiber. Diode laser pumps used as pump source. Erbium doped fiber amplifier reduce the system cost and enhance network performance.

The advantages of the EDFA's are:
1. High gain ($\approx$ 50 dB).
2. High output gain (> 100 mW).
3. Low noise figure (~ 4 dB).
4. Less gain variation.
5. Wide bandwidth of operation.
6. Inherent compatibility to transmission fiber with low insertion loss.
7. Low power requirement on the pump source.

3.6.2 Semiconductor Optical Amplifiers

Semiconductor optical amplifier or semiconductor laser amplifiers uses laser diode to amplify the light. The laser diodes are biased just below oscillation. It has not enough gain to oscillate. The insertion loss of these amplifiers tend to be 6 dB or more when they are placed in a fiber link. It introduces cross talk in multichannel system. Non-linearities in the gain medium affect the amplification process.

3.7 Optical Networks

Optical networks are high capacity telecommunication networks based on optical technology. Optical networks can be linked to wavelength division multiplexing which provide additional capacity on existing fibers. Networks can be divided into the three categories which are –

(a) **Local Area Network:** It interconnects users in a localized area such as a department, a building, or a campus.
(b) **Metropolitan Area Networks:** It interconnects users within a city or the metropolitan area surrounding a city.
(c) **Wide Area Networks:** It interconnects users within a large geographical area.

3.7.1 Network Topologies

The are three common topologies used for fiber optic system. These are the star network, the linear bus network and the ring network.

(a) Star Network:

In star network, all nodes are joined at a single point called the central node or hub. The central node are of two types active or passive. Active hub can control all routing messages in the network. A heavy switching burden can be placed on an active hub. In a passive central node, a power splitter is used at the hub to divide the incoming optical signals among all the outgoing lines to the attached stations. The star network is shown in Fig. 3.12.

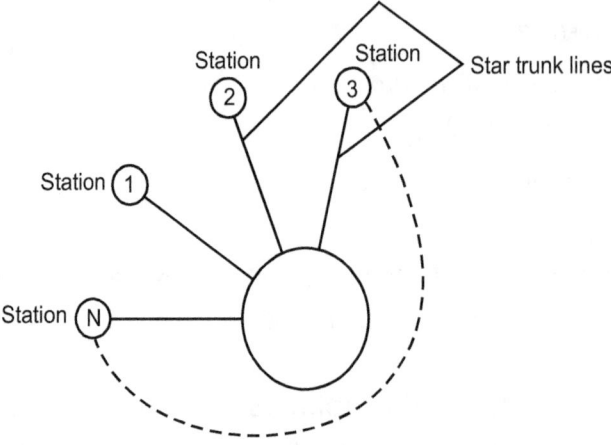

Fig. 3.12: Star Network

In a star network, each station has its own transmitter and receiver. The disadvantage of the start network, if star network damaged, it can disrupt the entire network. It has the advantage of making it relatively simple to add terminals to the network.

(b) Linear Bus Network:

In the linear bus network, the network takes the form of a backbone with individual stations receiving or adding data as required. It is difficult to implement. Optical data bus can be accessed by means of a coupling elements, which can be either active or passive. The linear bus network is shown in Fig. 3.13.

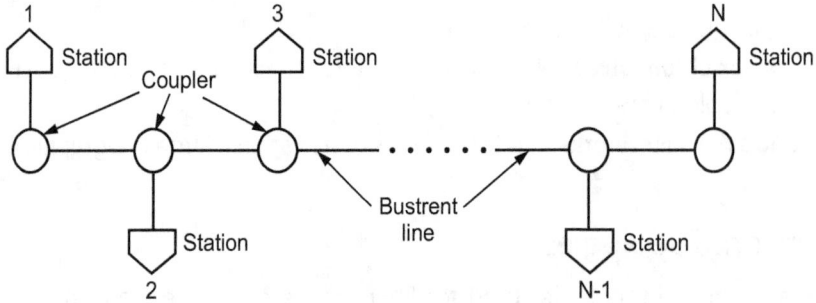

Fig. 3.13: Linear Bus Network

(c) Ring Network:

The ring network is shown in Fig. 3.14. In the ring network, the stations are arranged into a continuous circuit. Each station receives a message from its upstream neighbour. If the message is not the addressee, the same message repeats to its downstream neighbour. The disadvantage of the ring network that damage to any station on the ring will disrupt the entire network unless by pass switches or network redundancy are built it.

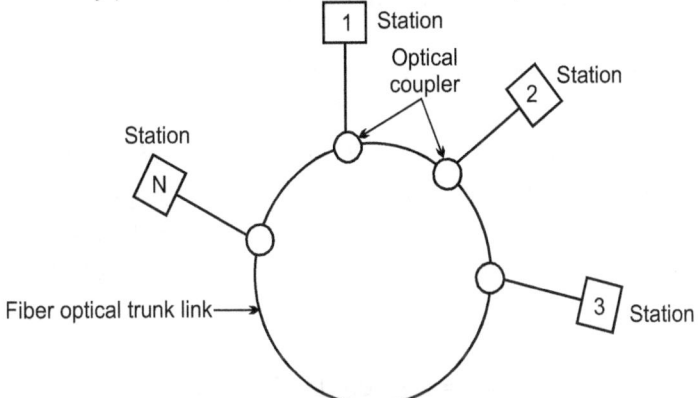

Fig. 3.14: Ring Network

3.7.2 Performance of Passive Linear Buses

The losses encountered in a passive linear bus coupler consisting of a cascaded combination of two directional coupler where two ports are not used as shown in Fig. 3.15. The coupler has four ports, two for connecting the coupler onto the fiber bus, one for receiving tapped-off light and one for inserting an optical signal on to the line after the tap-off to keep the signal out of the local receiver. If a fraction of optical power is lost at each port of the coupler, then the connecting loss and is given by,

$$L_C = -10 \log (1 - F_C)$$

where, L_C = Connecting loss

F_C = Fraction of optical power loss

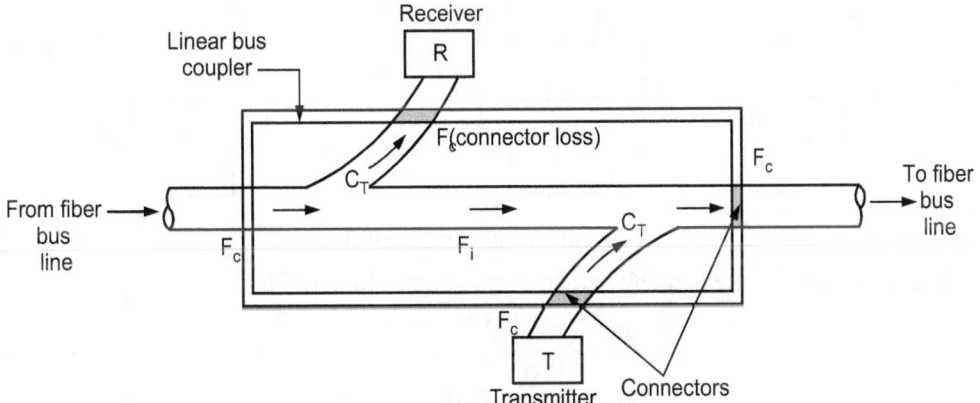

Fig. 3.15: Passive Linear Bus

If the fraction of power is removed from the bus and delivered to the detector port. The power extracted from the bus is called as a tap loss and is given by,

$$L_{tap} = -10 \log C_T$$

where,

L_{tap} = Tap loss

C_T = Fraction of power removed from the bus

In a symmetric coupler C_T is also the fraction of power which is coupled from the transmitting input port to the bus. If P_0 is the optical power launched from the source flyhead, the power coupled to the bus is $C_T P_0$. In calculation of the throughput power for intermediate stations, the transmission path through the bus coupler passes two tap points. The optical power is extracted at both the receiving and transmitting taps of the device. The power removed at the transmitting tap goes out of the unused port and thus is lost from the system, which is given by,

$$L_{thru} = -10 \log (1 - C_T)^2$$
$$L_{thru} = -20 \log (1 - C_T) \text{ (in dB)}$$

where,

L_{thru} = Throughput coupling loss

There is an intrinsic transmission loss associated with each bus coupler which is given by,

$$L_i = -10 \log (1 - F_i)$$

where,

L_i = Intrinsic transmission loss

F_i = Fraction of power loss in coupler

Consider a simplex linear bus of N station uniformly separated by a distance L, as shown in Fig. 3.16.

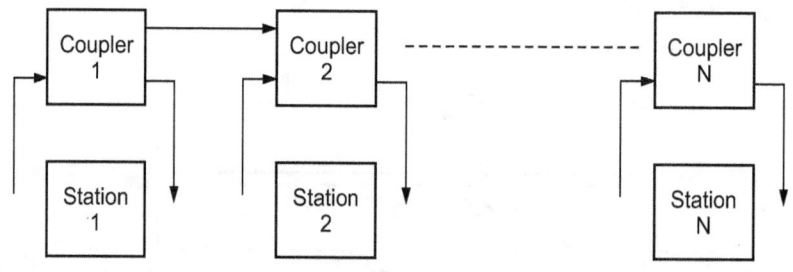

Fig. 3.16: Simplexed Linear Bus

The fiber attenuation between any two adjacent stations in decibels is,

$$L_{Fiber} = -10 \log A_0 = \alpha L$$

and

$$A_0 = \frac{P(x)}{P(o)} = 10^{-\alpha x/10}$$

where,

α = Fiber attenuation in units of dB/km
L = Separation of station

3.7.3 Nearest Neighbour Power Budget

The power budget can be obtained by examining the link in terms of fractional power losses at each link element. There should be smallest distance between adjacent stations. Such as station 1 and station 2. If P_0 is the optical power launched from a source flyhead at station 1, then the power received at station 2 is,

$$P_2 = A_0 \, C_T^2 \, (1 - F_C)^4 \, (1 - F_i)^2 \, P_0$$

The losses encounters in optical link such as,
(a) Fiber path attenuation (A_0).
(b) Coupling efficiency at tap points of both the transmitters and the receiver.
(c) For passive linear bus coupler, four connecting points each of which passes a fraction of the power entering them $(1 - F_C)$.
(d) The fraction of power loss in the coupler (F_i).

From the definition connecting loss (L_C), tap loss (L_{tap}), intrinsic transmission loss (L_i) and the power received at station 2, the expression of the power loss between station 1 and station 2 can be expressed in logarithmic form as,

$$10 \log \left(\frac{P_0}{P_2} \right) = \alpha L + 2 \, L_{tap} + 4 L_C + 2 L_i$$

3.7.4 Large Distance Power Budget

The largest distance occurs between station 2 and station N for transmitted and received power. The fractional power coupled from the transmitter flylead through the bus coupler at station 1 is,

$$F_1 = (1 - F_C)^2 \, C_T \, (1 - F_i) \qquad \text{... (a)}$$

At station N, the fraction of power from the bus coupler input port that emerges from the receiver is,

$$F_N = (1 - F_C)^2 \, C_T \, (1 - F_i) \qquad \text{... (b)}$$

The fraction of power passing through each coupling module for each of the (N − 2) intermediate stations is,

$$F_{coup} = (1 - F_C)^2 \, (1 - C_T)^2 \, (1 - F_i) \qquad \text{... (c)}$$

From the input to the output of each coupler, the power flow encounters two connector losses, the tap loss and one intrinsic losses. The power received at station N from station 1 is given by,

$$P_{1,N} = A_o^{N-1} F_1 F_{coul}^{N-2} F_N P_o$$
$$= A_o^{N-1} (1-F_C)^{2N} (1-C_T)^{2(N-2)} C_T^2 (1-F_i)^N P_o$$

From the link losses, the power budget for this link then is,

$$10 \log \left(\frac{P_o}{P_{1,N}} \right) = (N-1)\alpha L + 2N L_C + (N-2) L_{thru} + 2 L_{tap} + N L_i$$
$$= (\text{Fiber + Connector + Coupler throughput + Taploss + Intrinsic}) \text{ Losses}$$
$$= N(\alpha L + 2 L_C + L_{thru} + L_i) - \alpha L - 2 L_{thru} + 2 L_{tap}$$

(in decibels)

The losses of the linear bus increase linearly with the number of stations N.

3.7.5 Dynamic Range

In a linear bus, the optical power available at a particular node decreases with increasing distance from the source. Thus, the performance of an optical link can be termed as system dynamic range. The dynamic range is the maximum optical power range to which any detector must be able to respond. The dynamic range for worst case can be written as,

$$DR = 10 \log \left(\frac{P_{1,2}}{P_{1,N}} \right)$$
$$= 110 \log \left\{ \frac{1}{[A_o (1-F_C)^2 (1-C_T)^2 (1-F_i)]^{N-2}} \right\}$$
$$DR = (N-2)(\alpha L + 2 L_C + L_{thru} + L_i)$$

where,

DR = Dynamic Range

3.7.6 Performance of Star Architecture

A star coupled applied to a given network and examine the various optical power losses associated with the coupler. For the coupler, the excess loss is the ratio of the input power to the total power. It is the fraction of power lost in the process of coupling light from the input port to all the output ports.

$$\text{Fiber star excess loss} = L_{excess} = 10 \log \left[\frac{P_{in}}{\sum_{i=1}^{N} P_{out,i}} \right]$$

where,

P_{in} = Single input power

$P_{out,i}$ = N output powers

In star coupler the optical power from any input is equally divided to the output ports. The total loss of the device consists of the splitting loss and the excess loss in each path through the star. Therefore, the splitting loss is expressed in decibels as,

$$\text{Splitting loss} = L_{split} = -10 \log\left(\frac{1}{N}\right)$$
$$= 10 \log N$$

The power balance equation for a particular link between two stations in a star network is given by,

$$P_S - P_R = L_{excess} + \alpha(2L) + 2L_C + L_{split}$$

where,

P_S = The fiber coupled output power from source in dBm

P_R = The minimum optical power in dBm required at the receiver

α = Fiber attenuation

L = Distance between the station and star coupler

L_{excess} = Fiber star excess loss

$$P_S - P_R = L_{excess} + \alpha(2L) + 2L_C + 10 \log N$$

From the above equation, a star network loss increases much slower as log N. Fig. 3.17 shows the loss versus station for star and linear bus.

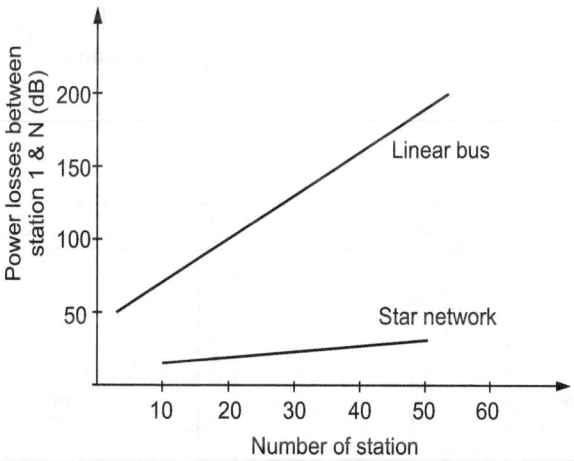

Fig. 3.17: Power Loss as a Function of Station for Linear Bus and Star Architecture

3.7.7 SONET/SDH

The synchronous optical network (SONET) standard has been proposed by American National Standard Institute (ANSI). The international version of SONET is called the Synchronous Digital Hierarchy (SDH). The standard has the several consideration, the optical interface that specifies the operating wavelength power levels etc.; operations specifications and the rate and format specifications that give the data format, the frame size etc.

3.7.7.1 SONET Optical Specifications

The optical parameter specification are –
    (a)   The nominal wavelength within a range of 1280 nm to 1340 nm.
    (b)   The maximum spectral width is about 9 nm.
    (c)   The signal extinction ratio is 10: 1.
    (d)   The NRZ coding is used.

3.7.7.2 Transmission Format and Speeds

SONET uses a basic transmission rate of STS-1-equivalent to 51.84 Mb/s. The frame format of STS-1 SONET is shown in Fig. 3.18. The basic signal of SONET is the synchronous transport signal level 1 or STS-1. The STS format is composed of 9 rows of 90 columns of 8-bit bytes or 810 bytes. The byte transmission order is row by row, left to right. A frame length of 125 μs (888 frames per second) is possible in SONET. The first three columns of the STS-1 frame are for the transport overhead. The three column each contain nine bytes. Of these, nine bytes are overhead for the section layer and 18 bytes are overhead for the line layer. The remaining 87 columns constitutes the STS-1. Envelope capacity i.e. payload and path overhead. Therefore, the transmission bit rate of the basic SONET signal can be obtained by,

$$\text{STS-1} = \frac{(90 \text{ bytes/row}) (9 \text{ rows/frame}) (8 \text{ bits/byte})}{(125 \text{ μs/frame})}$$

$$\text{STS-1} = 51.84 \text{ Mb/s}$$

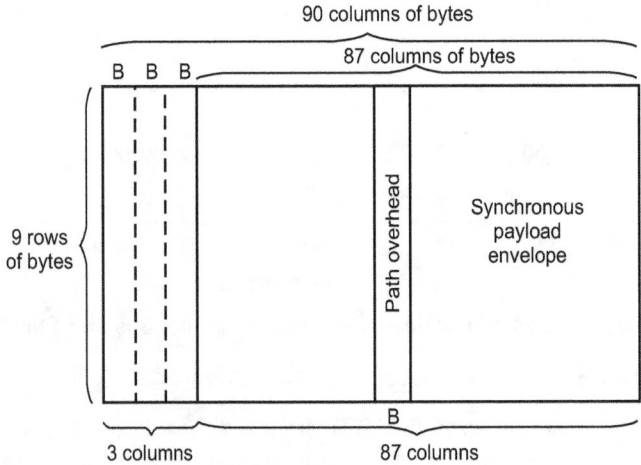

Fig. 3.18: STS-1 Frame Element

The Synchronous Payload Envelope (SPE) can be divided into two parts, STS path overhead and the payload. The payload is the revenue-producing traffic being transported and routed over the SONET network. Once the payload is multiplexed into the synchronous payload envelope, it can be transported and switched through SONET without having to be examined and possibly demultiplexed at intermediate nodes. Thus, SONET is said to be service independent or transparent. The optical equivalent of STS-1 is known as OC-1, and its used for transmission across the fiber. The OC stands for optical carrier. The SONET signals are integer multiplers of STS-1 bitrate. Thus, STS-N signal has a bit rate equal to N times 51.84 Mb/s. In SDH the basic rate is equivalent to STS-3 or 155.52 Mb/s which is called as synchronous transport module level-1 (STM-1). The higher bit rate are designed by STM-M module.

3.7.7.3 Feature of SONET/SDH
1. It has ability to access directly lower tributaries in higher bit streams.
2. Achieves intercompatibility among the different standard.
3. A basic rate of 155 Mb/s in STM-1 in the case of SDH and 51.84 Mb/s in case of SONET.
4. It has Add/Drop multiplexer (feature).
5. It is forward compatible to increase bit rates, it is also backward compatible down to the basic voice channel data rate of 64 kb/s.
6. It has built in ability to manage network capacity dynamically in response to traffic needs.
7. It has comprehensive operation, administration and maintenance feature.

3.7.7.4 Advantages of SONET
1. It has standardized equipment and interface.
2. It has broadband capability owing to a fiber medium.
3. Multiservice/multivendor operations.
4. It has large number of easily accessible overheads bytes.
5. It has extensive operation, administration and maintenance capabilities.
6. Simple mux/demux operation.

3.7.7.5 SONET Network Elements
(a) Terminal Multiplexer:
The path terminating element (PTE), an entry level path terminating terminal multiplexer, acts as a concentrator of DS 1s as well as other tributary signals. Its simplest deployment would involve two terminal multiplexers linked by fiber with or without a regenerator in the link. This implementation represents the simplest SONET link. (See Fig. 3.19).

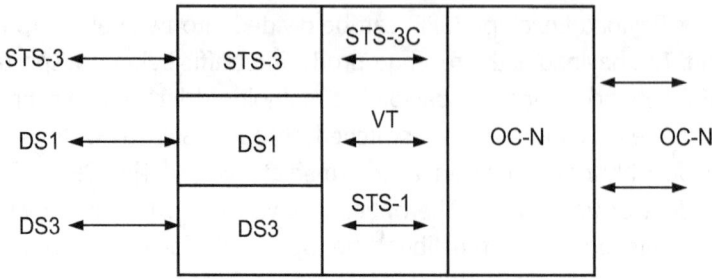

Fig. 3.19: Terminal Multiplexer

(b) Regenerator:

A regenerator is needed when, due to the long distance between multiplexers, the signal level in the fiber becomes too low.

The regenerator clock itself off of the received signal and replaces the Section Overhead bytes before re-transmitting the signal. The Line Overhead, payload, and Path Overhead are not altered. See Fig. 3.20.

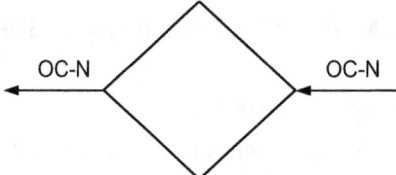

Fig. 3.20: Regenerator

(c) Add/Drop Multiplexer (ADM):

Although network elements (NEs) are compatible at the OC-N level, they may differ in features from vendor to vendor. SONET does not restrict manufacturers to providing a single type of product, nor require them to provide all types. For example, one vendor might offer an add/drop multiplexer with access at DS1 only, whereas another might offer simultaneous access at DS1 and DS3 rates. See Fig. 3.21.

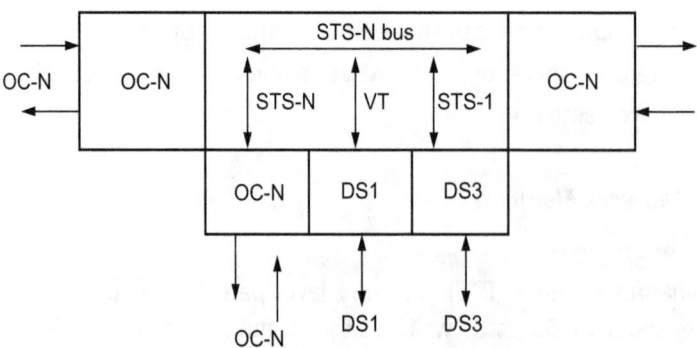

Fig. 3.21: Add/drop Multiplexer

A single-stage multiplexer/demultiplexer can multiplex various inputs into an OC-N signals. At an add/drop site, only those signals that need to be accessed are dropped or inserted. The remaining traffic continues through the network element without requiring special pass-through units or other signal processing.

In rural applications, an ADM can be deployed at a terminal site or any intermediate location for consolidating traffic from widely separated locations. Several ADMs can also be configured as a survivable ring.

SONET enables drop and repeat (also known as drop and continue) - a key capability in both telephony and cable TV applications. With drop and repeat, a signal terminates at one node, is duplicated (repeated) and is then sent to the next and subsequent nodes.

In ring-survivability applications, drop and repeat provides alternate routing for traffic passing through interconnecting rings in a "matched-nodes" configuration. If the connection cannot be made through one of the nodes, the signal is repeated and passed along an alternate route to the destination node.

In multi-node distribution applications, one transport channel can efficiently carry traffic between multiple distribution nodes. When transporting video, for example, each programming channel is delivered (dropped) at the node and repeated for delivery to the next and subsequent nodes. Not all bandwidth (program channels) need be terminated at all the nodes. Channels not terminating at a node can be passed through without physical intervention to the nodes.

The add-drop multiplexer provides interfaces between the different network signals and SONET signals. Single-stage multiplexing can multiple/demultiplex or more tributary (DS1) signals into/from an STS-N signal. It can be used in terminals sites, intermediate (add-drop) sites, or hub configurations. At an add-drop site, it can drop lower-rate signals to be transported on different facilities, or it can add lower-rate signals into the higher-rate STS-N signal. The rest of the traffic simply continues straight through.

(d) Wideband Digital Cross-Connects:
A SONET cross-connect accepts various optical carrier rates, accesses the STS-1 signals, and switches at this level. Its ideally used at a SONET hub. One major difference between a cross-connect and an add-drop multiplexer is that a cross-connect may be used to interconnect a much larger number of STS-1s. The broadband cross-connect can be used for grooming (consolidating or segregating) of STS-1s or for broad-band traffic management. For example, it may be used to segregate high-bandwidth from low-bandwidth traffic and send them separately to the high-bandwidth (e.g. video) switch and a low-bandwidth (voice)

switch. It's the synchronous equivalent of a DS3 digital cross-connect and supports hubbed network architectures.

This type is similar to the broadband cross-connect except that the switching is done at VT levels (similar to DS1/DS2 levels). It is similar to a DS3/1 cross-connect because it accepts DS1s, DS3s, and is equipped with optical interfaces to accept optical carrier signals. It's suitable for DS1 level grooming applications at hub locations. One major advantage of wideband digital cross-connects is that less demultiplexing and multiplexing is required because only the required tributaries are accessed and switched.

The Wideband Digital Cross-Connect (W-DCS) is a digital cross-connect that terminates SONET and DS3 signals, as well as having the basic functionality of VT and DS1-level cross-connections. It's the SONET equivalent to the DS3/DS1 digital cross-connect, and accepts optical OC-N signals as well as STS-1s, DS1s and DS3s.

In a Wideband Digital Cross-Connect, the switching is done at the VT level (i.e. it cross-connects the constituent VTs between STS-N terminations).

Because SONET is synchronous, the low-speed tributaries are visible and accessible within the STS-1 signal. Therefore, the required tributaries can be accessed and switched without demultiplexing, which isn't possible with existing digital cross-connects. As well, the W-DCS cross-connects the constituent DS1s between DS3 terminations, and between DS3 and DS1 terminations.

The feature of the W-DCS make it useful in several applications. Because it can automatically cross-connect VTs and DS1s, the W-DCS can be used as a network management system. This capability, in turn, makes the W-DCS ideal for grooming at a hub location. See Fig. 3.22.

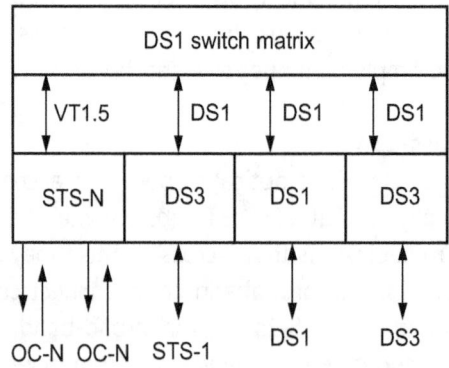

Fig. 3.22: Wideband Digital Cross-connect

(e) Broadband Digital Cross-Connect:

The Broadband Digital Cross-Connect interfaces various SONET signals and DS3s. It accesses the STS-1 signals, and switches at this level. It's the synchronous equivalent of the DS3 digital cross-connect, except that the broadband digital cross-connect accepts optical signals and allows overhead to be maintained for integrated OAM&P (asynchronous systems prevent overhead from being passed from optical signal to signal).

The Broadband Digital Cross-Connect can make two-way cross-connections at the DS3, STS-1, and STS-Nc levels. It's best used as a SONET hub, where it can be used for grooming STS-1s, for broadband restoration purposes, or for routing traffic. See Fig. 3.23.

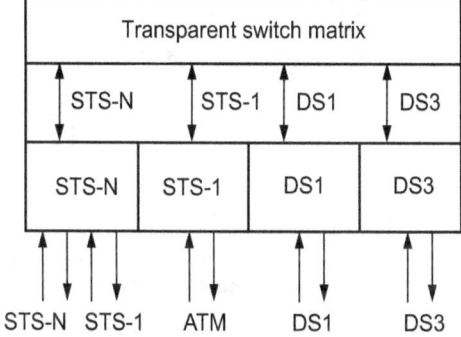

Fig. 3.23: Broadband Digital Cross-connect

(f) Digital Loop Carrier:

The Digital Loop Carrier (DLC) may be considered a concentrator of low-speed services before they are brought into the local central office for distribution. If this concentration were not done, the number of subscribers (or lines) that a central office could serve would be limited by the number of lines served by the CO. The DLC itself is actually a system of multiplexers and switches designed to perform concentration from the remote terminals to the community dial office and from there, to the central office.

Whereas a SONET multiplexer may be deployed at the customer premises, a DLC is intended for service in the central office or a controlled environment vault (CEV) that belongs to the carrier. Bellcore document TR-TSY-000303 describes a generic Integrated Digital Loop Carrier (IDLC), which consists of intelligent Remote Digital Terminals (RDTs) and digital switch elements called Integrated Digital Terminals (IDTs), which are connected by a digital line. The IDLCs are designed to more efficiently integrated DLC systems with existing digital switches. See Fig. 3.24.

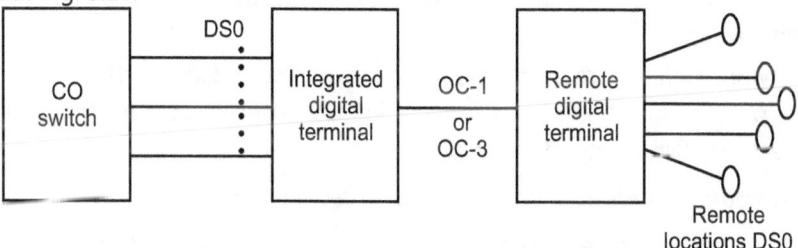

Fig. 3.24: Integrated Digital Loop Carrier

3.7.7.6 SONET Network Configurations

(a) Point-to-Point:

The SONET multiplexer, an entry level path terminating terminal multiplexer, acts as a concentrator of DS1s as well as other tributaries. Its simplest deployment involves two terminal multiplexers linked by fiber with or without a regenerator in the link. This implementation represents the simplest SONET configuration.

In this configuration, (Fig. 3.25), the SONET path and the Service path (DS1 or DS3 links end-to-end) are identical and this synchronous island can exist within an asynchronous network world. In the future, point-to-point service path connections will span across the whole network and will always originate and terminate in a multiplexer.

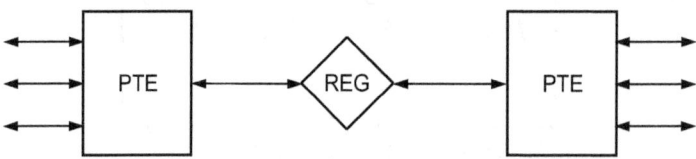

Fig. 3.25: Point-to-Point

(b) Point-to-Multipoint:

A point-to-multipoint (linear add/drop) architecture includes adding and dropping circuits along the way. The SONET ADM (add/drop multiplexer) is a unique network element specifically designed for this task. It avoids the current cumbersome network architecture of demultiplexing, cross-connecting, adding and dropping channels, and than remultiplexing. The ADM is typically placed along a SONET link to facilitate adding and dropping tributary channels at intermediate points in the network. See Fig. 3.26.

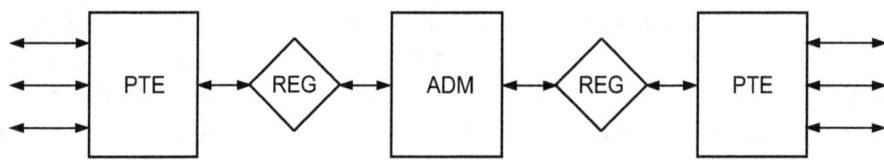

Fig. 3.26: Point-to-Multipoint

(c) Hub Network:

The hub network architecture accommodates unexpected growth and change more easily than simple point-to-point networks. A hub (Fig. 3.27) concentrates traffic at a central site and allows easy reprovisioning of the circuits.

There are two possible implementations of this type of network:

1. Using two or more ADMs, and a wideband cross-connect switch which allows cross-connecting the tributary services at the tributary level.

2. Using a broadband digital cross-connect which allows cross-connecting at both the SONET level and the tributary level.

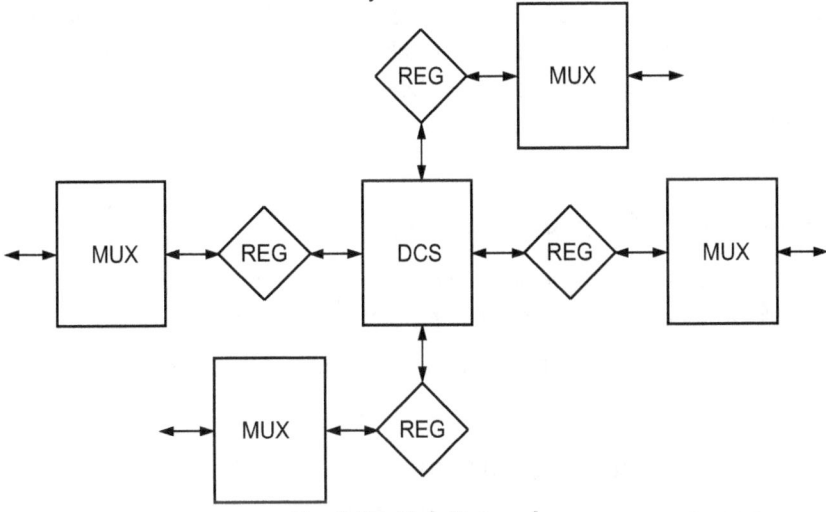

Fig. 3.27: Hub Network

(d) Ring Architecture:
The SONET building block for a ring architecture is the ADM. Multiple ADMs can be put into a ring configuration for either bi-directional or uni-directional traffic (See. Fig. 3.28). The main advantage of the ring topology if its survivability; if a fiber cable is cut, the multiplexers have the intelligence to send the service affected via. an alternate path through the ring without interruption.

The demand for survivable services, diverse routing of fiber facilities, flexibility to rearrange services to alternate serving nodes, as well as automatic restoration within seconds, have made rings a popular SONET topology.

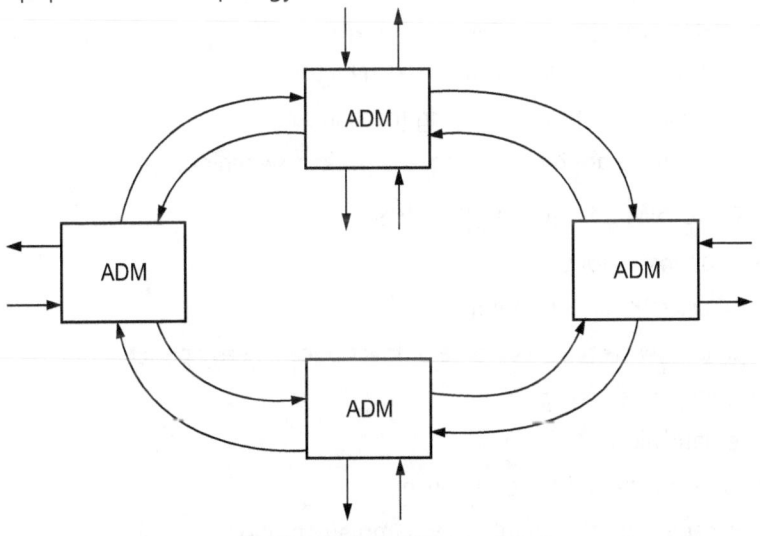

Fig. 3.28: Ring Architecture

3.8 Photonic Switching

The photonic switching technology provide the future high speed, broadband services etc. In fiber optic communication, electronic switching takes place by converting the optical signal to electrical and converting back to the optical form for transmission purpose. The photonic switching devices used typical two input/two output (2 × 2) devices.

3.8.1 Limitations of Photonic Switches

1. The power required for switching is the ratio of the switching energy to the switching time. The shorter switching time require more power.
2. The spontaneous switching occur due to thermal energy present in a device.

3.8.2 Features of Photonic Switching

Basic Switch Element:
1. Control mechanism which is electrically controlled.
2. Guided wave type.
3. Back optic form or integrated optic form.
4. N × N input output configuration.

Switch Arrays:
1. Logical interconnection of basic switch elements.
2. Switching array architectures are cross point, tree, planar, benes, class etc.
3. Photonic switching switching architecture are space switching, time division switching, code division switched architectures.
4. Centralised or distributed routing mechanism.
5. Switching used are bit switching and packed switching.

3.8.3 Photonic Switching Properties

1. Insertion loss is low.
2. Low cross talk/high isolation.
3. Required low switching voltage or low optical energy per change.
4. Switching speed is high.
5. Wide bandwidth.
6. Good reliability and fault tolerance.
7. It has capability of high integrated implementations.

3.8.4 Characteristics of Photonic Switching Architecture

1. **Signal-to-Noise Ratio:** It is the ratio of the signal power to the noise power due to cross talk. Photonic switching devices have a finite extinction ratio.
2. **Insertion Loss:** The insertion loss is the difference in the input power and the output power.
3. **Switching Time:** The transition time (T_t) holding time are considered. The duration in which state changes called transition time and in a holding time data pass through the switching fabric.
4. **Fault Tolerance:** The fault tolerance is the minimum number of switches that must be faulty for dynamic full access connectivity.

3.8.5 Types of Photonic Switches

Photonic switches are broadly classified as mechanically operated, magneto optic, acoustic optic and electro-optic switches.

3.8.5.1 Mechanically Activated Optical Switching

The mechanical forces are used to move an incoming fiber to one of many positions, causing it to couple to one of the corresponding outgoing fibers. The mechanical force is generated by an electrically activated solenoid as shown in Fig. 3.29. These switches have a good cross talk figure of merit. The switching speed is very less in order of milliseconds.

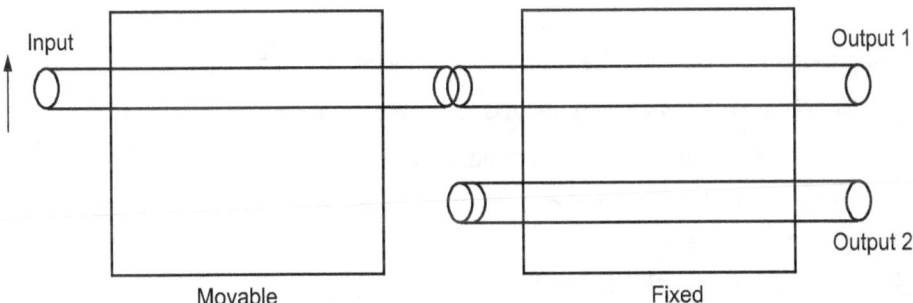

Fig. 3.29: Mechanically Activated Switch

3.8.5.2 Magneto Optic Switch

In this switches the magneto optic effect in an Yttrium Iron Garnet is used. The switching can take place by the linearly polarized light which is first rotated through a 45° Faraday rotator of the YIG single crystal. The rotation and its direction can be controlled by the magnetic field. The optical path is determined by the polarization separator.

It function as optical switch. The Faraday rotator is in the form of thin plate, which can be operate on low strength magnetic field. Internal cross talk can be minimised by using the coated surface of the thin crystal plate with optical interference films.

3.8.5.3 Acousto-Optic Switching

In this switching, the incoming optical beam is allowed to interact with an acoustic wave. The acoustic waves are generated in using interdigital electrodes in planar form. The diffraction angle is dependent on the grating spacing, which is depended on acoustic wave frequency. Therefore, the switching can be done by controlling the acoustic frequency.

3.8.5.4 Electro-Optic Switch

The switching can be done by combining electro optic effect and optical waveguide. Guided optical waves propagate in a thin film with a thickness in the range of optical wavelengths. The refractive index of the film must be higher than that of the substrate material so that light can be tapped in the film by the total internal reflection. Optical direction coupler is used.

3.9 Applications of Fiber Optic Sensors

Fiber optic sensors are being developed and used in two major ways. The first is as a direct replacement for existing sensors where the fiber sensors offers significantly improved performance, reliability, safety and/or cost advantages to the end user. The second area is the development and deployment of fiber optic sensors in new market areas.

Fiber optic sensors are being embedded into or attached to materials –
 (1) During the manufacturing process to enhance process control systems,
 (2) To augment non-destructive evaluation once parts have been made,
 (3) To form health and damage assessment systems once parts have been assembled into structures and
 (4) To enhance control systems.

Applications of fiber optic sensors are as follows:
 (1) In the area of fly-by-light, the conventional electronic sensor technology are targeted to be replaced by equivalent fiber optic sensor technology that offers sensors with relative immunity to electromagnetic interference, significant weight savings and safety improvements.
 (2) In manufacturing, fiber sensors are being developed to support process control. Often times, the selling points for these sensors are improvements in environmental ruggedness and safety, especially in areas where electrical discharges could be hazardous.

(3) One other area where fiber optic sensors are being mass-produced in the field of medicine, where they are being used to measure blood gas parameters and dosage levels. Because these sensors are completely passive they pose no electrical shock threat to the patient and their inherent safety has lead to a relatively rapid introduction.

(4) The automotive industry, construction industry and other traditional users of sensors remain relatively untouched by fiber sensors, mainly because of cost considerations. This can be expected to change as the improvements in optoelectronics and fiber optic communications continue to expand along with the continuing emergence of new fiber optic sensors.

(5) Fiber optic sensor and communication systems capable of monitoring the status of buildings, bridges, highways and factories over widely dispersed areas. Functions such as fire, police, maintenance scheduling and emergency response to earthquakes, hurricanes and tornadoes could be readily integrated into very wide area networks of sensors.

(6) It is also possible to use fiber optic sensors in combination with fiber optic communication links to monitor stress build up in critical fault locations and dome build up of volcanoes. These widely dispersed fiber networks may offer the first real means of gathering information necessary to form prediction models for these natural hazards.

3.10 Optical Time-Domain Reflectometry

End users use optical time-domain reflectometry to characterize optical fiber and optical connection properties in the field. In optical time-domain reflectometry, an **OTDR** transmits an optical pulse through an installed optical fiber. The OTDR measures the fraction of light that is reflected back due to Rayleigh scattering and Fresnel reflection. By comparing the amount of light scattered back at different times, the OTDR can determine fiber and connection losses. When several fibers are connected to form an installed cable plant, the OTDR can characterize optical fiber and optical connection properties along the entire length of the cable plant. A **fiber optic cable plant** consists of optical fiber cables, connectors, splices, mounting panels, jumper cables, and other passive components. A cable plant does not include active components such as optical transmitters or receivers.

The OTDR displays the back scattered and reflected optical signal as a function of length. The OTDR plots half the power in decibels (dB) versus half the distance. Plotting half the power in dB and half the distance corrects for round trip effects. By analyzing the OTDR plot, or trace, end users can measure fiber attenuation and transmission loss between any two points along the cable plant. End users can also measure insertion loss and reflectance of any optical connection. In addition, end users use the OTDR trace to locate fiber breaks or faults.

Fig. 3.30 shows an example OTDR trace of an installed cable plant. OTDR traces can have several common characteristics. An OTDR trace begins with an initial input pulse. This pulse is a result of Fresnel reflection occurring at the connection to the OTDR. Following this pulse, the OTDR trace is a gradual downsloping curve interrupted by abrupt shifts. Periods of gradual decline in the OTDR trace result from Rayleigh scattering as light travels along each fiber section of the cable plant. Periods of gradual decline are interrupted by abrupt shifts called point defects. A **point defect** is a temporary or permanent local deviation of the OTDR signal in the upward or downward direction. Point defects are caused by connectors, splices, or breaks along the fiber length. Point defects, or faults, can be reflective or non-reflective. An output pulse at the end of the OTDR trace indicates the end of the fiber cable plant. This output pulse results from Fresnel reflection occurring at the output fiber-end face.

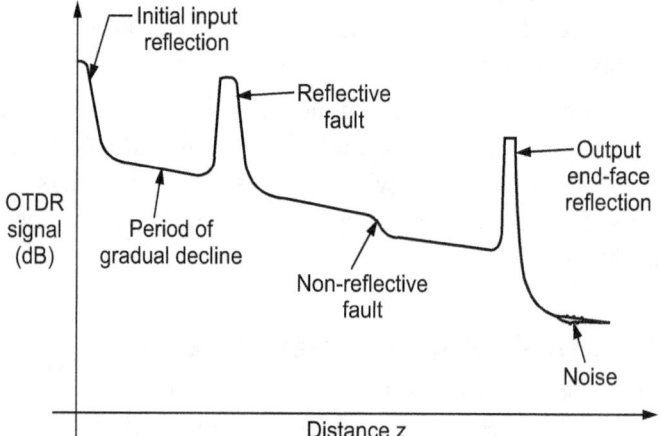

Fig. 3.30: OTDR Trace of an Installed Cable Plant

3.10.1 Attenuation

The fiber optic test method for measuring the attenuation of an installed optical fiber using an OTDR. The accuracy of this test method depends on the user entering the appropriate source wavelength, pulse duration, and fiber length (test range) into the OTDR. In addition, the effective group index of the test fiber is required before the attenuation coefficient and accurate distances can be recorded. By entering correct test parameters, OTDR fiber attenuation values will closely coincide with those measured by the cutback technique.

Test personnel can connect the test fiber directly to the OTDR or to a **dead-zone** fiber. This dead-zone fiber is placed between the test fiber and OTDR to reduce the effect of the initial reflection at the OTDR on the fiber measurement. The dead-zone fiber is inserted because minimizing the reflection at a fiber joint is easier than reducing the reflection at the OTDR connection.

Fig. 3.31 illustrates the OTDR measurement points for measuring the attenuation of the test fiber using a dead-zone fiber. Fiber attenuation between two points along the test fiber is measured on gradual downsloping sections on the OTDR trace. There should be no point defects present along the portion of fiber being tested.

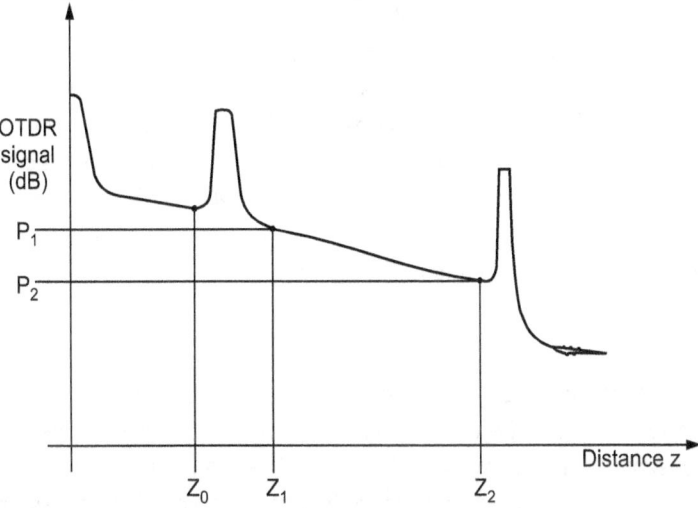

Fig. 3.31: OTDR measurement points for measuring fiber attenuation using a dead-zone fiber

OTDRs are equipped with either manual or automatic cursors to locate points of interest along the trace. In Fig. 2.44, a cursor is positioned at a distance z_0 on the rising of the reflection at the end of the dead-zone fiber. Cursors are also positioned at distances z_1 and z_2. The cursor positioned at z_1 is just beyond the recovery from the reflection at the end of the dead-zone fiber. Since no point defects are present in Fig. 3.31, the cursor positioned at z_2 locates the end of the test fiber. Cursor z_2 is positioned just before the output pulse resulting from Fresnel reflection occurring at the end of the test fiber.

The attenuation of the test fiber between points z_1 and z_2 is $(P_1 - P_2)$ dB. The attenuation coefficient (α) is,

$$a = \frac{(P_1 - P_2)}{(z_2 - z_1)} \text{ dB/km}$$

The total attenuation of the fiber including the dead zone after the joint between the dead-zone fiber and test fiber is,

$$\text{Attenuation} = (P_1 - P_2) \frac{(z_1 - z_0)}{(z_2 - z_1)} \text{ dB}$$

If fiber attenuation is measured without a dead-zone, z_0 is equal to zero ($z_0 = 0$).

At any point along the length of fiber, attenuation values can change depending on the amount of optical power back scattered due to Rayleigh scattering. The amount of back scattered optical power at each point depends on the forward optical power and its

backscatter capture coefficient. The backscatter capture coefficient varies with length depending on fiber properties. Fiber properties that may affect the backscatter coefficient include the refractive index profile, numerical aperture (multimode), and mode-field diameter (single mode) at the particular measurement point. The source wavelength and pulse width may also affect the amount of backscattered power.

By performing the OTDR attenuation measurement in each direction along the test fiber, test personnel can eliminate the effects of backscatter variations. Attenuation measurements made in the opposite direction at the same wavelength (within 5 nm) are averaged to reduce the effect of backscatter variations. This process is called bidirectional averaging. Bidirectional averaging is possible only if test personnel have access to both fiber ends. OTDR attenuation values obtained using bidirectional averaging should compare with those measured using the cutback technique in the laboratory.

3.10.2 Point Defects

Point defects are temporary or local deviations of the OTDR signal in the upward or downward direction. A point defect, or fault, can be reflective or non-reflective. A point defect normally exhibits a loss of optical power. However, a point defect may exhibit an apparent power gain. In some cases, a point defect can even exhibit no loss or gain.

Refer back to Fig. 3.32, it illustrates a reflective fault and a non-reflective fault, both exhibiting loss. Fig. 3.32 shows a non-reflective fault with apparent gain and a reflective fault with no apparent loss or gain.

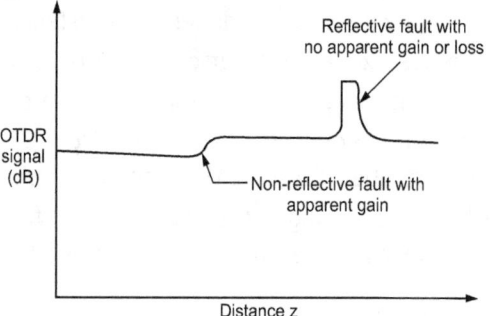

Fig. 3.32: An OTDR Trace showing a Non-reflective Fault with Apparent Gain and a Reflective Fault with no Apparent Loss or Gain

Test personnel must enter the appropriate input parameters including the source wavelength, the pulse duration, and the fiber or cable group index into the OTDR. The nature of fiber point defects depends on the value of each parameter entered by the end user. The pulse duration usually limits the length of the point defect while other input parameters, such as the wavelength, can vary its shape.

If the length of the fiber point defect changes with the pulse duration, then the OTDR signal deviation is in fact a point defect. If the length remains the same, then the OTDR signal deviation is a region of high fiber attenuation. Regions of high fiber attenuation are referred to as **attenuation non-uniformities**.

Fiber point defects occur from factory fiber splices or bends introduced during cable construction or installation. For shipboard applications, manufacturers are not allowed to splice fibers during cable construction. Fiber joints are natural sources of OTDR point defects. However, fiber breaks, cracks, or microbends introduced during cable installation are additional sources of point defects.

Point defects that occur at fiber joints are relatively easy to identify because the location of a fiber joint is generally known. A reflective or non-reflective fault occurs at a distance equal to fiber joint location. In most circumstances, an optical connector produces a reflective fault, while an optical splice produces a non-reflective fault.

Reflective and non-reflective faults occurring at distances other than fiber joint locations identify fiber breaks, cracks, or microbends. A fiber break produces a reflective fault because fiber breaks result in complete fiber separation. Fiber cracks and microbends generally produce non-reflective faults.

A point defect may exhibit apparent gain because the backscatter coefficient of the fiber present before the point defect is higher than that of the fiber present after. Test personnel measure the signal loss or gain by positioning a pair of cursors, one on each side of the point defect. Fig. 3.33 illustrates the positioning of the cursors for a point defect showing an apparent signal gain. The trace after the point defect is extrapolated as shown in Fig. 3.33. The vertical distance between the two lines in Fig. 3.33 is the apparent gain of the point defect.

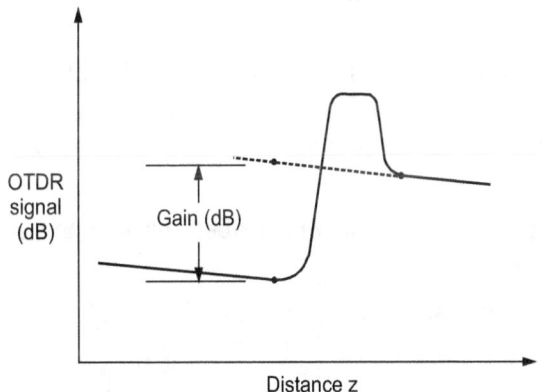

Fig. 3.33: Extrapolation for a Point Defect Showing an Apparent Signal Gain

Points defects exhibiting gain in one direction will exhibit an exaggerated loss in the opposite direction. Fig. 3.34 shows the apparent loss shown by the OTDR for the same point defect shown in Fig. 3.34 when measured in the opposite direction. Bidirectional measurements are conducted to cancel the effects of backscatter coefficient variations. **Bidirectional averaging** combines the two values to identify the true signal loss. Bidirectional averaging is possible only if test personnel have access to both ends of the test sample.

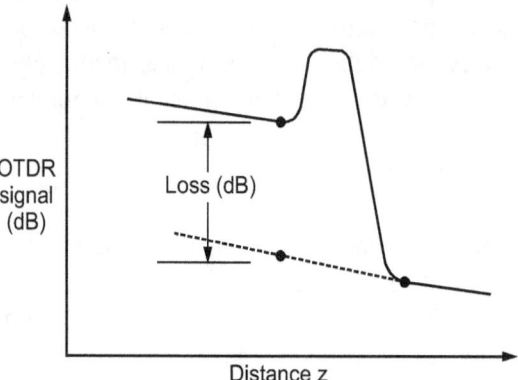

Fig. 3.34: The Exaggerated Loss Obtained at Point Defects Exhibiting Gain in One Direction by Conducting the OTDR Measurement in the Opposite Direction

OTDRs can also measure the return loss of a point defect. However, not all OTDRs are configured to make the measurement. To measure the return loss of a point defect, the cursors are placed in the same places as for measuring the loss of the point defect. The return loss of the point defect is displayed when the return loss option is selected on the OTDR. The steps for selecting the return loss option depend upon the OTDR being used.

3.10.3 Measurable Parameters

From an OTDR you can quickly determine the following characteristics of the fiber link under test:

1. **The length of the fiber:** This is not as precise as it sounds. What you can calculate is the length of the fiber itself. Most long distances cables employ "loose tube" construction and the fiber length is between 5% and 10% longer than the cable itself.
2. The attenuation in dB of the whole fiber link and the attenuation of separate sections of fiber (if any).
3. The attenuation characteristics of the basic fiber itself.
4. The locations of connectors, joints and faults in the cable

These locations are measured from the beginning of the fiber and can be as accurate as a few metres.

1. **Advantages:**

The major advantage of the OTDR is that tests can be done from one end of the link and you don't need access to the other end. This means you don't need two people to do the test and you save the problem of co-ordinating between people. Also the testing is much quicker. So even simple tests which could be performed with a basic optical source at one end of the link and a power meter at the other are often performed with an OTDR.

2. Characteristics:

OTDRs today are extremely sophisticated devices and come with many options. They can be large fixed laboratory instruments or small portable ones about the size of a laptop computer. Different models are available for multimode and single-mode fibers. Of course different models have different levels of sensitivity (and price). There is always a range of options for the user to control such as wavelength used for the test, timescales, pulse duration etc.

Many modern OTDRs come with additional functions such as optical power meter or laser source so that a good OTDR often has all of the function needed by a technician in the field. In addition many OTDRs offer computer output so that you can collect OTDR data in the form of digital readings and analyse it later on a computer.

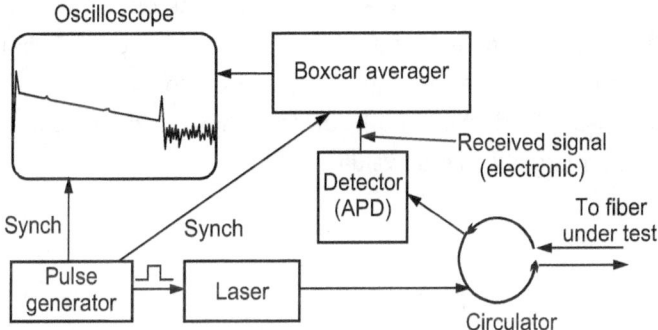

Fig. 3.35: OTDR Operational Logic

The principle of operation of a typical OTDR is shown in Fig. 3.35. In the figure a circulator has been used to enable transmission and reception of the pulse from the single strand of fiber under test. Other means of signal splitting/combining are used but circulators offer the least attenuation.

As might be expected the big problem with an OTDR is that the returning signal is very low level especially on long distance fiber sections. We can't use signal pulses of too high a power for many reasons and so pulses of 10-20 mW are typically sent. The problem of low return power is addressed in two ways:

   1. A very sensitive APD detector is used. As noted elsewhere in this book detectors double in sensitivity every time you halve the digital bit rate. Thus an APD becomes very sensitive indeed at the very low pulse rates used. The penalty for using APDs is additional noise but this is mitigated by the averaging process.

   2. A "boxcar averager" circuit is used to average many thousands of returning pulses. The averaging process removes a large amount of noise. (Most of the noise comes from the APD and its associated circuitry). In some (very sensitive, long distance) OTDRs the averaging time can be of the order of several minutes! The averager provides logarithmic scaling of its output so that the vertical scale on the display can be displayed in dBm.

The pulse rates used are quite slow ! Since the optical signal propagates at approximately 5 microseconds per kilometer we have to allow 10 microseconds per kilometer of fiber length. So for 20 km of fiber we need to wait at least 200 microseconds between pulses and so a pulse rate of 5000 pulses per second would be the maximum possible.

SOLVED PROBLEMS

Problem 3.1:

An optical fiber link having a silicon pin photodiode operating at 850 nm, the required received power is 42 dB. A LED can couple a 50 µW average optical power level into a fiber flyhead with a 50 µm core diameter. Allowable power loss is 29 dB. A 1 dB loss occurs when a fiber flyhead is connected to the cable and another 1 dB connector loss occurs at the cable photodetector interface. Find the length of transmission path having attenuation of 2.4 dB/km and system margin is of 6 dB value.

Solution:

Given data:

$$L = ?$$
$$\text{System margin} = 6 \text{ dB}$$
$$\text{Fiber attenuation}, \alpha_f = 2.4 \text{ dB/km}$$
$$\text{Connector loss}, l_c = 1 \text{ dB}$$
$$\text{Total power loss}, P_T = 29 \text{ dB}$$

We have,

Total optical power loss = $P_T = P_S - P_R$

$$P_T = 2l_c + \alpha_f L + \text{System margin}$$
$$29 = 2(1) + 2.4 (L) + 6$$
$$29 - 8 = 2.4 L$$
$$L = \mathbf{8.75 \text{ km}}$$

Therefore, the required transmission path is 8.75 km.

Problem 3.2:

Optical fiber glass cable of 21 km length is employed in transmission of digital signals at 565 Mbps. The cable loss is 0.3 dB/km splices at 1 km intervals have loss of 0.10 dB/splice. Connectors at transmitter and receiver end have 1.0 dB and 1.3 dB loss respectively. Source is launching at −9 dBm. Receiver is p-i-n photodiode and has sensitivity of −26 dBm. Safety margin is 4.5 dB. Prepare a power budget.

Solution:

Given data:

$$\text{Cable loss, } \alpha_f = 0.3 \text{ dB/km}$$
$$\text{Splice loss, } l_{sp} = 0.10 \text{ dB/splice}$$
$$\text{Source output, } P_{in} = -9 \text{ dBm}$$
$$\text{Connector loss} = 1.3 \text{ dB}$$
$$\text{System margin} = 4.5 \text{ dB}$$
$$\text{Receiver sensitivity} = -26 \text{ dBm} = 2.5 \text{ }\mu\text{W}$$

Link power budget

$$\text{Total power loss} = 2 \times l_c + \alpha_f L + \text{System margin}$$
$$P_T = (2 \times 1.3) + (0.3 \times 21) + 4.5$$
$$\mathbf{P_T = 13.4 \text{ dB}} \qquad \ldots \text{Ans.}$$

The maximum allowable system loss

$$P_{max} = \text{Optical source output power} - \text{Optical receiver sensitivity}$$
$$= -9 \text{ dBm} - (-26 \text{ dBm})$$
$$P_{max} = -9 \text{ dBm} + 26 \text{ dBm}$$
$$\mathbf{P_{max} = 17 \text{ dBm}} \qquad \ldots \text{Ans.}$$

The actual system loss is less than the allowable loss. Hence, the system is functional.

Problem 3.3:

In fiber optic link, a 1400 nm laser diode launch a 3 dBm optical power into a fiber flylead, an In GaAs APD having sensitivity of −52 dBm at 2.5 Gb/s, and a 60 km long optical cable with a 0.4 dB/km attenuation. A short optical jumper cable is attached between the end of the transmission cable and the SONET, each jumper cable introduces a loss of 30 dB and 1 dB connector loss occurs at each fiber joint. Determine the loss margin.

Solution:

Given data:

$$\text{Source optical power} = 3 \text{ dBm (2 mW)}$$
$$\text{Receiver sensitivity} = -52 \text{ dBm}$$
$$\text{Length of optical cable} = 60 \text{ km}$$
$$\text{Attenuation, } \alpha = 0.4 \text{ dB/km}$$
$$\text{Connector loss, } l_c = 1 \text{ dB}$$
$$\text{Jumper cable loss} = 3 \text{ dB}$$
$$\text{Allowed maximum power loss} = \text{Source optical power} - \text{Sensitivity}$$

$$\text{Allowed maximum power loss} = 3 \text{ dBm} - (-52 \text{ dBm})$$
$$= 55 \text{ dBm}$$

Total loss = Source connector loss + 2 (Jumper + Connector loss) + Attenuation + Receiver connector loss

$$= 1 + 2(3 + 1) + (0.4 \times 60) + 1$$
$$= 10 + (24)$$

Total loss = 34

Loss Margin = Allowed maximum power loss − Total loss
$$= 55 - 34$$
$$= 21 \text{ dBm}$$

Loss margin = **21 dBm** ... **Ans.**

Problem 3.4:

Consider a LED source of emitted power 1 mW with rise time 10 ns and spectral width of 10 nm. A pin diode is used as detector having rise time of 1 ns and sensitivity is −30 dBm. A step index multimode fiber of core index 1.46, NA = 0.2 and length is of 2 km available. A source coupling loss is 3 dB, detector coupling loss is 1 dB, system splice is 6 dB, splice loss is 0.2 dB per splice and attenuation is 2 dB/km at 850 nm. Determine the maximum permissible link length and data rate.

Solution:

Given data:

Source power = 1 mW = 0 dBm
$t_{rise, LED}$ = 10 ns
Spectral width = 6 = 10 nm
$t_{rise, pin}$ = 1 ns
Receiver sensitivity = −30 dBm
Core index, n_1 = 1.46
Numerical Aperture NA = 0.2
Length available = 2 km
Source coupling loss = 3 dB
Detector coupling loss = 1 dB
System margin = 6 dB
Splice loss = 0.2 dB

Attenuation, α = 2 dB/km
Wavelength, λ = 850 nm
Link length, L = ?
Bit rate or data rate = ?
Available power = Source power – Sensitivity
= 0 dBm – (–30 dBm)
= 30 dBm
= **30 dB**   … **Ans.**

The total loss can be calculated by adding source and detector coupling loss and system margin.

∴ Total loss = (Source coupling loss) + Detector coupling loss + System marging
= 3 dB + 1 dB + 6 dB
Total loss = 10 dB
Loss margin = Available power – Total loss
= 30 – 10
= **20 dB**   … **Ans.**

If the L km is the link length of the length of each fiber section is only 2 kms there are $\left(\frac{L}{2}-1\right)$ splices in the link.

By equating the total loss of the fiber cable attenuation to the loss margin, we get length of link.

∴ $\left(\frac{L}{2}-1\right) \times NA + L \times \alpha$ = 20 dB

$\left(\frac{L}{2}-1\right) \times (0.2) + L \times 2$ = 20

$\left[\frac{L-2}{2} \infty\, 0.2\right] + 2L$ = 20

$[(L-2)(0.1)] + 2L$ = 20

$0.1\,L - 0.2 + 2L$ = 20

$1.9\,L$ = 20.2

L = 10.632 km

The maximum permissible link length is 10.632 km i.e. approximately 11 km.

Bit rate can be calculated by rise time consideration. For the fiber of step index multimode type, the modal dispersion calculated is,

$$t_{mod} = \frac{L \cdot (NA)^2}{2 \cdot (n_1)}$$

$$= \frac{11 \times (0.2)^2}{2 \times 2.998 \times 10^5 \times 1.46}$$

$$= 502.6 \text{ ns}$$

$$t_{mod} = 503 \text{ ns}$$

$$\text{Bit rate} = \frac{1}{t_{mod}}$$

$$= \frac{1}{503}$$

Bit rate = 1.9896 Mb/s ... Ans.

Problem 3.5:

Calculate a rise time budget for a multimode fiber link, a LED drive circuit has a rise time of 12 ns, LED spectral width of 40 nm, a material dispersion related rise time degradation of 21 ns over the 6 km link. The receiver has a 25 MHz bandwidth and its rise time degradation is 14 ns. A fiber has a 400 MHz · km bandwidth distance product and the modal dispersion induced fiber rise time is 3.8 ns.

Solution:

Given data:

Transmitter rise time, t_{tx} = 12 ns

Material dispersion rise time, t_{mat} = 21 ns

Receiver rise time, t_{rx} = 14 ns

Modal dispersion rise time, t_{mod} = 3.8 ns

$$t_{sys} = [t_{tx}^2 + t_{mat}^2 + t_{rx}^2 + t_{mod}^2]^{1/2}$$

$$t_{sys} = [(12 \text{ ns})^2 + (21 \text{ ns})^2 + (14 \text{ ns})^2 + (3.8 \text{ ns})^2]^{1/2}$$

$$= [7.9544 \times 10^{-16}]^{1/2}$$

t_{sys} = 28.2 ns ... Ans.

Problem 3.6:

Consider a laser diode together with its drive circuit has a rise time of 0.025 ns. A laser diode spectral width of 0.1 nm at 1550 nm and an average dispersion of 2 ps/(nm · km) for the fiber. A group velocity dispersion rise time degradation of 12 ps over a 50 km long optical cable A In GaAs - APD - based receiver has 92.5 GHz bandwidth and the receiver rise time is 0.12 ns. Calculate the system rise time.

Solution:

Given data:

Source rise time, t_{tx} = 0.025 ns
GVD rise time, t_{GVD} = 12 ps = 0.012 ns
Receiver rise time, t_{rx} = 0.12 ns
System rise time, t_{sys} = ?

$$t_{sys} = [(t_{rx})^2 + (t_{tx})^2 + (t_{GVD})^2]^{1/2}$$
$$= [(0.025 \text{ ns})^2 + (0.12 \text{ ns})^2 + (0.012 \text{ ns})^2]^{1/2}$$

t_{sy} = 0.12 ns ... Ans.

Problem 3.7:

The optical bandwidth is $\Delta\vartheta$ = 14 THz for a usable spectral band $\Delta\lambda$ = 80 nm and Δv = 15 THz. For a usable spectral band $\Delta\lambda$ = 120 nm. Determine the total available window.

Solution:

Given data:

$\Delta\vartheta$ = 14 THz and $\Delta\lambda$ = 80 nm
Δv = 15 THz and $\Delta\lambda$ = 120 nm
λ = ?

$$|\Delta\vartheta| = \left|\frac{c}{\lambda^2}\right| |\Delta\lambda|$$

Case – I:

$$14 \times 10^{12} = \frac{3 \times 10^8}{\lambda^2} \times 80 \times 10^{-9}$$

λ = 1309 nm ... Ans.

Case – II:

$$15 \times 10^{12} = \frac{3 \times 10^8}{\lambda^2} \times 120 \times 10^{-9}$$

λ = 1549 nm ... Ans.

The source is operating in 1309 nm to 1549 window.

Problem 3.8:

A 2 × 2 biconical tapered fiber coupler has an input optical power P_0 = 300 μW. The output powers at the three other ports are P_1 = 150 μW, P_2 = 65 μW and P_3 = 8.3 nW. Calculate the splitting ratio, excess loss, insertion loss and cross talk for this coupler.

Solution:

Given data:

$$P_0 = 300 \ \mu W$$
$$P_1 = 150 \ \mu W$$
$$P_2 = 65 \ \mu W$$
$$P_3 = 8.3 \ nW$$

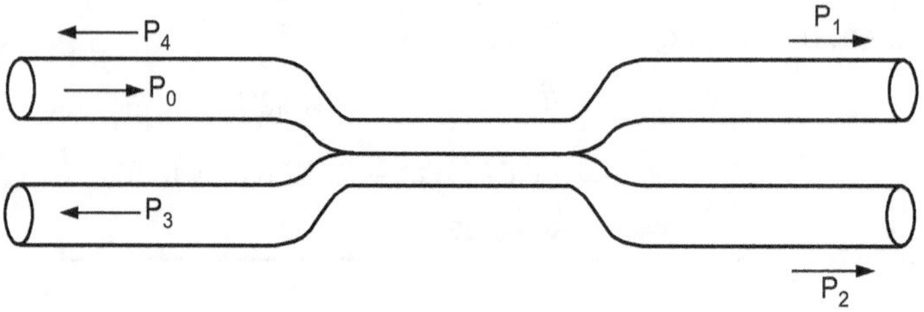

Fig. 3.36

The structure of coupler is shown in Fig. 3.36.

(1) $\quad$ Splitting ratio $= \left(\dfrac{P_2}{P_1 + P_2}\right) \times 100\%$

$\qquad\qquad\qquad\quad\ = \left(\dfrac{65}{150 + 65}\right) \times 100\%$

$\qquad$ Splitting ratio $= \mathbf{30.23\%}$ $\qquad\qquad\qquad\qquad$ ... **Ans.**

(2) $\quad$ Excess loss $= 10 \log \left(\dfrac{P_0}{P_1 + P_2}\right)$

$\qquad\qquad\qquad\ = 10 \log \left(\dfrac{300}{150 + 65}\right)$

$\qquad$ Excess loss $= \mathbf{1.4468 \ dB}$ $\qquad\qquad\qquad\qquad$ ... **Ans.**

(3) $\quad$ Insertion loss $= 10 \log \left(\dfrac{P_i}{P_j}\right)$

$\qquad\qquad\qquad i$ = Input port
$\qquad\qquad\qquad j$ = Output port

Insertion loss for port 0 to port 1.

i.e. $\qquad$ Insertion loss $= 10 \log \left(\dfrac{P_0}{P_1}\right)$

$\qquad\qquad\qquad\qquad\ = 10 \log \left(\dfrac{300}{150}\right)$

$\qquad\qquad$ **Insertion loss** $= \mathbf{3.0103 \ dB}$ **for P_0 to P_1** $\qquad$ ... **Ans.**

For port 0 to port 2.

$\qquad\qquad$ Insertion loss $= 10 \log \left(\dfrac{P_0}{P_2}\right)$

$\qquad\qquad\qquad\qquad\ = 10 \log \left(\dfrac{300}{65}\right)$

(4) Insertion loss = 6.642 dB

Cross talk = $10 \log \left(\dfrac{P_3}{P_0}\right) = 10 \log \left(\dfrac{8.3 \times 10^{-9}}{300 \times 10^{-6}}\right)$

Cross talk = –45.58 dB ... Ans.

Problem 3.9:

A symmetric waveguide coupler has a coupling coefficient K = 0.5 mm^{-1}. Find the coupling length, for m = 1.

Solution:

Given data:

Coupling coefficient, K = 0.5 mm^{-1} = 0.5×10^3

Coupling length, L = ? at m = 1

$$L = \dfrac{\pi}{2K}(m+1)$$

$$= \dfrac{3.14}{2 \times 0.5 \times 10^3}(1+1)$$

L = 6.28×10^{-3}

L = 6.28 mm ... Ans.

Problem 3.10:

A 32 × 32 single mode coupler mode from cascade of 3 dB fused fiber 2 × 2 couplers. If 4% of power is lost in each element. Determine the total loss in the coupler.

Solution:

Given data:

N = 32

Power loss = 4%

Total loss = ?

There are two method to solve this numerical, in first method.

Total loss = Splitting loss + Excess loss

∴ Splitting loss = $-10 \log \left(\dfrac{1}{N}\right)$

= 10 log N

= 10 log 32

Splitting loss = 15.05 dB

Excess loss = $-10 \log \left(F_T^{\log_2 N}\right)$

$F_T = \dfrac{100 - 4}{100} = 0.94$

∴ Excess loss $= -10 \log \left(F_T^{\log_2 N} \right)$

$= -10 \log \left[(0.94)^{\log_2 32} \right]$

Excess loss $= 1.34$ dB

Total loss $= 15.05 + 1.34$

Total Loss $= \mathbf{16.39}$ **dB**

In Second Method

Total loss $= 10 (1 - 3.322 \log F_T) \log N$

$= 10 (1 - 3.322 \log 0.94) \log 32$

Total loss $= 16.39$ dB ... Ans.

Problem 3.11:

Determine the power budget of LAN having 5 station. Assume that $C_T = 10\%$, $L_{tap} = 10$ dB, $L_{thru} = 0.9$ dB. $L_i = 0.5$ dB and $L_c = 1.0$ dB. If the stations are 800 m apart and an attenuation of 0.4 dB/km at 1300 nm the fiber loss is 0.2 dB. Also determine the dynamic range.

Solution:

Power budget for the link i.e. $10 \log \left(\dfrac{P_0}{P_{1,N}} \right)$

$10 \log \left(\dfrac{P_0}{P_{1,N}} \right)$ = [Fiber + Connector + Coupler throughput + ingrees/egrees + Coupler intrinsic] losses

i.e. total loss

$N = 5$

Given data:

Connector loss, $L_c = 1.0$ dB

Tap loss, $L_{tap} = 10$ dB

$C_T = 10\%$

Throughput coupling loss $= 0.9$ dB

Intrinsic loss, $L_i = 0.5$ dB

For 5 station calculation

Total loss $= N (\alpha \cdot L + 2L_c + L_{thru} + L_i) - \alpha_L - 2L_{thru} + 2L_{tap}$

$N = 5$

$L = 800 = 0.8$ km

$\alpha = 0.4$ dB/km

$= 5 [(0.4 \times 0.8) + (2 \times 1) + 0.9 + 0.5]$
$- (0.4 \times 0.8) - (2 \times 0.9) + (2 \times 10)$

$= 18.6 - 0.32 - 1.8 + 20$

Total loss = 36.48 dB ... Ans.

This is the power budget for 5 station.

The dynamic range (DR) can be calculated as,

$$DR = (N - 2)(\alpha L + 2L_c + L_{thru} + L_i)$$
$$DR = (5 - 2)[(0.4 \times 0.8) + (2 \times 1) + 0.9 + 0.5]$$
$$= 3[0.32 + 2 + 1.4]$$

Dynamic range = 11.16 dB ... Ans.

Problem 3.12:

A two star network having 20 and 60 stations respectively. A station is located at 800 m from the star coupler and the fiber attenuation is 0.4 dB/km. The excess loss is 0.75 dB for the 20 stations and 1.25 dB for 60 station network and the connector loss is 1 dB. Determine the power margin between the transmitter and receiver.

Solution:

Given data:

$$N = 20 \text{ and } 60$$
$$\text{Length, } L = 800 \text{ m} = 0.8 \text{ km}$$
$$\text{Attenuation, } \alpha = 0.4 \text{ dB/km}$$
$$\text{Excess loss} = 0.75 \text{ dB for 20 station network}$$
$$\text{Excess loss} = 1.25 \text{ dB for 60 station network}$$
$$\text{Connector loss} = 1 \text{ dB}$$

The power margin between transmitter and receiver is given by,

$$P_S - P_R = L_{excess} + \alpha(2L) + 2L_c + L_{split}$$
$$P_S - P_R = L_{excess} + \alpha(2L) + 2L_c + 10 \log N$$

For N = 20 station

$$P_S - P_R = 0.75 + (0.4 \times 2 \times 0.8) + (2 \times 1) + 10 \log 20$$
$$= 0.75 + 0.64 + 2 + 13.01$$
$$P_S - P_R = \mathbf{16.40 \text{ dB}}$$ ... Ans.

For N = 60 station

$$P_S - P_R = L_{excess} + \alpha(2L) + 2L_c + 10 \log N$$
$$= 1.25 + (0.4 \times 2 \times 0.8) + (2 \times 1) + 10 \log 60$$
$$= 1.25 + 0.64 + 2 + 17.78$$
$$P_S - P_R = \mathbf{21.67 \text{ dB}}$$ ... Ans.

Problem 3.13:

A star coupled optical fiber network with 16 inputs and 16 outputs operating at 12 Mb/s.

Given: Connector loss = 1 dB

Star coupler insertion loss = 3 dB

and Fiber loss = 4 dB/km

The optical source has an output of −15 dBm from flylead. The photodetector has sensitivity of − 50 dBm. Assuming a 6 dB system margin, what is the maximum transmission distance if transmission and reflection star coupler is used?

Solution:

Given data:

$$\text{Connector loss, } L_c = 1 \text{ dB}$$
$$\text{Star coupler insertion loss, } L_s = 3 \text{ dB}$$
$$\text{Fiber loss, } \alpha_f = 4 \text{ dB/km}$$
$$\text{Transmitter power, } P_S = -15 \text{ dBm}$$
$$\text{Receiver sensitivity, } P_R = -50 \text{ dBm}$$
$$\text{System margin} = 6 \text{ dB}$$
$$P_S - P_R = L_s + 2\alpha_f L + 4 L_c + 10 \log N + \text{System margin}$$

(i) If transmission star coupler is used N = 16.

∴
$$(-15 + 50) \text{ dBm} = 3 + (2 \times 4 \text{ dB/km}) L + 4 (1) + 10 \log_{10} 16 + 6$$
$$35 \text{ dBm} = 13 + 8 L \text{ dB/km} + 10 \log_{10} 16$$
$$8 L \text{ dB/km} = 35 - 13 - 12$$
$$L \text{ (km)} = \frac{10}{8}$$

Length of fiber, L = 1.25 km ... Ans.

(ii) If reflection star coupler is used then, N = 32.

$$(-15 + 50) \text{ dBm} = 3 + 2 (4 \text{ dB/km}) L + 4 (1) + 10 \log_{10} 32 + 6$$
$$35 \text{ dBm} = 13 + 8 \text{ LdB/km} + 10 \log_{10} 32$$
$$8 \text{ LdB/km} = 35 - 13 - 15$$
$$L = \frac{7}{8}$$
$$\text{Length, L (km)} = 0.875$$

L = 0.875 km ... Ans.

Problem 3.14:

An optical fiber system is to be designed to operate an 8 km length without repeaters. The rise times of the chosen components are:

Source (LED): 8 ns.
Fiber cable: Intermodal : 5 ns/km
                  Intramodal : 1 n/km
             Detector (p-i-n) : 6 ns

Estimate maximum bit rate that may be achieved on the link when using NRZ and RZ format.

Solution:

Given data:

$$\text{Source rise time, } t_{tx} = 8 \text{ ns}$$
$$\text{Rise time intermodal, } t_{intermod} = 55 \text{ ns/km}$$
$$\text{Rise time interamodal, } t_{intramod} = 1 \text{ n/km}$$
$$\text{Detector rise time} = 6 \text{ ns} = t_{rx}$$
$$\therefore \text{ Total modal dispersion rise time } t_{mod} = 5 + 1$$
$$= 6 \text{ ns}$$
$$\text{System rise time, } t_{sys} = [(t_{tx})^2 + (t_{rx})^2 + (t_{mod})^2]^{1/2}$$
$$t_{sys} = [8^2 + 6^2 + 6^2]^{1/2}$$
$$= [64 + 36 + 36]$$
$$t_{sys} = 11.66 \text{ ns}$$
$$\text{Bandwidth, } B_{sys} = \frac{350}{t_{sys}} = \frac{350}{11.66}$$
$$= 30 \text{ MHz}$$
$$\text{Bandwidth length product} = 30 \text{ MHz} \times 8 \text{ km}$$
$$= 240 \text{ MHz} \cdot \text{km}$$
$$\therefore \quad \textbf{Maximum bit rate} = \textbf{240 Mbps} \quad \text{... Ans.}$$

Problem 3.15:

An analog optical fiber system employs and LED, which emits 3 dBm mean optical power into air. However, a coupling loss of 17.5 dB is encountered when launching into a fiber cable. The fiber cable which extends for 6 km without repeaters exhibit a loss of 5 dB/km. It is spliced every 1.5 km with an average loss of 1.1 dB per splice. In addition there is a connector loss at the receiver of 0.8 dB. The PIN-FET receiver has a sensitivity of − 54 dBm at the operating bandwidth of the system. Assuming there is no dispersion-equalization penalty, perform an optical power budget for the system and establish a safety margin.

Solution:

Given data:

$$\text{LED source data} = 3 \text{ dBm}$$
$$\text{Coupling loss, } l_c = 17.5 \text{ dB}$$
$$\text{Length (L)} = 6 \text{ km}$$
$$\text{Fiber cable loss } (\alpha) = 5 \text{ dB/km}$$
$$\text{Spliced every 1.5 km, Average loss } (l_s) = 1.1 \text{ dB per splice.}$$
$$\text{Connector loss at receiver} = 0.8 \text{ dB}$$

PIN FET receiver sensitivity = -54 dBm

Allowed maximum power loss = (Source optical power) − (Sensitivity)

$\qquad\qquad\qquad\qquad\qquad = 3 - (-54)$

$\qquad\qquad\qquad\qquad\qquad = 57$

Allowed maximum power = 57 dBm

Loss margin = (Allowed maximum power loss) − (Total loss)

$\qquad\qquad\qquad = 57 -$ Total loss

Total loss = (Coupling loss) + (Attenuation loss × Length) + Splice loss + Receiver connector loss

$\qquad\quad = 17.5 + (5 \times 6) + (4 \times 1.1) + 0.8$

Total loss = 52.7

∴ Loss margin = 57 − 52.7

$\qquad\qquad\quad = 4.3$ dBm

Loss margin = System margin = 4.3 dBm ... Ans.

SUMMARY

- A basic point to point fiber optic data link consists of an optical transmitter, optical fiber and an optical receiver.
- Fiber optic links are classified according to the modulation type.
- Digital modulation implies that the optical signal consists of discrete level.
- Analog modulation implies that the intensity of the optical signal is proportional to a continuously varying electrical input.
- Modulation is the process of varying one or more characteristics of an optical signal to encode and convey information.
- A digital signal is a discontinuous signal that changes from one state to another in discrete steps.
- Binary, or two level digital modulation is a popular form of digital modulation.
- Line coding is the process of arranging symbols that represents for transmission. The most common types of line coding used in fiber optic communications include non-return to zero (NRZ), return to zero (RZ) and biphase or manchester.
- Digital transmission offers an advantage with regard to the acceptable SNR at the optical receiver.

- Most analog fiber optic communication system intensity modulate the optical source.
- In intensity modulation, the intensity of the optical sources output signal is directly modulated by the incoming electrical analog baseband signal.
- A baseband signal is a signal that is in its original form and has not been changed by a modulation technique.
- Fiber optic system that have complex architecture can be simplified into a collection of point to point data link.
- Link analysis involves calculating each links power budget and rise time budget.
- Calculating a power budget involves identifying all of the sources of loss in the fiber optic link. These losses and an additional safety margin are then compared to the difference between the transmitter output power and the receiver sensitivity.
- Calculating the rise time budget involves calculating the rise time of the link transmitter and the optical fiber.
- NRZ code represents binary 1's and 0's by two different light that are constant during a bit duration. The presence of a high light level in the bit duration represents a binary 1, while a low light level represents a binary 0.
- RZ coding uses only half the bit duration for data transmission.
- In manchester encoding, a high to low light level transition occurring in the middle of the bit duration represents a binary 1. A low to high light level transition occurring in the middle of the bit duration represents a binary 0.
- A star coupler is a passive device that distributes optical power from more than two input ports among several output ports.
- A linear bus topology consists of a single transmission line that is shared by a number of equipment.
- A ring topology consists of equipment attached to one another in a closed loop or ring.
- The two main optical amplifier types can be classified as semiconductor optical fiber and active fiber or doped fiber amplifier.
- SONET/SDH means synchronous optical network/synchronous digital hierarchy.
- The technology of combining a number of wavelength onto the same fiber is known as wavelength division multiplexing or WDM.
- In fiber optic communication, switching can be implemented in the electronic domain by converting the optical signal to electrical signal, switching electronically and converting back to the optical form for transmission purpose.

POINTS TO REMEMBER

- A basic point to point fiber optic data link consists of an optical transmitter, optical fiber and an optical receiver.
- Fiber optic links are classified according to the modulation type.
- Digital modulation implies that the optical signal consists of discrete level.
- Analog modulation implies that the intensity of the optical signal is proportional to a continuously varying electrical input.
- Modulation is the process of varying one or more characteristics of an optical signal to encode and convey information.
- A digital signal is a discontinuous signal that changes from one state to another in discrete steps.
- Binary, or two level digital modulation is a popular form of digital modulation.
- Line coding is the process of arranging symbols that represents for transmission. The most common types of line coding used in fiber optic communications include non-return to zero (NRZ), return to zero (RZ) and biphase or manchester.
- Digital transmission offers an advantage with regard to the acceptable SNR at the optical receiver.
- Most analog fiber optic communication system intensity modulate the optical source.
- In intensity modulation, the intensity of the optical sources output signal is directly modulated by the incoming electrical analog baseband signal.
- A baseband signal is a signal that is in its original form and has not been changed by a modulation technique.
- Fiber optic system that have complex architecture can be simplified into a collection of point to point data link.
- Link analysis involves calculating each links power budget and rise time budget.
- Calculating a power budget involves identifying all of the sources of loss in the fiber optic link. These losses and an additional safety margin are then compared to the difference between the transmitter output power and the receiver sensitivity.
- Calculating the rise time budget involves calculating the rise time of the link transmitter and the optical fiber.

- NRZ code represents binary 1's and 0's by two different light that are constant during a bit duration. The presence of a high light level in the bit duration represents a binary 1, while a low light level represents a binary 0.
- RZ coding uses only half the bit duration for data transmission.
- In manchester encoding, a high to low light level transition occurring in the middle of the bit duration represents a binary 1. A low to high light level transition occurring in the middle of the bit duration represents a binary 0.
- A star coupler is a passive device that distributes optical power from more than two input ports among several output ports.
- A linear bus topology consists of a single transmission line that is shared by a number of equipment.
- A ring topology consists of equipment attached to one another in a closed loop or ring.
- The two main optical amplifier types can be classified as semiconductor optical fiber and active fiber or doped fiber amplifier.
- SONET/SDH means synchronous optical network/synchronous digital hierarchy.
- The technology of combining a number of wavelength onto the same fiber is known as wavelength division multiplexing or WDM.
- In fiber optic communication, switchig can be implemented in the electronic domain by converting the optical signal to electrical signal, switching electronically and converting back to the optical form for transmission purpose.

QUESTIONS

1. What do you mean by receiver sensitivity?
2. What is response time?
3. Sketch an RZ, NRZ, manchester pattern for 1 1 0 0 1 0 1 0 1 1 1 0 1.
4. What are the sources of receiver sensitivity degradation?
5. What is dynamic range?
6. Write down and explain the link design equations in a point-to-point communication link, based on power budget and rise time budget consideration.
7. What are the underlying principles of the WDM technique? What are its various advantages?

8. Explain the photonic switching? What are its features? What are its limitations?
9. What are the types of photonic switches?
10. How does photonic switching differ from electro-optic-switching? Discuss various kinds of switch being used in fiber optical communication systems?
11. Compare the performance of fiber optic digital transmission system and analog transmission system.
12. Write short notes on SONET/SDH.
13. Explain in brief OTDR.
14. Explain with neat diagram working of OTDR.
15. What are the two important performance parameter of OTDR?

✱✱✱

Unit IV

MICROWAVE WAVEGUIDES AND COMPONENTS

4.1 Introduction to Microwaves

Microwaves are electromagnetic waves whose frequency range from 1 GHz to 1000 GHz (1 GHz = 10^9 Hz), for comparison the signal from an AM station is 1 MHz and the signals from FM radio station is 100 MHz.

Microwaves are so called since they are defined in terms of their wavelengths in the sense that micro refers to tinyness referring to the wavelengths and the period of cycle of a cm wave. In other words, the wavelengths (λ) of a cm waves at microwave frequencies are very short, typically from a few tens of cm to a fraction of a mm.

The higher frequency edge of microwaves border on the infrared and visible light regions or spectrum. Therefore, microwaves behave more like rays of light than ordinary radio waves. Due to this unique behaviour, microwave frequencies are classified separately from radio waves.

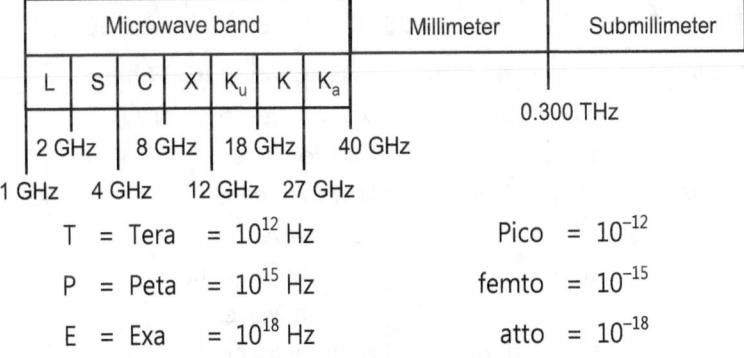

Fig. 4.1: IEEE Microwave Frequency Band

Microwave Frequency Band in Radio Spectrum:
The whole electromagnetic spectrum is broadly divided into two regions namely:
(1) The radio spectrum from 0 to 300 GHz and
(2) The optical spectrum extending from 300 GHz to ∞.

The term microwaves is commonly used to designate for those frequency ranging from 300 MHz to 300 GHz or with wave lengths ranging from 100 cm to 1 mm in radio spectrum.

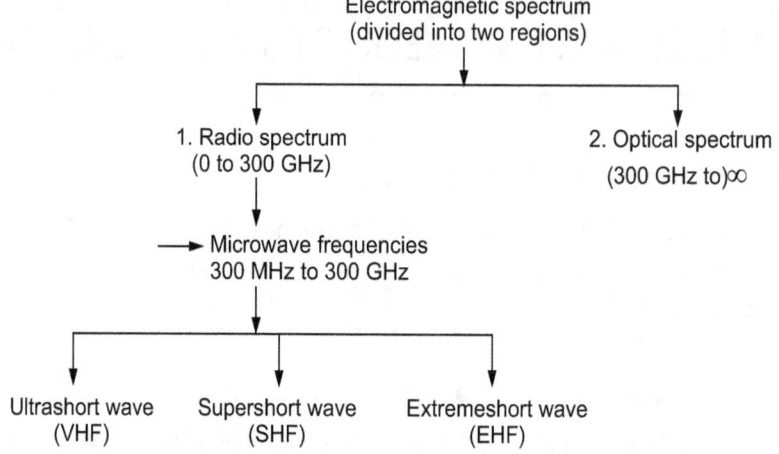

Fig. 4.2: Classification of electromagnetic spectrum

Microwave region has been further divided into three bands:
1. UHF (Ultra short wave)
2. SHF (Super short wave)
3. EHF (Extreme short wave)

4.1.1 Position of Microwave Bands in Entire Radio Spectrum

Frequency band	Wavelength	Designation (CCIR band)	Remarks
1. 0-30 kHz	x to 10^4 m	VLF very low frequency/ Very long wave	–
2. 30 to 30 kHz	10^4 to 10^3 m	Low frequency/ Long wave	–
3. 30 to 300 kHz	10^3 to 10^2 m	Medium frequency/ Medium waves	–
4. 3 to 30 MHz	100 to 10 m	High frequency/ Short wave	–
5. 30 M to 300 MHz	10 to 1 m	VHF/Very short waves	
6. 0.3 to 3 GHz	1 to 0.1 m	UHF/Ultra short wave	Microwave
7. 3 to 30 GHz	10 to 1 cm	SHF/Super short waves	Microwave
8. 30 to 300 GHz	10 to 1 mm	EHF/Extreme short waves	Microwave
9. 300 to 3000 GHz	1 to 0.1 mm	Submillimeter wave	–

4.2 Microwave Systems

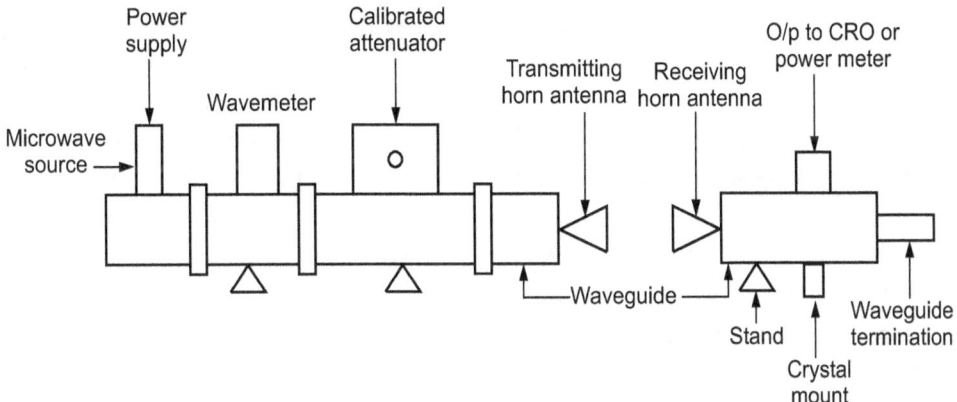

Fig. 4.3: Typical Microwave System

Fig. 4.3 shows a typical microwave system. It has a transmission subsystem, which is normally consists of microwave generator, waveguides, wavemeter, attenuator, transmitting antenna and a receiver subsystem which normally consists of receiving antenna, waveguides, a microwave amplifier, detector.

Three major areas of study in microwave are,
1. Microwave transmission lines and waveguides.
2. Microwave circuit elements.
3. Microwave sources, amplifiers and detectors.

4.3 Basic Microwave Concepts

1. Microwave Transmission:

Conventional two conductor line cannot be used for microwave transmission. Hollow metal tubes called waveguides are used for microwave transmission. The energy propagation in these structures is basically a reflection phenomena.

The waveguide transmission of microwaves is associated with a number of interesting problems such as coupling of power to another system, say from generator to line, exciting of microwave waves in a waveguide etc. To overcome these problems three basic coupling methods, viz. electrical coupling (probe), magnetic coupling (loop) and aperture coupling (waveguide to waveguide) have been evolved. The basic feature of these methods is that one can control the amount of coupling as these structures have small antennas that radiate into the waveguide to be coupled.

2. Microwave Circuit Elements:

Conventional circuit elements such as resistors, capacitors and inductors do not respond well at microwave frequencies. A coil of wire may be an excellent inductor at 1 MHz but at 500 MHz it may be an equally good capacitor because of the predominating effect of inter-turn capacitance. However, this does not mean that energy dissipating (resistors) and storing (capacitors and inductors) elements cannot be constructed at microwave frequencies but their geometrical shape will be quite different. A section of microwave line (distributed parameters), offers reactances varying from $-\infty$ to $+\infty$ if its length is suitably chosen.

Similarly, conventional resonant and antiresonant circuits are replaced by resonant microwave line sections known as **resonant cavities.** Often resonant cavities are used as circuit elements with varying properties.

When a number of such a microwave circuit elements are connected together, we have a microwave circuit.

3. Generation and amplification of microwaves:

The operation of conventional vacuum tubes and solid state devices is limited by transit time effect. However, the frequency range of operation of these devices can be extended to the lower edge of microwave spectrum but there is a noise characteristics.

Number of new principles of operation such as velocity modulation, interaction of space charge waves with electromagnetic fields were proposed. It evolves the transfer of power from a source of direct voltage to a source of alternating voltage by means of a density modulation of electrons resulting in development of Klystron, magnetron and travelling wave tube.

The interaction of impact ionization avalanche and the transit time of charge carriers was used to develop **Reed diode**, IMPATT, TRAPTT diode. Quantum mechanical tunneling was used to develop tunnel diode. Transferred electron techniques were used to develop Transferred Electron Device (TED). In all solid state devices, the negative resistance character is used for microwave generation and amplification.

4.4 Advantages of Microwaves

There are some unique advantages of microwave over low frequencies.

1. Increased Bandwidth Availability:

Microwaves have large bandwidth (1 GHz to 10^3 GHz) compared to the common bands namely MW, SW, UHF waves. The advantage of large bandwidth is that frequency range of information channels will be small percentage of the carrier frequency and more information can be transmitted in low frequency ranges.

Microwave region is very useful since the lower band of frequency is already crowded.

Infact, microwave region (1000 GHz) contains thousand sections of frequency band $0\text{-}10^9$ Hz and hence any one of these thousand sections may be used to transmit all the Television, radio and other communications that is presently transmitted by $0\text{-}10^9$ Hz band. TV = 5-7 MHz, telegraph ch = 120-240 Hz, Bandwidth of speech = 4 kHz, Music = 10 – 15 kHz).

Microwave communication is also used in telephone networks, TV networks. Space communication, telementry, defence, railway etc. FM and digital modulation scheme also needs higher bandwidth.

2. Improved Directive Properties:

As frequency increases, directivity increases and beamwidth decreases. Hence, the beamwidth of radiation θ is proportional to λ/D.

At low frequency bands, the size i.e. diameter of antenna becomes very large if it is required to get sharp beams of radiation.

However, at microwave frequencies, antenna size of several wavelength leads to smaller beamwidths and an extremely directed beam just the same way as an optical lens focusses light rays, therefore microwave frequencies are said to possess quasi optical properties.

For example, for a parabolic antenna,

$$B = \frac{140°}{(D/\lambda)}$$

where,

    B = Beamwidth in degrees
    D = Diameter of antenna in cm
    λ = Wavelengths of antenna in cm

At 30 GHz (λ = 1 cm), for 1° beamwidth,

$$D = \frac{140}{B} \times \lambda$$

$$= \frac{140}{1} \times 1$$

$$\boxed{D = 140 \text{ cm}}$$

At 300 MHz (λ = 100 cm) for 1° beamwidth,

$$D = \frac{140}{1} \times 100$$

$$= 140 \text{ m}$$

$$\boxed{D = 140 \text{ m}}$$

From the above example, it is clear that antenna size is small for microwave frequencies.

3. Fading Effect and Reliability:

Fading effect is due to the change in the transmission medium and it is more effective at low frequency. Due to line of slight propagation (LOS) and high frequencies there is less fading effect and hence, microwave communication is more reliable.

4. Power Requirements:

Transmitter/Receiver power requirements are very low at microwave frequencies compared to that at short wave band.

5. Transparency Property of Microwaves:

Microwaves frequency band ranging from 300 MHz-10 GHz are capable of freely propagating through the ionized layers surrounding the earth as well as through the atmosphere.

The presence of such a transparent window in microwave band is useful for study of microwave radiation from the sun and stars in radio astronomical research of space. It also makes it possible for duplex communication and exchange of information between ground stations and space vehicles.

4.5 Applications of Microwaves

Microwaves have a broad range of applications in modern technology. Most important among them are in long distances communication system, radar, radio astronomy, navigation etc.

1. **Telecomm:** Intercontinental Telephone and TV space communication (earth to space and space to earth), telemetry communication link for railways etc.
2. **Radars:** It detects aircraft, track/guide supersonic missiles, observe/track weather patterns, air traffic control (ATC), burglar alarms, garage door openers, police speed detectors etc.
3. **Commercial and industrial applications use heat property of microwaves:**
    (i) Microwave oven (2.4 GHz, 600 W).
    (ii) Drying machines: Textile, food and paper industry for drying clothes, potato chips and printing matters.
    (iii) Food processing industry.
    (iv) Rubber industry/plastics/chemical/forest product industry.
    (v) Biomedical applications.

4.6 Microwave Waveguides and Components

Waveguides:

A hollow metallic tube of uniform cross-section for transmitting electromagnetic (EM) waves by successive reflections from the inner walls of the tube is called a **'waveguide'**.

Waveguides are used for transmitting electro-magnetic fields in the ultra high frequency (UHF) and microwave frequency (μW) frequency region (3-300 GHz). In the microwave region the transmission lines such as co-axial cable and parallel wires become inefficient due to skin effect and dielectric losses. Waveguides are used to obtain larger bandwidth and lower signal attenuation. In waveguides the electric and magnetic fields are confined to the space within the guides. Thus, no power is lost through radiation, and even the dielectric loss is negligible, since the guide are normally air-filled. However, there is some power loss as heat in the walls of the guides, but the loss is very small. No TEM (Transverse electromagnetic) wave can exist in a waveguide but Transverse Electric (TE) and Transverse Magnetic (TM) waves can exist. Induced currents in the walls of the waveguide gives rise to power loss and to minimize these losses, the waveguides (WG) wall resistance is made as low as possible. Hence, the inner surface of the waveguide is usually coated with either gold or silver to improve the conductivity and minimise losses inside the waveguide because of roughness. The waveguide is manufactured generally by using copper. They are superior to the co-axial cables at UHF and higher frequencies, can handle greater power and possess less resistance.

4.7 Types of Waveguides

Any shape of cross-section of a waveguide can support EM waves. But irregular shape are difficult to analyse.

Most widely used waveguides are:
1. Rectangular waveguide.
2. Circular waveguide.

Rectangular waveguide shown in Fig. 4.4 (a) is most common type of waveguide. Circular waveguide tends to twist the waves as these travel through them. However, circular waveguides are used with rotational antenna as in radars. Circular waveguide is shown in Fig. 4.4 (b).

Elliptical shape shown in Fig. 4.4 (b) is often preferred in flexible waveguide. Flexible waveguides will be required whenever the waveguide section should be capable of movement like bending, stretching or twisting. A copper tube having an elliptical cross-section is good example of a flexible waveguide.

Ridging is a convenient method of reducing the waveguide dimensions and thereby increasing the critical wavelength. However, the presence of ridge has the disadvantage of increased attenuation, reduced power handling capacity and introducing distortions. Single and double ridge waveguides have been shown in Fig. 4.4 (d) and (e) respectively. Also the useful frequency range of waveguide is increased by ridging. It also helps in reducing the phase velocity. As disadvantages are more than advantages, therefore they are not used for standard applications.

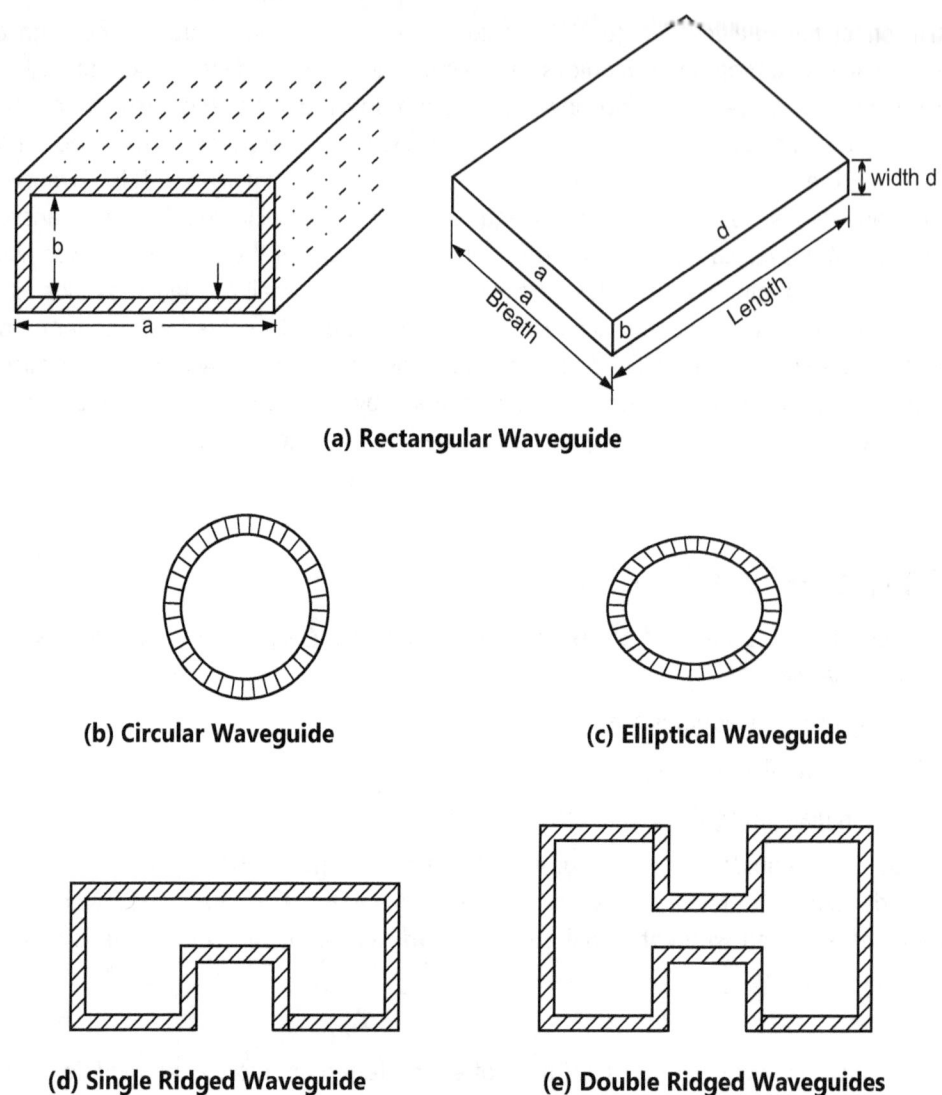

Fig. 4.4: Types of Waveguides

4.7.1 Rectangular Waveguide

A rectangular waveguide is a hollow metallic tube with a rectangular cross section. The conducting walls of the guide confine the electromagnetic field and thereby guide the electromagnetic wave. The electromagnetic wave inside a waveguide can have an infinite number of patterns which are called **'mode'.** An electromagnetic wave consists of magnetic and electric fields which are always perpendicular to each other. The fields in the waveguides which make up these mode pattern must obey certain physical laws. At the surface of conductor, the electric field cannot have a component parallel to the surface of conductor.

This indicates that the electric field must always be perpendicular to the surface at a conductor. The magnetic field is always on the parallel to the surface of the conductor and cannot have a component perpendicular to it at the surface.

In a waveguide, two kinds of modes (wave) are:
1. TE Wave or Transverse Electric Wave.
2. TM Wave or Transverse Magnetic Wave.

1. TE Wave: The electric field is always transverse to the direction of propagation and is called Transverse Electric of TE Wave or TE Mode.

2. TM Wave: The magnetic field is always transverse to the direction of propagation and is called the Transverse Magnetic or (TM Mode) Wave.

In TE mode, no electric lines is in the direction of propagation i.e. $E_z = 0$, if z is the direction of propagation. But $H_z \neq 0$.

In TM mode, no magnetic lines in the direction of propagation i.e. $H_z = 0$ but $E_z \neq 0$.

Thus, a component of either electric or magnetic field in the direction of propagation of the resultant wave, therefore the wave is no longer a transverse electromagnetic (TEM) wave.

Fig. 4.5 shows that any uniform plane wave in a lossless guide may be resolved into TE and TM waves.

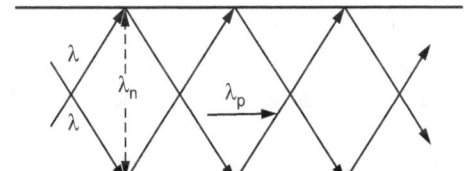

Fig. 4.5: Plane Wave Reflected in a Waveguide

When the wavelength λ is in the direction of propagation of the incident wave, there will be one component λ_n in the direction normal to the reflecting plane and another λ_p parallel to the plane.

These components are:

$$\lambda_n = \frac{\lambda}{\cos \theta} \quad \ldots (4.1)$$

$$\lambda_p = \frac{\lambda}{\sin \theta} \quad \ldots (4.2)$$

where, θ = Angle of incidence
λ = Wavelength of the impressed signal in unbounced medium

In rectangular waveguide the two mode TE and TM are designated TE_{mn} or TM_{mn}, where the integer 'm' denotes the number of half waves of electric or magnetic field in the x-direction and 'n' is the number of half waves in the y-direction if, the propagation of the wave is assumed in the positive z-direction integer m indicates the number of half wave variations of electric field (or magnetic field in TM) across the wider dimension 'a' of waveguide (x-direction) and integer n indicates the number of half-wave variations of electric or magnetic fields across the narrow dimension 'b' i.e. y-direction.

4.7.2 Propagation of Waves in Rectangular Waveguides

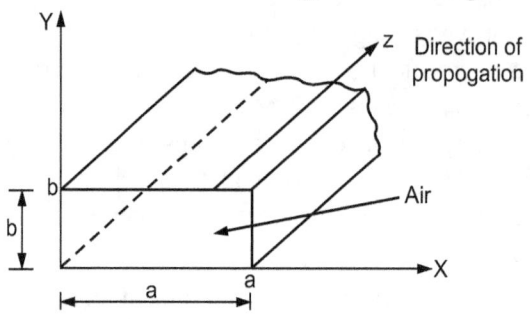

Fig. 4.6: Propagation through Rectangular Waveguides

Consider a rectangular waveguide situated in the rectangular co-ordinate system with its breath along X-axis (a), width along Y-axis (b) and wave is assumed to be propagate along the z-direction and the waveguide is filled with air as dielectric as shown in Fig. 4.6.

The wave equations for TE and TM waves are given by,

$$\nabla^2 H_z = -\omega^2 \mu \varepsilon H_z \text{ for TE wave } (E_z = 0) \quad \text{... (4.3)}$$

$$\nabla^2 E_z = -\omega^2 \mu \varepsilon E_z \text{ for TM wave } (H_z = 0) \quad \text{... (4.4)}$$

Expanding $\nabla^2 E_z$ in rectangular co-ordination system and using Maxwell's equations (4.1) and (4.2), finally we get,

$$E_x = \frac{-\gamma}{h^2} \frac{\partial E_z}{\partial x} - \frac{j\omega\mu}{h^2} \frac{\partial H_z}{\partial y} \quad \text{... (4.5)}$$

$$E_y = \frac{-\gamma}{h^2} \frac{\partial E_z}{\partial y} - \frac{\partial \omega\mu}{h^2} \frac{\partial H_z}{\partial x} \quad \text{... (4.6)}$$

$$H_x = \frac{-\gamma}{h^2} \frac{\partial H_z}{\partial x} + \frac{j\omega\varepsilon}{h^2} \frac{\partial E_z}{\partial y} \quad \text{... (4.7)}$$

and

$$H_y = \frac{-\gamma}{h^2} \frac{\partial H_z}{\partial y} - \frac{j\omega\varepsilon}{h^2} \frac{\partial E_z}{\partial x} \quad \text{... (4.8)}$$

These equations give a general relationship for field components within a waveguide.

4.7.3 Propagation of TEM Waves

For TEM wave, $E_z = 0$ and $H_z = 0$.

Putting these values in above equations from equation (4.5) to equation (4.8), all field components along x and y directions E_x, E_y, H_x, H_z vanish and therefore a TEM wave cannot exist inside a waveguide.

4.7.4 TE Modes in Rectangular Waveguide

Fig. 4.7 (b) shows the field pattern for a TE wave solid line indicates electric field lines or voltage lines and dotted lines indicate magnetic field lines. As already mentioned above that subscript are used for designating a particular mode.

Referring to TE pattern shown in above Fig. 4.7 (a), it can be seen that the voltage varies from 0 to maximum and maximum to 0 across the wide dimension 'a'. This is one half variation. Hence m = 1.

Across the narrow dimension there is no variation in voltage 'V'. Hence, n = 0. Therefore, this mode is TE_{10} mode.

1. TE_{10} mode:

TE_{10} mode is a mode having highest cut-off wavelength known as **'dominant mode'** of waveguide and all other modes are called higher modes. It is the mode which is used for practically all electromagnetic transmission in a rectangular waveguide. TE_{10} is the dominant mode for the TE wave. Dominant mode is almost low-loss, distortionless transmission and higher modes result in significant loss of power and also undesirable harmonic distortion.

Radiation pattern for TE_{10} mode is shown in Fig. 4.8 and sketches of some high order TE modes are shown in Fig. 4.9.

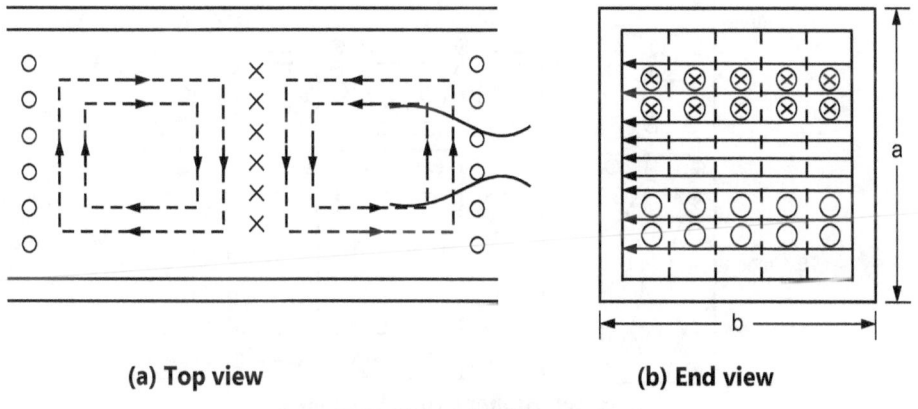

(a) Top view **(b) End view**

Fig. 4.7: Field Pattern of a TE Mode

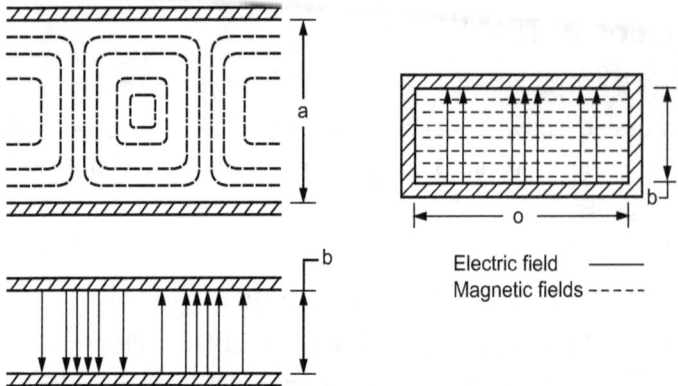

Fig. 4.8: Radiation Patterns for TE10 Mode

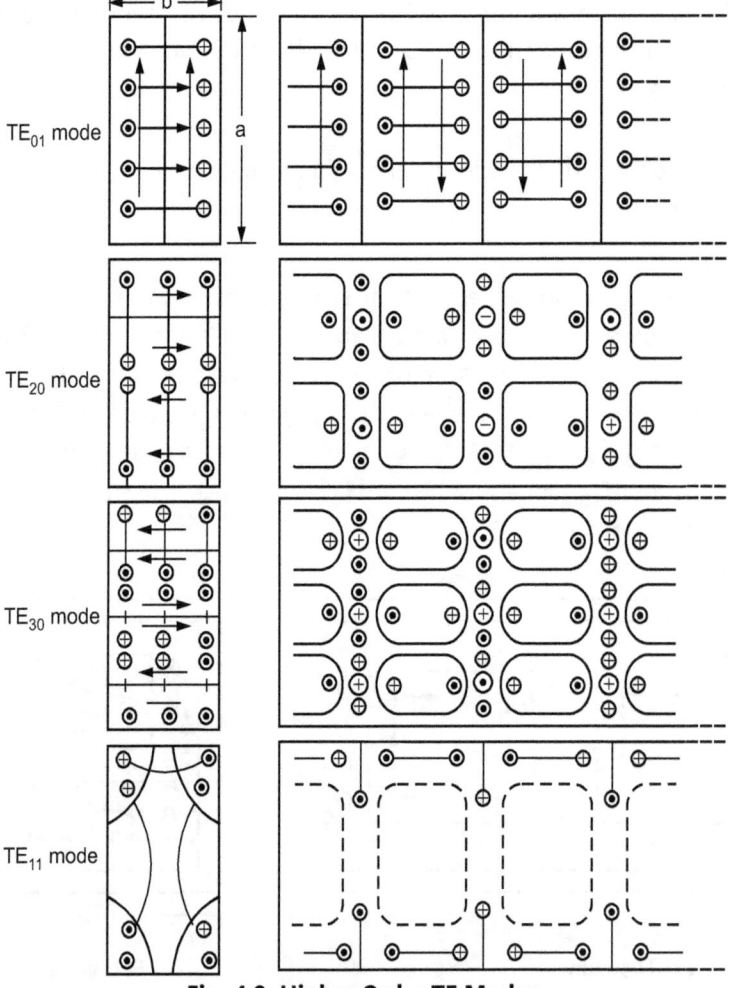

Fig. 4.9: Higher Order TE Modes

2. **TE$_{00}$ mode:**

For m = 0 and n = 0, i.e. number of half wave variations along the wider dimensions are zero and narrow dimensions are zero. Therefore, all field components vanished inside the waveguide. Therefore, this mode cannot exist.

3. **TM Modes in Rectangular Waveguide:**

Depending on the values of m and n, there are various modes in TM waves. In general, we represent the modes as TM$_{mn}$.

4. **Various TM$_{mn}$ modes:**

   (i) **TM$_{00}$ mode:** [m = 0 and n = 0]. If m = 0 and n = 0 are substituted in E_x, E_y, H_x and H_y in equation (4.5) and equation (4.8), we see that all of them vanish and hence TM$_{00}$ mode cannot exist.

   (ii) **TM$_{01}$ mode:** [m = 0 and n = 1]. Again, if we put value of m = 0 and n = 1 in E_x, E_y, H_x and E_y equation, then all of them vanish, so TM$_{01}$ mode cannot exist.

   (iii) **TM$_{10}$ mode:** [m = 1 and n = 0]. Again, all field components vanish hence, this mode cannot exist.

   (iv) **TM$_{11}$ mode:** [m = 1 and n = 1]. Now, we have all E_x, E_y, H_x and H_y components i.e. TM$_{11}$ mode exists and for all higher values of m and n, component exists, i.e. all higher modes do exist.

4.8 Waveguide Parameters

Following are the waveguide parameters.

1. **Cut-off wavelength (λ_c):**

Cut-off wavelength is the wavelength of signal below which the propagation of the wave occurs and above which there is attenuation or no propagation. The cut-off wavelength is denoted by 'λ_c'.

The cut-off wavelength for rectangular waveguide for both TE$_{mn}$ and TM$_{mn}$ is given by,

$$\lambda_c = \frac{2}{\sqrt{\left(\frac{m}{a}\right)^2 + \left(\frac{n}{b}\right)^2}}$$

where,

   a = Wide dimension of waveguide

   b = Narrow dimension of waveguide

Therefore, the operating frequency must be above the cut-off frequency in order to propagate the wave in waveguide.

The frequency associated with cut-off wavelength is called cut-off frequency and denoted as 'f_c',

$$f_c = \frac{1}{2\sqrt{\mu\varepsilon}} \sqrt{\left(\frac{m}{a}\right)^2 + \left(\frac{n}{b}\right)^2}$$

This is cut-off frequency for both TE_{mn} and TM_{mn} mode.

where,

μ = Permeability of free space

ε = Permittivity of free space

2. Dominant Mode:

It is the mode for both TE and TM which offers highest cut-off wavelength (λ_o) or lowest cut-off frequency (f_o) in a particular waveguide.

For TM_{mn} mode, TE_{10} is the dominant mode and

For TM_{mn} mode, TM_{11} is the dominant mode.

As mention earlier, dominant mode is almost a low loss, distortion transmission while higher modes contains losses and harmonic distortion. For practically, electromagnetic transmission TE_{10} and TM_{11} modes are used.

3. Guide Wavelength (λ_g):

It is defined as the distance travelled by the wave in order to undergo a phase shift of 2π radians. It is shown in Fig. 4.10.

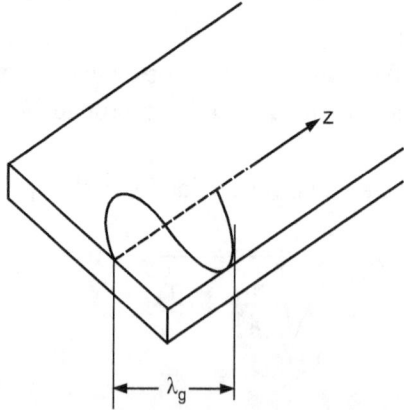

Fig. 4.10: Guide Wavelength

It is related to the phase constant by relation,

$$\lambda_g = \frac{2\pi}{\beta}$$

The wavelength in the waveguide is different from the wavelength in free space. In fact, it is related to free space wavelength λ_o and cut-off wavelength λ_c by,

$$\frac{1}{\lambda_g^2} = \left(\frac{1}{\lambda_o^2} - \frac{1}{\lambda_c^2}\right)$$

or

$$\lambda_g = \frac{\lambda_o}{\sqrt{1 - \left(\frac{\lambda_o}{\lambda_c}\right)^2}}$$

This equation is valid for any waveguide mode.

4. Group velocity (V_g):

If there is modulation in the carrier, the modulation envelope actually travels at velocity slower than that of carrier and slower than speed of light. The velocity of modulation envelope is called the group velocity 'V_g'. This happens when modulated signal travels in a waveguide, the modulation goes on slipping backward with respect to carrier.

Group velocity 'V_g' is defined as the rate at which the wave propagates through the waveguide and is given by,

$$V_g = \frac{d\omega}{d\beta}$$

In an air filled or hollow waveguide,

$$V_g = \frac{\lambda_o}{\lambda_g} \cdot c$$

Putting value of λ_g,

$$V_g = \frac{c}{\sqrt{1 - \left(\frac{f_c}{f}\right)^2}}$$

where,

c = Velocity of light
f_c = Cut-off frequency

$$f = \frac{c}{\lambda}$$

5. Phase Velocity (V_p):

Phase velocity (V_p) is defined as the rate at which the wave changes its phase, in terms of guide wavelength.

i.e.

$$V_p = \frac{\lambda_g}{\text{Unit time}}$$

$$= \lambda_g \cdot f$$
$$= \frac{2\pi \lambda_g \cdot f}{2\pi}$$
$$= \frac{2\pi f \lambda_g}{2\pi}$$
$$= \frac{2\pi f}{2\pi/\lambda_g}$$
$$V_p = \frac{\omega}{\beta}$$

where,
$$2\pi f = \omega$$
and $\quad 2\pi/\lambda_g = \beta$

For a wave travelling through the waveguide the speed with which a particular phase of wave travels in the propagation direction is defined as **phase velocity (V_p)**.

$$V_p = \frac{c}{\sqrt{1 - \left(\frac{f_c}{f}\right)^2}}$$

or
$$V_p = \frac{f}{\sqrt{1 - \left(\frac{\lambda_o}{\lambda_c}\right)^2}}$$

6. Wave Impedance:

Wave impedance is defined as the ratio of transverse electric field to the transverse magnetic field at any point in the waveguide. Wave impedance is also known as a characteristics impedance.

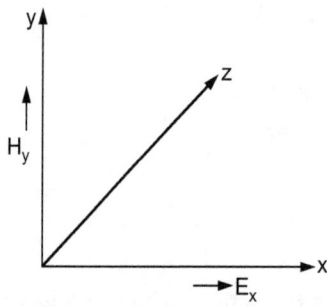

Fig. 4.11: Wave Impedance

$$Z_g = \frac{E_x}{H_y} = \frac{-E_y}{H_x}$$

Wave impedance, for TM wave in rectangular waveguide.

$$Z_{TM} = \eta \sqrt{1 - \left(\frac{\lambda_o}{\lambda_c}\right)^2}$$

Wave impedance for TE wave in rectangular waveguide,

$$Z_{TE} = \frac{\eta}{\sqrt{1 - \left(\frac{\lambda_o}{\lambda_c}\right)^2}}$$

where,

η = Intrinsic impedance for free space for air $\eta = \sqrt{\frac{\mu}{\varepsilon}} = 120\pi$

4.8.1 Difference between TE and TM Mode

TE Mode	TM Mode
1. In TE mode, TE_{10} is dominant mode.	1. In TM mode, TM_{11} is dominant mode.
2. Wave impedance for TE mode, $Z_{TE} = \dfrac{\eta}{\sqrt{1 - \left(\frac{\lambda_o}{\lambda_c}\right)^2}}$	2. Wave impedance TM mode, $Z_{TM} = \eta \sqrt{1 - \left(\frac{\lambda_o}{\lambda_c}\right)^2}$
3. Attenuation in waveguide for TE_{mn} is $\alpha_g = \dfrac{\alpha}{\sqrt{1 - (\lambda_o/\lambda_c)^2}}$	3. Attenuation in waveguide for TM_{mn} is $\alpha_g = \alpha \sqrt{1 - (\lambda_o/\lambda_c)^2}$

Cut-off wavelength, $\lambda_c = \dfrac{2}{\sqrt{\left(\frac{m}{a}\right)^2 + \left(\frac{n}{b}\right)^2}}$ is same for both TE and TM mode.

Guide wavelength, $\lambda_g = \dfrac{\lambda_o}{\sqrt{1 - \left(\frac{\lambda_o}{\lambda_c}\right)^2}}$ is valid for any waveguide mode

4.8.2 Power Transmission in the Rectangular Waveguide

The power transmitted through a waveguide and power loss in the guide walls can be calculated by means of complex Poynting theorem. We assume that:
1. The waveguide is terminated in such a way that there is no reflection from receiving end or
2. The waveguide is infinitely long as compare with its wavelength.

Then the power transmitted through the waveguide of dimensions a × b, from the sending end is given by complex Poynting theorem as,

$$P_{tr} = \oint \cdot ds \qquad \left(\oint \text{Closed surface integration}\right)$$

where,
$$P = E \times H^*$$

$$\therefore \quad P_{tr} = \oint (E \times H^*) ds$$

This theorem gives the complex power transmitted across the surface enclosed by the volume. Then the real power transmitted is given by,

$$P = \frac{1}{2} \oint (E \times H^*) ds$$

where, real value of H^* is taken.

We know that, Z_g = Wave impedance, it is also denoted as Z_z,

$$Z_g = Z_z = \frac{E_x}{H_y}$$

$$\therefore \quad P_{tr} = \frac{1}{2 Z_z} \int_a |E|^2 da$$

$$= \frac{Z_z}{2} \int_a |H|^2 da$$

where,

$$Z_z = \frac{E_x}{H_y} = \frac{-E_y}{H_x}$$

$$|E|^2 = |E_x|^2 + |E_y|^2$$

$$|H|^2 = |H_x|^2 + |H_y|^2$$

4.9 Power Losses in Waveguide

As the electromagnetic wave propagates through a waveguide, the wave intensity gets attenuated because of losses in the waveguides.

There are two types of losses in the waveguide which causes attenuation of transmitted signal.
1. Power loss in dielectric filling.
2. Power loss in waveguide walls.

1. Power loss in dielectric filling:

When the guide is completely filled with a low loss dielectric ($\sigma << \mu\varepsilon$), the attenuation constant 'α' in the guide due to dielectric loss is,

$$\alpha = \frac{\sigma}{2}\sqrt{\frac{\mu}{\sigma}}$$

where, σ = (sigma) conductivity of metal wall, μ = Permeability, ε = Permittivity.
But, η = Intrinsic impedance in an unbounded dielectric is given as,

$$\eta = \sqrt{\frac{\mu}{\varepsilon}}$$

$\therefore$ For free space, $\alpha = \dfrac{\sigma\eta}{2}$

The attenuation in waveguide 'α_g' for TE_{mn} and TM_{mn} mode is given by,
For TE_{mn} mode,

$$\alpha_g = \frac{\sigma\eta}{2\sqrt{1-\left(\frac{f_c}{f}\right)^2}} = \frac{\alpha}{\sqrt{1-\left(\frac{\lambda}{\lambda_c}\right)^2}}$$

For TM_{mn} mode,

$$\alpha_g = \frac{\sigma\eta}{2}\sqrt{1-\left(\frac{f_c}{f}\right)^2} = \alpha\sqrt{1-\left(\frac{\lambda}{\lambda_c}\right)^2}$$

2. Power loss in waveguide walls:

In waveguide the wave is propagated by reflections from walls. The tangential component of electric field and normal component magnetic field develops losses in the walls. Due to this the average power in the waveguide is dissipated.
The attenuation in the waveguide α_g is given by,

$$\alpha_g = \frac{P_L}{2\,P_{tr}}$$

where,
P_L = Power loss per unit length
P_{tr} = Power transmitted through the waveguide

When the waveguide sections are joined and if the joint is not proper or misaligned, there will be some loss due to reflection.

4.10 Microwave Cavity Resonator

When one end of the waveguide is terminated in a shorting plate there will be reflections and hence standing waves as shown in Fig. 4.12. When another shorting plate is kept at a distance of **"multiple of $\lambda_g/2$"** then the hollow space so formed can support a signal which bounces back and forth between the two shorting plates. This results in a resonance and hence hollow space is called cavity and hence resonator as **"cavity resonator"**.

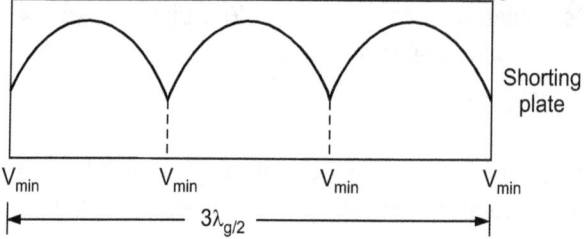

Fig. 4.12: Standing Waves

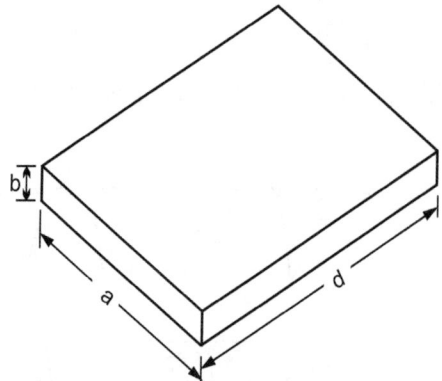

Fig. 4.13: Rectangular Cavity Resonator

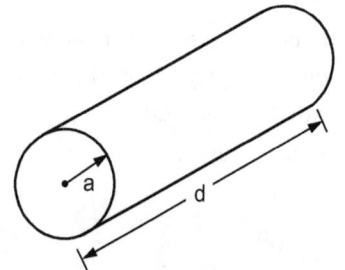

Fig. 4.14: Circular Cavity Resonator

In microwave applications, the commonly used cavity resonators are:
1. Rectangular cavity resonator.
2. Circular cavity resonator.
3. Re-entrant cavity resonator.

Rectangular and circular cavity waveguides are shown in Fig. 4.13 and Fig. 4.14 respectively. Just like a parallel resonator circuit, cavity resonator can resonate at only one particular frequency.

In Fig. 4.12, $d = \frac{3\lambda_g}{2}$, for a given resonator and mode a, b, m and n are constants. Therefore, λ_c (cut-off wavelength) is also fixed and λ_o (free space wavelength) will also have a fixed value. But, $\lambda_o = \frac{c}{f_o}$ and f will also have a constant value equal to f_o, which is a resonant frequency of cavity resonator.

In rectangular cavity resonator, resonant frequency is same for both TE and TM mode and given as,

$$f_o = \frac{1}{2p\sqrt{\mu\varepsilon}}\left[\left(\frac{mp}{a}\right)^2 + \left(\frac{np}{b}\right)^2 + \left(\frac{Pp}{d}\right)^2\right]^{1/2}$$

$$f_o = \frac{c}{2}\left[\left(\frac{mp}{a}\right)^2 + \left(\frac{np}{b}\right)^2 + \left(\frac{Pp}{d}\right)^2\right]^{1/2}$$

where,
- m = Number of half wave variation in X-direction
- n = Number of half wave variation in Y-direction
- P = Number of half wave variation in Z-direction

4.11 Quality Factor (Q) of Cavity Resonators

Q-factor is the measure of frequency selectivity of circuit, Q is defined by equation,

$$Q = \frac{\omega_o W}{P}$$

where,
- W = Maximum energy stored
- ω_o = Resonant frequency
- P = Average power loss (or dissipated power)

i.e.
$$Q = 2\pi \frac{\text{Maximum energy stored per cycle}}{\text{Energy dissipated per cycle}}$$

The Q i.e. quality factor of a perfect or ideal cavity resonator is infinite. Since in a perfect conductor forming the cavity, P (power losses) would be zero and also once energised it would resonate for ever.

$$Q_o = \frac{\omega_o L}{R}$$

This equation is true for cavity resonator i.e. resonant at one frequency only. If there is more than one resonant frequency, there will be different values of Q for the various values of frequency. Normally, coupling loops are used to couple the energy in and out of a cavity resonator. This coupling has the effect of an imperfectly reflecting wall and so is the finite termination or the load of the cavity. This would also change the value of Q. This Q that takes into account the coupling between the cavity and coupling paths is known as the loaded Q_L.

So, Q_L is given by,

$$\frac{1}{Q_L} = \frac{1}{Q_0} + \frac{1}{Q_{ext}}$$

where,

Q_0 = Q of an unloaded cavity
Q_{ext} = Q due to external ohmic losses

There are three types of coupling resulting in –
1. Critically coupled.
2. Under coupled and
3. Over coupled.

4.12 Application of Cavity Resonators

They can be used as tuned circuits in Klystron amplifier/oscillators, in UHF tubes, cavity magnetron, in duplexers of radars, cavity wavemeters in measurement of frequency etc.

4.12.1 Re-entrant Cavity

In order to maintain resonance at operating frequency and for efficient energy transfer into the cavity resonator the inductance and capacitance must be reduced. The re-entrant cavities are specially designed to maintain such a requirement.

In re-entrant cavity metallic boundaries extend into the interior of cavity. One of the commonly used re-entrant cavity is co-axial cavity. In this not only inductance is reduced but resistance losses are also reduced and shelf shielding enclosure prevents radiation losses. Fig. 4.14 shows co-axial re-entrant cavity.

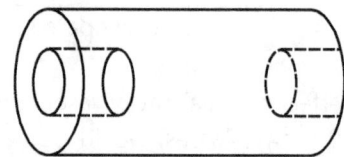

Fig. 4.15: Co-axial Re-entrance Cavity

Applications:

Re-entrant cavities are used in Klystron and other microwave tubes.

4.12.2 Coupling of Cavity Resonator

Field inside a cavity cannot exist inside completely enclosed resonators unless the energy is supplied by some means of coupling into the resonator from the outside. There are several ways of coupling.

1. **Loop Coupling: (Mechanical Coupling)**

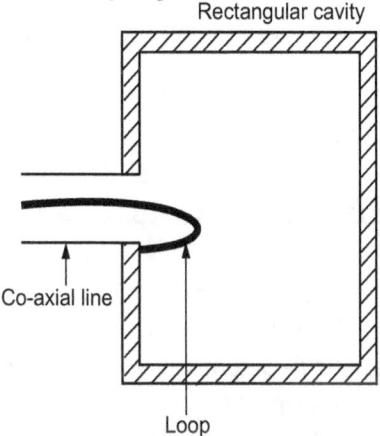

Fig. 4.16: Loop Coupled Cavity

Rectangular cavity, loop coupled to a co-axial line is shown in Fig. 4.16.

The loop size is very small and the current in the loop can be considered to be constant. The conductor current in the loop produces a linking magnetic field. The loop is capable of exciting any cavity mode. The plane of the loop is placed perpendicular to the magnetic flux lines.

2. **Probe Coupling: (Electrical Coupling)**

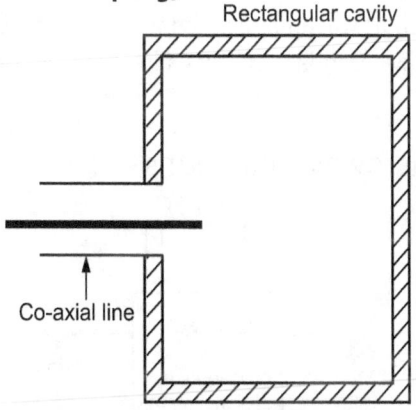

Fig. 4.17: Probe Coupled Cavity

A rectangular cavity probe coupled to a co-axial line is shown in Fig. 4.17. Any cavity mode having an electric field component parallel to the probe can be excited by this coupling arrangement.

3. **Aperture/Iris Coupling:**

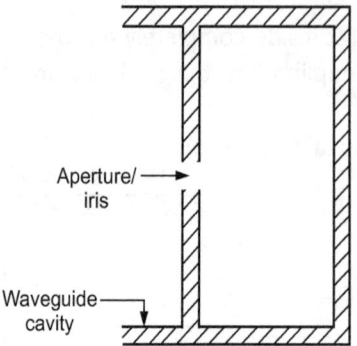

Fig. 4.18: Aperture Coupled Cavity Resonator

In aperture coupling, cavity resonator is excited by means of a small centred hole in the transverse wall. Such a type of coupling is also called as iris coupling. Fig. 4.18 shows Aperture/Iris coupling. A magnetic field component that is parallel to the long dimension of the slot will be coupled through the aperture.

4.13 Microwave Components

Microwave systems normally consists of several microwave components including the source and the load being connected to each other by waveguide or co-axial or transmission line systems. All these components must be built with low standing wave ratios, lower attenuator, lower insertion losses and other character to achieve the desired transmission of microwave signal.

Microwave components such as waveguide junction, joints, corners, drives, posts and screws, directional coupler ferrite devices, phase shifters, filters etc. are given in this topic.

4.13.1 Waveguide Microwave Junctions

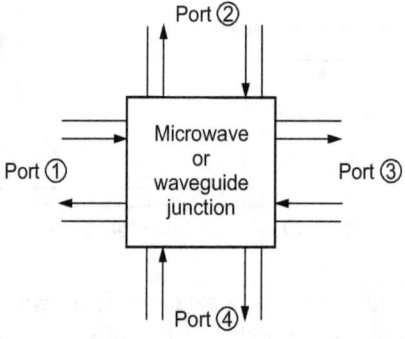

Fig. 4.19: Microwave Junction

At a certain position in the waveguide system, many a times it becomes necessary to split all or a part of the microwave energy into a particular directions. This is achieved by microwave junctions. These are combined to form coupler units that direct the energy as required. Alternately, the same junction may be used to combine two or more signals. We can say that microwave junction is an interconnection of two or more microwave components as shown in Fig. 4.19.

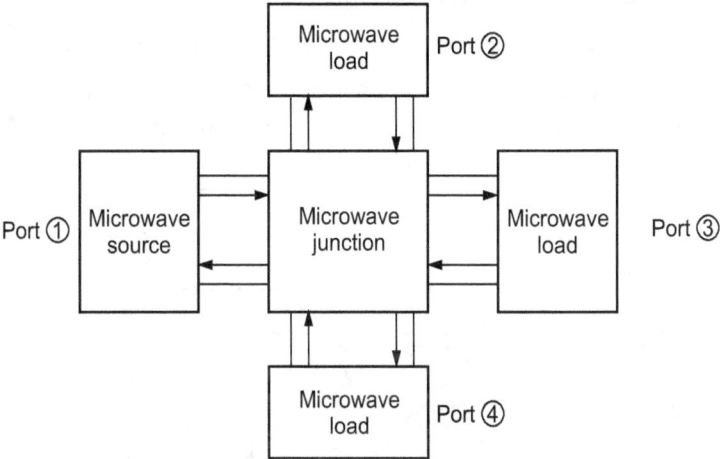

Fig. 4.20: Microwave Junction with 4-port

This junction has four ports similar to low frequency two-ports networks. Fig. 4.20 shows a microwave source at port (1) and microwave loads at ports (2), (3) and (4).

In microwave junction when input from microwave source is applied at port (1) a part of it comes out of port (2) another part out of port (3) some part out of port (4) and the remaining part may come out of port (1) itself-due to mismatch between port (1) and microwave junction.

4.13.2 Scattering (S) Parameters

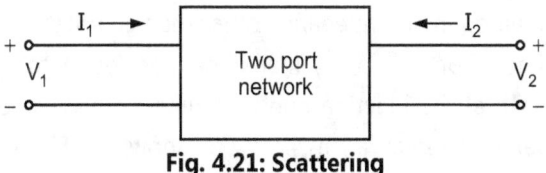

Fig. 4.21: Scattering

Low frequency circuits can be described by two-port networks and their parameters such as Z, Y, ABCD, H etc. Here, network parameters are defined in terms of voltage and circuits.

Similarly, at microwave frequencies, travelling waves are associated with power-instead of voltage and circuits and the microwave junction can be defined by S-parameter or scattering parameters (similar to Z, Y, H and ABCD parameters).

From Fig. 4.20, it is seen that, for an input at port (1), we have four outputs. Similarly, if we apply inputs to all ports, we have 16 combinations, which are represented in a matrix form and that matrix is called as **scattering matrix.**

Scattering matrix is a square matrix which gives all the combinations of power relationships between the various input and output of a microwave junction. The elements of this matrix are called scattering coefficients or scattering (S) parameter.

To obtain the relationship between the scattering matrix and the input-output powers at different ports, consider a junction of 'n' number of transmission lines where i^{th} line (i can be any line from 1 to n) is connected in a source as shown in Fig. 4.22.

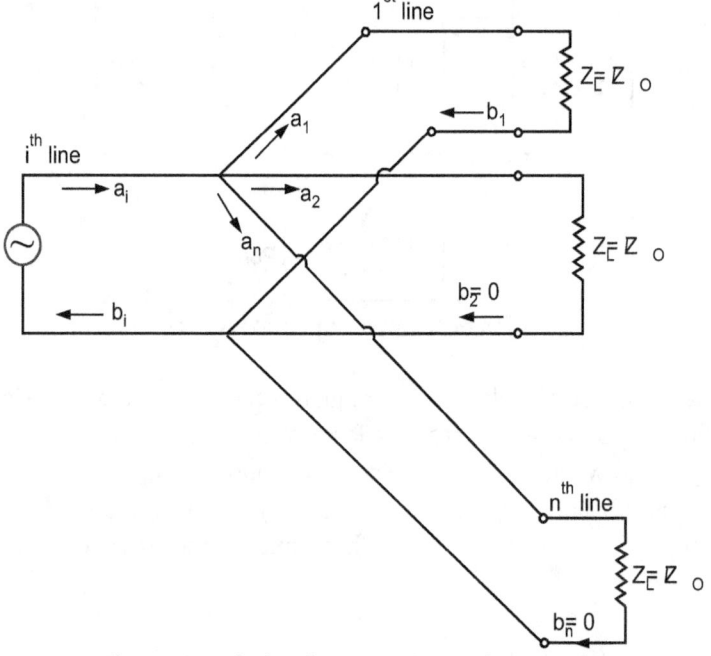

Fig. 4.22: Relation between Scattering Matrix

Case I:

Let the 1st line be terminated in an impedance other than character impedance (i.e. $Z_L \ne Z_0$) and all the remaining lines (from 2nd to n^{th}) in an impedance equal to Z_0 (i.e. $Z_L = Z_0$).

If a_i be the incident wave at the junction due to source at the ith line, then it divides itself among (n – 1) number of lines as $a_1, a_2, ... a_n$ as shown in Fig. 4.22. There will be no reflections from 2nd to n^{th} line and the incident waves are absorbed since their impedances are equal to character impedance (Z_0). But, there is a mismatch at the 1st line and hence there will be a reflected wave b_1 going back into the junction.

b_1 is related to a_1 by,

$$b_1 = \text{Reflection coefficient} \times a_1$$
$$= S i_1 a_1$$

where,

$$S_{i_1} = \text{Reflection coefficient of } 1^{st} \text{ line}$$
$$1 = \text{Reflection from } 1^{st} \text{ line and}$$
$$i = \text{Source connected at } i^{th} \text{ line.}$$

∴ Outward travelling wave in the ith line is given by,

$$b_i = S_{i_1} a_1 \qquad [\because b_2 = b_3 = \ldots = b_n = 0]$$

Case II:

Let all the $(n-1)$ lines be terminated in an impedance other than Z_o (i.e. $Z_L \neq Z_o$) for all lines. Then, there will be reflections into the junction from every line and hence the total contribution to the outward travelling wave in the ith line is given by,

$$b_i = S_{i_1}a_1 + S_{i_2}a_2 + S_{i_3}a_3 + \ldots + S_{i_n}a_n \qquad \ldots (4.9)$$

$i = 1$ to n since i can be any line from 1 to n.

Therefore, we have,

$$b_1 = S_{11}a_1 + S_{12}a_2 + S_{13}a_3 + \ldots + S_{1n}a_n$$
$$b_2 = S_{21}a_1 + S_{22}a_2 + S_{23}a_3 + \ldots + S_{2n}a_n$$
$$\vdots$$
$$b_n = S_{n1}a_1 + S_{n2}a_2 + S_{n3}a_3 + \ldots + S_{nn}a_n$$

In matrix form,

$$\begin{bmatrix} b_1 \\ b_2 \\ \vdots \\ \vdots \\ b_n \end{bmatrix} = \begin{bmatrix} S_{11} & S_{12} & \ldots & S_{1n} \\ S_{21} & S_{22} & \ldots & S_{2n} \\ \vdots & \vdots & & \vdots \\ \vdots & \vdots & & \vdots \\ S_{n1} & S_{n2} & & S_{nn} \end{bmatrix} \begin{bmatrix} a_1 \\ a_2 \\ \vdots \\ \vdots \\ a_n \end{bmatrix} \qquad \ldots (4.10)$$

Column-Matrix [b] corresponding to reflected waves or output

Scattering column matrix [S] or order $n \times n$

Matrix [a] corresponding to incident waves or input

∴ $\qquad [b] = [S][a] \qquad \ldots (4.11)$

Here, 'a' represents input to particular port.

'b' represents output to particular port.

S_{ij} is corresponding to scattering coefficient resulting due to input at i^{th} port and output taken out of jth port.

S_{ii} denotes how much of power is reflected back from the junction into the ith port when input power is applied at the ith port itself.

4.13.3 Properties of S-Matrix

1. [S] is always a square matrix of order (n × n).
2. [S] is a symmetric matrix.
   i.e., $S_{ij} = S_{ji}$
3. [S] is a unitary matrix.
   i.e., $[S][S^*] = [I]$
   [I] = Unit matrix or identity matrix of the same order as that of [S].
4. The sum of the products of each term of any row (or column) multiplied by the coupler conjugate of the corresponding of any other row (or column) is zero.

   i.e. $\sum_{i=1}^{n} S_{ik} S_{ij}^* = 0$ for $k \neq j$ $\begin{bmatrix} k = 1, 2, 3, ..., n \\ j = 1, 2, 3, ..., n \end{bmatrix}$

5. If any of the terminal or reference planes (say the kth port) are moved away from the junction by an electric distance $B_k l_k$, each of the coefficients. S_{ij} involving k will be multiplied by the factor $e^{-jB_k l_k}$.

4.14 Microwave T-Junctions

A T-junction is an intersection of three waveguide in the form of alphabet "T". These are several types of Tee junctions.

1. H-plane Tee Junction.
2. E-plane Tee Junction.
3. E-H Plane Tee Junction (Hybrid/T-junction or Magic-T Junction).
4. Rat-Race Junction.

4.14.1 H-plane Tee Junction

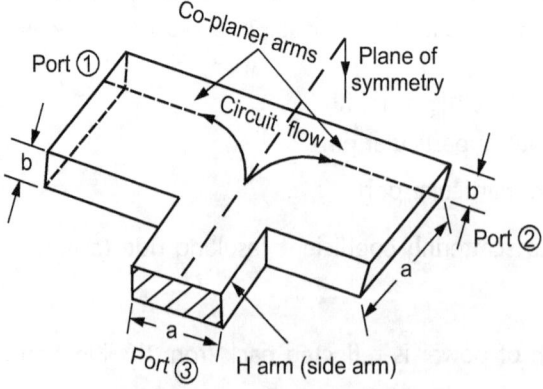

Fig. 4.23: H-plane Tee Junction

Port (1) and port (2) of the main waveguide are called collinear ports and port is the H-arm or side arm.

H-plane Tee is called as H-plane because the axis of the side arm is parallel to the planes of the main transmission line. As all three arms of the H-planes Tee lie in the plane of magnetic field, the magnetic field divides itself into the arms. This is also called as **current junction.**

The properties of the H-plane Tee can be completely defined by its [S] matrix. The order of scattering matrix is 3×3 since there are three possible inputs and three possible outputs.

$$\therefore \quad [S] = \begin{bmatrix} S_{11} & S_{12} & S_{13} \\ S_{21} & S_{22} & S_{23} \\ S_{31} & S_{32} & S_{33} \end{bmatrix}$$

Now we determine the S-parameter, S_{ij}

where, $\quad i = 1, 2, 3$

and $\quad j = 1, 2, 3$

By applying the properties of S-matrix.

1. Because of the plane of symmetry of the junction scattering coefficients S_{13} and S_{23} must be equal.

$$\therefore \quad S_{13} = S_{23}$$

2. From the symmetric property,

$$S_{ij} = S_{ji}$$

$$\therefore \quad S_{12} = S_{21}$$

$$S_{23} = S_{32} = S_{13}$$

$$S_{13} = S_{31}$$

3. Since port is perfectly matched to the junction.

$$\therefore \quad S_{33} = 0$$

With these properties [S] matrix becomes,

$$[S] = \begin{bmatrix} S_{11} & S_{12} & S_{13} \\ S_{21} & S_{22} & S_{23} \\ S_{31} & S_{32} & S_{33} \end{bmatrix} = \begin{bmatrix} S_{11} & S_{12} & S_{13} \\ S_{12} & S_{22} & S_{13} \\ S_{13} & S_{13} & 0 \end{bmatrix}$$

Now we have four unknown.

4. From the unitary property,

$$[S][S^*] = [I]$$

i.e. $\begin{bmatrix} S_{11} & S_{12} & S_{13} \\ S_{12} & S_{22} & S_{13} \\ S_{13} & S_{13} & 0 \end{bmatrix} \begin{bmatrix} S_{11}^* & S_{12}^* & S_{13}^* \\ S_{12}^* & S_{22}^* & S_{13}^* \\ S_{13}^* & S_{13}^* & 0 \end{bmatrix} = \begin{bmatrix} 1 & 0 & 0 \\ 0 & 1 & 0 \\ 0 & 0 & 1 \end{bmatrix}$

$$R_1 C_1 = S_{11} S_{11}^* + S_{12} S_{12}^* + S_{13} S_{13}^* = 1$$

or $\quad |S_{11}|^2 + |S_{12}|^2 + |S_{13}|^2 = 1$ ... (4.12)

$$R_2 C_2 = S_{12} S_{12}^* + S_{22} S_{22}^* + S_{13} S_{13}^* = 1$$ ... (4.13)

$\therefore \quad |S_{12}|^2 + |S_{22}|^2 + |S_{13}|^2 = 1$

$$R_3 C_3 = |S_{13}|^2 + |S_{13}|^2 = 1$$ ... (4.14)

$\therefore \quad 2|S_{13}|^2 = 1$

$\therefore \quad S_{13} = \dfrac{1}{\sqrt{2}}$ ... (4.15)

$$R_3 C_1 = S_{13} S_{11}^* + S_{13} S_{12}^* = 0$$ ... (4.16)

Comparing equation (4.12) and equation (4.13),

$|S_{11}|^2 = |S_{22}|^2$

$\therefore \quad S_{11} = S_{22}$ ... (4.17)

From equation (4.16),

$S_{13}(S_{11}^* + S_{12}^*) = 0$

Since, $\quad S_{13} \neq 0$

$\therefore \quad S_{11}^* + S_{12}^* = 0$

or $\quad S_{11}^* = -S_{12}^*$

or $\quad S_{11} = -S_{12}$

or $\quad S_{12} = -S_{11}$

From equation (4.12),

$|S_{11}|^2 + |S_{12}|^2 + |S_{13}|^2 = 1$

$|S_{11}|^2 + |S_{11}|^2 + \dfrac{1}{2} = 1$

or $\quad 2|S_{11}|^2 = 1 - \dfrac{1}{2} = \dfrac{1}{2}$

$\therefore \quad S_{11} = \dfrac{1}{2}$

$\because$ $S_{11} = S_{22}$

$\therefore$ $S_{22} = \dfrac{1}{2}$

and $S_{11} = -S_{12}$

$\therefore$ $S_{12} = -\dfrac{1}{2}$

Substituting all these values in [S] matrix,

$$[S] = \begin{bmatrix} \dfrac{1}{2} & -\dfrac{1}{2} & \dfrac{1}{\sqrt{2}} \\ -\dfrac{1}{2} & \dfrac{1}{2} & \dfrac{1}{\sqrt{2}} \\ \dfrac{1}{\sqrt{2}} & \dfrac{1}{\sqrt{2}} & 0 \end{bmatrix} \qquad \ldots (4.18)$$

We know that, $[b] = [S][a]$

$\therefore$
$$\begin{bmatrix} b_1 \\ b_2 \\ b_3 \end{bmatrix} = \begin{bmatrix} \dfrac{1}{2} & -\dfrac{1}{2} & \dfrac{1}{\sqrt{2}} \\ -\dfrac{1}{2} & \dfrac{1}{2} & \dfrac{1}{\sqrt{2}} \\ \dfrac{1}{\sqrt{2}} & \dfrac{1}{\sqrt{2}} & 0 \end{bmatrix} = \begin{bmatrix} a_1 \\ a_2 \\ a_3 \end{bmatrix}$$

i.e. $b_1 = \dfrac{1}{2} a_1 - \dfrac{1}{2} a_2 + \dfrac{1}{\sqrt{2}} a_3$ ... (4.19)

$b_2 = -\dfrac{1}{2} a_1 + \dfrac{1}{2} a_2 + \dfrac{1}{\sqrt{2}} a_3$ ... (4.20)

$b_3 = \dfrac{1}{\sqrt{2}} a_1 + \dfrac{1}{\sqrt{2}} a_2$ ... (4.21)

Case I: $a_3 \neq 0$, $a_1 = 0$ and $a_2 = 0$.

Input is given at port (3) and no input at port (1) and port (2).

$\therefore$ $b_1 = \dfrac{a_3}{\sqrt{2}}$

$b_2 = \dfrac{a_3}{\sqrt{2}}$

and $b_3 = 0$

Let P_3 be the power input which is corresponding to a_3 at port (3). Then this power divides equally between port (1) and port (2) in phase i.e. $P_1 = P_2$ and $P_3 = P_1 + P_2 = 2P_1 = 2P_2$.

The amount of power coming out of port (1) or port (2) due to input at port (3),

$$= 10 \log_{10} \frac{P_1}{P_3}$$

$$= 10 \log_{10} \frac{P_1}{2P_1}$$

$$= 10 \log_{10} \left(\frac{1}{2}\right)$$

$$= -10 \log_{10} 2$$

$$= -10 (0.3010) \cong -3 \text{ dB}$$

Hence, the power coming out of port (1) or port (2) is 3 dB down with respect to input power at port (3), hence H-plane Tee is called as **3-dB splitter**.

When TE_{10} mode is allowed to propagate into port (3), the electric field lines do not change their direction when they come out of ports (1) and port (2) hence called H-plane Tee i.e. the waves that comes out of port (1) and (2) are equal in magnitude and phase.

Case II:

$a_1 = a_2 = a, a_3 = 0$.

∴

$$b_1 = \frac{a}{2} - \frac{a}{2} = 0$$

$$b_2 = -\frac{a}{2} + \frac{a}{2} = 0$$

$$b_3 = \frac{a}{\sqrt{2}} + \frac{a}{\sqrt{2}}$$

i.e. the output at port (3) is addition of the two inputs at port (1) and port (2) these are added in phase.

4.14.2 E-plane Tee Junction

Fig. 4.24 (a) shows E-plane Tee ports (1) and (2) and the collinear arms and port (3) is the E-arm.

When TE_{10} mode is mode to propagate into port (3), the two outputs at port (1) and port (2) will have a phase shift of 180° as shown in Fig. 4.24 (b). As the electric field lines change their directions, when they come out of port (1) and (2) therefore it is called a E-plane Tee. E-plane Tee is a voltage or series junction symmetrical about the central arm.

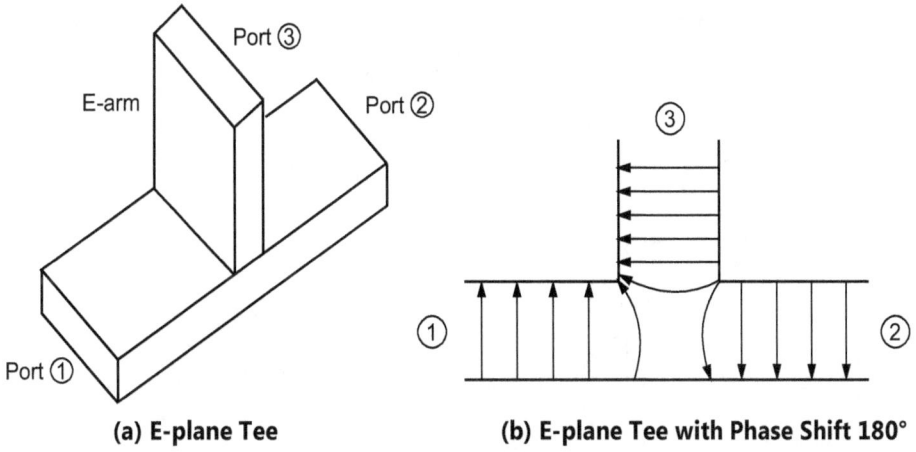

(a) E-plane Tee (b) E-plane Tee with Phase Shift 180°

Fig. 4.24: E-plane Tee

Properties of E-plane Tee can be described by using scattering matrix.

The power out of port (3) i.e. side or E-arm is proportional to the difference between instantaneous powers entering from ports (1) and port (2).

When powers entering the main arm i.e. ports (1) and (2) are in phase opposition, maximum energy comes out of port (3) or E-arm.

It is a 3 port junction, scattering matrix can be derived as follows:

1. There are three ports.

∴ [S] is a 3 × 3 matrix.

$$[S] = \begin{bmatrix} S_{11} & S_{12} & S_{13} \\ S_{21} & S_{22} & S_{23} \\ S_{31} & S_{32} & S_{33} \end{bmatrix}$$

2. The scattering coefficients.

$$S_{23} = -S_{13}$$

As outputs at ports (1) and (2) are out of phase by 180° with an input at port (3).

3. If port (3) is perfectly matched to the junction,

$$S_{33} = 0$$

4. From symmetric property,

$$S_{ij} = S_{ji}$$

∴

$$S_{12} = S_{21}$$

$$S_{13} = S_{31}$$

$$S_{23} = S_{32}$$

∴ [S] matrix becomes,

$$[S] = \begin{bmatrix} S_{11} & S_{12} & S_{13} \\ S_{12} & S_{22} & -S_{13} \\ S_{13} & -S_{12} & 0 \end{bmatrix}$$

5. From unitary property,

$$[S][S^*] = [I]$$

i.e. $\begin{bmatrix} S_{11} & S_{12} & S_{13} \\ S_{12} & S_{22} & -S_{13} \\ S_{13} & -S_{13} & 0 \end{bmatrix} \begin{bmatrix} S_{11}^* & S_{12}^* & S_{13}^* \\ S_{12}^* & S_{22}^* & -S_{13}^* \\ S_{13}^* & -S_{13}^* & 0 \end{bmatrix} = \begin{bmatrix} 1 & 0 & 0 \\ 0 & 1 & 0 \\ 0 & 0 & 1 \end{bmatrix}$

$$R_1C_1 = |S_{11}|^2 + |S_{12}|^2 + |S_{13}|^2 = 1$$

$$R_2C_2 = |S_{12}|^2 + |S_{22}|^2 + |S_{13}|^2 = 1$$

$$R_3C_3 = |S_{13}|^2 + |S_{13}|^2 = 1$$

$$R_3C_1 = S_{13}S_{11}^* - S_{12}^* S_{13} = 0$$

$$R_1C_1 = R_2C_2 = 1$$

∴ $\quad S_{11} = S_{22}$

$$S_{11} = S_{12} = S_{22}$$

$$R_3C_3 = 2|S_{13}|^2 = 1$$

∴ $\quad S_{13} = \dfrac{1}{\sqrt{2}}$ ... **Ans.**

∴ $\quad S_{11} = \dfrac{1}{2}$ ... **Ans.**

$$R_3C_1 = S_{13}(S_{11}^* - S_{12}^*) = 0 \text{ as } S_{13} \neq 0$$

$$R_1C_1 = |S_{11}|^2 + |S_{11}|^2 + \left|\dfrac{1}{\sqrt{2}}\right|^2 = 1$$

∴ $\quad S_{11}^* = S_{12}^* = 0$

∴ $\quad S_{11} = S_{12}$

$$\therefore \quad [S] = \begin{bmatrix} \frac{1}{2} & \frac{1}{2} & \frac{1}{\sqrt{2}} \\ \frac{1}{2} & \frac{1}{2} & -\frac{1}{\sqrt{2}} \\ \frac{1}{\sqrt{2}} & -\frac{1}{\sqrt{2}} & 0 \end{bmatrix}$$

$$\therefore \quad [b] = [S] \cdot [a]$$

$$\therefore \quad \begin{bmatrix} b_1 \\ b_2 \\ b_3 \end{bmatrix} = \begin{bmatrix} \frac{1}{2} & \frac{1}{2} & \frac{1}{\sqrt{2}} \\ \frac{1}{2} & \frac{1}{2} & -\frac{1}{\sqrt{2}} \\ \frac{1}{\sqrt{2}} & -\frac{1}{\sqrt{2}} & 0 \end{bmatrix} \begin{bmatrix} a_1 \\ a_2 \\ a_3 \end{bmatrix}$$

$$b_1 = \frac{1}{2} a_1 + \frac{1}{2} a_2 + \frac{1}{\sqrt{2}} a_3$$

$$b_2 = \frac{1}{2} a_1 + \frac{1}{2} a_2 - \frac{1}{\sqrt{2}} a_3$$

$$b_3 = \frac{1}{\sqrt{2}} a_1 - \frac{1}{\sqrt{2}} a_2$$

Case I: $a_1 = a_2 = 0$, $a_3 \neq 0$: Power is applied from port (3) i.e. E-arm.

$$\therefore \quad b_1 = \frac{1}{\sqrt{2}} a_3$$

$$b_2 = -\frac{1}{\sqrt{2}} a_3$$

$$b_3 = 0$$

i.e. when input is applied at port (3) it is equally divided among port (1) and port (2) with a phase shift of 180° between them. Hence, E-plane Tee is acts as **3 dB splitter**.

Case II: $a_1 = a_2 = a$ and $a_3 = 0$

$$\therefore \quad b_1 = \frac{a}{2} + \frac{a}{2}$$

$$b_2 = \frac{a}{2} + \frac{a}{2}$$

$$b_3 = \frac{1}{\sqrt{2}} a - \frac{1}{\sqrt{2}} a = 0$$

When equal inputs are applied also port (1) and (2), no output at port (3).

Case III: $a_1 \neq 0, a_2 = 0, a_3 = 0.$

$\therefore$
$$b_1 = \frac{a_1}{2}$$

$$b_2 = \frac{a_1}{2}$$

$$b_3 = -\frac{a_1}{\sqrt{2}}$$

Similarly, we have all combinations of inputs and outputs.

4.14.3 E-H Plane Tee Junction (Hybrid or Magic Tee)

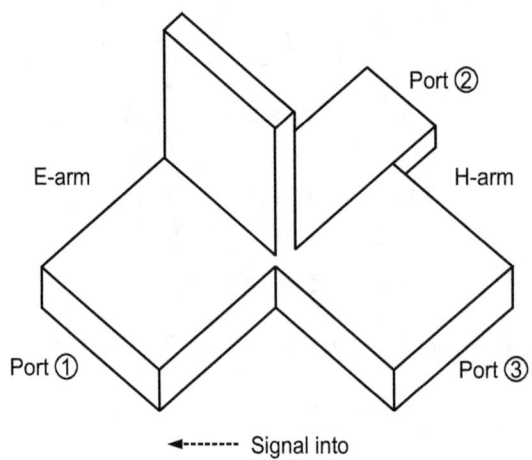

(a)

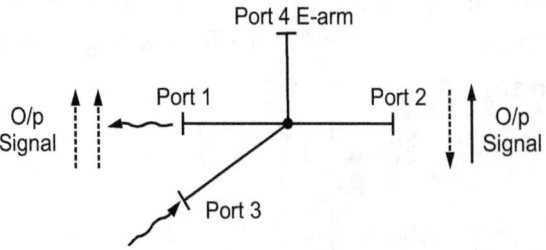

(b) Signal into H-arm

Fig. 4.25: E-H Plane

Fig. 4.25 (a) shows E-H plane Tee. Port (1) and (2) are collinear arms, port (3) is the H-arm and port (4) is the E-arm.

Such a device is used to obtaining a completely matched 3-port tee junction. It uses the power diving properties of both H-plane Tee and E-plane tee as shown in Fig. 4.25 (b) and advantages of this device is that the completely matched at all its ports. This has several applications.

(i) $[S] = 4 \times 4$ matrix as these are four ports.

$$\therefore \quad [S] = \begin{bmatrix} S_{11} & S_{12} & S_{13} & S_{14} \\ S_{21} & S_{22} & S_{23} & S_{24} \\ S_{31} & S_{32} & S_{33} & S_{34} \\ S_{41} & S_{42} & S_{43} & S_{44} \end{bmatrix}$$

(ii) Because of H-plane Tee section,

$$S_{23} = S_{13}$$

(iii) Because of E-plane Tee section,

$$S_{24} = -S_{14}$$

(iv) Because of the geometry of the junction an input at port (3) cannot come out of port (4). Since they are isolated ports and vice-versa.

$$\therefore \quad S_{34} = S_{43} = 0$$

(v) From symmetric property,

$S_{ij} = S_{ji}$, $S_{12} = S_{21}$, $S_{13} = S_{31}$, $S_{23} = S_{32}$, $S_{14} = S_{41}$, $S_{24} = S_{42}$, $S_{34} = S_{43}$

(vi) If ports (3) and (4) are perfectly matched ports.

$$\therefore \quad S_{33} = S_{44} = 0$$

$$\therefore \quad [S] = \begin{bmatrix} S_{11} & S_{12} & S_{13} & S_{14} \\ S_{12} & S_{22} & S_{23} & S_{24} \\ S_{13} & S_{23} & 0 & S_{34} \\ S_{14} & S_{24} & S_{34} & 0 \end{bmatrix}$$

$$= \begin{bmatrix} S_{11} & S_{12} & S_{13} & S_{14} \\ S_{12} & S_{22} & S_{13} & -S_{14} \\ S_{13} & S_{13} & 0 & 0 \\ S_{14} & -S_{14} & 0 & 0 \end{bmatrix}$$

(vii) From unitary property,

$$[S][S^*] = [I]$$

$$\therefore \begin{bmatrix} S_{11} & S_{12} & S_{13} & S_{14} \\ S_{12} & S_{22} & S_{13} & -S_{14} \\ S_{13} & S_{13} & 0 & 0 \\ S_{14} & -S_{14} & 0 & 0 \end{bmatrix} \begin{bmatrix} S_{11}^* & S_{12}^* & S_{13}^* & S_{14}^* \\ S_{12}^* & S_{22}^* & S_{13}^* & -S_{14}^* \\ S_{13}^* & S_{13}^* & 0 & 0 \\ S_{14}^* & -S_{14}^* & 0 & 0 \end{bmatrix} = \begin{bmatrix} 1 & 0 & 0 & 0 \\ 0 & 1 & 0 & 0 \\ 0 & 0 & 1 & 0 \\ 0 & 0 & 0 & 1 \end{bmatrix}$$

$$R_1C_1 = |S_{11}|^2 + |S_{12}|^2 + |S_{13}|^2 + |S_{14}|^2 = 1 \quad \ldots (4.22)$$

$$R_2C_2 = |S_{12}|^2 + |S_{22}|^2 + |S_{13}|^2 + |S_{14}|^2 = 1 \quad \ldots (4.23)$$

$$R_3C_3 = |S_{13}|^2 + |S_{13}|^2 = 1$$

$$R_4C_4 = |S_{14}|^2 + |S_{14}|^2 = 1$$

Comparing equations (4.22) and (4.23),

$$\therefore \quad S_{11} = S_{22}$$

$$\therefore \quad S_{13} = \frac{1}{\sqrt{2}}, \; S_{14} = \frac{1}{\sqrt{2}}$$

$$R_1C_1 = R_2C_2$$

$$\therefore \quad S_{11} = S_{22} = 1$$

$$|S_{11}|^2 + |S_{12}|^2 + \frac{1}{2} + \frac{1}{2} = 1$$

$$\therefore \quad |S_{11}|^2 + |S_{12}|^2 = 0$$

$$S_{11} = S_{12} = 0$$

$$\therefore \quad S_{22} = 0 \quad (\because S_{11} = S_{22})$$

As $S_{11} = S_{22} = 0$, this means port (1) and (2) are the perfectly matched to the junction. Hence, in any four port junction, if any two ports are perfectly matched to the junction, then the remaining two ports are automatically matched to the junction.

Such a junction where all four ports are perfectly matched to the junction is called a **Magic-Tee**.

$$[S] = \begin{bmatrix} 0 & 0 & \frac{1}{\sqrt{2}} & \frac{1}{\sqrt{2}} \\ 0 & 0 & \frac{1}{\sqrt{2}} & -\frac{1}{\sqrt{2}} \\ \frac{1}{\sqrt{2}} & \frac{1}{\sqrt{2}} & 0 & 0 \\ \frac{1}{\sqrt{2}} & -\frac{1}{\sqrt{2}} & 0 & 0 \end{bmatrix}$$

$$[b] = [S] \cdot [a]$$

$$\therefore \begin{bmatrix} b_1 \\ b_2 \\ b_3 \\ b_4 \end{bmatrix} = \begin{bmatrix} 0 & 0 & \frac{1}{\sqrt{2}} & \frac{1}{\sqrt{2}} \\ 0 & 0 & \frac{1}{\sqrt{2}} & -\frac{1}{\sqrt{2}} \\ \frac{1}{\sqrt{2}} & \frac{1}{\sqrt{2}} & 0 & 0 \\ \frac{1}{\sqrt{2}} & -\frac{1}{\sqrt{2}} & 0 & 0 \end{bmatrix} \begin{bmatrix} a_1 \\ a_2 \\ a_3 \\ a_4 \end{bmatrix}$$

$$b_1 = \frac{1}{\sqrt{2}}(a_3 + a_4); \quad b_3 = \frac{1}{\sqrt{2}}(a_1 + a_2)$$

$$b_2 = \frac{1}{\sqrt{2}}(a_3 - a_4); \quad b_4 = \frac{1}{\sqrt{2}}(a_1 - a_2)$$

Properties of Magic Tee for some important cases:

Case I: $a_3 \neq 0$, $a_1 = a_2 = a_4 = 0$

$$b_1 = \frac{a_3}{\sqrt{2}}$$

$$b_2 = \frac{a_3}{\sqrt{2}}$$

$$b_3 = b_4 = 0$$

This is the property of H-plane Tee.

Case II: $a_4 \neq 0$ $a_1 = a_2 = a_3 = 0$

$$b_1 = \frac{a_4}{\sqrt{2}}$$

$$b_2 = -\frac{a_4}{\sqrt{2}}$$
$$b_3 = b_4 = 0$$

This is the property of E-plane.

Case III: $a_1 \neq 0, a_2 = a_3 = a_4 = 0$

$$\therefore \quad b_1 = 0, b_2 = 0, b_3 = \frac{a_1}{\sqrt{2}}, b_4 = \frac{a_1}{\sqrt{2}}$$

i.e. when power is fed into port (1) nothing comes out port (2). Hence, port (1) and port (2) are called as **isolated port**. Similarly, when input is applied to port (2) nothing comes out at port (1), similarly E and H ports are isolated ports.

Case IV: $a_3 = a_4, a_1 = a_2 = 0$

$$b_1 = \frac{1}{\sqrt{2}}(2a_3)$$
$$b_2 = 0$$
$$b_3 = 0$$
$$b_4 = 0$$

This is nothing but additive property.

Equal inputs applied at port (3) and (4) results in an output at port 4.

Case V: $a_1 = a_2, a_3 = a_4 = 0$

$$\therefore \quad b_1 = 0$$
$$b_2 = 0 = b_2 = b_4$$
$$b_3 = \frac{1}{\sqrt{2}}(2a_1)$$

This is similar as case IV. When input is applied at (1) and (2) port than we will get output at port (3) and no output port (1), (2) and (4). This is **additive property**.

4.14.4 Applications of Magic Tee

A Magic Tee has several applications.

(a) Measurement of Impedance: A Magic Tee has been used in the form of bridge as shown in Fig. 4.25 (c) for measuring impedance.

Microwave source is connected in arm (3) and a null detector in arm (4). The unknown impedance is connected to arm (2) and a standard variable known impedance in arm (1). Using the properties of Magic Tee, the power from microwave source (a_3) gets divided equally between arms (1) and (2) $\left(\frac{\alpha_3}{\sqrt{2}}\right)$ (to the unknown impedance and standard variable impedances). These impedances are not equal to characteristic impedance Z_0 and hence there will be reflections from arms (1) and (2). If ρ_1 and ρ_2 are the reflection coefficients, powers $\dfrac{\rho_1 a_3}{\sqrt{2}}$ and $\dfrac{\rho_2 a_3}{\sqrt{2}}$ enter the Magic Tee jnction from arms (1) and (2) as shown in Fig. 4.25 (c).

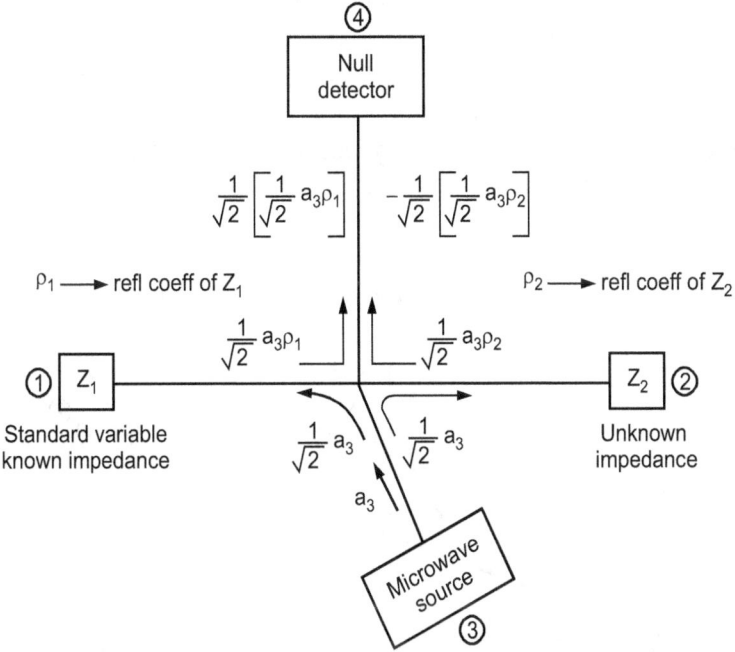

Fig. 4.25 (c): Magic Tee for Measurement of Impedances

The resultant wave into arm (4) i.e., the null detector can be calculated as follows:

The net wave reaching the null detector (Refer Fig. 4.25 (c)).

$$= \frac{1}{\sqrt{2}} \left(\frac{1}{\sqrt{2}} a_3 \rho_1 \right) - \frac{1}{\sqrt{2}} \left(\frac{1}{\sqrt{2}} a_3 \rho_2 \right) = \frac{1}{2} a_3 (\rho_1 - \rho_2)$$

For perfect balancing of the bridge (null detection) from above equation is equated to zero.

i.e. $\quad \dfrac{1}{2} a_3 (\rho_1 - \rho_2) = 0$

or $\quad \rho_1 - \rho_2 = 0$

or $\quad \rho_1 = \rho_2$

or $\quad \dfrac{Z_1 - Z_z}{Z_1 + Z_z} = \dfrac{Z_2 - Z_z}{Z_2 + Z_z}$

$\therefore$
i.e. $\quad Z_1 = Z_2$
$\quad R_1 + jX_1 = R_2 + jX_2$

or $\quad R_1 = R_2$ and $X_1 = X_2$

Thus, the unknown impedance can be measured by adjusting the standard variable impedance till the bridge is balanced and both impedances become equal.

(b) Magic Tee as a Duplexer: The transmitter and receiver are connected in port (2) and (3) respectively, antenna in the E-arm or port (4) and port (3) of Magic Tee is terminated in a matched load as shown in Fig. 4.25 (d). During transmission half the power reaches the antenna from where it is radiated into space. Other half reaches the matched load where it is absorbed without reflections. No transmitter power reaches the receiver since port (1) and (2) are isolated ports in a Magic Tee. During reception, half of the received power goes to the receiver and the other half to the transmitter are isolated during reception as well as during transmission.

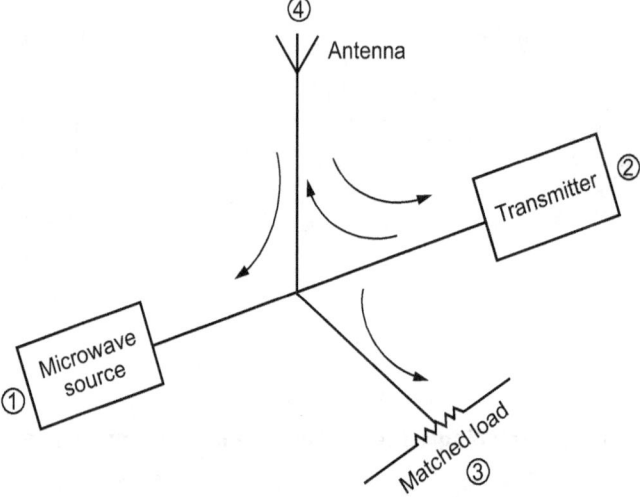

Fig. 4.25 (d): Magic Tee as a Duplexer

(c) Magic Tee as a Mixer: A Magic Tee can also be used in microwave receivers as a mixers where the signal and local oscillator are fed into the E and H arms as shown in Fig. 4.25 (e).

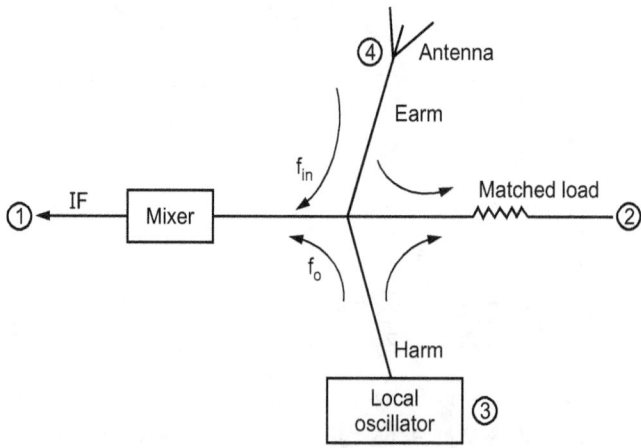

Fig. 4.25 (e): Magic Tee as a Mixer

Half of the local oscillator power and half of the received power from antenna goes to the mixer where they are mixed to generate the IF frequency.

$$IF = f_{in} \sim f_o$$

Other applications of Magic Tee's are,
- Discriminator.
- Microwave bridge.

4.15 Directional Couplers

Directional couplers are flanged, built in waveguide assemblies which can sample a small amount of microwave power for measurement purposes. They can be designed to measure incident or reflected power, SWR (standing wave ratio) values, provides a single path to the receiver or perform other desirable operations. They can be unidirectional or bi-directional. Unidirectional measuring only incident power while bi-directional measuring incident as well as reflected powers.

In its most common form, the directional couplers is a four port waveguide junction consisting of a primary main waveguide and a secondary auxiliary waveguide as shown in Fig. 4.26 (a).

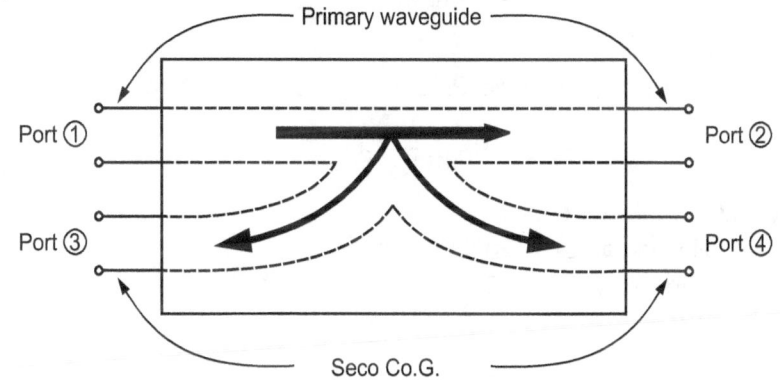

(a) Schematic of D.C. Received Power

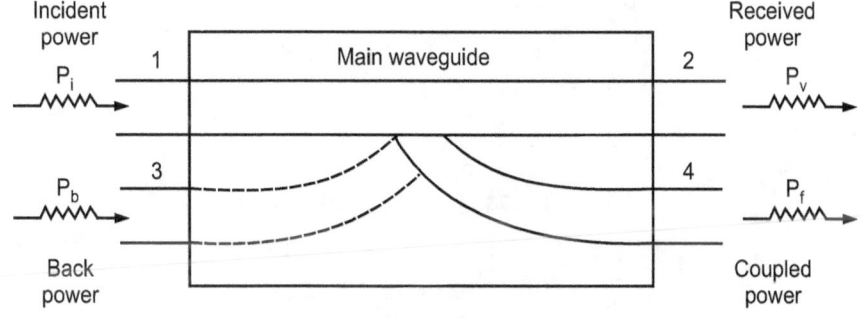

(b) D.C. Indicating Power

Fig. 4.26: Directional Couples

With matched terminations at all ports, the properties of ideal direction coupler.
1. A portion of power travelling from port (1) to port (2) is coupled to port (4) but not to port (3).
2. A portion of power travelling from port (2) to port (1) is coupled to port (3) but not to port (4).
3. A portion of power incident on port (3) is coupled to port (2) but not to port (1) and a portion of the power incident on port (4) is coupled to port (1) but not to port (2).

A small portion of input power at port (1) is coupled to port (4) so that measurement of this small power is possible. Ideally, no power should come out of port (3). Fig. 4.26 (b) indicates various inputs/output powers.

P_i = Incident power at port (1)
P_r = Received power at port (2)
P_f = Forward coupled power at port (4)
P_b = Back power at port (3)

The performance of directional coupler are usually defined by two parameters:

1. **Coupling factor C:**
It is the ratio of incident power to the forward power measure in dB.
$$C = 10 \log_{10} \frac{P_i}{P_f} \text{ dB}$$

2. **Directivity D:**
It is the ratio of the forward power P_f to the back power P_b expressed in dB.
$$D = 10 \log_{10} \frac{P_f}{P_b} \text{ dB}$$

For a typical Directional Coupler
Coupling factor, C = 20 dB
Directivity, D = 60 dB

i.e. $C = 20 = 10 \log \frac{P_i}{P_f}$

∴ $\frac{P_i}{P_f} = 10^2 = 100$

or $P_f = \frac{P_i}{100}$

Also, D = 60 dB

$60 = 10 \log \frac{P_f}{P_b}$

$\frac{P_f}{P_b} = 10^6$

or $P_b = \frac{P_f}{10^6} = \frac{P_i}{10^8}$

Since, $P_b = \dfrac{P_i}{10^8}$ which is very small and can be neglected.

The coupling factor is measure of how much of the incident power is being sampled while directivity is a measure of how well the Directional Coupler distinguishes between forward and reverse travelling powers.

3. Isolation:

Isolation is the another parameter of Directional Coupler.

It is the ratio of incident power to the back power and expressed in dB.

$$I = 10 \log_{10} \dfrac{P_i}{P_b} \text{ dB}$$

Isolation in dB = Coupling factor + Directivity

In addition to the above parameters, Standing Wave Ratio (SWR), frequency range and transmission loss are also specified for a directional coupler. Low SWR ensures minimum mismatch errors, wide frequency range eliminates the need for several octave band couplers to cover the broad band range and minimum transmission loss for significance power availability for measurement setup.

There are several types of directional couplers such as:

1. Two hole cross guide coupler.
2. Two hole branching guide coupler.
3. Short-slot coupler.
4. Loop directional coupler.
5. Single hole directional coupler.

1. Two-hole directional coupler:

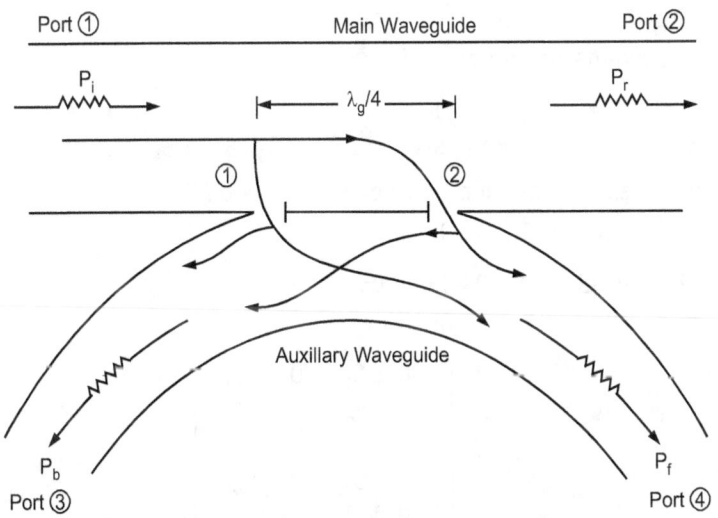

Fig. 4.27: Two-hole Directional Coupler

The principle of operation of a two hole directional coupler is shown in Fig. 4.27. It consists of two guides the main and auxilliary with two tiny holes common between them as shown in Fig. 4.24. The two holes are at distance of $\lambda_g/4$ where, λ_g is the guide wavelength.

The two leakages out of holes (1) and (2) both in phase at position of 2nd holes and hence they added up contributing to forward coupled power. But the two leakages are out of phase by 180° at position of 1st hole and hence they cancel each other making back power (P_b) = 0 (ideally). The magnitude of the power coming out of two holes depends upon the dimension of the two holes. Since the distance between the two holes is $\lambda_g/4$, P_b (Back power) is made zero {since the incident power will have to travel a distance of $\lambda_g/4 + \lambda_g/4 = \lambda_g/2$, when it comes back from hole (2) resulting in 180° phase shift, with incident power leakage through hole (1) entering port (3)}.

The number of holes can be one i.e. single hole direction coupler or two or more. The degree of coupling is determined by size and location of the holes in the waveguide.

4.16 Scattering Matrix of a Directional Coupler

1. Directional Coupler is four port network.

    $\therefore$ [S] = 4 × 4 matrix

    i.e. $[S] = \begin{bmatrix} S_{11} & S_{12} & S_{13} & S_{14} \\ S_{21} & S_{22} & S_{23} & S_{24} \\ S_{31} & S_{32} & S_{33} & S_{34} \\ S_{41} & S_{42} & S_{43} & S_{44} \end{bmatrix}$

2. In the Directional Coupler all four ports are perfectly matched to the junction.

    $\therefore \quad S_{11} = S_{22} = S_{33} = S_{44} = 0$

3. From the symmetric property,

    $S_{ij} = S_{ji}$

    $\therefore \quad S_{12} = S_{21}, S_{13} = S_{31}, S_{14} = S_{41}, S_{23} = S_{32}, S_{24} = S_{42}, S_{34} = S_{43}$

4. Ideally, there is no coupling between port (1) and (3).

    $\therefore \quad S_{13} = S_{31} = 0$

    And no coupling between (2) and (4).

    $\therefore \quad S_{24} = S_{42} = 0$

    $\therefore \quad [S] = \begin{bmatrix} 0 & S_{12} & 0 & S_{14} \\ S_{12} & 0 & S_{23} & 0 \\ 0 & S_{23} & 0 & S_{34} \\ S_{14} & 0 & S_{34} & 0 \end{bmatrix}$

5. Since $[S][S^*] = I$

$$\therefore \begin{bmatrix} 0 & S_{12} & 0 & S_{14} \\ S_{12} & 0 & S_{23} & 0 \\ 0 & S_{23} & 0 & S_{34} \\ S_{14} & 0 & S_{34} & 0 \end{bmatrix} \begin{bmatrix} 0 & S_{12}^* & 0 & S_{14}^* \\ S_{12}^* & 0 & S_{23}^* & 0 \\ 0 & S_{23}^* & 0 & S_{34}^* \\ S_{14}^* & 0 & S_{34}^* & 0 \end{bmatrix} = \begin{bmatrix} 1 & 0 & 0 & 0 \\ 0 & 1 & 0 & 0 \\ 0 & 0 & 1 & 0 \\ 0 & 0 & 0 & 1 \end{bmatrix}$$

R_1C_1: $|S_{12}|^2 + |S_{14}|^2 = 1$ ... (4.24)

R_2C_2: $|S_{12}|^2 + |S_{23}|^2 = 1$ ... (4.25)

R_3C_3: $|S_{23}|^2 + |S_{34}|^2 = 1$ ... (4.26)

R_4C_4: $|S_{14}|^2 + |S_{34}|^2 = 1$

R_1C_3: $S_{12}S_{23}^* + S_{14}S_{34}^* = 0$ ... (4.27)

Comparing equations (4.24) and (4.25),

$$S_{14} = S_{23}$$

Comparing equations (4.25) and (4.26),

$$S_{12} = S_{34}$$

Let us assume S_{12} is real and positive $= P$.

$$S_{12} = S_{34} = P = S_{34}^*$$

$\therefore$ Equation (4.27) becomes,

$$P S_{23}^* + S_{23} P = 0$$

$$P [S_{23}^* + S_{23}] = 0$$

Since, $P \neq 0$

$\therefore$ $S_{23} + S_{23}^* = 0$

$$S_{23} = jy$$

and $S_{23}^* = -jy$

i.e. S_{23} must be imaginary.

Let, $S_{23} = jq = S_{14}$

$\therefore$ $S_{12} = S_{34}$ (Transmission parameter)

and $S_{23} = S_{14} = jq$

Also, $P^2 + q^2 = 1$

$$\therefore \quad [S] = \begin{bmatrix} 0 & P & 0 & jq \\ P & 0 & jq & 0 \\ 0 & jq & 0 & P \\ jq & 0 & P & 0 \end{bmatrix}$$

4.17 Waveguide, Bends, Corners, Transitions and Twists

Waveguide bends, corners and twists are shown in Figs. 4.28, 4.29, 4.30, 4.31. These components are useful for changing the directions of the guide by a desired angle. The bends can be H-bend or E-bend. If the bend is in the direction of the wide dimension, the H lines are affected (H-bend) and if the bend is in the direction of narrow dimension, the E lines are affected (E-bend). The bending radius must be atleast $2\lambda_g$ to avoid SWR. R_{min} = 1.5 b for an E-bend and R_{min} = 1.5a for H-bend for small reflection. Sharp 90° bends create total reflection resulting in infinite standing wave ratio. Therefore, bends should be gradual.

At lower frequencies, the bends have to be very long and in such a cases corners are preferred. These are two corners.

1. H-plane corner: where, d = 0.65 D.
2. E plane corners: Smaller value of 'd' produces arcing and hence not common in order to minimize reflections the mean length L must be add number of quarter wavelength. So that the reflected wave from both ends of the waveguide are completely cancelled.

i.e.
$$L = (2n + 1)\frac{\lambda_g}{4}$$

where,
$$n = 0, 1, 2, 3, \ldots$$

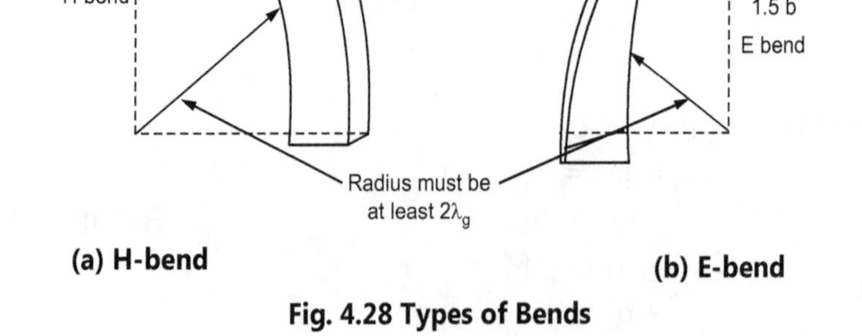

(a) H-bend

(b) E-bend

Fig. 4.28 Types of Bends

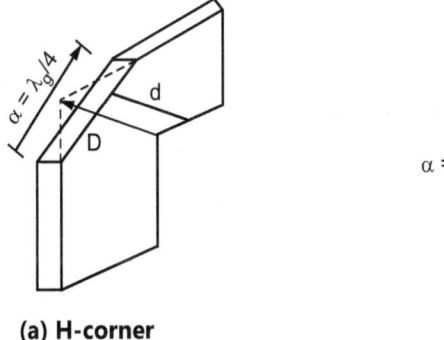

(a) H-corner (b) E-corner

L = (2n + 1) · g/4 to avoid reflections from both ends of waveguide

Fig. 4.29: Types of Corners

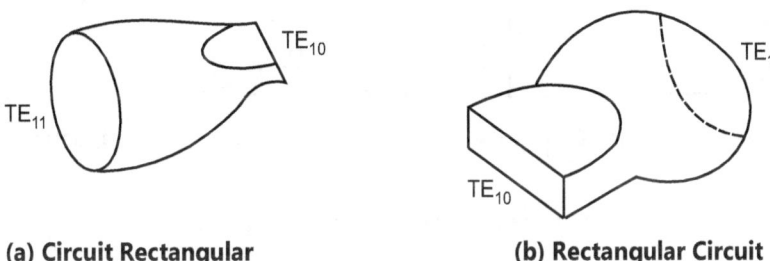

(a) Circuit Rectangular (b) Rectangular Circuit

Fig. 4.30: Transitions or Tapers

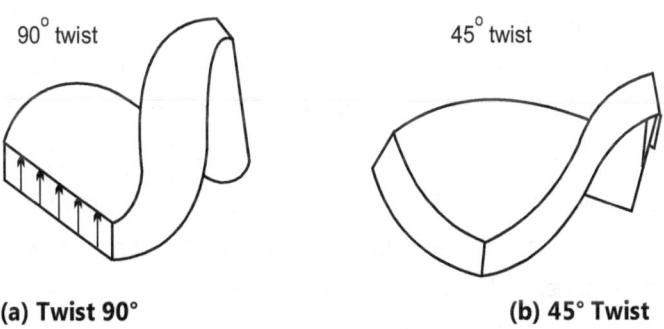

(a) Twist 90° (b) 45° Twist

Fig. 4.31: Types of Twist

Fig. 4.30 shows waveguide transitions or tapers. These are required whenever it is required to join two waveguide sections that have different shapes for their cross-sectional areas, for example, a circular to rectangular waveguide transition.

Waveguide twists such as 90° and 45° twists are helpful in converting vertical to horizontal polarization or vice-versa. Twists can also be used along with bends.

4.18 Waveguide Irises

In any waveguide system, when there is a mismatch there will be reflections. In transmission lines in order to overcome this mismatch dumped impedances or stub of required value are placed at a particular points. In waveguides also, there is mismatch causes reflection and avoid this we need some matching. Any susceptance appears across the guide, causing, mismatch and produces standing waves and needs to be cancelled by introducing another susceptance of the same magnitude but of opposite nature. Irises (also called as windows, apertures, obstacles or diaphragms) are made for this purpose.

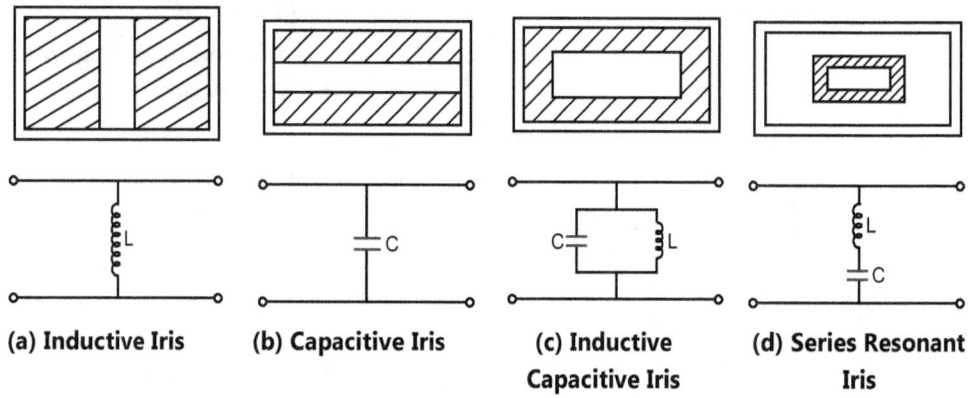

Fig. 4.32: Types of Waveguide Irises

An inductive iris Fig. 4.32 (a) allows a current to flow where none flowed before. The iris is placed in a position where the magnetic field is strong (or where electric field is relatively weak. Since the plane of polarization of electric field is parallel to the plane of iris, the current flow due to iris causes a magnetic field to be set up. Energy storage of magnetic field takes place and there is an increase in inductance at that point of the waveguide.

In capacitive iris as shown in Fig. 4.32 (b), it is seen that the potential which existed between the top and bottom walls of the waveguide now exists between surfaces which are closer and therefore the capacitance has increased at that point. The capacitive iris is placed in a position where the electric field is strong.

The inductive and capacitive irises if combined suitably the inductive and capacitive reactances introduced will be equal and iris becomes a parallel resonant circuit. For the dominant mode, the iris presents a high impedance and the shunting effect for this mode will be negligible. Other modes are completely attenuated and the resonant iris acts as a Band Pass Filter (BPF) to suppress unwanted modes.

Fig. 4.32 (d) shows series resonant iris which is supported by a non-metallic material and is transparent to flow of microwave energy.

4.19 Terminators

There are two types of terminations used in the waveguide and transmission line.

1. Match load and
2. Variable short circuit, which produces an adjustable reactive load.

These terminations are widely used in the laboratory when measuring the impedance or scattering parameters of a microwave circuit element.

The matched load provides a termination, that absorbs all the incident power and hence is equivalent to terminating the line in its character impedance. The variable short circuit is a termination that reflects all the incident power. The phase of the reflected wave is varied by changing the position of the short circuit, and this is required to changing the reactance of the termination.

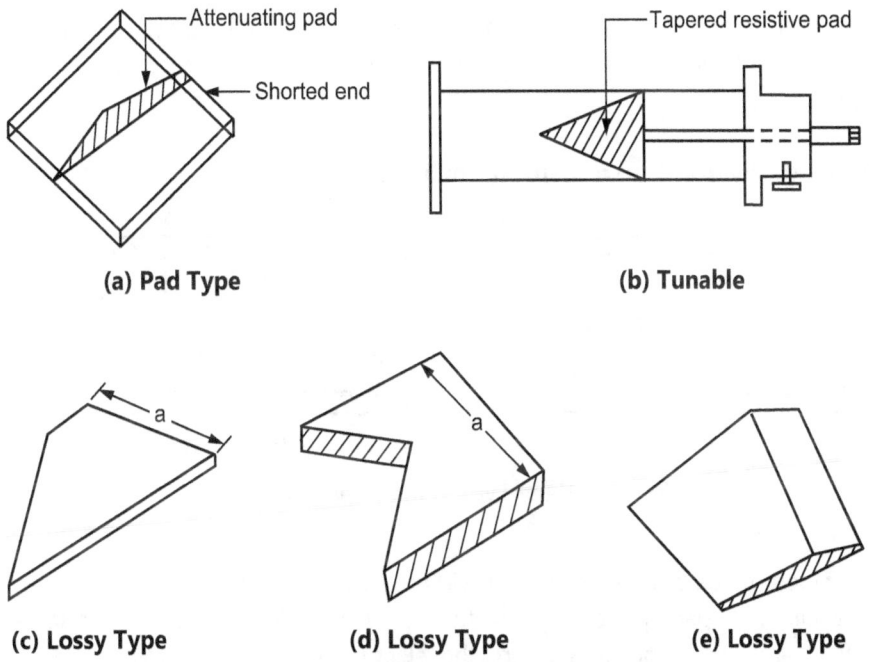

Fig. 4.33: Waveguide Matched Terminations

Matched Terminations:

Matched waveguide terminations are constructed by mounting a power absorbing card or pad in the space near the closed end of a waveguide section as shown in Fig. 4.33 (a). The reflections arising from the end are minimized by tapering the card. The card is placed parallel to the dominant. TE_{10} mode at a place where the electric field is maximum to have maximum attenuation. As the card has finite thickness, the reflections arising from it cannot be ruled out. Moreover, it is located at E_{max} which will give maximum reflected power. To avoid this, the pad is kept closed to the side wall and its length is increased. Tunable matched termination is shown in Fig. 4.33 (b).

Matched loads may also be designed by loading the whole of the waveguide with lossy materials such as powdered metal, lossy dielectric, wood, flowing water, sand etc. as shown in Fig. 4.33 (c), (d) and (e).

4.20 Attenuators

The passive elements used to control the amount of microwave power transferred from one point to another on a microwave transmission line are called **microwave attenuators**. Generally, these elements control the flow of microwave power either by reflecting and/or absorbing it in some dissipative elements, attenuators may be fixed or variable depending on the requirements.

An ideal attenuator when placed in a transmission line, must present a good impedance match at both the terminals, i.e. it should be a **well-matched reciprocal device.** As attenuation is a function of frequency, therefore, care should be taken if standard attenuator is desired.

Fixed Type Attenuator (Flap or Card Attenuator):

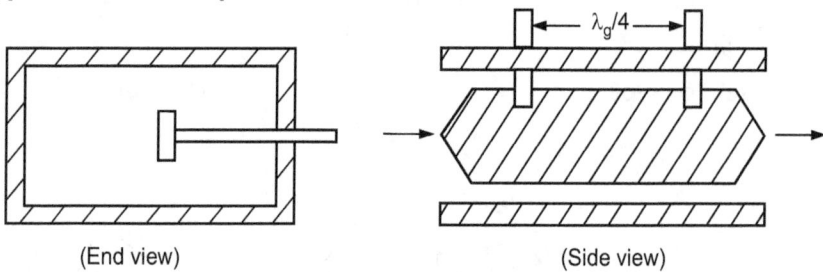

(End view) (Side view)

Fig. 4.34: Fixed Type Flap or Card Attenuator

The fixed type attenuators are used to provide fixed amount of attenuation. It consists of a dissipative element (pad) placed in a section of waveguide with its plane parallel to the electric field and at the position where the electric field of the dominant TE_{10} mode is maximum. The dissipating element is generally in the form of card or pad. The card is held parallel to the electric field by means of two thin metal rods.

To minimize reflections, the rods are held normal to the electric field and spaced quarter wavelength apart and the ends of the pad are tapered. When TE_{10} dominant mode enters the waveguide attenuator, the electric field tangential of the pad causes a dissipative circuit and it is thus absorbed. The amount of microwave power thus dissipated or the attenuation produced depends upon the strength of the electric field i.e. location of the pad within the waveguide, area of the pad intercepted by the electric field and the frequency.

Variable Attenuator:

For bridge setups used to measure transmission coefficient, the variable attenuator is used. These are variant types of the variable attenuators. But the most precise variable attenuator is the **variable rotary attenuator** as shown below. It consists of the following components:

1. The first part is the tapered rectangular to circular waveguide transition, having an attenuating pad placed parallel to the broad wall of the rectangular waveguide.

This component transforms, the dominant mode TE_{10} in rectangular waveguide to a TM_{11} mode in a cylindrical waveguide, with negligible reflections. The orthogonal polarization of the TM_{11} mode, having its electric field parallel to the plane of attenuating pad is absorbed while the other polarizations having electric field perpendicular to the plane of the pad passes without any attenuation.

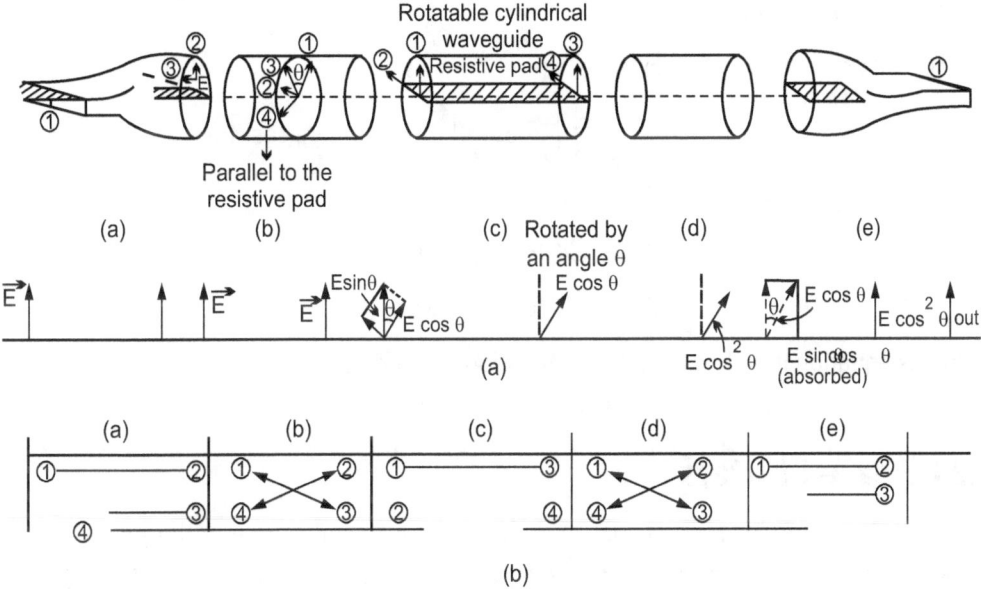

Fig. 4.35: Precision Variable Attenuator (a) Component Form with Working Principle (b) Equivalent Circuit

2. The second part is a plane circular waveguide section. This section only changes the reference polarizations (ports) as shown in the equivalent circuit (b). The scattering matrix of the component is,

$$[S] = \begin{bmatrix} 0 & 0 & \cos\theta & \sin\theta \\ 0 & 0 & \sin\theta & \cos\theta \\ \cos\theta & \sin\theta & 0 & 0 \\ -\sin\theta & \cos\theta & 0 & 0 \end{bmatrix}$$

3. The third and the main component of the instrument is a rotatable circular waveguide section having a **tapered resistive pad.** At the minimum attenuation condition, the plane of this pad is the same as that of the pad in component (a). If the plane of the pad in section (c) is rotated through an angle θ, the electric field component E sin θ, parallel to the resistive pad will be absorbed while the electric field perpendicular to the resistive pad, E cos θ passes without attenuation.

4. The fifth component is symmetrical with section (b).

5. The electric field E cos θ coming out of section (d) makes an angle (90 – θ) with the resistive pad of section (e), consequently the normal component of this electric field i.e. (E cos θ) cos θ = E cos² θ passes without any attenuation, while the tangential component (E cos θ) sin θ is absorbed.

The power transmitted is given by,

$$P_{trans} = \frac{1}{R} \left| E \cos^2 \theta \right|^2 = P_{incident} \cos^2 \theta$$

or the attenuation is,

$$A = -20 \log_{10} \cos^2 \theta$$
$$A = -40 \log_{10} \cos \theta \text{ db}$$

From this equation it is clear that the attenuation depends only on the angle of rotation θ.

4.21 Phase Shifters

A phase shifter is an instrument that produces an adjustable change in the phase angle of the wave transmitted through it. Ideally, it should be perfectly matched to the input and output lines and should produce zero attenuation. There are variety of designs for phase shifters of the mechanically adjustable type. The rotary phase shifters is the best class.

Electronically controlled phase shifters using PIN diodes as switches have been popular for use in phased-array antennas. In a phase-array antennas there are many radiating elements such as printed circuit dipoles and the radiated beam can be scanned in direction by varying the phase of excitation of each element in the array. In large array this requires many phase shifters, so a design that is small, electronically controlled and can be economically produced in large quantities using integrated circuit technique is desirable. The PIN diode phase shifters meet these requirements.

4.22 Rotary Phase Shifter

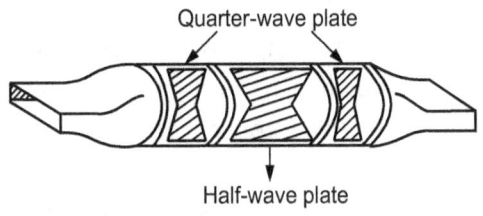

(a) Compact Form

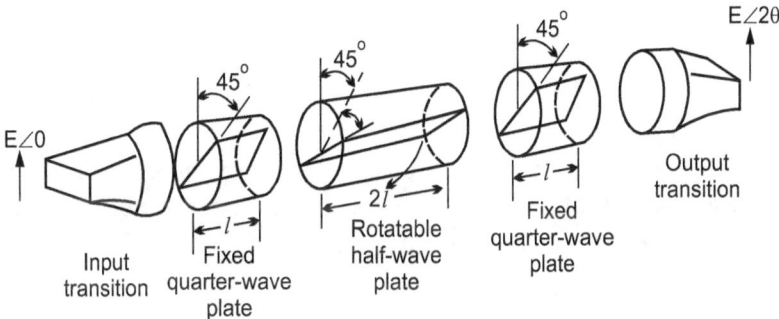

(b) Component Form

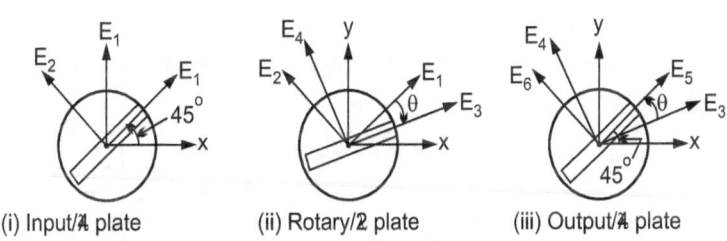

(i) Input/4 plate   (ii) Rotary/2 plate   (iii) Output/4 plate

(c) Vector-Phasor

Fig. 4.36: Precision Rotary Phase Shifter

A precision rotary phase shifter is shown in Fig. 4.36. The instrument consists of two rectangular to circular waveguide tapered transitions, together with two quarter-wave sections on both the sides of the free rotatable central half-wave section. The quarter-wave sections are oriented at an angle 45° relative to the broad wall of the rectangular waveguide. The incoming linearly polarized TE_{11} mode is decomposed into two modes polarized parallel and perpendicular to the quarter-wave section. When a half-wave section is at its zero set position, the outgoing wave suffers a total phase of 90° + 180° = 270°. Consequently, the wave going out of the second quarter-wave section suffers a total phase 270° + 90° = 360° i.e. no phase change under ideal conditions. However, when the central half section is rotated by an angle θ, the outgoing wave suffers a phase delay of 2θ.

The basic operation of the device can be understood with reference to Fig. 4.36 (a) which almost shows all components except transitions.

$E_i < 0$ represents the vertically polarized input wave in the input quarterwave section. It is decomposed into two transverse component one E_1 polarized parallel and other E_2 polarized perpendicular to quarterwave plate. After propagation through the quarter wave plate these two components are,

$$E_1 = E_i \cos 45° \, e^{-j\beta_1 l} = E_o \, e^{-j\beta_1 l}$$

$$E_2 = E_i \sin 45° \, e^{-j\beta_2 l} = E_o \, e^{-j\beta_2 l} \quad \ldots (4.28)$$

where,

$$E_o = \frac{E_1}{\sqrt{2}}$$

The length l is adjusted such that these two components will have equal magnitude but a differential phase change of $(\beta_1 - \beta_2) \, l = 90°$. Thus, after propagation through the quarterwave plate these two field components become,

$$E_1 = E_o \, e^{-j\beta_2 l}$$

$$E_2 = jE_o \, e^{-j\beta_2 l} = -jE_1 = E_1 \, e^{j\pi/2} \quad \ldots (4.29)$$

Now, it is noted that, the quarterwave section converts a linearly polarized TE_{11} wave to a circularly polarized wave and vice-versa.

After propagation through that wave plate the field components parallel to perpendicular to the half wave plates are as,

$$E_3 = (E_1 \cos \theta - E_2 \sin \theta) \, e^{-j2\beta_1 l} = E_o \, e^{-j\theta} \, e^{-j3\beta_1 l} \quad \ldots (4.30)$$

and $E_4 = (E_2 \cos \theta + E_1 \sin \theta) \, e^{-j2\beta_2 l} = E_o e^{-j\theta} \, e^{-3\beta_1 l} \, e^{-j\pi/2}$

Since, $2(\beta_1 - \beta_2) \, l = \pi$ or $-2\beta_2 l = (\pi - 2\beta_1 l)$

These two field components (E_3 and E_4) are again decomposed after propagation through half-wave plate into two TE_{11} modes, polarized parallel perpendicular to the output quarterwave plate, the decompose components can be written as,

$$E_5 = (E_3 \cos \theta + E_4 \sin \theta) \, e^{-j\beta_1 l} = E_o \, e^{-j2\theta} \, e^{-j4\beta_1 l}$$

$$E_6 = (E_4 \cos \theta - E_3 \sin \theta) \, e^{-j\beta_2 l} = E_o \, e^{-j2\theta} \, e^{-j4\beta_1 l} \quad \ldots (4.31)$$

From equation (4.31) it is seen that parallel component equal to perpendicular component E_6 at the output end in magnitude as well as in the phase. Therefore, these two will produce a resultant field which is linearly polarized TE_{11} wave.

$$E_{out} = \sqrt{2} \, E_o \, e^{-j2\theta} \, e^{-j4\beta_1 l}$$

$$= E_i \, e^{-j2\theta} \, e^{-j4\beta_1 l} \quad \ldots (4.32)$$

which has the same direction of polarization as the incident field E_1 with a phase change of $(2\theta + 4\beta_1 l)$. At a given frequency and structure θ can be varied and $4\beta_1 l$ is fixed, a phase shift of 2θ can be obtained by rotating the halfwave plate precisely through an angle θ with respect to the quarter wave plate.

The simple dependence of the phase change on a mechanical rotation may be used to calibrate the phase changer precisely and is the advantage of the rotary phase shifter.

4.23 Microwave Filters

Filters are frequency selective network that are made of reactive elements and are of four types:

(a) Low pass (b) High pass (c) Band pass (d) Band stop

To get desired responses, more than one cavity will be cascaded. Such a filter is known as multicavity filter. Microwave filters are built using a high Q cavity in contrast to low frequency counterpart.

Coupling is achieved by using irises or slots and tuning is dependent on depth of penetration of screw.

The construction of a multi-cavity filter is as shown in the figure below.

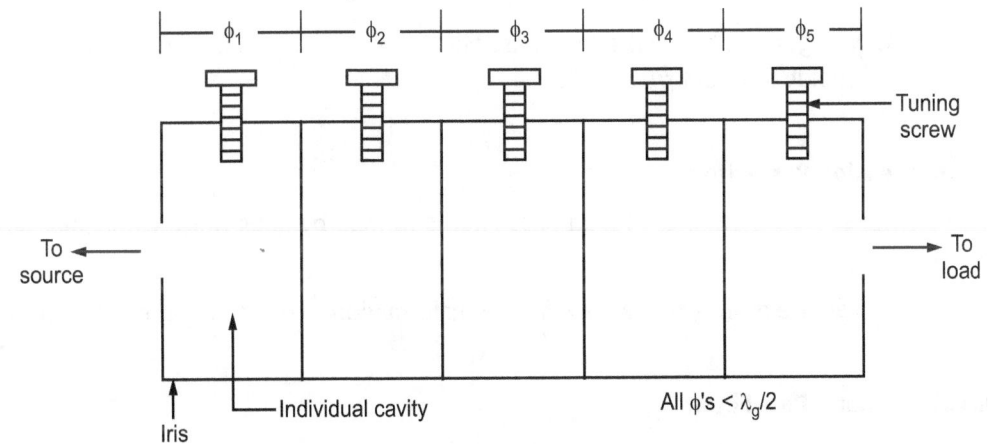

Fig. 4.37 (a)

Factors that affect the characteristic of filters are –

(a) Resonant frequency.
(b) Loaded Q of each cavity.
(c) Susceptance of each slot iris.
(d) Input and output impedances of filter.
(e) Degree of coupling between neighouring cavities.

The difference between microwave filters and other filters is that microwave circuit uses distributed elements and conventional filters use lumped elements.

The filter elements in microwave are realized by waveguide sections, co-axial lines, microstip lines, etc.

Microwave Low Pass Filter:

- Low pass filters are implemented using co-axial lines and we can use microstrip lines.
- A circuit that shows microwave low pass filter is as given below which uses co-axial line as a element.

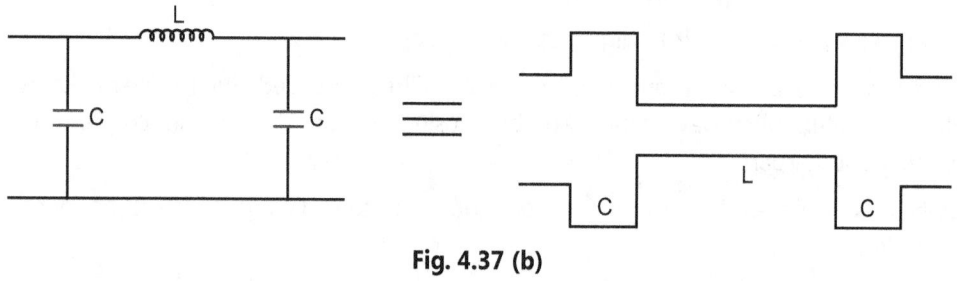

Fig. 4.37 (b)

- As waveguide is basically a high pass filter so it is not possible to have a design of waveguide form of low pass filter.

Microwave High Pass Filter:

- The series capacitance in high pass filter is formed by gaps which as of small size ($< \lambda_g/4$).
- We can use prorotype low pass filter transformation to design high pass filter.

Microwave Band Pass Filter:

- These are same as multicavity filters which are explained previously.

4.24 Faraday's Rotation Principle

Faraday's principle states that if a circularly polarized wave (TE_{11}) in a cylindrical waveguide is made to pass through a ferrite rod, which has been influenced by an axial magnetic field B, the axis of polarization gets tilted in clockwise direction and the amount of tilt depends upon the strength of magnetic field and geometry of the ferrite. This principle is illustrated in Fig. 4.38.

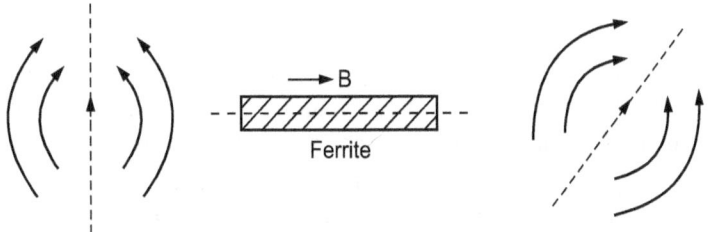

(a) Circularly Polarized Wave (b) Tilted Polarized Wave

Fig. 4.38: Faraday's Principle

Microwave components which make use, of this phenomenon are,
1. Isolator
2. Circulator and
3. Gyrator

1. Isolator:

An isolator is a two port device which provides a very small amount of attenuation for transmission from port (1) to port (2) but provides maximum attenuation for transmission from port (2) to port (1). This requirement is very much desirable when we want to match a source with a variable load.

In most microwave generators, the output amplitude and frequency tend to fluctuate very significantly with changes in load impedance. This is due to mismatch of generator output to the load resulting in reflected wave from load. But these reflected waves should not be allowed to reach the microwave generator, which will cause amplitude and frequency instability the microwave generator.

When isolator is inserted between generator and the load, the generator is coupled to the load with zero attenuation and reflections if any from the load side are completely absorbed by the isolator without affecting this generator output. Hence, the generator appears to be matched for all loads in the presence of isolator so that there is no change in frequency and output power due to variation in the load. This is shown in Fig. 4.39.

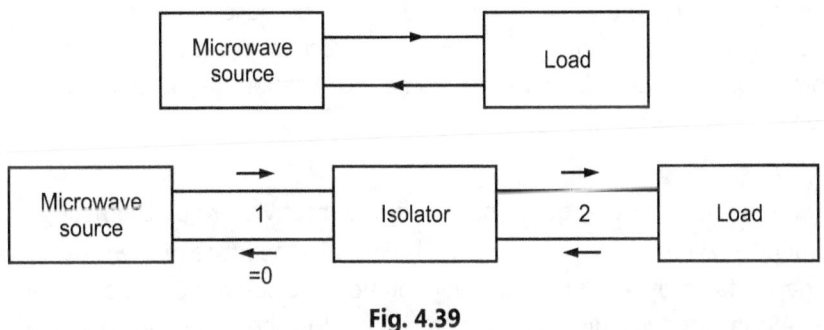

Fig. 4.39

Construction:

The construction of isolator is shown in Fig. 4.40. Isolator consists of resistive card, 45° twisted rectangular waveguide and faraday rotation ferrite rod is placed along the larger dimension of the rectangular waveguide, so as to absorb any wave whose plane of polarization is parallel to the plane of resistive card. The resistive card does not absorb any wave whose plane of polarization is perpendicular to its own plane.

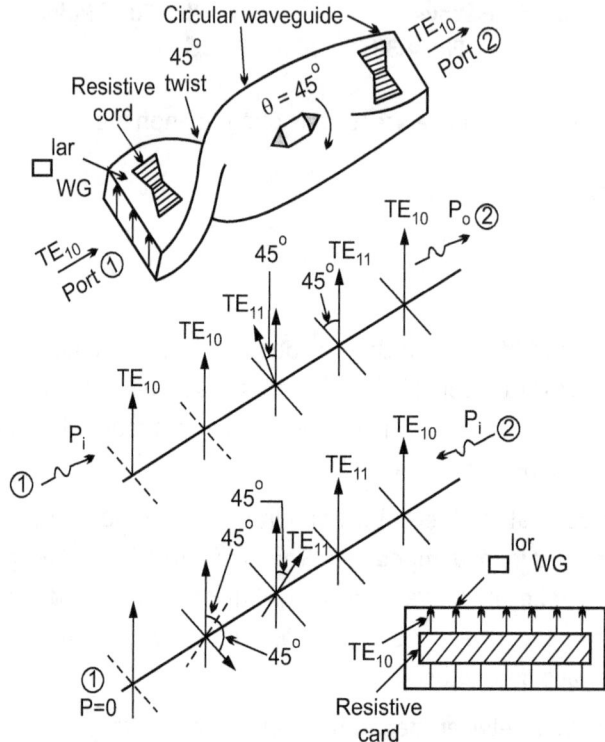

Fig. 4.40: Constructional Details of Isolator

Operation:

A TE_{10} wave passing from port (1) through the resistive card and is not attenuated. After coming out of the card, the wave gets shifted by 45° because of the twist in anticlockwise direction and then by another 45° in clockwise direction because of the ferrite rod and hence comes out of port (2) with the same polarization as at port (1) without any attenuation.

But TE_{10} wave fed from port (2) gets a pass from the resistive card placed near port (2), since the plane of polarization of the wave is perpendicular to the plane of the resistive card. Then the wave gets rotated by 45° due to faraday rotation in clockwise direction and further gets rotated by 45° in clockwise direction due to the twist in the waveguide. Now, the plane of polarization of the wave will be parallel with that of the resistive card and hence the wave will be completely absorbed by the resistive card and the output at port (1) will be zero. This power is dissipated in the card as heat. In practice, 20 to 30 dB isolation is obtained for transmission from port (2) to port (1).

4.25 Circulators

A circulator is a four port microwave device in which its one port is connected to its next port by an anticlockwise direction i.e. port (1) is connected to port (2) but not to (3) and (4), port (2) connected to port (3) but not to (4) and (1) and so on. There is no restriction on the number of ports. But four port is commonly used in circulator.

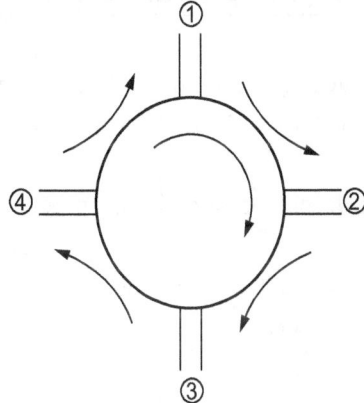

Fig. 4.41: Circulators

Application:

Parametric amplifier, tunnel diode duplexer in radar.

Construction:

A four port faradays, rotation circulator is shown in Fig. 4.42.

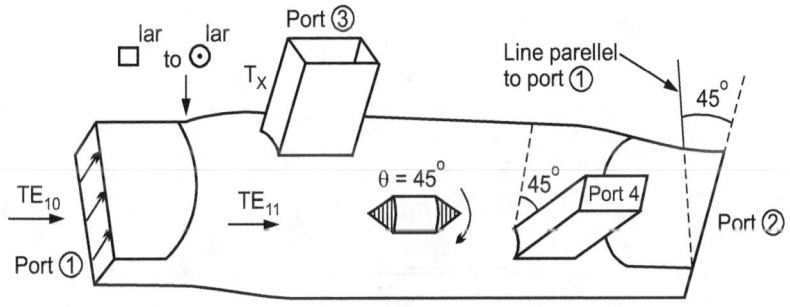

Fig. 4.42: Four Port Circulator

The power entering at port (1) is TE_{10} and its converted to TE_{11} mode because of gradual rectangular to circular transition. This power passes port (3) unaffected since the electric field is not significantly cut and is rotated through 45° due to ferrite rod, passes through the port (4) unaffected because again the fields are not significantly cut. Finally power comes out of port (2). Power from port (2) will have plane of polarization already tilted by 45° with respect to port (1). This power passes port (4) unaffected because again the electric field is not significantly cut. This wave gets rotated by another 45° due to the ferrite rod in clockwise direction. Now, this power whose plane of polarization gets tilted by 90° emerges out of port (3). Similarly, port (3) is coupled only to port (4) and port (4) to port (1).

SOLVED PROBLEMS

Problem 4.1:

When the dominant mode is propagated in an air filled rectangular waveguide, the guide wavelength for a frequency of 9000 MHz is 4 cm. Calculate breath of guide?

Solution:

For rectangular waveguide the dominant mode is TE_{10} mode, TE_{10} mode can propagate at a lower frequency.

Given:
$$f = 9000 \text{ MHz} = 9 \text{ GHz}$$
$$\lambda_g = 4 \text{ cm}$$

For TE_{10} mode $\lambda_c = 2a$

$$\lambda_g = \frac{\lambda_o}{\sqrt{1 - \left(\frac{\lambda_o}{\lambda_c}\right)^2}}$$

$$\lambda_o = \frac{c}{f}$$

where,
c = Velocity of light in cms/sec.
$= 3 \times 10^{10}$ cm/sec.
$f = 9$ GHz
$= 9 \times 10^9$ Hz

$\therefore \quad \lambda_o = \dfrac{c}{f} = \dfrac{3 \times 10^{10}}{9 \times 10^9}$

$= \mathbf{3.333}$ **cm** ... Ans.

$$\lambda_g = \frac{\lambda_o}{\sqrt{1 - \left(\frac{\lambda_o}{\lambda_c}\right)^2}}$$

Putting the values of λ_g and λ_o in equation (4.33),

$$4 = \frac{3.333}{\sqrt{1-\left(\frac{3.333}{\lambda_c}\right)^2}}$$

$$\lambda_c = 6.0302 \text{ cm}$$

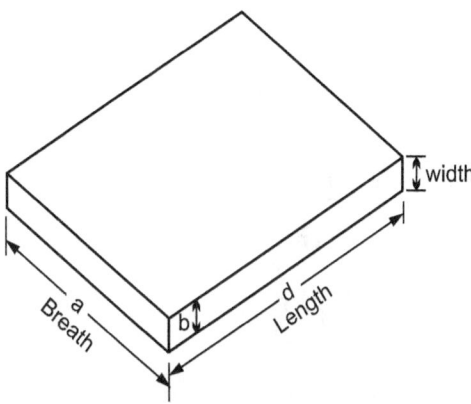

Fig. 4.43

As $\lambda_c > \lambda_o$, the wave propagates and

$$\boxed{\lambda_c = 2a} \text{ (For TE}_{10}\text{ mode)}$$

∴ $a = \dfrac{\lambda_c}{2} = \dfrac{6.0302}{2}$

$= \mathbf{3.0151}$ **cms** ... Ans.

∴ Breath = 3.0151 cms
= 3 cms

Also, width = $b = \dfrac{\lambda_c}{4}$

∴ $\boxed{a = 2b}$

∴ $b = \dfrac{3.0151}{2}$

= 1.50755 cms
= **1.5 cms** ... Ans.

Problem 4.2:
Determine the cut-off wavelength for the dominant mode in a rectangular waveguide of breadth 10 cms. For a 2.5 GHz signal propagated in this waveguide in the dominant mode, calculate the guide wavelength, the group and the phase velocities.

Solution:
In a rectangular waveguide, TE$_{10}$ in dominant mode and for TE$_{10}$,

$$\lambda_c = 2a$$

Given: f = 2.5 GHz
Cut-off wavelength = λ_c = 2a
∴ λ_c = 2 × 10 cm
∴ $\boxed{\lambda_c = 20 \text{ cm}}$

(i) Guide wavelength = λ_g:

$$\lambda_g = \frac{\lambda_0}{\sqrt{1 - \left(\frac{\lambda_0}{\lambda_c}\right)^2}}$$

and $\lambda_0 = \frac{c}{f} = \frac{3 \times 10^{10}}{2.5 \times 10^9}$

= 12 cms

∴ $\lambda_g = \dfrac{12}{\sqrt{1 - \left(\frac{12}{20}\right)^2}}$

= **15 cms**

(ii) Phase velocity = v_p:

$$v_p = \frac{c}{\sqrt{1 - \left(\frac{\lambda_0}{\lambda_c}\right)^2}}$$

$$v_p = \frac{3 \times 10^{10}}{\sqrt{1 - \left(\frac{12}{20}\right)^2}}$$

∴ v_p = **3.75 × 10¹⁰ cms/sec.** ... Ans.

(iii) Group velocity = v_g:

$v_p \cdot v_g = c^2$

∴ $v_g = \dfrac{c^2}{v_p} = \dfrac{(3 \times 10^{10})^2}{3.75 \times 10^{10}}$

= **2.4 × 10¹⁰ cms/sec.** ... Ans.

Problem 4.3:

The TE_{10} mode is propagated in a rectangular waveguide of dimensions a = 6 cms and b = 4 cms. Distance between a maximum and minimum is found to be 4.55 cms. Find the frequency of the wave.

Solution: Given: a = 6 cms
and b = 4 cms

Distance between maximum and minimum = 4.5 cms = $\lambda_g/4$.

For TE_{10} mode $\lambda_c = 2a = 2 \times 6 = 12$ cms.

Guide wavelength, $\lambda_g = \dfrac{\lambda_o}{\sqrt{1 - \left(\dfrac{\lambda_o}{\lambda_c}\right)^2}}$ ... (4.34)

$$\dfrac{\lambda_g}{4} = 4.55 \text{ cms}$$

∴ $\lambda_g = 4.55 \times 4$

$\lambda_g = $ **18.2 cms** ... Ans.

Substituting these values in equation (4.34), as $\lambda_o < \lambda_c$

$\lambda_o \approx 10$

$\lambda_o = \dfrac{c}{f}$

$10 = \dfrac{3 \times 10^{10}}{f}$

∴ $f = \dfrac{3 \times 10^{10}}{10}$

$= 3 \times 10^9$

$f = $ **3 GHz** ... Ans.

Problem 4.4:

A rectangular waveguide has dimensions 4×2 cms. Determine the guide wavelength, phase velocity and phase constant β at a wavelength of 6 cms for the dominant mode.

Solution:

In rectangular waveguide TE_{10} is the dominant mode.

$\lambda_c = 2a$

$= 2 \times 4$

$= 8$ cms

and free space wavelength, $\lambda_o = 6$ cms.

∴ $\lambda_g = \dfrac{\lambda_o}{\sqrt{1 - \left(\dfrac{\lambda_o}{\lambda_c}\right)^2}}$

$= \dfrac{6}{\sqrt{1 - (6|8)^2}}$

$= $ **9.07 cm** ... Ans.

Now, phase velocity = v_p

$$v_p = \frac{c}{\sqrt{1 - \left(\frac{\lambda_o}{\lambda_c}\right)^2}}$$

$$= \frac{3 \times 10^{10}}{\sqrt{1 - (6\!/\!8)^2}}$$

$$= 4.53 \times 10^{10} \text{ cm/sec.} \quad \ldots \text{Ans.}$$

β = Phase constant,

$$\beta = \frac{1}{c}\sqrt{\omega_o^2 - \omega_c^2}$$

$$= \frac{1}{c}\sqrt{\left(\frac{2\pi c}{\lambda_o}\right)^2 - \left(\frac{2\pi c}{\lambda_c}\right)^2}$$

$$= \frac{2\pi}{\lambda_o \lambda_c}\sqrt{\lambda_c^2 - \lambda_o^2}$$

$$= \frac{2 \times 3.14}{8 \times 6}\sqrt{(8)^2 - (6)^2}$$

$$\beta = \frac{3.14}{24} \times 2\sqrt{7}$$

$$\beta = 0.692 \text{ radians} \quad \ldots \text{Ans.}$$

Problem 4.5:

A hollow rectangular waveguide has dimensions a = 1.5 cm and b = 1 cm. Calculate the amount of attenuation if the frequency of the signal is 6 GHz.

Solution:

For dominant mode i.e. TE_{10},

$$\lambda_c = 2a = 2 \times 1.5 = 3 \text{ cm}$$

$$f_{c10} = \frac{c}{\lambda_{c10}}$$

$$= \frac{3 \times 10^{10}}{3}$$

$$= 10 \text{ GHz}$$

Thus, the 6 GHz signal will not pass through the waveguide will get attenuated. α, the attenuation is given by,

$$\alpha = \sqrt{\left(\frac{m\pi}{a}\right)^2 + \left(\frac{n\pi}{b}\right)^2 - \omega^2 \mu \varepsilon}$$

$$= \sqrt{\left(\frac{1\times\pi}{0.015}\right)^2 + 0 - (2\pi\times 6\times 10^9)^2 \times 4\pi\times 10^{-7}\times 8.854\times 10^{-12}}$$

$$= \sqrt{43876.281 - (12\pi)^2 \times 10^{18} \times 4\pi\times 10^{-7} \times 8.854\times 10^{-12}}$$

$$= \sqrt{43876.281 - 15819.054}$$

$$= 167.5 \text{ nepers/meter}$$

$$= \mathbf{1453.23 \text{ dB/m}} \quad \text{... Ans.}$$

Problem 4.6:

Given rectangular waveguide 3 × 1 cm operating at a frequency of 9 GHz in TE_{10} mode. Calculate the maximum power handling capacity of the waveguide if the maximum potential gradient of the signal is 3 kV/cm.

Solution:

$$\lambda_o = \frac{c}{f_o}$$

$$= \frac{3\times 10^{10}}{9\times 10^9}$$

$$= \frac{10}{3}$$

$$= 3.33 \text{ cm}$$

$$\lambda_{c_{10}} = 2a = 2\times 3$$

$$= 6 \text{ cm}$$

$$\lambda_g = \frac{\lambda_o}{\sqrt{1-\left(\frac{\lambda_o}{\lambda_c}\right)^2}}$$

$$= \frac{3.33}{\sqrt{1-\left(\frac{3.33}{6}\right)^2}}$$

$$\approx 5 \text{ cm}$$

Power handling capacity of the rectangular waveguide is given by,

$$P = (6.63\times 10^{-4})\, E_{max}^2\, ab\left(\frac{\lambda_o}{\lambda_g}\right)$$

$$= (6.63\times 10^{-4})\,(3\times 10^3)^2\,(3)\,(1)\left(\frac{3.33}{5}\right)$$

$$P = \mathbf{11.922 \text{ kW}} \quad \text{... Ans.}$$

Problem 4.7:

Design a rectangular waveguide to propagate 10 GHz signal under dominant mode.

Solution:

$$f = 10 \text{ GHz}$$
$$= 10 \times 10^9 \text{ Hz}$$

For rectangular waveguide TE_{10} is the dominant mode,

$$TE_{mn} = TE_{10}$$

$\therefore$ m = 1 and n = 0

$$\lambda_0 = \text{Wavelength of free space}$$
$$= \frac{c}{f_0}$$

$\therefore$
$$\lambda_0 = \frac{3 \times 10^{10}}{10 \times 10^9}$$
$$= 3 \text{ cm}$$

Typically, $\lambda_0 > a > \frac{\lambda_0}{2}$

3 cm > a > 1.5 cm

Let a = 2 cm

For standard rectangular waveguide the aspect ratio is 2: 1 i.e.

$$a = 2b$$

$\therefore$
$$b = \frac{a}{2}$$
$$= \frac{2}{2}$$
$$= 1 \text{ cm} \qquad \text{... Ans.}$$

So the dimensions of rectangular waveguide is 2 cm × 1 cm.

Problem 4.8:

A rectangular waveguide has a = 3 cm and carries dominant mode of a signal 7.63 GHz. Find the characteristics wave impedance.

Solution:

For rectangular waveguide TE_{10} is the dominant mode.

Given:
$$a = 3 \text{ cm}$$
$$f_0 = 7.63 \text{ GHz}$$
$$= 7.63 \times 10^9 \text{ Hz}$$

Find: Z_{TE} = ?

We know that,

λ_c = Cut-off wavelength,

$$= \frac{2}{\sqrt{\left(\frac{m}{a}\right)^2 + \left(\frac{n}{b}\right)^2}}$$

$$= \frac{2}{\sqrt{\left(\frac{1}{3}\right)^2 + 0}}$$

As m = 1 and n = 0 for TE_{10} mode.

λ_c = **6 cm** ... Ans.

Wavelength in free space λ_o,

$$\lambda_o = \frac{c}{f_o}$$

$$= \frac{3 \times 10^8}{7.63 \times 10^9}$$

λ_o = **3.93 cm** ... Ans.

Characteristics wave impedance for TE_{10} mode, = Z_{TE}.

$$Z_{TE} = \frac{\eta}{\sqrt{1 - \left(\frac{\lambda_o}{\lambda_c}\right)^2}}$$

$$= \frac{120\pi}{\sqrt{1 - \left(\frac{3.93}{6}\right)^2}}$$

∴ Z_{TE} = **498.94 Ω** ... Ans.

Problem 4.9:

For an air-filled rectangular waveguide of 2 cm × 1 cm, calculate the cut-off wavelength λ_c for TE_{10} and TM_{11} modes. Also calculate guide wavelength at 10 GHz.

Solution:

Given: a = 2 cm, b = 1 cm.

λ_c = Cut-off wavelength is given by,

$$\lambda_c = \frac{2}{\sqrt{\left(\frac{m}{a}\right)^2 + \left(\frac{n}{b}\right)^2}}$$

(i) For TE$_{10}$ mode:

$$\lambda_c = \frac{2}{\sqrt{\left(\frac{1}{2}\right)^2 + 0}}$$

{∵ m = 1 and n = 0 for TE$_{10}$ mode}

∴ $\lambda_c = 2a = 2 \times 2$

= 4 cm ... Ans.

(ii) For TM$_{11}$ mode:

$$\lambda_c = \frac{2}{\sqrt{\left(\frac{1}{a}\right)^2 + \left(\frac{1}{b}\right)^2}}$$

$$\lambda_c = \frac{2ab}{\sqrt{a^2 + b^2}}$$

$$= \frac{2 \infty 2 \infty 1}{\sqrt{(2)^2 + (1)^2}}$$

= 1.79 cms ... Ans.

(iii) **Guide wavelength (λ_g):**

$$\lambda_g = \frac{\lambda_o}{\sqrt{1 - \left(\frac{\lambda_o}{\lambda_c}\right)^2}}$$

$$\lambda_o = \frac{c}{f_o}$$

$$= \frac{3 \times 10^{10}}{10 \times 10^9}$$

= 3 cms ... Ans.

$$\lambda_g = \frac{3}{\sqrt{1 - \left(\frac{3}{4}\right)^2}}$$

= 4.5 cms ... Ans.

Problem 4.10:

Determine the scattering parameters for a 10 dB directional coupler. The directivity D = 30 dB. Assumes that it is lossless and the VSWR at each port is 1.0 under matched conditions. Designate the ports in the main guide as 1 or 2 and the ports in the auxiliary guide as 3 and 4.

Solution:

Given: Directivity, D = 30 dB
VSWR = 1.0

Directional coupler is 10 dB.

$$C = \text{Coupling factor}$$

$$C = -10 \log \frac{P_1}{P_4}$$

where,
P_i = Incident power = P_1
and P_f = Coupled power = P_4

∴
$$C = -10 \log \frac{P_1}{P_4}$$

$$= -10 \log \frac{P_i}{P_f}$$

$$10 = -10 \log \frac{P_1}{P_4}$$

∴
$$-10 = 10 \log \frac{P_1}{P_4}$$

or
$$10^{-1} = \frac{P_1}{P_4} = |S_{41}^2|$$

∴
$$S_{41} = \sqrt{10^{-1}}$$
$$= \sqrt{0.1}$$
$$= \mathbf{0.3162} \qquad \text{... Ans.}$$

or $S_{41} = S_{14} = 0.3162$ ...(4.35)
as all four ports are matched and lossless.

Now, D = Directivity = $10 \log \dfrac{P_4}{P_3}$

$$= 10 \log \frac{P_f}{P_b}$$

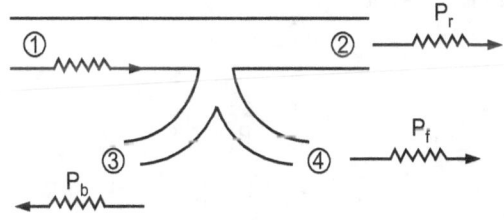

Fig. 4.44

where,

$$P_f = \text{Coupled power}$$

and

$$P_b = \text{Back power}$$

$$\therefore \quad 30 = 10 \log \frac{|S_{41}^2|}{|S_{31}^2|}$$

$$10^3 = \frac{|S_{41}^2|}{|S_{31}^2|}$$

or

$$|S_{31}^2| = \frac{(0.3162)^2}{10^3}$$

or

$$|S_{31}| = \mathbf{0.01}$$

or

$$\mathbf{S_{31} = S_{13} = 0.01} \quad \text{(As all ports are perfectly matched and lossless)}$$

$$\ldots (4.36)$$

$$\text{VSWR} = 1.0$$

$$S_{11} = \frac{\text{VSWR} - 1}{\text{VSWR} + 1}$$

$$= 0$$

Since all ports are perfectly matched to the junction.

$$\therefore \quad S_{11} = S_{22} = S_{33} = S_{44} = 0 \qquad \ldots (4.37)$$

$$\text{S-matrix} = \begin{bmatrix} S_{11} & S_{12} & S_{13} & S_{14} \\ S_{21} & S_{22} & S_{23} & S_{24} \\ S_{31} & S_{32} & S_{33} & S_{34} \\ S_{41} & S_{42} & S_{43} & S_{44} \end{bmatrix} = \begin{bmatrix} 0 & S_{12} & 0.01 & 0.3162 \\ S_{12} & 0 & S_{23} & S_{24} \\ 0.01 & S_{23} & 0 & S_{34} \\ 0.3162 & S_{24} & S_{34} & 0 \end{bmatrix}$$

$$\ldots (4.38)$$

∵ Main guides 1 and 2 ports and auxiliary guide as 3 and 4 port;

∴ $\mathbf{S_{13} = S_{31}, S_{12} = S_{21}, S_{23} = S_{32}, S_{42} = S_{24}, S_{43} = S_{34}}$ ... **Ans.**

Consider P_1 = Input power at port (1).

$$\therefore \quad P_1 = P_2 + P_3 + P_4$$

$$\therefore \quad \frac{P_1}{P_1} = \frac{P_2}{P_1} + \frac{P_3}{P_1} + \frac{P_4}{P_1}$$

$$\therefore \quad 1 = |S_{21}|^2 + |S_{31}|^2 + |S_{41}|^2$$

$$\therefore \quad 1 = |S_{21}|^2 + |0.01|^2 + |0.3162|^2$$

$$\therefore \quad |S_{121}|^2 = 0.8999$$
$$S_{21} = 0.9486$$
$$S_{21} = S_{12} = 0.9486$$

Using unitary property i.e. identify proper [S] [S*] = [I] on rows (II), (III) and (IV).

$$\left.\begin{array}{l} S_{12}^2 + S_{23}^2 + S_{24}^2 = 1 \\ (0.01)^2 + S_{23}^2 + S_{34}^2 = 1 \\ (0.3162)^2 + S_{24}^2 + S_{34}^2 = 1 \end{array}\right\}$$

and $\quad S_{12}^2 + S_{23}^2 + S_{24}^2 = 1$

Putting value of S_{23}, we get,

$$S_{12}^2 + S_{24}^2 - 10^{-4} = S_{34}^2$$

and $\quad S_{24}^2 + 10^{-1} = 1 - S_{34}^2$

$$S_{12}^2 - 10^{-1} - 10^{-4} = 2 S_{34}^2 - 1$$

or $\quad 2 S_{34}^2 = 1 + S_{12}^2 - 10^{-1} - 10^{-4}$

$$S_{34}^2 = \frac{1}{2}(1 + 0.899 - 0.1 - 0.0001)$$

$\therefore \quad S_{34} = S_{43} = 0.9486$

Now, from (4.39 A)

$$S_{23}^2 = 1 - S_{34}^2 - 10^{-4}$$
$$= 1 - 0.8999 - 10^{-4}$$
$$S_{23}^2 = 0.1$$

and $\quad S_{23} = S_{32} = 0.3162$

Also, $S_{24}^2 = 1 - 10^{-1} - S_{34}^2$
$$= 1 - 0.1 - 0.8999$$

$\Rightarrow \quad S_{24}^2 = 10^{-4}$ or $S_{24} = S_{42} = 0.01$

Thus, from equations (1) to (8), we have,

$$S_{11} = S_{22} = S_{33} = S_{44} = 0$$
$$S_{12} = S_{21} = 0.9486$$
$$S_{13} = S_{31} = 0.01$$
$$S_{14} = S_{41} = 0.3162$$

$S_{23} = S_{32} = 0.3162$

$S_{24} = S_{42} = 0.01$

$S_{34} = S_{43} = 0.9486$

Thus, the required S-parameters for 10 dB directional coupler are,

$$\begin{bmatrix} 0 & 0.9486 & 0.01 & 0.3162 \\ 0.9486 & 0 & 0.3162 & 0.01 \\ 0.01 & 0.3162 & 0 & 0.9486 \\ 0.3162 & 0.01 & 0.9486 & 0 \end{bmatrix}$$

Problem 4.11:

A signal of power 32 mW is fed into one of the collinear ports of a loss-less H-plane tee. Determine the powers in the remaining ports when other ports are terminated by means of matched load.

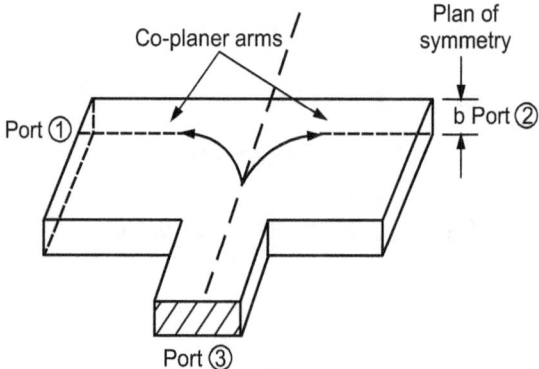

Fig. 4.45

Solution:

In H-plane tee port (1) and port (2) are the collinear ports.

Consider 32 mW power is fed into the port (1) of H-plane tee. Then port (2), which is the other collinear port and port (3) which is the side arm are terminated in matched load.

∴ $a_1 = 32$ mW and $a_2 = a_3 = 0$.

S-matrix for H-plane tee is,

$$[S] = \begin{bmatrix} \frac{1}{2} & -\frac{1}{2} & \frac{1}{\sqrt{2}} \\ -\frac{1}{2} & \frac{1}{2} & \frac{1}{\sqrt{2}} \\ \frac{1}{\sqrt{2}} & \frac{1}{\sqrt{2}} & 0 \end{bmatrix}$$

As we know,

$$[b] = [S] \cdot [a]$$

$$\begin{bmatrix} b_1 \\ b_2 \\ b_3 \end{bmatrix} = \begin{bmatrix} \dfrac{1}{2} & -\dfrac{1}{2} & \dfrac{1}{\sqrt{2}} \\ -\dfrac{1}{2} & \dfrac{1}{2} & \dfrac{1}{\sqrt{2}} \\ \dfrac{1}{\sqrt{2}} & \dfrac{1}{\sqrt{2}} & 0 \end{bmatrix} \begin{bmatrix} 32 \text{ mW} \\ 0 \\ 0 \end{bmatrix}$$

b_1 = Power at port (1),

$$b_1 = \frac{1}{2} a_1 - \frac{1}{2} a_2 + \frac{1}{\sqrt{2}} a_3$$

$$= \left(\frac{1}{2}\right)^2 \times 32 = \left(\frac{1}{2}\right)^2 |a_1|$$

$$= \frac{1}{4} \times 32$$

$$= 8 \text{ mW} \qquad \ldots \text{Ans.}$$

b_2 = Power at port (2),

$$b_2 = -\frac{1}{2} a_1 + \frac{1}{2} a_2 + \frac{1}{\sqrt{2}} a_3$$

$$b_2 = \left(\frac{1}{2}\right)^2 |a_1| = \left(-\frac{1}{2}\right)^2 \times 32$$

$$= 8 \text{ mW} \qquad \ldots \text{Ans.}$$

b_3 = Power at port (3),

$$b_3 = \frac{1}{\sqrt{2}} a_1 + \frac{1}{\sqrt{2}} a_2 + 0$$

$$\left(\frac{1}{2}\right)^2 |a_1| = b_3 = \frac{1}{2} \times 32$$

$$= 16 \text{ mW} \qquad \ldots \text{Ans.}$$

As we know that in the H-plane tee the output at port (3) is addition of the two inputs at port (1) and port (2) and these are added in phase.

i.e. $b_3 = b_1 + b_2$ i.e. 8 mW + 8 mW = 16 mW

Problem 4.12:

The collinear ports (1) and (2) of a magic tee are terminated by impedances of reflection coefficients $P_1 = 0.5$ and $P_2 = 0.6$. The difference port (4) is terminated by an impedance with reflection coefficient of 0.8. If 1 W power is feed at sum port (3). Calculate the power reflected at port (3) and the power divisions at the other ports.

Solution:

In Magic Tee,
[b] = [S] [a] is given by,

$$\begin{bmatrix} b_1 \\ b_2 \\ b_3 \\ b_4 \end{bmatrix} = \begin{bmatrix} 0 & 0 & \frac{1}{\sqrt{2}} & \frac{1}{\sqrt{2}} \\ 0 & 0 & \frac{1}{2} & -\frac{1}{\sqrt{2}} \\ \frac{1}{\sqrt{2}} & \frac{1}{\sqrt{2}} & 0 & 0 \\ -\frac{1}{\sqrt{2}} & \frac{1}{\sqrt{2}} & 0 & 0 \end{bmatrix} \begin{bmatrix} a_1 \\ a_2 \\ a_3 \\ a_4 \end{bmatrix}$$

$$\begin{bmatrix} \text{Reflected} \\ \text{power} \end{bmatrix} = \begin{bmatrix} \text{Scattering} \\ \text{matrix} \end{bmatrix} \begin{bmatrix} \text{Incident} \\ \text{power} \end{bmatrix}$$

$\rho_1 = \frac{a_1}{b_1}, \rho_2 = \frac{a_2}{b_2}$

$\therefore \quad a_1 = \rho_1 b_1, a_2 = \rho_2 b_2, |a_3|^2 = 1$ Watt and

$a_4 = \rho_4 b_4$

$\therefore \quad a_1 = 0.5 b_1, a_2 = 0.6 b_2, |a_3|^2 = 1$ Watt or

$$\therefore \begin{bmatrix} b_1 \\ b_2 \\ b_3 \\ b_4 \end{bmatrix} = \begin{bmatrix} 0 & 0 & \frac{1}{\sqrt{2}} & \frac{1}{\sqrt{2}} \\ 0 & 0 & \frac{1}{2} & -\frac{1}{\sqrt{2}} \\ \frac{1}{\sqrt{2}} & \frac{1}{\sqrt{2}} & 0 & 0 \\ -\frac{1}{\sqrt{2}} & \frac{1}{\sqrt{2}} & 0 & 0 \end{bmatrix} \begin{bmatrix} 0.5 b_1 \\ 0.6 b_2 \\ 1 b_3 \\ 0.8 b_4 \end{bmatrix}$$

By solving above matrix,

$b_1 = 0.6566$ V, $b_2 = 0.7576$ V, $b_3 = 0.6536$ V and $b_4 = 0.0893$ V.

$$\therefore \quad P_1 = |b_1|^2 = 0.4309 \text{ W}$$
$$P_2 = |b_2|^2 = 0.5738 \text{ W}$$
$$P_3 = |b_3|^2 = 0.3065 \text{ W}$$
$$P_4 = |b_4|^2 = 0.00797 \text{ W}$$

Problem 4.13:

An isolator has an insertion loss of 0.5 dB and an isolation of 30 dB. Determine the scattering matrix of the isolator if the isolated ports are perfectly matched to the junction.

Solution:

Given: Insertion loss $= 0.5 \text{ dB} = -20 \log |S_{21}|$

$$S_{21} = 10^{-0.5/20} = 10^{-0.025}$$

Isolation $= 30 \text{ dB} = -20 \log |S_{12}|$

or $\quad S_{12} = 10^{-30/20} = 10^{-1.5}$

$$S_{11} = S_{22} = 0$$

$\therefore \quad [S] = \begin{bmatrix} S_{11} & S_{12} \\ S_{21} & S_{22} \end{bmatrix} = \begin{bmatrix} 0 & 10^{-1.5} \\ 10^{-0.025} & 0 \end{bmatrix}$

Problem 4.14:

Determine the [S] of a 3-port circulator. Given insertion loss of 0.5 dB, isolation of 20 dB and VSWR of 2.

Solution:

Given: Insertion loss $= 0.5 \text{ dB}$

$$= -20 \log [S_{21}]$$

or $\quad |S_{21}| = 10^{-0.5/20}$

$$= 10^{-0.025}$$

Similarly, $\quad |S_{21}| = |S_{32}| = |S_{13}| = 10^{-0.025}$

Isolation $= 20 \text{ dB} = -20 \log |S_{12}|$

$$|S_{12}| = 10^{-20/20}$$
$$= 10^{-1}$$
$$= 0.1$$

Similarly, $\quad |S_{23}| = |S_{31}| = 0.1$

$$\rho = \frac{\text{VSWR} - 1}{\text{VSWR} + 1} = \frac{S - 1}{S + 1}$$

$$= \frac{2-1}{2+1}$$

$$= \frac{1}{3}$$

$$= 0.333$$

$$= |S_{11}| = |S_{22}| = |S_{33}|$$

$$\therefore \quad [S] = \begin{bmatrix} S_{11} & S_{12} & S_{13} \\ S_{21} & S_{22} & S_{23} \\ S_{31} & S_{32} & S_{33} \end{bmatrix} = \begin{bmatrix} 0.33 & 0.1 & 10^{-0.025} \\ 10^{-0.025} & 0.33 & 0.1 \\ 0.1 & 10^{-0.025} & 0.33 \end{bmatrix}$$

For a perfectly matched, non-reciprocal, lossless 3-port-circulator the [S] is given by,

$$[S] = \begin{bmatrix} 0 & 0 & S_{13} \\ S_{21} & 0 & 0 \\ 0 & S_{32} & 0 \end{bmatrix}$$

The terminal planes are so chosen as to make the phase angles of S_{13}, S_{21} and S_{23} zero.

i.e. $\quad S_{13} = S_{21} = S_{32} = 1$

$$\therefore \quad [S] = \begin{bmatrix} 0 & 0 & 1 \\ 1 & 0 & 0 \\ 0 & 1 & 0 \end{bmatrix}$$

Problem 4.15:

A directional coupler has the scattering matrix is given below. Find directivity, coupling, isolation.

$$[S] = \begin{bmatrix} 0.05 < 30 & 0.96 < 0 & 0.1 < 90 & 0.05 < 90 \\ 0.96 < 0 & 0.05 < 30 & 0.05 < 90 & 0.1 < 90 \\ 0.1 < 90 & 0.05 < 90 & 0.04 < 30 & 0.96 < 0 \\ 0.05 < 90 & 0.1 < 90 & 0.96 < 0 & 0.05 < 30 \end{bmatrix}$$

Solution:

$$\text{Coupling factor} = C = 10 \log \frac{P_1}{P_3}$$

$$= -20 \log |S_{13}|$$

$$C = -20 \log 0.1$$

$$= 20 \text{ dB}$$

$$\text{Directivity, D} = 10 \log\left(\frac{P_3}{P_4}\right)$$

$$= 20 \log \frac{|S_{13}|}{|S_{14}|} \text{ dB}$$

$$D = 20 \log \frac{0.1}{0.05}$$

$$= 6.02 \text{ dB}$$

$$\text{Isolation} = I = 10 \log \frac{P_3}{P_4}$$

$$= 10 \log \frac{P_1}{P_4}$$

$$I = -20 \log |S_{14}| \text{ dB}$$

$$= -20 \log |0.05|$$

$$I = 26.02 \text{ dB} \quad \text{... Ans.}$$

We know that,

$$I = D + C \text{ in dB}$$

Problem 4.16:

Double minimum method is used to determine the VSWR value on a waveguide. If the separation between two nulls is 3.5 cm and that between twice minimum power point is 2.5 mm. Determine the value of VSWR.

Solution:

$$\text{Distance between two minimas} = \frac{\lambda_g}{2} = 3.5 \text{ cm}$$

$$\therefore \quad \lambda_g = \text{Guide wavelength} = 7 \text{ cm}$$

$$d_2 - d_1 = 2.5 \text{ m}$$

$$\text{VSWR} = \frac{\lambda_g}{\pi (d_2 - d_1)} = \frac{7}{\pi \times 2.5 \times 10^{-1}}$$

$$= 89126$$

$$\therefore \quad \text{VSWR} = S = 8.9126 \quad \text{... Ans.}$$

Problem 4.17:

A section of transfer-band waveguide with dimensions a = 2.286 cm and b = 1.016 cm has perfectly conducting walls and is filled with a lossy dielectric whose conductivity is 367.5 µs/m and permittivity is 2.1 and permeability is 1.0. Find the attenuation factor of this waveguide in dB/m. For the dominant mode of propagation at a frequency of 9 GHz.

Solution:

Given:

$$a = 2.286 \text{ cm}$$

$$b = 1.016 \text{ cm}$$

$$\sigma = 367.5 \text{ µs/m}$$

$$\varepsilon_r = 2.1$$
$$\mu_r = 1.0$$
$$f = 9 \text{ GHz} = 9 \times 10^9 \text{ Hz}$$

For dominant mode (TE_{10}),

$$f_c = \frac{c}{2a}$$
$$= \frac{3 \times 10^8}{2 \times 2.286 \times 10^{-2}}$$
$$\mathbf{f_c = 6.5 \text{ GHz}}$$

$$\eta = \sqrt{\frac{\mu_0 \mu_r}{\varepsilon_0 \varepsilon_r}}$$
$$= \sqrt{\frac{4\pi \times 10^{-7} \times 1}{8.85 \times 10^{-12} \times 2.1}}$$
$$\mathbf{\eta = 260}$$

α_g = Attenuation for TE_{mn} mode because of low-loss dielectric in rectangular waveguide.

$$\alpha_g = \frac{\sigma \eta}{2\sqrt{1 - \left(\frac{f_c}{f}\right)^2}}$$

$$\alpha_g = \frac{367.5 \times 260}{2\sqrt{1 - \left(\frac{6.5}{9}\right)^2}}$$

$$\mathbf{\alpha_g = 96.7 \text{ dB/m}} \quad \text{... Ans.}$$

Problem 4.18:
A rectangular waveguide with dimensions 4 cm × 2.5 cm is excited by a microwave source propagating in the dominant mode. Following were the observations with a slotted line having the same dimensions of the above waveguide. Distance between two consecutive maxima is 1.618 cm. Calculate the frequency of operation.

Solution:
$$a = 4 \text{ cm}$$
$$b = 2.5 \text{ cm}$$

As mode is dominant.
∴ $TE_{mn} = TE_{10}$
∴ m = 1 and n = 0.

(i) Cut-off wavelength, λ_c:

$$\lambda_c = \frac{2}{\sqrt{\left(\frac{m}{a}\right)^2 + \left(\frac{n}{b}\right)^2}}$$

$$\lambda_c = \frac{2}{\sqrt{\left(\frac{1}{4}\right)^2 + 0}}$$

$$\lambda_c = 8 \text{ cm} \quad \text{... Ans.}$$

(ii) Guide wavelength, λ_g:

$$\lambda_g = \frac{\lambda_o}{\sqrt{1-\left(\frac{\lambda_o}{\lambda_c}\right)^2}}$$

$$\lambda_g^2 = \frac{\lambda_o^2}{1-\left(\frac{\lambda_o}{\lambda_c}\right)^2}$$

$$\lambda_g^2 - \left(\lambda_g \cdot \frac{\lambda_o}{\lambda_c}\right)^2 = \lambda_o^2$$

$$\lambda_g^2 = \lambda_o^2 + \left(\frac{\lambda_g \cdot \lambda_o}{\lambda_c}\right)^2$$

$$\lambda_g^2 = \lambda_o^2 \left(1 + \frac{\lambda_g^2}{\lambda_c^2}\right)$$

$$\lambda_o = \frac{\lambda_g}{\sqrt{1+\left(\frac{\lambda_g}{\lambda_c}\right)^2}}$$

$$\lambda_g = 1.618 \text{ cm} \quad \text{(Given)}$$

$$\therefore \quad \lambda_o = \frac{1.618}{\sqrt{1+\frac{(1.618)^2}{(8)^2}}}$$

$$\lambda_o = 1.58 \text{ cm} \quad \text{... Ans.}$$

$$\lambda_o = \frac{c}{f_o}$$

$$\therefore \quad 1.58 = \frac{3 \times 10^{10}}{f_o}$$

f_o = Frequency of operation

f_o = **18.6 GHz** ... Ans.

Problem 4.19:

An air filled rectangular waveguide has dimensions of 6 cm × 4 cm. It propagates a signal at 3 GHz. Compute the following for TE_{10} mode.

    (i) Cut-off frequency   (ii) Guide wavelength
    (iii) Phase constant   (iv) Phase velocity
    (v) Group velocity   (vi) Wave impedance.

Solution:

Given:
$$a = 6 \text{ cm}^2 = 6 \times 10^{-2} \text{ m}$$
$$b = 4 \text{ cm} = 4 \times 10^{-2} \text{ m}$$
$$f_o = 3 \text{ GHz} = 3 \times 10^9 \text{ Hz}$$

For rectangular waveguide TE_{10} is dominant mode (as $TE_{mn} = TE_{10}$, therefore, m=1 and n=0).

(i) Cut-off frequency, f_c:

f_c, for an air-filled waveguide operating at dominant mode is given by,

$$f_c = \frac{c}{2a} = \frac{3 \times 10^8}{2 \times 6 \times 10^{-2}}$$

$$f_c = 2.5 \text{ GHz} \qquad \text{... Ans.}$$

$$\therefore \quad \lambda_c = 0.12 \text{ m} \qquad \text{... Ans.}$$

(ii) Guide wavelength:

$$\lambda_o = \frac{c}{f_o}$$

$$\therefore \quad \lambda_o = \frac{3 \times 10^8}{3 \times 10^9}$$

$$\lambda_o = 0.1 \text{ m} \qquad \text{... Ans.}$$

$$\lambda_g = \frac{\lambda_o}{\sqrt{1 - \left(\frac{f_c}{f_o}\right)^2}} = \frac{0.1}{\sqrt{1 - \left(\frac{2.5}{3}\right)^2}}$$

$$\lambda_g = 0.18 \text{ m}$$

$$\lambda_g = 0.18 \qquad \text{... Ans.}$$

(iii) Phase constant (β_g):

$$\beta_g = \frac{\omega}{c}\sqrt{1 - \left(\frac{f_c}{f_o}\right)^2}$$

$$\beta_g = \frac{2\pi \times 3 \times 10^9}{3 \times 10^8}\sqrt{1 - \left(\frac{2.5}{3}\right)^2}$$

$$\beta_g = 34.74 \text{ nepers/m} \qquad \text{... Ans.}$$

(iv) Phase velocity, v_p:

$$v_p = \frac{c}{\sqrt{1 - \left(\frac{f_c}{f_o}\right)^2}}$$

$$= \frac{3 \times 10^8}{\sqrt{1 - \left(\frac{2.5}{3}\right)^2}}$$

∴ $v_p = 5.4 \times 10^8$ m/sec. ... Ans.

(v) Group velocity, (v_g):

$$v_p = \frac{\lambda_o}{\lambda_g} \times c$$

$$= \frac{0.1}{0.18} \times 3 \times 10^8$$

$v_g = 1.67 \times 10^8$ m/sec. ... Ans.

(vi) Wave impedance (Z_{TE}):

$$Z_{TE} = \frac{\eta}{\sqrt{1 - \left(\frac{\lambda_o}{\lambda_c}\right)^2}}$$

$$Z_{TE} = \frac{120\pi}{\sqrt{1 - \left(\frac{0.1}{0.18}\right)^2}}$$

$$= \frac{120\pi}{0.5528}$$

$Z_{TE} = 681.97\ \Omega$ ... Ans.

Problem 4.20:

An air filled rectangular waveguide of inside dimensions 7×3.5 cm operates in the dominant TE_{10} mode:

   (i) Find the cut-off frequency.
   (ii) Determine phase velocity of wave in the guide at 3.5 GHz.
   (iii) Determine the guide wavelength at the same frequency.

Solution:

Given:
     $a = 7$ cm $= 7 \times 10^{-2}$ m
     $b = 3.5$ cm $= 3.5 \times 10^{-2}$ m

For dominant mode, $m = 1, n = 0$.

(i) Cut-off frequency:

For an air filled waveguide,

$$f_c = \frac{c}{2a}$$

$$f_c = \frac{3 \times 10^8}{2 \times 7 \times 10^{-2}}$$

$$= 2.14\ \text{GHz}$$ ... Ans.

(ii) **Phase velocity, v_p:**

$$v_p = \frac{c}{\sqrt{1-\left(\frac{f_c}{f}\right)^2}}$$

$$= \frac{3 \times 10^8}{\sqrt{1-\left(\frac{2.14}{3.5}\right)^2}}$$

$$v_p = 3.78 \times 10^8 \text{ m/s} \qquad \ldots \text{Ans.}$$

(iii) **Guide wavelength, λ_g:**

$$\lambda_g = \frac{\lambda_o}{\sqrt{1-\left(\frac{f_c}{f_o}\right)^2}}$$

$$\lambda_o = \frac{c}{f_o}$$

$$= \frac{3 \times 10^8}{3.5 \times 10^9}$$

$$\therefore \quad \lambda_g = \frac{\frac{3 \times 10^8}{3.5 \times 10^9}}{\sqrt{1-\left(\frac{2.14}{3.5}\right)^2}}$$

$$\lambda_g = 10.9 \text{ cms} \qquad \ldots \text{Ans.}$$

SUMMARY

- This unit mainly consists of introduction to microwave systems, its advantages, frequency range and applications. Types of waveguides and the mode and parameters of rectangular waveguide is explained thoroughly along with the various field patterns. It also gives idea about the different microwave components like Tees with their s-parameter. Here, the concept of microwave filter and cavity resonator is also discussed.

POINTS TO REMEMBER

1. **Waveguide:** Waveguide is a hollow metallic tube of uniform cross-section for transmitting microwave frequencies.
2. **Most widely used waveguides:**

(i) Rectangular waveguide and (ii) Circular waveguide
3. **Modes:** The electromagnetic (EM) wave inside a waveguide can have an infinite number of patterns, called modes.
4. Waveguide support TE mode and TM mode.
5. In rectangular waveguide TEM mode does not exist.
6. Waveguide parameters are –
   (a) Cut-off wavelength (λ_c)
   (b) Guide wavelength (λ_g)
   (c) Phase velocity (V_p)
   (d) Wave impedance (Z_g) and
   (e) Dominant mode
7. **Waveguide excitation:** Waveguide excitation in desired mode is done by using coupling probes.
8. **Cavity resonator:** It is a metallic enclosure formed by shorting two ends of a section of a waveguide.
9. **Microwave attenuators:** It controls flow of microwave power either by reflecting it or absorbing it.
10. **Types of attenuators:** (i) Fixed attenuator, (ii) Variable type.
11. **Tee junction:** A T-junction is an intersection of three waveguide in the form of alphabet 'T'.
12. **Types of Tee junctions:**
    (i) H-plane Tee junction
    (ii) E-plane Tee junction
    (iii) E-H plane Tee junction (Magic-Tee junction)
    (iv) Rat-Race junction.
13. **H-plane Tee:** H-plane Tee is so called because the axis of the side arm is parallel to the H-field of the main transmission line.
14. **E-plane Tee:** E-plane Tee is so called because the axis of its side arm is parallel to the E-field of the main transmission line.
15. **Magic Tee:** It is also called as E-H plane tee or Hybrid Tee.
16. **Directional Coupler:** It is used to sample a small amount of microwave power.
17. **Performance parameters of directional couplers:**
    (i) Coupling factor (C)
    (ii) Directivity (D)
    (iii) Isolation (I)
18. **Isolator:** An isolator is (2) port device which provides very small amount of attenuation for transmission from port (1) to port (2) but provides maximum attenuation for transmission from port (2) to port (1).
19. **Circulator:** It is (3) or more port device that passes signals in one direction to the next adjacent port.
- Microwaves are electromagnetic waves whose frequency is range from 1 GHz to 1000 GHz.

- Microwaves are so called because the wavelength (λ) of a cm waves at microwave frequencies are very short.
- Applications of microwave –
  - (a) Broadcasting
  - (b) Communication
  - (c) Microwave heating
  - (d) Radar
  - (e) Radio Astronomy and
  - (f) Navigations

QUESTIONS

1. What is a waveguide?
2. What is a mode in waveguide?
3. What is TE and TM mode of propagation?
4. Why TEM mode cannot exist in the rectangular waveguide?
5. Draw different field patterns for TE mode.
6. Write a note on:
   (a) Waveguide transitions
   (b) Matched terminations
7. Explain the different power losses takes place in the rectangular waveguide.
8. What is a waveguide excitation?
9. Explain the neat sketch TE_{10} field pattern.
10. Explain the need of coupling probes and loops.
11. Write a note on microwave attenuators.
12. What is the significance of scattering matrix?
13. State and explain properties of s-parameters.
14. What are the various losses in a network? Give their expressions in term of s-parameters.
15. What are waveguide tees?
16. Explain E-plane and H-plane tees.
17. Explain magic tee and its applications.
18. What is directional coupler?
19. Write a note on microwave filter.
20. Explain the performance parameters of a directional coupler.
21. State the principle of Faraday's rotation.
22. Explain the construction and working of circulator.
23. Explain the construction and working of isolator.
24. Write a note on waveguide Iris.
25. Define re-entrant cavity.
26. Write a note on match terminations.
27. What is the need of waveguide twists and bends?

***

Unit V

MICROWAVE TUBES

5.1 Introduction

The conventional vacuum tubes, such as triodes, tetrodes and pentodes are still used as a single sources of low output power at low microwave frequencies. These tubes at microwave frequency range becomes less effective when used as an amplifier and oscillator. The output of oscillator drops rapidly with increase in frequency and an amplifier requires greater amount of driving power therefore the gain which is the ratio of output power to input power, falls. These are many factors which deteriorate the performance of the conventional tube (triodes, tetrode and pentodes) at ultral high frequency (UHF - 300-3000 MHz) or at microwave frequency. Special types of tubes such as two cavity klystron, multicavity klystron, reflex klystron, travelling wave tube and magnetron are used to overcome the high frequency limitations of conventional tubes.

5.2 High Frequency Limitations of Conventional Tubes

In order to see whether the conventional device like triode or transistor works satisfactorily at UHF or at microwave frequencies, consider a simple LC thank circuit and increase its operating frequency. Now, in this case we need to decrease the tank circuit parameters i.e. L or C $\left(\text{as } f = \dfrac{1}{2\pi\sqrt{LC}}, \text{ as f increases, L or C decreases}\right)$. But there is a certain limit upto which the values of L and C can be decrease below that point, the component lead inductance and intermediate capacitance affects the operation of circuit i.e. the circuit condition required for operation as an oscillator or as an amplifier may not be satisfied and the device at these frequencies become useless as an oscillator or as an amplifier.

Following are the reasons because of which conventional tubes cannot be used for frequencies higher than 100 MHz.

1. Interelectrode Capacitance Effect.
2. Lead Inductance Effect.
3. Transit Time Effect.
4. Gain Bandwidth Limitation.
5. Effect due to RF Losses.
6. Effect due to Radiation Losses.

1. Interelectrode Capacitance Effect:

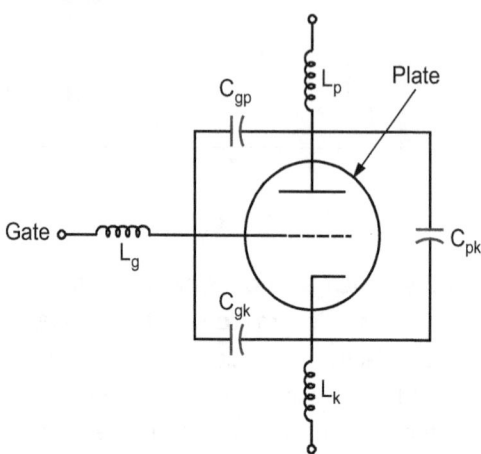

Fig. 5.1: Interelectrode Capacitance Effect

As frequency increases, the reactance of capacitance $X_c = \dfrac{1}{2\pi f_c}$, decreases and the output voltage decreases due to shunting effect. Because at higher frequencies X_c becomes almost a short. In Fig. 5.1 C_{gp}, C_{gk} and C_{pk} are the interelectrode capacitance i.e. the capacitance between the leads which comes into effect.

The effect of interelectrode capacitance can be minimised by reducing the interelectrode capacitances C_{gk}, C_{pk} and C_{gp}. These can be reduced by decreasing the area of the electrodes ($\because C = \varepsilon_o \varepsilon_r A/d$) or by increasing the distance between electrodes.

2. Lead Inductance Effect:

As frequency increases, the reactance $X_L = 2\pi f_L$ increases and hence the voltages appearing at the active electrode are less than the voltages at the base pins. This results in reduced gain for the tube amplifier. L_g, L_p and L_k are the lead inductance as shown in Fig. 5.1 that limit the performance of the tube.

The effect of lead inductance can be minimised by decreasing L. As $L = l/\mu_o\mu_r A$ therefore, L can be decreased by increasing A and decreasing 'l'. But this reduces the power handling capability.

3. Transit Time Effect:

Transit time is the time taken for electron to travel from cathode to anode as shown in Fig. 5.2.

$$\text{Transit time, } \tau = \frac{d}{v_o}$$

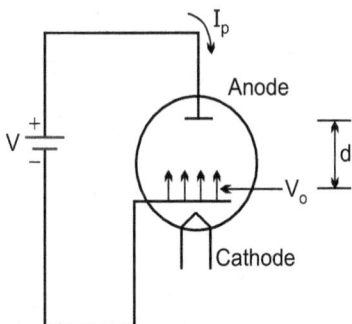

Fig. 5.2: Transit Time Effect

At low frequencies transit time is negligible, but at higher frequencies, the transit time 'τ' is appreciable which reduces the output.

To minimise transit time 'd' the separation between electrodes can be decreased and the plate to cathode potential 'V' can be increased. But as the distance between plate and cathode 'd' decreased, interelectrode capacitance. Therefore, a compromise is required between transit time and interelectrode capacitance.

4. **Gain Bandwidth Product Limitation:**

When the tuned circuit is not at resonance, at that time maximum gain is achieved. Consider the equivalent circuit shown in Fig. 5.3.

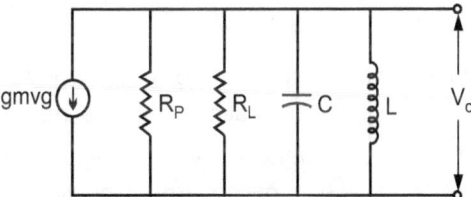

Fig. 5.3: Equivalent Circuit

Apply Laplace transform to equivalent circuit, then,

$$\frac{1}{z_0(s)} = y_0(s) = C_s + \frac{1}{L_s} + \frac{1}{R} \qquad \left(\text{where, } R = \frac{1}{R_L} + \frac{1}{R_p}\right)$$

$$= \frac{S^2 LCR + LS + R}{RLS}$$

$$z_0(s) = \frac{S/C}{S^2 + \frac{S}{CR} + \frac{1}{LC}}$$

If we find the roots of the quadratic equation in the denominator of $z_0(s)$, we will get two roots.

ω_1 and ω_2, $\omega_1 = -\dfrac{1}{2CR} - \sqrt{\left(\dfrac{1}{2CR}\right)^2 - \dfrac{1}{LC}}$

and

$\omega_2 = -\dfrac{1}{2CR} + \sqrt{\left(\dfrac{1}{2CR}\right)^2 - \dfrac{1}{LC}}$

$G = \dfrac{1}{R}$

∴ $\omega_1 = -\dfrac{G}{2CR} - \sqrt{\left(\dfrac{G}{2C}\right)^2 - \dfrac{1}{LC}}$

and $\omega_2 = -\dfrac{G}{2C} + \sqrt{\left(\dfrac{G}{2C}\right)^2 - \dfrac{1}{LC}}$

Bandwidth (BW) $= \omega_2 - \omega_1$

$= \dfrac{G}{C}$ for $\left(\dfrac{G}{2C}\right)^2 >> \dfrac{1}{LC}$

The maximum gain at resonance is $A_{max} = gm/G$.

∴ Gain bandwidth product $= A_{max} \cdot BW$

$= \dfrac{gm}{G} \times \dfrac{G}{C}$

$= gm/C$

The gain bandwidth product is thus independent of frequency. As gm and C are fixed for a particular circuits or tube, higher gain can be achieved by decreasing bandwidth.

In microwave circuit gain bandwidth limitation can be overcome by use of (i) re-entrant cavities, (ii) slow wave tubes for large gain over a large bandwidth.

5. Effect due to RF Losses:

RF losses are of two types:
1. Skin effect losses (conductor loss).
2. Dielectric losses.

   1. Skin effect losses: These losses occurs at higher frequencies at which the current has the tendency to confine itself to a smaller cross-section of the conductor towards its outer surface.

These losses can be reduced by increasing the size of the conductor.

   2. Dielectric losses: This occurs in various types of insulating materials used in the of device i.e. spacers, glass envelope, silicon or plastic encapsulations etc. As frequency increases dielectric losses are also increases.

These losses can be reduced by eliminating the tube base of reducing the surface area of glass.

6. Effect due to Radiation Losses:

Radiation losses increases with increase in frequency. This losses are reduced by using proper shielding or the tubes and its circuitry.

5.3 Classification of Tubes at Microwave Frequency

Microwave tubes are constructed so as to overcome the limitations of conventional and Ultra High Frequency (UHF) tubes. They differ from them in that, they make use of the transit time effect. In fact, large transit time is required for their operation.

The basic principle of operation of the microwave tubes involves transfer of power from source of D.C. voltage to a source of A.C. voltage by means of current density modulated electron beam. The same is achieved by accelerating electrons in a static electric field and retarding them in an A.C. field. The density modulation of the electron beam allows more electrons to be retarded by A.C. field than accelerated by A.C. field which therefore makes possible a net energy to be delivered to the A.C. electric field.

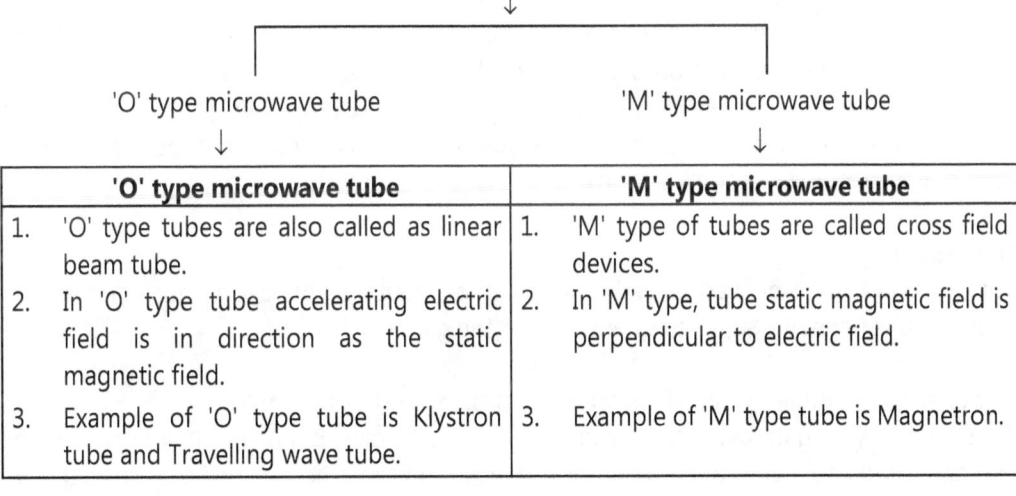

'O' type microwave tube	'M' type microwave tube
1. 'O' type tubes are also called as linear beam tube.	1. 'M' type of tubes are called cross field devices.
2. In 'O' type tube accelerating electric field is in direction as the static magnetic field.	2. In 'M' type, tube static magnetic field is perpendicular to electric field.
3. Example of 'O' type tube is Klystron tube and Travelling wave tube.	3. Example of 'M' type tube is Magnetron.

5.4 Klystrons

A klystron is a vacuum tube that can be used as generator or amplifier at microwave frequencies. There are two basic configurations of Klystron amplifier.

1. Two cavity or multicavity klystron and it is used as a low power microwave amplifier.
2. Reflex Klystron: It is used as low power microwave oscillator.

5.4.1 Two Cavity Klystron Amplifier

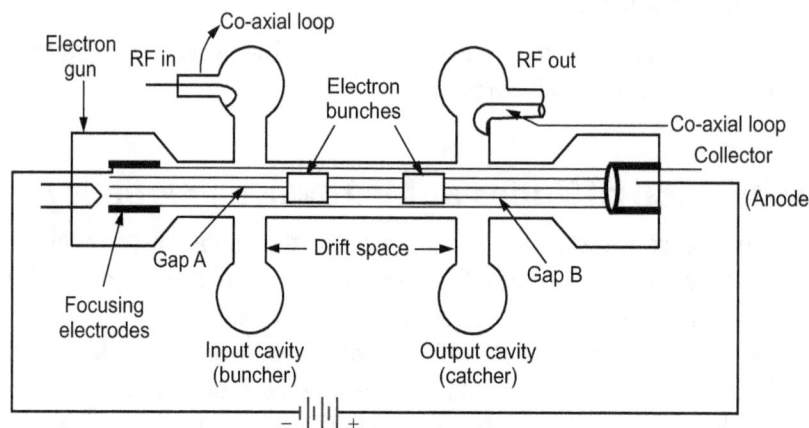

Fig. 5.4: Two Cavity Klystron Amplifier

A two cavity klystron amplifier is shown in Fig. 5.4 which is basically a velocity modulated tube. Here a high velocity electron beam is formed, focussed and send down along a glass tube, through an input cavity (buncher cavity), a field free drift space and an output cavity (catcher) to the collector electrode/anode. The anode is kept at a positive potential with respect to cathode. The electron beam passes through a gap 'A' consisting of two grids of the buncher cavity separated by a very small distance and two other grids of the catcher cavity with a small gap 'B'. The input and output are taken from the tube via. resonant cavities with addition of coupling loops.

Operation:
The RF signal to be amplified is used for exciting the input buncher cavity which develops an alternating voltage of a signal frequency across the gap 'A'.

Effect of gap voltage on the electron beam passing through gap 'A':
Consider an Applegate diameter shown in Fig. 5.5. At point 'B' on the RF input cycle, the alternating voltage is zero and going positive. At this instant, the electric field across gap 'A' is zero and an electron which passes through gap 'A' at this instant is unaffected by the RF signal. Let this electron be called the **reference electron 'e_R'** which travels with an unchanged velocity $v_0 = \sqrt{\dfrac{2eV}{m}}$ where, v = Anode to cathode voltage.

At point 'C' of an RF input cycle an electron which leaves gap 'A' later than reference electron e_R called **later electron 'e_l'** is subjected to the maximum positive RF voltage and hence travels towards gap 'B' with an increased velocity (v > v₀) and this electron tries to overtake the reference electron e_R.

Similarly, an early electron e_e that passes the gap A slightly before the reference electron e_R is subjected to a maximum negative field. Hence, this early electron is decelerated and travels with a reduced velocity 'v_0'. This electron e_e falls back and reference electron e_R catches up with the early electron.

Therefore, the velocity of electron varies in accordance with RF input voltage, resulting in **velocity modulation** of electron beam. As a result of these actions, the electrons in the bunching limit (i.e. between point A' and C') gradually bunch together as they travel down the drift space, from gap A to gap B. The pulsating stream of electrons pass through gap 'B' and excite oscillations in the output cavity (cathcer cavity). The density of electrons passing the gap 'B' vary cyclically with time i.e. electron beam contains an A.C. current and that is modulated. The drift space converts the velocity modulation into current modulation.

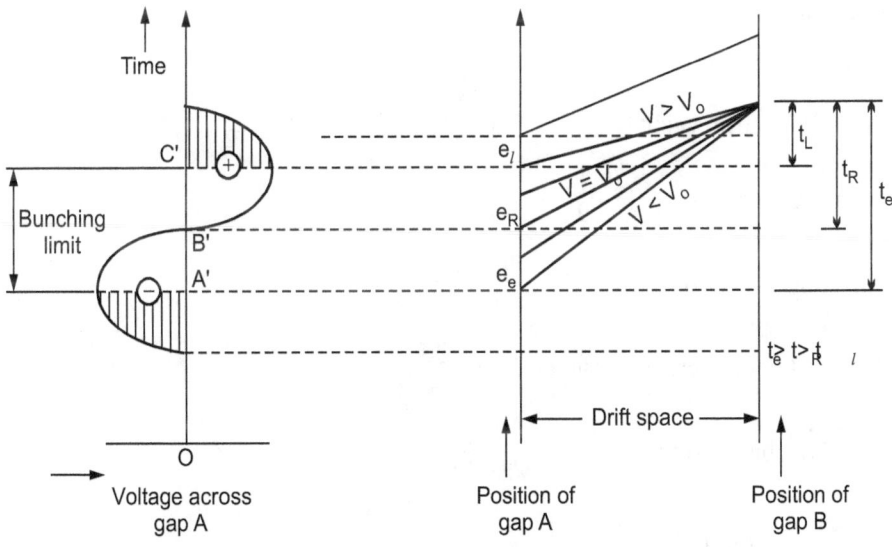

Fig. 5.5: Apple Gate Diameter of Klystron Amplifier

Bunching occurs only once/cycle, centered around the reference electron. With proper design, (optimum gap width, anode to cathode voltage, drift space lengths etc.), a little RF power applied to the buncher cavity results in large beam currents at the catcher cavity with a considerable power gain.

Performance Characteristics:
1. Frequency: 250 MHz to 100 GHz (60 GHz nominal).
2. Power: 10 kW to 500 kW (CW), 30 MW (pulsed).
3. Power gain: 15 dB - 70 dB (60 dB nominal).
4. Bandwidth: Limited 10-60 MHz because of cavity resonator are being used and generally used in fixed frequency applications.
5. Noise figure: 15-20 dB.
6. Theoretical efficiency: 58% (30 to 40% nominal)

Multicavity Klystron use more than two cavities (upto six), with more bunching, voltage amplification and hence more power and gain, efficiency (η) and Bandwidth (BW).

Applications:
1. As power output tube –
    (i) In UHF TV transmitters.
    (ii) In trophosphere scatter transmitters.
    (iii) Satellite communication ground stations.
    (iv) Radar transmitters.
2. As power oscillator (5-50 GHz) if used as Klystron oscillator.

Important Formula:
Cavity Klystron Amplifier:

$$\text{Electron velocity, } v_0 = \sqrt{\frac{2eV_c}{m}} = 0.593 \times 10^3 \sqrt{v_0}$$

$$\text{Gap transit angle, } \theta_g = \omega \frac{d}{v_0}$$

$$\text{Beam coupling coefficients, } \beta_1 = \frac{\sin(\theta_g/2)}{\theta_g/2}$$

$$\text{D.C. transit angle between cavities, } \theta_c = \frac{\omega L}{v_0}$$

$$\text{Bunching parameter, } X = \frac{\beta_i v_i}{2v_0} \theta_0$$

$$\text{Input voltage, } V = \frac{2v_0}{\beta_0 \theta_0}$$

$$\text{Voltage gain, } A_v = \frac{|v_2|}{|v_1|} = \frac{\beta_0 I_2 R_{sh}}{v_1} = \frac{\beta_0^2 \theta_0 J_1(x)}{R_0(x)} R_{sh}$$

$$\text{Efficiency, } \eta = \frac{P_{out}}{P_{in}} = \frac{\beta_0 I_2 v_2}{\beta_0 I_0 v_0} = \frac{0.58 \, v_2}{v_0}$$

$$\text{Electron gain anode voltage for maximum power transfer} = \left(\frac{v_1}{v_0}\right)_{max} = \frac{3.68}{2n\pi - \pi/2}$$

Output Current and Power of Two Cavity Klystron:

$$I_2 = \frac{1}{2} \frac{I_0 \omega}{V_0 \omega_q} \beta_o^2 |v_1|$$

$$P_{out} = |I_2|^2 R_{sh\ell} = \frac{1}{4} \left(\frac{I_0 \omega}{V_0 \omega_q}\right)^2 \beta_o^2 |v_1|^2 R_{sh\ell}$$

$$\eta = \frac{P_{out}}{P_{in}} = \frac{P_{out}}{I_0 V_0} = \frac{1}{4}\left(\frac{I_0}{V_0}\right)\left(\frac{v_1 \omega}{V_0 \omega_n}\right)^2 \beta_o^2 R_{sh\ell}$$

5.4.2 Two Cavity Klystron Oscillator

A Klystron amplifier can be covered into an oscillator by feeding back a part of catcher output into the buncher in proper phase so as to satisfy **Barkhausen Criterion.** The schematic is same as Klystron amplifier except that a feedback loop needs to be added. The feedback must be so adjusted to give correct polarity and amplitude which basically depends on the cavity tuning and the various D.C. voltages. It 'θ' is the total phase shift in the resonators and the feedback cable, the criterion for oscillation is,

$$\theta + \alpha + \pi/2 = 2\pi n \text{ radians} \qquad \ldots (5.1)$$

Also, a small change in D.C. accelerating voltage causes a change in frequency since then transit angle 'α' varies. In that case the frequency of oscillation will shift in such a way to obtain a new value of 'θ' so as to satisfy equation (5.1). Since two resonators having the same resonant frequency are coupled here, the input impedance looking into either resonator circuits will vary with frequency as shown in Fig. 5.6.

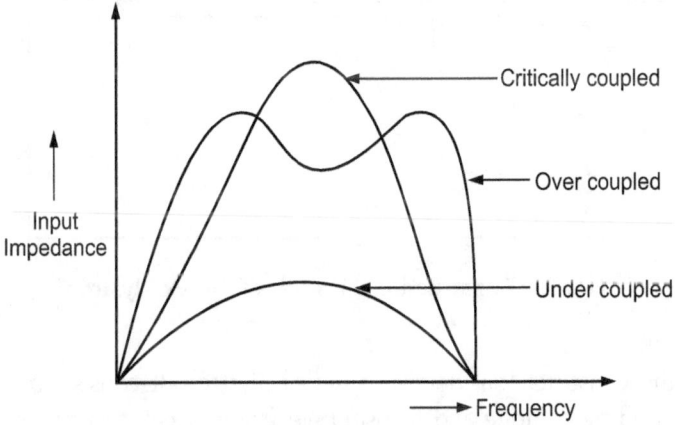

Fig. 5.6: Frequency Vs. Impedance

When the resonators are over coupled the oscillators can be obtained over wide range. If the resonators are critically coupled then almost linear variation in frequency with accelerating voltage, making frequency modulation possible.

High frequency stability of oscillator is obtained by controlling the temperature of the resonators and also by use of regulated power supply.

Tuning of oscillator is done by adjusting grid voltage, D.C. accelerating voltage and the tuning of the two resonators.

5.4.3 Reflex Klystron

The reflex klystron is single cavity variable frequency microwave generator of low power and low efficiency.

This is widely used in application where variable frequency is desired, such as:
1. In Radar receiver.
2. Local oscillator in microwave receivers.
3. Signal source in microwave generator of variable frequency.
4. Portable microwave links and
5. Pump oscillators in parametric amplifier.

Construction:

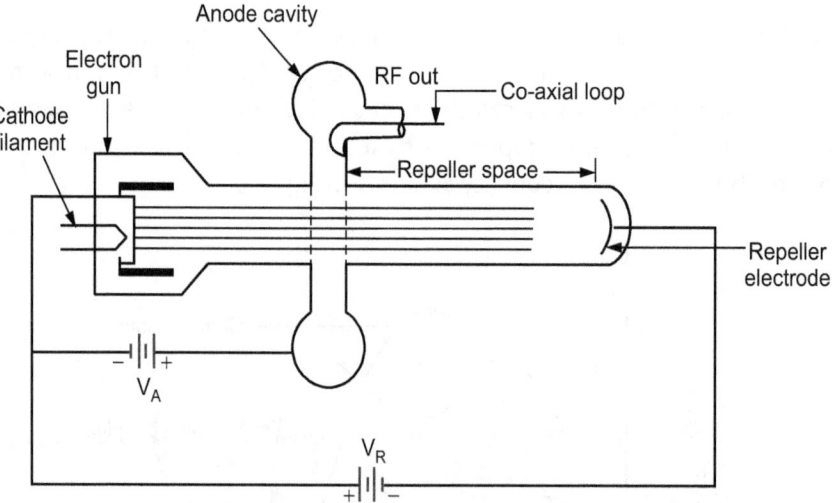

Fig. 5.7: Constructional Details of Reflex Klystron

Fig. 5.7 shows the constructional details of Reflex Klystron. It consists of an electron gun, filament surrounded by cathode and focusing electrode at cathode potential. The electron beam is accelerated towards the anode cavity which is at positive potential. After passing the gap in the cavity, electrons travel towards a repeller electrode which is at higher negative potential V_R. The electrons never reach the repeller because of negative field and returned back towards the gap. Under suitable conditions the electrons give more energy to the gap than they took from the gap on their forward journey and oscillations are sustained.

Operation:

It is assumed that the oscillations are set up in the tube initially due to noise or switching transients and these oscillations are sustained by device operation. This can be explained by apple gate diagram as shown in Fig. 5.8.

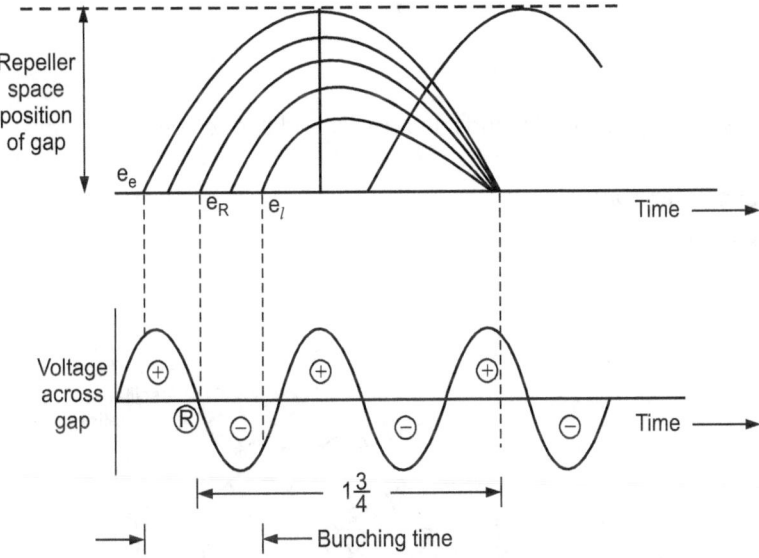

Fig. 5.8: Apple Gate Diagram

The RF voltage that produced across the gap by the cavity oscillations act on the electron beam to cause velocity modulation. 'e_R' is reference electron that passes through the gap when the gap voltage is '0' and going negative. Electron 'e_R' is unaffected by the gap voltage. This moves towards the repeller and gets reflected by the negative voltage on the repeller. It returns and passes through the gap for a second time.

The early electron 'e_e' that passes through the gap before the reference electron 'e_R' experiences a maximum positive voltage across the gap and this electron is accelerated. It moves with greater velocity and penetrates deep into repeller space. The return time for electron 'e_e' is greater as the depth of penetration into the repeller space is more. Hence, 'e_e' and 'e_R' appears at the gap for the second time at the same time.

The late electron 'e_l' that passes the gap later than reference electron 'e_R' experiences a maximum negative voltage and moves with a retarding velocity. The return time is shorter as penetration into repeller space is less and catches up with e_R and e_e electrons forming electron bunch. Bunches occurs once per cycle centered around the reference electron 'e_R' and these bunches transfer maximum energy to gap to get sustained oscillation.

For oscillations to be sustained, the time taken by electrons to travel into repeller space and back to the gap (called transit time) must have an optimum value. This factor is not important in a Klystron amplifier but it assumes a great importance here.

In general, the optimum transit time should be,

$$\tau = n + \frac{3}{4}$$

where,
n is any integer. This depends on repeller and anode voltage.

Operating Characteristics:
1. Voltage Characteristics:

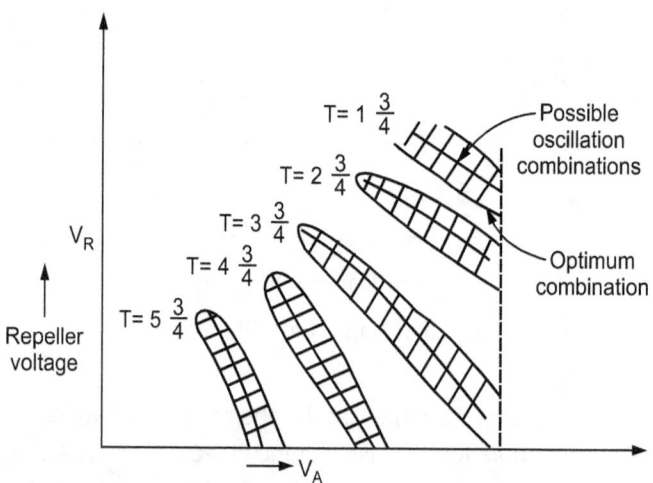

Fig. 5.9: Voltage Characteristics of Reflex Klystron

Oscillations can be obtained only for specific combinations of anode and repeller voltage that gives a favourable transit time ($\tau = n + 3/4$).

The shaded areas show possible oscillation combinations and heavy linear shows optimum combinations. if n = 1, 2, 3, ..., then there is a different modes such as $1\frac{3}{4}, 2\frac{3}{4}, 3\frac{3}{4}$. The earlier modes i.e. $1\frac{3}{4}$, this mode which gives the larger power which is the advantage but this mode also required higher voltage and increases insulation problems and reduces the efficiency (η). As a result the modes corresponding to n = 2 or n = 3 are most widely used. Because these mode needs moderate voltage.

2. **Power Output and Frequency Characteristics:**

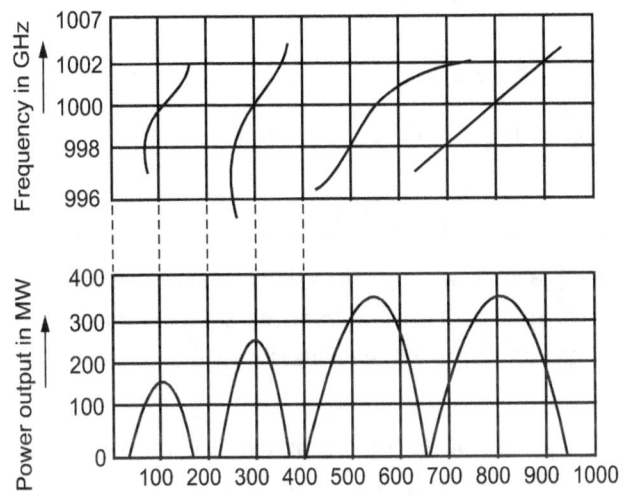

Fig. 5.10: Power Output and Frequency Characteristics of Reflex Klystron

Fig. 5.10 shows two characteristics.
1. Repeller voltage Vs. Output power i.e. mode curve and
2. Repeller voltage Vs. Frequency i.e. frequency characteristics.

The frequency of resonance of the cavity decides the frequency of oscillations. If the repeller voltage changes, there is slightly variations in frequency. Therefore, it is possible to use reflex klystron as a voltage tuned oscillator or frequency modulated oscillator.

5.4.4 Equivalent Circuit of Reflex Klystron

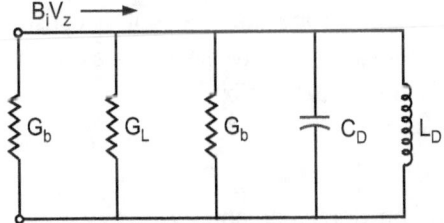

Fig. 5.11: Equivalent Circuit of Reflex Klystron

The equivalent circuit of a reflex klystron is shown in Fig. 5.11. It consists of klystron in parallel with beam loading conductance 'G_b', copper cavity losses G_o, load conductance 'G_L' and parallel tuned circuit.

5.4.5 Performance Characteristics of Reflex Klystron
1. Frequency range: 4 to 200 GHz.
2. Output power: 1.0 mW to 2.5 W.
3. Theoretical efficiency (η): 22.78%.
4. Practical efficiency (η): 10% to 20%.
5. Tuning range: 5 GHz at 2 Watts to 30 GHz at 10 mW.

5.5 Travelling Wave Tube (TWT)

Klystrons are essentially a narrow band devices whereas TWTs are broadband devices in which there is no cavity resonators. The interaction space in the TWT is extended and the electron beam exchanges energy with the RF wave over the full length of the tube.

The TWT makes the use of distributed interaction between an electron beam and a travelling wave. To prolong the interaction between an electron beam and the RF field it is necessary to ensure that they are both travelling in the same direction with nearly with the same velocity. Thus, it differs from the Klystron in which the electron beam travels and RF field remains stationary.

The electron beam travels with a velocity governed by the anode voltage. The RF field propagates with a velocity equals to the velocity of light. The interaction between the RF field and the moving electron beam will take place only when the RF field is retarded by some means. Normally, slow wave structures are utilized to retard the RF field, like helix or a waveguide arrangement.

5.5.1 Constructional Features of TWT
Fig. 5.12 shows the schematic electrode arrangement. It consists of electron gun which is used to produce a narrow constant velocity electron beam. This electron beam is in turn passed through the center of a long axial helix.

A magnetic focussing field is provided to –
1. prevent the beam from spreading and
2. guide it through the center of the helix.

Helix: Helix is a loosely wound thin conducting helical wire, which acts as a slow wave structure.

The signal which is to be amplified is applied to the one end of the helix and output is take at the other end of helix under appropriate operating conditions.

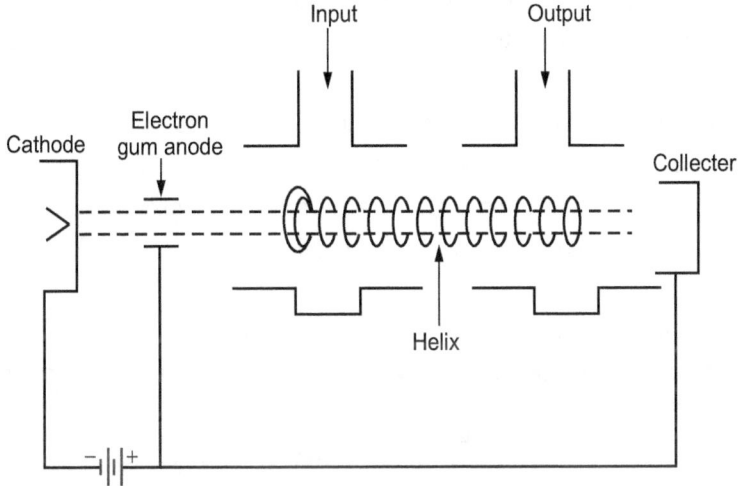

Fig. 5.12: Schematic Electrode Arrangement of TWT

Operation:

When the applied RF signal propagates around the turns of the helix, it produces an electric field at the center of the helix. The RF field propagates with the velocity of light. The axial electric field due to RF signals travels with velocity of light multiplied by the ratio of helix pitch/helix circumference when the velocity of electron beam travelling through the helix is at the same rate as that of the axial field, then interaction takes place between them in such a way that on an average the electron beam delivers energy to the RF wave on the helix.

Thus, the signal wave grows and amplified output is obtained at the output of the TWT.

The axial phase velocity 'v_p' is given by,

$$v_p = v_c (Pitch/2\pi r)$$

where, r = Radius of the helix which is essentially constant over a range of frequency. This characteristics of helix slow wave structure enables TWT to have broadband operation.

Advantages of Helix:

It provides less change in 'v_p' with frequency, therefore, it is preferred over other slow wave structure for TWT.

As electron passes across the gap, velocity modulation and bunching take place. When electron enters the helix tube, an interaction takes place between the moving axial electric field and the moving electrons. The electrons transfer energy to the wave on the helix. This interaction causes the signal wave on the helix to become larger. The electrons entering the helix at zero field are not affected by the signal wave, those electrons entering the helix as the accelerating field are accelerated and those at retarding field are decelerated.

As electrons travel further along the helix, the bunching process continues and the bunching shifts the phase by $\pi/2$. The microwave energy of the electrons is delivered by electron bunch to the wave on the helix and the RF wave on the helix grows exponentially and also reaches its maximum at the output end. Thus, amplification of RF wave is accomplished.

5.5.2 Wave Modes in TWT

The slow wave structure helix can be represented by a distributed loss-less transmission line.

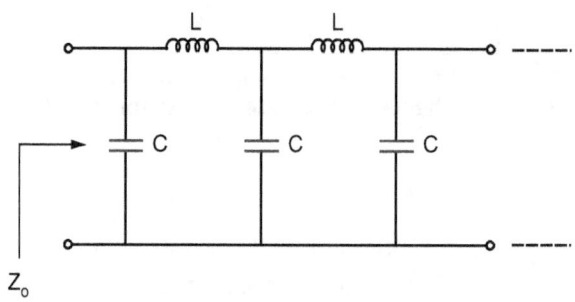

Fig. 5.13

Basically, there are four modes of traveling wave in TWT. Therefore, four propagation constants 'γ' for four modes of travelling wave are given by,

1. $\qquad \gamma_1 = -\beta_e C \cdot \dfrac{\sqrt{3}}{2} + j\beta_e [1 + C/2] \qquad$ ... (5.2)

2. $\qquad \gamma_2 = \beta_e C \cdot \dfrac{\sqrt{3}}{2} + j\beta_e [1 + C/2] \qquad$ ... (5.3)

3. $\qquad \gamma_3 = j\beta_e [1 - C] \qquad$ ... (5.4)

4. $\qquad \gamma_4 = -j\beta_e [1 - C^3/4] \qquad$ ... (5.5)

where,

$$C = \left[\dfrac{I_0 Z_0}{4 V_0}\right]^{1/3} \qquad \text{Travelling wave gain parameter}$$

$$\beta_e = \dfrac{\omega}{\beta_0} \qquad \text{Phase constant of velocity}$$

From equation (5.2) to equation (5.5) it is concluded that,

1. The wave corresponds to γ_1 is a forward wave and its amplitude grows exponentially with distance. The growing wave propagates at a phase velocity slightly lower than the electron beam velocity and the energy flows from electron beam to the wave.

2. Wave corresponds to γ_2 is also a forward wave, but its amplitude decays exponentially. The decaying wave propagates at a phase velocity slightly lower than the electron beam velocity but the energy flows from waves to electron beam.

3. Wave corresponds to γ_3 is also a forward wave, but its amplitude remains constant. The constant amplitude wave travels at a velocity slightly higher than the electron beam velocity but no net energy exchange occurs between wave and electron beam.

4. Wave corresponds to γ_4, is a backward wave and there is no change of amplitude. The backward wave progresses in the negative z-direction with a velocity slightly higher than the velocity of electron beam.

5.5.3 Comparison between Klystron Tube and TWTA (Travelling Wave Table Amplifier)

	Klystron Tube		TWTA
1.	It is a narrowband device.	1.	It is a wideband device.
2.	Cavity resonators are used for velocity modulation.	2.	Non-resonant slow wave structures are used for velocity modulation.
3.	Interaction between electron beam and RF field occurs only across the cavity gap.	3.	Continuous interaction between electron beam and RF field takes place.
4.	The wave in Klystron is not a propagating wave.	4.	The wave in TWTA is propagating wave.
5.	An average output power is 500 kW.	5.	Upto 10 kW average output power.
6.	Power gain is about 30 dB.	6.	Power gain is about 60 dB.
7.	Efficiency is about 20 to 40%.	7.	Efficiency is about 5 to 20%.
8.	**Applications:** (i) Used as power output tube in radar transmitters and satellite ground stations. (ii) Used as power oscillator.	8.	**Applications:** (i) Used as low noise amplifier (RF) for broadband applications in microwave receiver. (ii) Used as repeater amplifier in co-axial cable.

5.6 Magnetrons

Magnetron is the cross-field type of microwave tube in which electric and magnetic fields are perpendicular to each other. Magnetrons provide microwave oscillation of very high peak power.

In magnetron, like a TWT the electrons are made to interact with RF field for a longer duration and because of which higher efficiency can be obtained. These are three types of magnetrons.

1. Negative Resistance Type.
2. Cyclotron Frequency Type.
3. Travelling Wave or Cavity Type.

1. Negative Resistance Magnetron: Make use of negative resistance between two anode segments but have low efficiency and are useful only at low frequencies. (< 500 MHz).

2. Cyclotron Frequency Magnetron: These are useful only for frequencies greater than 100 MHz.

3. Cavity Magnetron: Cavity magnetron depends upon the interaction of electrons with a rotating electro-magnetic field of constant angular velocity. These provide oscillations of very high peak power and hence are very useful in radar applications.

5.6.1 Cavity Magnetron

Cavity Magnetron is of cylindrical configuration with a thick cylindrical cathode at the centre and co-axial cylindrical block of copper as anode. In the anode block are cut a number of holes and slots which acts as resonant anode cavities. The space between the anode and cathode is the interaction space. One of the cavity is connected to a co-axial line or waveguide for extracting the output. It is a cross field device as the electric field between anode and cathode is radians whereas the magnetic field produced by a permanent magnetic is axial. The permanent magnet is placed such that the magnetic lines are parallel to the vertical cathode and perpendicular to the electric field between cathode and anode. The construction is shown in Fig. 5.14 and Fig. 5.15.

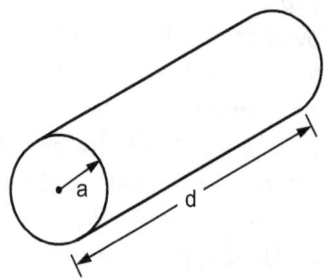

Fig. 5.14: Constructional Detail

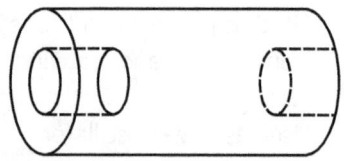

Fig. 5.15: Magnetic Flux Lines in Magnetron

Operation:

The cavity magnetron shown in Fig. 5.14 has 8 cavities that are tightly coupled to each other. If ϕ_V is the relative phase change of the A.C. electric field across adjacent cavities, then,

$$\phi_V = \frac{2\pi n}{N}$$

where,

$$n = 0, \pm 1, \pm 2, \pm \left(\frac{N}{2} - 1\right), \pm \frac{N}{2}$$

i.e. N/2 mode of resonance can exist if N is an even number.

If
$$n = \frac{N}{2}$$

$$\phi_V = \pi$$

This mode of resonance is called the π-mode.

If $n = 0$, $\phi_V = 0$.

This is the zero mode, meaning there will be no RF electric field between anode and cathode, called as the fringing field and is of no use in magnetron operation.

Depending on the relative strengths of the electric and magnetic fields, the electrons emitted from the cathode and moving the interaction space as shown in Fig. 5.16.

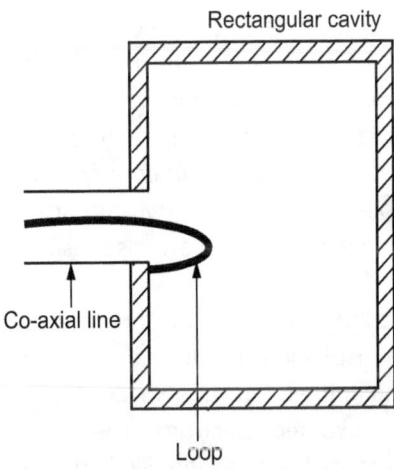

Fig. 5.16: Electron Trajectories in Presence of Crossed Electrical Magnetic Fields
(a) Electron Magnetic Field, (b) Small Magnetic Field, (c) Magnetic Field = B_c, (d) Excessive Magnetic Field

When magnetic field B = 0, the electron travels straight from cathode to the anode due to the radial electric field force acting on it which is indicated by trajectory 'a' in Fig. 5.16. If the magnetic field strength is increased slightly i.e. moderate value of B, it will exert a lateral force bending the path of electron as shown by path 'b' in Fig. 5.16. The radius of the path is given by $R = \dfrac{mV}{eB}$ that varies directly with electron velocity and inversely as the magnetic field strength.

If the strength of the magnetic field is made sufficiently high so as to prevent the electrons from reaching the anode as shown by path 'c' in Fig. 5.16, the anode current becomes zero. The magnetic field required to return electrons back to cathode just grazing the surface of the anode is called the **critical magnetic field (B_c), cut-off magnetic field**. If the magnetic field is made larger than the critical field ($B > B_c$), the electron experiences a greater rotational force and may return back to cathode quite faster. As such electrons may cause back heating of the cathode. This can be avoided by switching off the heater supply after commencement oscillation, which in turns avoid fall in the emitting efficiency of the cathode. All above explanation is for a static case is the absence of the RF field in the cavity of magnetron.

Assuming RF oscillations to have been initiated due to some noise transient within the magnetron, the oscillations will be sustained by device operation. Self consistent oscillations will be obtained if the phase difference between adjacent anode poles is $\dfrac{n\pi}{4}$, where n is an integer. When n = 4, results in π-mode of operation which is shown in Fig. 5.17. Here, the anode poles are π radians apart in phase. The **dotted electron paths refer to the case of static field with no RF field.** The solid paths refer to the electron trajectories in the presence of RF oscillations in the interaction space. The electron 'a' is seen to be slowed down in presence of oscillations thus transferring energy to the oscillations, during its longer journey from cathode to anode. Such electrons which participate in transferring energy to the RF field are called **favoured electrons** and are responsible for **bunching effect.**

An electron 'b' is accelerated by the RF field and instead of imparring energy to the oscillations takes energy from oscillations resulting in increased velocity. Hence, bends more sharply, spends very little time in the interaction space and is returned back to the cathode. Such electrons are called unfavoured electrons. These electrons do not participate in bunching process rather they cause back heating. Similarly, an electron 'c' which is emitted a little latter to be in correct position moves faster and tries to catch up with electron 'a' and an electron emitted at 'd' will be slowed down to fall back in step with electron 'a'. This results in all favoured electrons like a, c, d, to form a bunch one for each two anodes as shown in Fig. 5.18. This process is called **phase focussing effect** corresponds to reference electrons 'a'.

The phase focussing effect of these favoured electrons imparts enough energy to the RF oscillations so that they are sustained.

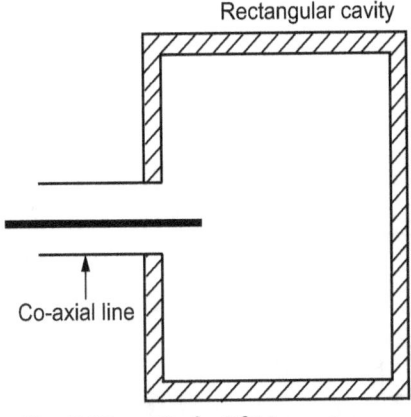

Fig. 5.17: π Mode Of Magnetron

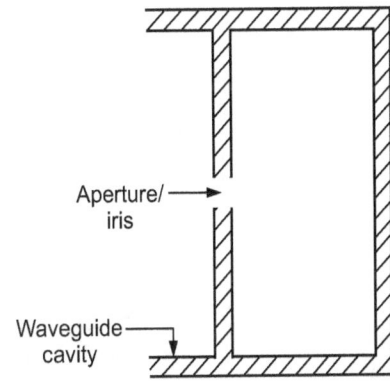

Fig. 5.18: Phase Focussing Effect

SOLVED PROBLEMS

Problem 5.1:

A 2-cavity Klystron amplifier has the following characteristics:

$$\begin{aligned}
\text{Voltage gain} &= 15 \text{ dB} \\
\text{Input power} &= 5 \text{ mV} \\
R_{sh} \text{ of input cavity} &= 30 \text{ k}\Omega \\
R_{sh} \text{ of output cavity} &= 40 \text{ k}\Omega \\
R_L \text{ (load impedance)} &= 40 \text{ k}\Omega
\end{aligned}$$

Determine:

(i) The input r.m.s. voltage

(ii) The output r.m.s. voltage.

(iii) The power delivered to the load.

Solution:

(i)
$$P_{in} = \frac{V_1^2}{R_{sh}}$$

or
$$V_1^2 = P_{in} \times R_{sh}$$

$$V_1^2 = 5 \times 10^{-3} \times 30 \times 10^3$$

$$= \mathbf{150 \text{ V}} \quad \text{... Ans.}$$

∴ $V_1 = \mathbf{12.25 \text{ V}}$

(ii) $$A_V = 20 \log \frac{V_2}{V_1} \text{ dB}$$

$$15 = 20 \log \frac{V_2}{12.25}$$

or $V_2 = $ **68.89 V** ... Ans.

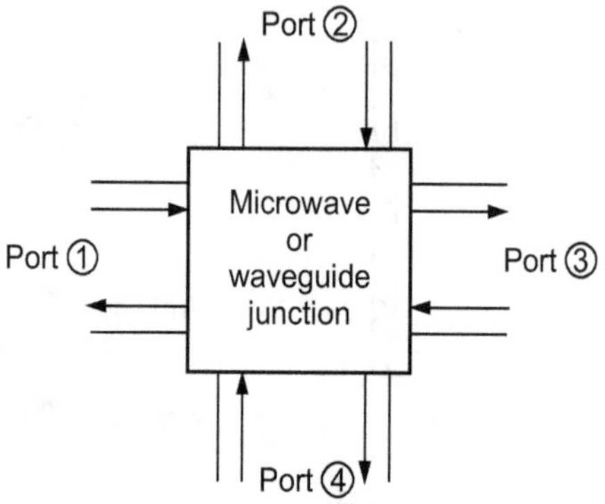

Fig. 5.19

(iii) $P_{out} = \dfrac{V_2}{R_{sh}}$

$= \dfrac{68.89}{20 \text{ K}}$

$\therefore \quad P_{out} = $ **237.3 mW** ... Ans.

Problem 5.2:

A two-cavity Klystron amplifier has the following specifications:

Beam voltage, V = 900 V
Beam current, I_0 = **30 mA**
Frequency, f = 8 GHz

Gap spacing in either cavity, d = 1 mm, Cavity spacing between centers of cavities, L = 4 cm, Effective shunt impedance, R_h = 40 kΩ.

Determine:
(i) The electron velocity.
(ii) The D.C. transit time of electron.
(iii) The input voltage for maximum output voltage.
(iv) The voltage gain in decibels.

Solution:

(i) Electron velocity, $v_0 = 0.593 \times 10^6 \sqrt{v_0}$

$= 0.593 \times 10^6 \sqrt{900}$

$= $ **17.79 × 10⁶ m/sec.** ... Ans.

(ii) D.C. transit time of electrons,

$$\theta_0 = \omega \tau_0 = \omega \frac{L}{v_0}$$

$$\tau_0 = \frac{L}{v_0} = 4 \times \frac{10^{-2}}{17.79 \infty 10^6}$$

$$= 0.225 \times 10^{-8} \text{ sec.} \quad \ldots \text{Ans.}$$

(iii) Maximum input voltage,

$$V_{1\,(max)} = \frac{V_0 \infty 3.68}{\beta_i \, \theta_0}$$

$$\theta_0 = \omega \tau_0 = 2\pi f \tau_0$$
$$= 2 \times \pi \times 8 \times 10^9 \times 0.22 \times 10^{-8}$$
$$= 113.1 \text{ rad.} \quad \ldots \text{Ans.}$$

Input beams coupling coefficient, β_i,

$$\beta_i = \sin \frac{\theta_g}{\frac{\theta_f}{2}}$$

$$\theta_g = \omega \frac{d}{v_0} = \frac{2\pi \times f \times d}{v_0}$$

$$= \frac{2\pi \times 8 \times 10^9 \times 10^{-3}}{17.79 \times 10^6}$$

$$= 2.825 \text{ rad.}$$

$$\frac{\theta_g}{2} = \frac{2.825 \text{ rad.}}{2}$$

$$= 1.413 \text{ rad.}$$

$$\sin \frac{\theta_g}{2} = \sin 1.413$$

$$= 0.988$$

$$\beta_0 = \beta_i = \frac{\sin \theta_g/2}{\theta_g/2}$$

$$= \frac{0.988}{1.413}$$

$$= 0.699$$

$$\therefore \quad V_{1\,(max)} = \frac{V_0 \times 3.68}{\beta_i \, \theta_0}$$

$$= \frac{900 \times 3.68}{0.699 \times 113.1}$$

$$= 41.894 \text{ V} \quad \ldots \text{Ans.}$$

(iv) Voltage gain, A_V:

$$A_V = \frac{V_2}{V_1} = \frac{\beta_o^2 \, \theta_n \left(\frac{J_1(x)}{x}\right)}{R_o} \times R_{sh}$$

For maximum output voltage,
$$J_1(x) = 0.582$$
$$x = \mathbf{1.841}$$

$$A_V = \frac{(0.699)^2 \, (113.1) \, (0.582) \times 40 \times 10^3}{30 \times 10^3 \times 1.841}$$

$$A_V = \mathbf{23.293 \text{ dB}} \quad \ldots \text{Ans.}$$

Problem 5.3:

A two cavity Klystron amplifier has the following parameters:

Beam voltage, V_o = 900 V,
Beam current, I_o = 30 mA,
Frequency, f = 8 GHz

Gap spacing in either cavity, d = 1 mm, Spacing between centers of cavities, L = 4 cm, Effective shunt impedance, R_{sh} = 40 kΩ.

Determine:
(i) The electron velocity.
(ii) The D.C. electron transit time.
(iii) The input voltage for maximum output voltage.
(iv) The voltage gain in decibels.

Solution:

(i)
$$v_o = \text{Electron velocity}$$
$$v_o = 0.593 \times 10^6 \sqrt{V_o}$$
$$= 0.593 \times 10^6 \sqrt{900}$$
$$= 17.79 \times 10^6$$
$$v_o = \mathbf{1.8 \times 10^7 \text{ m/s}} \quad \ldots \text{Ans.}$$

(ii) Transit time, τ_o:
$$\tau_o = \frac{d}{v_o} = \frac{1 \times 10^{-3}}{1.8 \times 10^7}$$
$$= \mathbf{0.55 \times 10^{-10} \text{ sec.}} \quad \ldots \text{Ans.}$$

(iii) Input voltage for maximum output voltage,
$$V_{1 \, (\text{max})} = \frac{2V_o}{\beta_o \theta_o} \, x$$

∴ Beam coupling coefficient, $\beta_i = \beta_o$

$$= \frac{\sin \theta_g/2}{\theta_g/2} = 0.704$$

D.C. transit angle, $\theta_o = \dfrac{\omega_L}{V_o}$

$$\theta_o = \frac{2\pi f_L}{V_o} = \frac{2 \times \pi \times 8 \times 10^9 \times 4 \times 10^{-2}}{1.8 \times 10^7}$$

$$\theta_o = 111.64 \text{ rad.} \quad \ldots \text{Ans.}$$

For maximum output voltage, V_2,

$$J_1(x) = 0.582$$

and $x = 1.841$

∴ $$V_{1\,(max)} = \frac{2V_o}{\beta_o \theta_o} \, x$$

$$= \frac{2 \times 900 \times (1.841)}{0.704 \times 111.64}$$

$$= 42.16 \text{ V} \quad \ldots \text{Ans.}$$

(iv) $$A_v = \frac{\beta_o^2 \, \theta_o \left(\dfrac{J_1(x)}{x}\right)}{R_o} \, R_{sh}$$

Assume, $R_o = 30 \text{ k}\Omega = 30 \times 10^3 \, \Omega$

$$A_v = \frac{(0.704)^2 \times 111.64 \times 0.582 \times 40 \times 10^3}{30 \times 10^3 \times 1.841}$$

$$A_v = 23.32 \text{ dB} \quad \ldots \text{Ans.}$$

Problem 5.4:

A two cavity Klystron is operated at 10 GHz with $V_o = 1200$ V, $I_o = 30$ mA, d = 1 mm, L = 4 cm, and $R_{sh} = 40$ kΩ. Neglecting beam loading, calculate –

(i) Input RF voltage, V_1 for a maximum output voltage,

(ii) Voltage gain and

(iii) Efficiency

Solution:

(i) The bunching parameter 'X' is given by,

$$X = \frac{V_1}{2V_o} \, \theta_o$$

where,

$$\theta_o = \frac{\omega_L}{\omega_o} = \text{Transit angle without RF voltage}$$

v_o = Velocity of reference electron

$v_o = 0.593 \times 10^6 \sqrt{V_o}$

$\quad\ = 0.593 \times 10^6 \sqrt{1200}$

$\quad\ = 20.54 \times 10^6$ m/s

$$\theta_o = \frac{2\pi \times f \times L}{v_o}$$

$$= \frac{2 \times \pi \times 10 \times 10^9 \times 4 \times 10^{-2}}{20.54 \times 10^6}$$

θ_o = **122.347 radians** ... Ans.

For maximum output power,

$X = 1.84$

$$V_{1\,(max)} = \frac{2x_1 V_o}{\beta_i \theta_o}$$

where,

$$\beta_i = \frac{\sin \theta_g/2}{\theta_g/2}$$

θ_g = Average gap transit angle = $\dfrac{\omega d}{v_o}$

$$\theta_g = \frac{2\pi f \times d}{v_o} = \frac{2 \times \pi \times 10 \times 10^9 \times 10^{-3}}{20.54 \times 10^6}$$

$\quad\ =$ **3.05 radians** ... Ans.

$$\beta_i = \frac{\sin \theta_g/2}{\theta_g/2} = \frac{\sin(1.5293)}{1.5293}$$

$\quad\ =$ **0.653** ... Ans.

∴ $V_{1\,(max)} = \dfrac{36.09}{0.653}$

$\quad\quad\quad\ =$ **55.268 V** ... Ans.

(ii) Voltage gain = $A_v = \dfrac{V_2}{V_1}$

where,

$V_2 = \beta_o I_o R_{sh}$

β_o = Output cavity coupling coefficient

$\beta_o = \beta_i$

and $I_2 = 2I_o J_1(x)$

For x = 1.84, $J_1(x)$ = 0.58

$$I_2 = 2 \times 30 \times 10^{-3} \times 0.58$$
$$V_2 = \beta_0 I_2 R_{sh}$$
$$= 0.653 \times 2 \times 30 \times 10^{-3} \times 0.58 \times 40 \times 10^3$$
V_2 = 909.49 V ... Ans.

$$A_v = \frac{V_2}{V_1} = \frac{909.49}{55.268}$$
$$= 16.45 \quad \text{... Ans.}$$

Gain in dB = $20 \log_{10}(16.45)$

A_v = 24.33 dB ... Ans.

(iii) Efficiency:

Maximum efficiency is given by,

$$\eta = 0.58 \times \frac{V_2}{V_0}$$
$$= \frac{0.58 \times 909.49}{1200}$$
η = 43.95% ... Ans.

Problem 5.5:

A reflex Klystron operates at the peak mode of n = 2 with V_0 = 280 V, I_0 = 22 mA and a signal voltage V_1 = 30 V.

Determine:

(i) The input power.

(ii) The output power and

(iii) Efficiency

Solution:

Given:
$$V_0 = 280 \text{ V}$$
$$I_0 = 22 \times 10^{-3} \text{ A}$$
$$V_1 = 30 \text{ V}$$
$$n = 2$$

(i) Input power i.e. P_{dc}

$$P_{dc} = V_0 I_0 = 280 \times 22 \times 10^{-3}$$
= 6.16 W ... Ans.

(ii) P_{ac} (output power) = $\dfrac{2 V_o I_o \, x' \, J_1(x')}{2n\pi - \pi/2}$

The factor $X' \, J_1(x')$ reaches a maximum value of 1.252 at $X' = 2.408$ and $J_1(x') = 0.52$. {The maximum power output is obtained when n = 2 or $1\dfrac{3}{4}$ mode}.

$$P_{ac} = \dfrac{2 \times 6.16 \times 2.408 \times 0.52}{2 \times 2 \times \pi - \pi/2}$$

∴ $$P_{ac} = \dfrac{2 \times 6.16 \times 1.25}{4\pi - \pi/2}$$

$$= \dfrac{15.4}{7\pi} \times 2$$

$$\boxed{P_{ac} = 1.4 \text{ W}} \qquad \text{... Ans.}$$

(ii) Efficiency (η):

$$\eta = \dfrac{P_{ac}}{P_{dc}} \times 100$$

$$= \dfrac{1.40}{6.16} \times 100$$

$$\boxed{\eta = 22.74\%} \qquad \text{... Ans.}$$

Problem 5.6:

A reflex Klystron operates at 8 GHz at peak of n = 2 mode with $V_o = 300$ V, $R_{sh} = 20$ kΩ and L = 1 mm. If the gap transit time and beam loading are neglected, find:
   (i) Repeller voltage,
   (ii) Beam current necessary to obtain an RF gap voltage of 200 V.

Solution:

(i) Repeller voltage 'V_R':

$$\dfrac{V_o}{(V_R - V_o)^2} = \dfrac{1}{8} \dfrac{1}{\omega^2 L^2} \dfrac{e}{m} (2\pi n - \pi/2)^2$$

$$= \dfrac{1}{8} \times \dfrac{(1.759 \times 10^{11})(2\pi \times 2 - \pi/2)^2}{(2\pi \times 8 \times 10^9)^2 (1 \times 10^{-3})^2}$$

$$= 0.00105$$

$$\dfrac{V_o}{(V_R - V_o)^2} = 0.00105$$

$$(V_R - V_o)^2 = \dfrac{300}{0.00105}$$

$$= 285 \times 1.34 \times 10^3$$

$$(V_R - V_O) = 533.98 \text{ V}$$
$$V_R = 533.98 + V_O$$
$$= 833.98 \text{ V} \quad \text{... Ans.}$$

(ii) Beam current (I_O):

$$I_O = \frac{V_1}{2 J_1(x') R_{sh}}$$
$$V_1 = I_2 \cdot R_{sh} = 2 I_O J_1(x') R_{sh}$$
$$\therefore \quad I_O = \frac{200}{2 \times 0.582 \times 20 \times 10^3}$$
$$I_O = 8.59 \text{ mA} \quad \text{... Ans.}$$

Problem 5.7:

A four-cavity Klystron amplifier has the following parameters:

- Beam voltage, V_O = 20 kV
- Beam current, I_O = 2A
- Operating frequency, f = 9 GHz
- D.C. charge density, ρ_o = 10^{-6} c/m³
- RF charge density, ρ = 10^{-8} c/m³
- Velocity perturbation, v = 10^5 m/s

Determine:
(i) The D.C. electron velocity
(ii) The D.C. phase constant.
(iii) The plasma frequency.
(iv) The reduced plasma frequency for R = 0.5
(v) The beam current density.
(vi) The instantaneous beam current density.

Solution:

(i) The D.C. electron velocity,

$$v_O = 0.593 \times 10^6 \sqrt{V_O}$$
$$= 0.593 \times 10^6 \sqrt{20 \times 10^3}$$
$$= 8.386 \times 10^7 \text{ m/s}$$

Problem 5.8:

A two-cavity Klystron amplifier has the following parameters:

- V_O = 1000 V
- R_O = 40 kΩ
- I_O = 25 mA
- f = 3 GHz

Gap spacing in either cavity, d = 1 mm, Spacing between the two cavities, L = 4 cm, Effective shunt impedance, excluding beam loading, R_{sh} = 30 kΩ.

(i) Find the input gap voltage to give maximum voltage V_2.

(ii) Find the voltage gain, neglecting the beam loading in the output cavity.

(iii) Find the efficiency of the amplifier, neglecting beam loading.

(iv) Calculate the beam loading conductance and show that neglecting it was justified in the preceding calculations.

Solution:

(i) For maximum V_2, $J_1(x)$ must be maximum. This means, $J_1(x)$ = 0.582 and X = 1.841.

Thus, electron velocity = v_0

$$v_0 = 0.593 \times 10^6 \sqrt{V_0}$$
$$= 0.593 \times 10^6 \sqrt{10^3}$$
$$= 1.88 \times 10^7 \text{ m/s} \quad \ldots \text{Ans.}$$

The gap transit angle is, θ_g.

$$\theta_g = \omega \frac{d}{v_0}$$
$$= 2\pi f \times \frac{d}{v_0}$$
$$\theta_g = 2 \times \pi \times 3 \times 10^9 \times \frac{10^{-3}}{1.88 \times 10^7}$$
$$= 1 \text{ rad.}$$

β_i = Beam coupling coefficient

$$\beta_i = \beta_0 = \frac{\sin(\theta_g/2)}{(\theta_g/2)}$$
$$= \frac{\sin(1/2)}{1/2}$$
$$= 0.952$$

θ_0 = D.C. transit angle between the cavities

$$\theta_0 = \omega\tau_0 = \omega\frac{L}{v_0} = 2\pi f \times \frac{L}{v_0}$$
$$= 2\pi \times 3 \times 10^9 \times \frac{4 \times 10^{-2}}{1.88 \times 10^7}$$
$$= \mathbf{40 \text{ rad.}}$$

The maximum input voltage 'V_1' is then given by,

$$V_{1\,(max)} = \frac{2 V_o X}{\beta_i \theta_o}$$

$$= \frac{2 \times 1000 \times 1.841}{0.952 \times 40}$$

$$= 96.5 \text{ V} \qquad \text{... Ans.}$$

(ii) The voltage gain, A_V and

$$A_V = \frac{\beta_o^2 \, \theta_o}{R_o} \, \frac{J_1(x)}{X} \, R_{sh}$$

$$= \frac{(0.952)^2 \times 40 \times 0.582 \times 30 \times 10^3}{40 \times 10^3 \times 1.841}$$

$$= 8.595 \text{ dB} \qquad \text{... Ans.}$$

(iii) Efficiency, η:

$$\eta = \frac{\beta_o I_2 V_2}{2 I_o V_o}$$

$$I_2 = 2 I_o J_1(x) = 2 \times 25 \times 10^{-3} \times 0.582$$
$$= 29.1 \text{ mA}$$

$$V_2 = \beta_o I_2 R_{sh} = 0.952 \times 29.1 \times 10^{-3} \times 30 \times 10^3$$
$$= 831 \text{ V}$$

$$\text{Efficiency, } \eta = \frac{\beta_o I_2 V_2}{2 I_o V_o}$$

$$= \frac{(0.952)(29.1 \times 10^{-3})(831)}{2 \times (25 \times 10^{-3}) \times 1000}$$

$$= 46.2\% \qquad \text{... Ans.}$$

(iv) Beam loading conductance (G_B).

$$G_B = \frac{G_o}{2} \left(\beta_o^2 - \beta_o \cos \frac{\theta_g}{2} \right)$$

$$= \frac{25 \times 10^{-6}}{2} [(0.952)^2 - (0.952) \cos (28.6°)]$$

$$G_B = 8.8 \times 10^{-7} \text{ mho} \qquad \text{... Ans.}$$

Beam loading resistance,

$$R_B = \frac{1}{G_B}$$

$$\therefore \quad R_B = \frac{1}{8.8 \times 10^{-7}}$$

$$R_B = 1.14 \times 10^6 \, \Omega \qquad \text{... Ans.}$$

In comparison with effective shunt resistance R_{sh}, the beam loading resistance is like an open circuit and thus can be neglected in the preceding calculations.

Problem 5.9:

A two-cavity Klystron has the following parameter:

Beam voltage, V_0 = 20 kV
Beam current, I_0 = 2 A
Operating frequency, f = 8 GHz
Beam coupling coefficient, $\beta_i = \beta_0 = 1$
D.C. electron beam current density, $\rho_0 = 10^{-6}$ c/m²
Signal voltage, V_1 = 10 V (r.m.s.)
Shunt resistance of cavity, R_{sh} = 10 kΩ
Total shunt resistance including load, R = 30 kΩ

Calculate:
(i) Plasma frequency.
(ii) The reduced plasma frequency for R = 0.5.
(iii) The induced current in the output cavity.
(iv) The induced voltage in the output cavity.
(v) The output power delivered to the load.
(vi) The power gain.
(vii) The electronic efficiency.

Solution:

(i) The plasma frequency = ω_p

$$\omega_p = \sqrt{\frac{e\rho_0}{m \, \epsilon_0}}$$

$$\omega_p = \sqrt{\frac{1.759 \times 10^{11} \times 10^{-6}}{8.854 \times 10^{-12}}}$$

$= 1.41 \times 10^8$ rad/sec. ... Ans.

(ii) The reduced plasma frequency is 'ω_q'.

$\omega_q = R\omega_p = 0.5 \times 1.41 \times 10^8$

$= 0.705 \times 10^8$ rad/sec. ... Ans.

(iii) The induced current in the output cavity,

$= |I_2|$

$I_2 = \beta_0 |i_2|$

where, $|i_2|$ is magnitude of RF convection current at output cavity for a 2-cavity Klystron.

$$|i_2| = \frac{1}{2} \frac{I_0 \omega}{V_0 \omega_q} \beta_i |V_1|$$

where, V_1 is magnitude of the input signal voltage.

$$|I_2| = \beta_0 |i_2| = \frac{1}{2} \frac{I_0 \omega}{V_0 \omega_q} \beta_0^2 |V_1|$$

$$= \frac{1}{2} \frac{2 \times 2 \times \pi \times 8 \times 10^9}{20 \times 10^3 \times 0.705 \times 10^8} \times (1)^2 \times |10|$$

$$|I_2| = 0.3565 \text{ A} \qquad \text{... Ans.}$$

(iv) The induced voltage in the output cavity is,

$$|V_2| = |I_2| R_{sh\ell}$$

where, $R_{sh\ell}$ is total shunt resistance including load.

$$\therefore \quad |V_2| = 0.3565 \times 30 \times 10^3$$
$$= 10.71 \text{ kV} \qquad \text{... Ans.}$$

(v) The output power delivered to the load,

$$P_{out} = |I_2|^2 \times R_{sh\ell}$$
$$= (0.3565)^2 \times 30 \times 10^3$$
$$= 3.82 \text{ kW} \qquad \text{... Ans.}$$

(vi) The power gain $= \dfrac{P_{out}}{P_{in}}$

$$\frac{P_{out}}{P_{in}} = \frac{P_{out}}{|V_1|^2/R_{sh}} = \frac{1}{4}\left(\frac{I_0 \omega}{V_0 \omega_q}\right)^2 \beta_o^4 \, R_{sh} \cdot R_{sh\ell}$$

$$\text{Gain} = \frac{1}{4}\left[\frac{2 \times 2\pi \times 8 \times 10^9}{20 \times 10^3 \times 0.705 \times 10^8}\right] (1)^4 \times 10 \times 10^3 \times 30 \times 10^3$$

$$= 3.83 \times 10^5$$
$$= 55.8 \text{ dB} \qquad \text{... Ans.}$$

(vii) Electronic efficiency, η

$$\eta = \frac{P_{out}}{P_{in}}$$
$$= \frac{3.82 \times 10^3}{I_0 \times V_0}$$
$$= \frac{3.82 \times 10^3}{2 \times 20 \times 10^3}$$
$$= 9.6\% \qquad \text{... Ans.}$$

Problem 5.10:

A helical TWT has diameter of 2 mm with 50 turns per cm. Calculate –

(i) Axial phase velocity,
(ii) The anode voltage at which the TWT can be operated for useful gain.

Solution:

(i)
$$v_p = \text{Phase velocity}$$

$$v_p = \text{Velocity of light} \times \frac{\text{Pitch}}{\text{Circumference}}$$

$$\text{Pitch} = \frac{1}{50 \text{ cm}} = 2 \times 10^{-4} \text{ m}$$

$$= \frac{1}{50 \times 10^{-2} \text{ m}}$$

$$\text{Circumference} = \pi \times D$$
$$= \pi \times 2 \times 10^{-3}$$
$$= 6.284 \times 10^{-3} \text{ m}$$

$$\therefore \quad v_p = 3 \times 10^8 \times \frac{2 \times 10^{-4}}{6.284 \times 10^{-3}}$$

(ii) Anode voltage, (V_o): $v_p = ?$

$$e V_o = \frac{1}{2} m v_p^2$$

$$\therefore \quad V_o = \frac{1}{2} \frac{m}{e} v_p^2$$

$$V_o = \frac{1}{2} \times 9.1 \times \frac{10^{-31}}{1.6 \times 10^{-19}} (0.9548 \times 10^7)^2$$

$$\therefore \quad \mathbf{V_o = 25.92 \text{ kV}} \qquad \ldots \text{Ans.}$$

Problem 5.11:

A reflex Klystron operates under the following conditions:
$$V_o = 600 \text{ V}$$
$$L = 1 \text{ mm}$$
$$R_{sh} = 15 \text{ KV}$$
$$f_r = 9 \text{ GHz}$$
$$\frac{e}{m} = 1.759 \times 10^{11} \text{ (MKS system)}$$

The tube is oscillating at f_r at the peak of the n = 2 mode of $1\frac{3}{4}$ mode. Assume that the transit time through the gap and beam loading can be neglected.

Find:
(i) Value of repeller voltage, V.
(ii) The direct current necessary to give a microwave gap voltage of 200 V.
(iii) What is the electronic frequency under this condition.

Solution:

(i)
$$\frac{V_o}{(V_o + V_r)^2} = \left(\frac{e}{m}\right) \frac{(2\pi n - \pi/2)^2}{8 \omega^2 L^2}$$

$$= (1.759 \times 10^{11}) \frac{(2\pi \times 2 - \pi/2)^2}{8 (2\pi \times 9 \times 10^9)^2 (10^{-3})^2}$$

$$= 0.832 \times 10^{-3}$$

$$(V_0 + V_r)^2 = \frac{600}{0.832 \times 10^{-3}}$$

$$= 0.721 \times 10^6$$

V_r = 250 V ... Ans.

(ii) Assume that, $\beta_0 = 1$.

Since, $V_2 = I_2 R_{sh}$

$$= 2 I_0 J_1(x') R_{sh}$$

I_0 = Direct current

$$I_0 = \frac{V_2}{2 J_1(x') R_{sh}} = \frac{200}{2(0.582)(15 \times 10^3)}$$ ... Ans.

I_0 = 11.45 mA ... Ans.

(ii) Efficiency (η):

$$\eta = \frac{2 x' J_1(x')}{2\pi n - \pi/2}$$

$$= \frac{2(1.841)(0.582)}{2\pi \times 2 - \pi/2}$$

%η = 19.49% ... Ans.

Problem 5.12:

A travelling wave tube (TWT) operates under the following parameters:

Beam voltage, V_0 = 3 kV
Beam current I_0 = 30 mA
Characteristic Impedance of helix z_0 = 10 Ω
Circuit length, N = 50
Frequency, f = 10 GHz

Determine:
(i) Gain parameter.
(ii) The output power gain A_p in decibels and
(iii) All four propagation constants.

Solution:

Gain parameter = C

(i) $$C = \left(\frac{I_0 z_0}{4 V_0}\right)^{1/3}$$

$$= \left(\frac{30 \times 10^{-3} \times 10}{4 \times 3 \times 10^3}\right)^{1/3}$$

= 2.92 × 10^{-2} ... Ans.

(ii) Output power gain (A_p),

$$A_p = -9.54 + 4.73 \, N_C$$
$$= -9.54 + 47.3 \times 50 \times 2.92 \times 10^{-2}$$
$$= 59.52 \text{ dB} \quad \text{... Ans.}$$

(iii) The four propagation constants are,
$\gamma_1, \gamma_2, \gamma_3$ and γ_4.

$$\beta_e = \frac{\omega}{v_o} = \frac{2\pi \times 10 \times 10^{10}}{0.593 \times 10^6 \sqrt{3 \times 10^3}}$$
$$= 1.93 \times 10^3 \text{ rad/s} \quad \text{... Ans.}$$

$$v_1 = -\beta_e C \frac{\sqrt{3}}{2} + j\beta_e \left(1 + \frac{C}{2}\right)$$

$$= -1.93 \times 10^3 \times 2.92 \times 10^{-2} \times 0.87 + j1.93 \times 10^3 \left(1 + \frac{2.92 \times 10^{-2}}{2}\right)$$

$$v_1 = -49.03 + j1952$$

$$\gamma_2 = \beta_e C \frac{\sqrt{3}}{2} + j\beta_e \left(1 + \frac{C}{z}\right)$$

$$= 49.03 + j19.52$$

$$\gamma_3 = j\beta_e (1 - C)$$
$$= j(1.93 \times 10^3)(1 - 2.92 \times 10^{-2})$$
$$\gamma_3 = j1872.25$$
$$\gamma_4 = j1872.25$$

$$\gamma_4 = -j\beta_e \left(1 - \frac{C^3}{4}\right)$$

$$= -j1.93 \times 10^3 \left[1 - \frac{(2.92 \infty 10^{-2})^3}{4}\right]$$

$$\gamma_4 = -j1930$$

Problem 5.13:

An transfer band conventional magnetron has the following operating parameters.

Anode voltage, V_o = 5.5 kV
Beam current, I_o = 4.5 A
Operating frequency, f = 9×10^9 Hz
Resonator conductance, G_r = 2×10^{-4} mho
Loaded conductance, G_l = 2.5×10^{-5} mho
Vane capacitance, C = 2.5 pf
Duty cycle, D_c = 0.002
Power loss, P_{loss} = 18.50 kW

Calculate:
- (i) Angular resonance frequency.
- (ii) Unloaded quality factor.
- (iii) The loaded quality factor.
- (iv) External quality factor.
- (v) Circuit efficiency.
- (vi) Electronic efficiency.

Solution:

(i) Angular resonance frequency = ω_r.

$$\omega_r = 2\pi f = 2 \times 9 \times 10^9$$
$$= 56.55 \times 10^9 \text{ rad.}$$

(ii) Unloaded quality factor, (Q_{un}):

$$Q_{un} = \frac{\omega_c}{G_r} = \frac{56.55 \times 10^9 \times 2.5 \times 10^{-12}}{2 \times 10^{-4}}$$

$$\boxed{Q_{un} = 707}$$

(iii) Loaded quality factor, Q_l:

$$Q_l = \frac{\omega_c}{G_r + G_l} = \frac{56.55 \times 10^9 \times 2.5 \times 10^{-12}}{2 \times 10^{-4} + 2.5 \times 10^{-5}}$$

$$\boxed{Q_l = 628}$$

(iv) External quality factor Q_{ext}:

$$Q_{ext} = \frac{\omega_c}{G_l} = \frac{56.55 \times 10^9 \times 2.5 \times 10^{-12}}{2.5 \times 10^{-5}}$$

$$\boxed{Q_{ext} = 5655}$$

(v) Circuit efficiency η_c :

$$\eta_c = \frac{1}{1 + Q_{ext}/Q_{un}}$$

$$= \frac{1}{1 + \frac{5655}{707}}$$

$$= \mathbf{11.11\%} \qquad \text{... Ans.}$$

(vi) Electronic efficiency (η_e):

$$\eta_e = \frac{V_o \times I_o - P_{loss}}{V_o \times I_o}$$

$$= \frac{5.5 \times 10^3 \times 4.5 - 18.5 \times 10^3}{5.5 \times 10^3 \times 4.5}$$

$$= \mathbf{25.25\%} \qquad \text{... Ans.}$$

Problem 5.14:

A normal circular magnetron has the following parameters.

   Inner radius = 0.15 m
   Outer radius = 0.45 m
   Magnetic flux density = 1.2 m weber/m^2

Determine:
(i) Hull cut-off voltage.
(ii) Hull cut-off magnetic flux density if the beam voltage is 6000 V.

Solution:

Given:
   a = 0.15 m
   b = 0.45 m
   β = 1.2 mwb/m^2

(i) Hull cut-off voltage:

$$V_{OC} = \frac{3}{8m} \beta_0^2 \, b^2 \left(1 - \frac{a^2}{b^2}\right)^2$$

$$V_{OC} = \frac{1.759 \times 10^{11}}{8} (1.2 \times 10^{-3})^2 (0.45)^2 \left(1 - \frac{(0.15)^2}{(0.45)^2}\right)^2$$

$$V_{OC} = 5065.92 \text{ V}$$

$$V_{OC} = \mathbf{5.06592 \text{ kV}} \quad \text{... Ans.}$$

(ii) Cut-off magnetic flux density:

$$\beta_{OC} = \frac{\left(8 V_0 \frac{m}{e}\right)^{1/2}}{b \left(1 - \frac{a^2}{b^2}\right)}$$

$$\beta_{OC} = \frac{\left(8 \times 6000 \times \frac{1}{1.759 \times 10^{11}}\right)^{1/2}}{0.45 \left(1 - \frac{(0.15)^2}{(0.45)^2}\right)}$$

$$\mathbf{B_{OC} = 10.43 \text{ m weber/m}^2} \quad \text{... Ans.}$$

Problem 5.15:

A normal circular magnetron has the following parameters.

   Cathode radius = 2 mm
   Anode radius = 4 mm

Determine the Hull cut-off voltage if the magnetic flux density is 0.3 wb/m^2 and the cut-off magnetic flux density if V_0 = 15 kV.

Solution:

Given:
$a = 2 \text{ mm} = 2 \times 10^{-3} \text{ m}$
$b = 4 \text{ mm} = 4 \times 10^{-3} \text{ m}$
$\beta_0 = 0.3 \text{ wb/m}^2$

Hull cut-off voltage,

$$V_{oc} = \frac{e}{8m} \beta_0^2 \, b^2 \left(1 - \frac{a^2}{b^2}\right)^2$$

$$= \frac{1.759 \times 10^{11}}{8} (4 \times 10^{-3})^2 \left(1 - \frac{(2)^2}{(4)^2}\right)^2$$

$V_{oc} = 23.746 \text{ kV}$ ... **Ans.**

Cut-off magnetic flux density = β_{oc},

$$\beta_{oc} = \frac{\left(8 V_0 \dfrac{m}{e}\right)^{1/2}}{b\left(1 - \dfrac{a^2}{b^2}\right)}$$

$$= \frac{\left(8 \times 5 \times 10^3 \times \dfrac{1}{1.759 \infty 10^{11}}\right)^{1/2}}{4 \times 10^{-3} \left(1 - \dfrac{(2)^2}{(4)^2}\right)}$$

$\beta_{oc} = 0.15486$

$\boldsymbol{\beta_{oc} = 154.86 \text{ m wb/m}^2}$ ... **Ans.**

SUMMARY

- This unit exposes limitations of conventional tubes.
- The various highlighted topics in this are classification of microwave tubes, construction and operation of microwave tubes, two cavity klystron amplifier, klystron oscillator and the travelling wave tube along with mathematical equations.
- The magnetron types and operation of two cavity magnetron is given along with various solved problems.

POINTS TO REMEMBER

1. Microwave tubes are constructed to overcome the limitations of the conventional and UHF (Ultra High Frequency) tubes.
2. Microwave tubes are classified as –
   (a) 'O' type: Linear beam tube.
      e.g. Klystron and travelling wave tube.
   (b) 'M' type: Cross field tube.
      e.g. Magnetron.
3. **Klystron tube:** Works on the principle of velocity and current modulation.
4. Two configurations of Klystrons are – (i) Two cavity or multicavity Klystron
   (ii) Reflex Klystron.
5. Klystron is normally a power amplifier but can be made to oscillate if an external feedback network is supplied.
6. Reflex Klystron is a single cavity device.
7. TWT uses a slow wave structure called Helix.

QUESTIONS

1. What are the limitations of conventional tubes at microwave frequencies? Explain how these limitations can be overcome.
2. What is the velocity modulation? Explain how velocity modulation is utilized in Klystron amplifier.
3. Starting from basic principles drive an expression for the efficiency of a two cavity Klystron amplifier.
4. What are the performance characteristics of a Klystron amplifier?
5. Explain construction and working of reflex Klystron.
6. What is a need of slow wave structure?
7. State the characteristics and operation of reflex Klystron.
8. Assuming reflex, Klystron, π-mode, explain how magnetron sustain its oscillations.
9. Discuss the performance of magnetron and list the important applications.
10. Explain how helical TWT achieves amplification.
11. Differentiate between Klystron and TWT.
12. Explain phase-focussing effect in magnetron.

Unit VI

SOLID-STATE MICROWAVE DEVICES

6.1 Classification of Semiconductor Microwave Devices

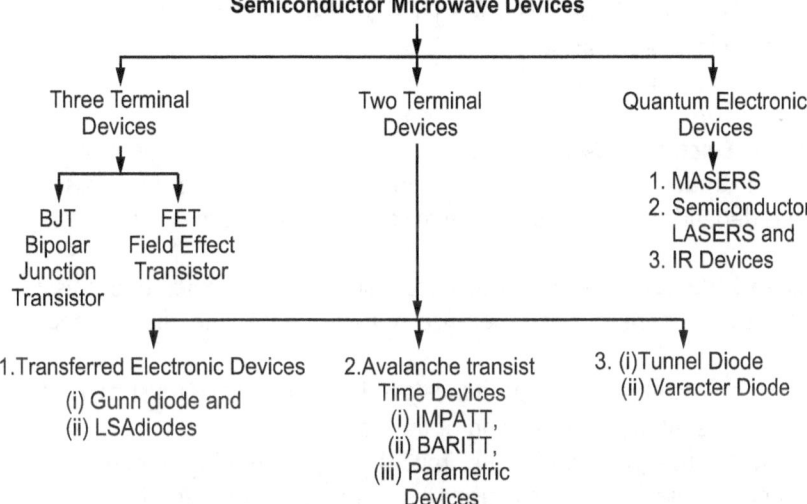

Fig. 6.1: Classification of Semiconductor Microwave Devices

Above Fig. 6.1 mentioned all solid state devices employ a negative resistance characteristics rather than the velocity modulation for their operation.

6.1.1 Advantages of Solid State Microwave Devices
1. Small size.
2. Low power consumption.
3. Large bandwidth.
4. Long working life.
5. Good stability and better noise figure.

6.1.2 Disadvantages of Solid State Microwave Devices
1. Power frequency limitation.
2. Voltage frequency limitations.
3. Current frequency limitations.

6.1.3 Applications of Solid State Microwave Devices
1. Modern communication system.
2. Radars.
3. Navigation.
4. Medical and biological equipment and
5. Other industrial electronic products.

6.1.4 High Frequency Limitation of Bipolar Transistor
1. Inter Electrode Capacitance.
2. Lead Inductance and
3. Transit Time.

1. Inter Electrode Capacitance: The high frequency response is limited by the **interelectrode capacitance** which makes α and β of transistor complex. Also the depletion layer which is depends on the bias voltage makes the problem much more complex than the tubes.

2. Lead Inductance: Lead inductance also has the similar effect as that in tubes i.e. signal losses but here it is less because transistors are small in size and have smaller leads.

The effect of interelectrode capacitance and lead inductance must be kept minimum by proper choice of geometry of packaging of transistors.

3. Transit Time: The transit time limits the high operating frequency as in tubes but here this effect is less because electrons have to travel smaller distance in a transistor. However, the ion mobility, bias voltages, emitter delay time, base transit time, collector transit time are the parameters which have to be controlled for better performance.

6.2 Microwave Transistors
6.2.1 Construction of Microwave Transistor

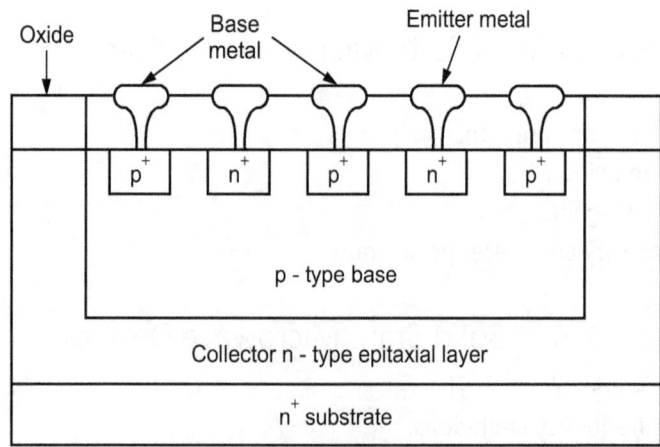

Fig. 6.2: n-p-n Silicon Double Diffused Epitaxial Transistor

Fig. 6.2 shows the silicon n-p-n transistor which provides adequate power at microwave frequency typically 5 Watt at 3 GHz frequency with gain of 5 dB. These are made in planar form as a double diffused epitaxial device.

It consists of n^+ substrate on which n-type epitaxial layer is grown, layer is thermally grown which is p-type base and heavily doped n-emitters are diffused into the base. Contacts are provided by opening in the oxide and connections are made in parallel. The surface geometry of such transistors can have –

1. Inter digitated.
2. Overlay or
3. Matrix forms as shown in Fig. 6.3.

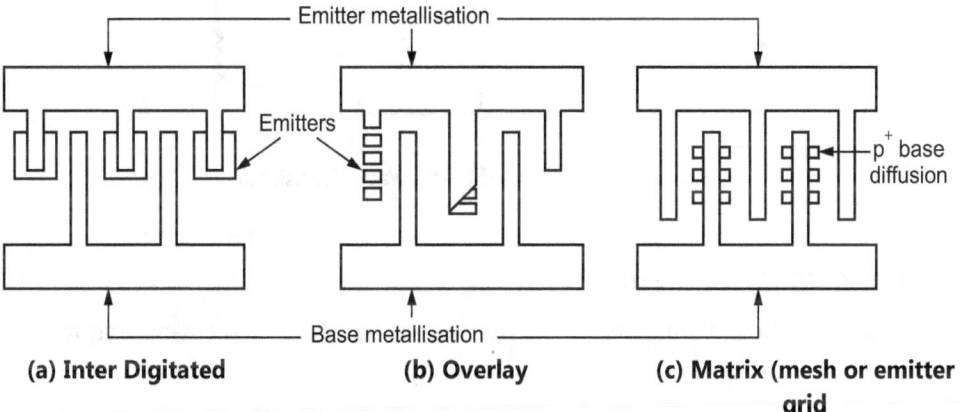

(a) Inter Digitated (b) Overlay (c) Matrix (mesh or emitter grid

Fig. 6.3: Surface Geometry of n-p-n Microwave Transistor

1. Inter Digitated Surface Geometry:

Small signal transistors uses inter digitated surface geometry while power transistors employ all three surfaces geometrices. Inter digitated surface geometry consists of large number of emitter strips alternating with base strips. Both of these are metalised. Inter digitated structure is suitable for small signal applications in the L, S and C bands.

2. Overlay Structure:

The overlay structure geometry has a large number of segmented emitters over laid through a number of wide metal strips.

3. Matrix or Mesh Geometry:

It is also called as emitter grid. Overlay and matrix structures are useful as power devices in the VHF and UHF regions.

Operation:

In the microwave transistor, initially the emitter-base and the collector base junctions are reversed biased corresponding to class C condition. The microwave signal is applied between emitter and base and forward bias this junction during positive portion of the signal. If p-n-p transistor is considered, the holes in the p-region diffuses and drift through the thin base region to the collector and accelerate to the negative terminal of the bias voltage between collector and base terminals. A pulse of current flows through the load connected in the collector circuit.

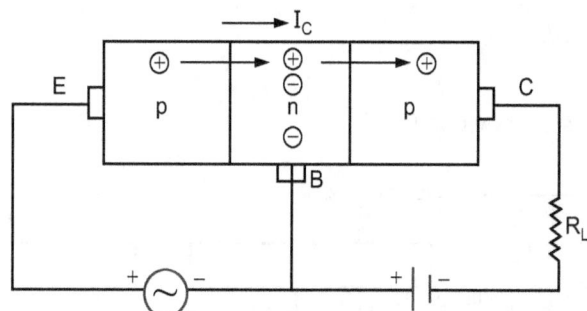

Fig. 6.4: Operation of Microwave Transistor

6.2.2 Performance Parameters

The behaviour of the low frequency transistor is defined by α, β and cut-off frequencies $f_{\alpha b}$ and $f_{\alpha e}$.

where, $\beta = \dfrac{\alpha}{1-\alpha}$ and $f_{\alpha e} = \dfrac{f_{\alpha b}}{\beta}$

while behaviour of microwave transistors is defined by f_T i.e. cut-off frequency and maximum possible frequency of oscillation f_{max}.

Cut-off frequency (f_T): Cut-off frequency is determined by,

$$f_T = \dfrac{1}{2\pi \tau_{ec}}$$

where,

$\tau_{ec} = \tau_e + \tau_b + \tau_d + \tau_c$

and
τ_e = Emitter base junction charging time

τ_b = Base transit time

τ_d = Collector depletion layer transit time and

τ_c = Collector depletion layer charging time

But, for microwave transistors, the cut-off frequency is f_T',
where,

$$f_T' = \frac{1}{\tau_{bec}} \qquad \ldots (6.2)$$

$$\tau_{bec} = \tau_{be} + \tau_{ec}$$

with $\tau_{be} = \gamma_B' C_e$ and the base is kept extremely narrow. Hence, $f_T' < f_T$.

f_T is a current gain bandwidth frequency which is a frequency at which β falls to unity i.e. the highest frequency at which current gain may be obtained.

Maximum Frequency of Oscillation (f_{max}):

f_{max} is higher than f_T because β has fallen to unity at this frequency and power gain has not i.e. β = 1, output impedance is higher than input impedance, voltage gain exists and hence both generation and oscillation are possible.

f_{max} is given by,

$$f_{max} = \sqrt{\frac{f_T}{8\pi\gamma_B' C_c}} \qquad \ldots (6.3)$$

where,

f_T = Cut-off frequency
γ_B' = Base resistance
C_c = Collector capacitance

6.2.3 Performance Characteristics

1. High output power at the lower bands of the microwave region.
2. High operating power efficiency.
3. Large operating bandwidth.
4. Lower signal distortion and noise levels.

However, structure of microwave transistors is quite complex than that of two terminal devices and also have problems of instability due to thermal runway and breakdown.

6.2.4 Power Frequency Limitations

As the frequency is increased, output power drops because of low impedance of junction capacitance $\left(X_c = \frac{1}{2\pi f_c}\right)$. This power frequency limitation was given by Johnsen and it is due to,

1. Maximum velocity of the charge carriers in a semiconductor.
2. Maximum electric field that can be applied to a semiconductor.
3. Width of the base that determines the maximum current.

6.2.5 Voltage Frequency Limitations

If V_m = Maximum allowable applied voltage, then,
$$V_m = E_m L_m$$
where,
E_m = Maximum electric field and
L_m = Maximum collector emitter distance

The charge carrier transit time cut-off frequency is given by,
$$f_c = \frac{1}{2\pi \tau_{av}}$$

τ_{av} = Base transit time (τ_B) + Base collector depletion layer transit time (τ_D).

$\therefore \quad f_c = \dfrac{V}{2\pi L_m}$

$\therefore \quad \tau_{av} = \dfrac{L_m}{V}$

As $\quad V_m = E_m \times L_m$

$\therefore \quad V_m = E_m \times \dfrac{V}{2\pi L_m}$

$\therefore \quad \boxed{V_m f_c = \dfrac{E_m V}{2\pi}} \qquad \ldots (6.4)$

This equation gives voltage frequency limitation.

where, V = Drift velocity

6.2.6 Current Frequency Limitations

$$V_m = I_m \times I_c$$

where, I_m = Maximum current limited by bandwidth.

$$X_c = \frac{1}{2\pi f_c C_o}$$

where, C_o = Collector base capacitance.

Consider above equation of V_m,

$$V_m f_c = \frac{E_m V}{2\pi}$$

$\therefore \quad I_m \times X_c \times f_c = \dfrac{E_m V}{2\pi}$

The power frequency limitation is given by the product of voltage frequency limitation and current frequency limitation i.e.

$$f_c \sqrt{P_m X_c} = \frac{E_m V}{2\pi}$$

As $E_m V$ = Constant for particular transistor.
As frequency is increased, maximum power capability decreases.
The power gain frequency limitation is given by,

$$f \sqrt{G_m V_{th} V_m} = \frac{E_m V}{2\pi}$$

where,

f = Frequency of operation
G_m = Maximum available power gain
V_{th} = kT/e with usual notations

6.3 Performance Characteristics of Microwave Transistor

1. Output power = 200 W to 150 W for frequency between 1 to 8 GHz.
2. Noise figure = 3.3 dB to 14 dB for frequency between 4 GHz to 8 GHz.
3. Power gain = 31 ± 1.5 dB over the frequency range 4 to 6 GHz.
4. Voltage frequency limitation = 2×10^{11} V/s for silicon and 1×10^{11} for Germanium.

6.4 Varactor Diodes

Varactor diode is short form of variable reactor which contains the voltage variable capacitance of a reverse biased junction. They have non-linearity of capacitance which is fast enough to follow microwaves. Varactor diode is a semiconductor device in which the junction capacitance can be varied by varying the bias voltage i.e. reverse voltage. The junction capacitance depends on the applied voltage and junction design. In some cases a junction with fixed reverse biased may be used as capacitance of fixed value. V-I character of a typical varactor diode is shown in Fig. 6.6 (b).

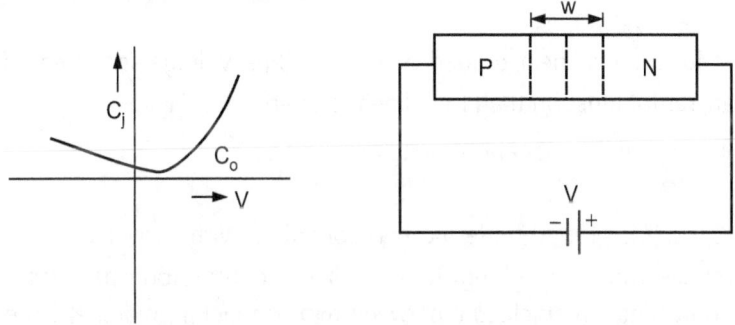

Fig. 6.5: Junction Capacitance C_j Vs. Voltage (V)

We know that,

$$C_j \propto V_r^{-n}$$

where,

C_j = Junction capacitance

V_r = Reverse bias voltage

and n = Parameter that decides the type of junction

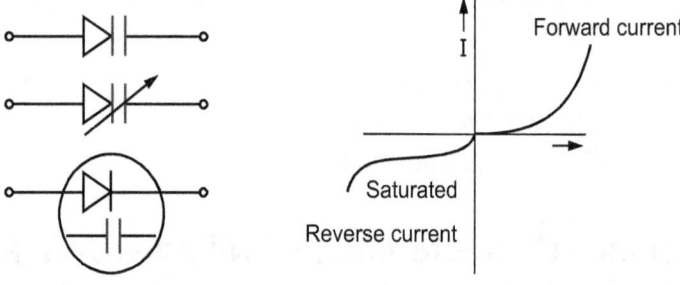

(a) Commonly Used Symbols   (b) V-I Characteristics

Fig. 6.6

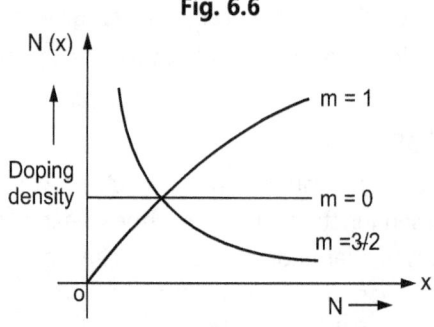

Fig. 6.6 (c): Doping Profiles

1. If p-n junction is abrupt, capacitance varies as a square root of reverse bias 'V_r' i.e. $n = 1/2$.
2. If p-n junction is linear graded one, $n = 1/3$ i.e. voltage sensitivity of C_j is greater for an abrupt junction than for a linear graded junction.
3. If p-n junction is hyper abrupt junction $n > 1/2$.

The graph of C_j Vs. V is plotted under no bias condition. With a reverse bias, the junction is depleted by mobile carriers resulting in capacitance i.e. the diode behaves as a capacitor with the junction acting as a dielectric between two conducting materials. The width of the depletion region (w) increases with reverse bias and capacitance decreases as the reverse bias increases.

6.4.1 Construction of Varactor Diode

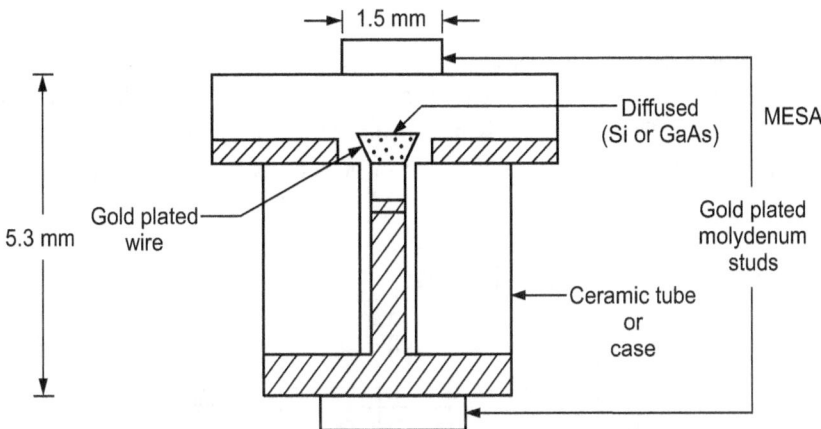

Fig. 6.7: Constructional Details of Varactor Diode

Diffused junction MESA 'Si' diodes are widely used at microwave frequency. They are capable of handling larger powers and larger reverse breakdown voltages, and have no noise. Frequency limit of Si diodes is upto 25 GHz. Varactors are made of GaAs have high operating frequency (over 90 GHz), and better functioning at lowest temperatures. However, manufacturing techniques are easier for Si.

6.4.2 Equivalent Circuit

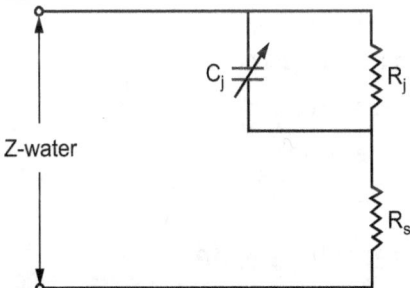

Fig. 6.8 (a): Electrical Equivalent Circuit of Varactor Diode

Electrical equivalent circuit of varactor diode is shown in Fig. 6.8. C_j = Junction capacitance which is function of applied bias.

R_j = Junction resistance is a function of applied bias.

R_s = Series resistance including resistance of wafer and resistance of the ohmic electrical leads and is the function of applied bias.

At microwave frequencies R_j is 10 MΩ and may be neglected compared to capacitive reactance.

Variation in junction capacitance is the most important characteristics of varactor diode these are parasitic resistances, capacitances and conductances associated with every practical encapsulated diode. The diode encapsulation contains electrical leads attached to wafer. Because of these, circuit of Fig. 6.8 (a) can be redrawn as a final equivalent circuit in Fig. 6.8 (b).

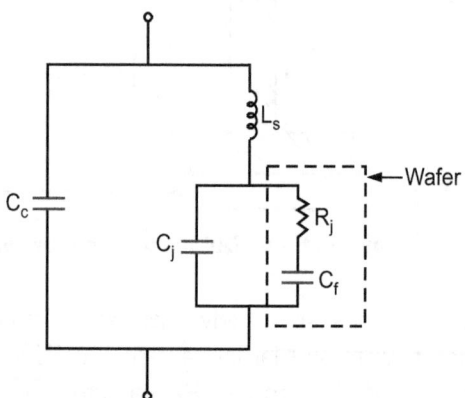

Fig. 6.8 (b): Final Equivalent Circuit of Varactor Diode

where,

C_c = Capacitance of ceramic case
C_f = Fringe capacitance
L_e = Lead inductance
C_j = Junction capacitance
R_s = Series resistance
R_j = 10 MΩ (neglected)

6.4.3 Applications of Varactor diode

1. Harmonic generation.
2. Microwave frequency multiplication.
3. Low noise amplification.
4. Pulse generation and pulse shaping.
5. Tuning stage of radio radar.
6. Active filters.
7. Switching circuits and modification of microwave signal.

6.5 Tunnel Diode (Esaki Diode)

Tunnel diode is a negative resistance semiconductor p-n junction diode in which p and n regions are the heavily doped junctions and the potential barrier is very thin here, it is possible for carrier to pass through or tunneling through the potential barrier.

This tunnel diode shows the negative resistance on the part of the forward characteristics. Tunneling effect takes place because of majority carrier. The operation of tunnel diode is very fast.

6.5.1 Operation of Tunnel Diode

1. **Open Circuit Condition:**

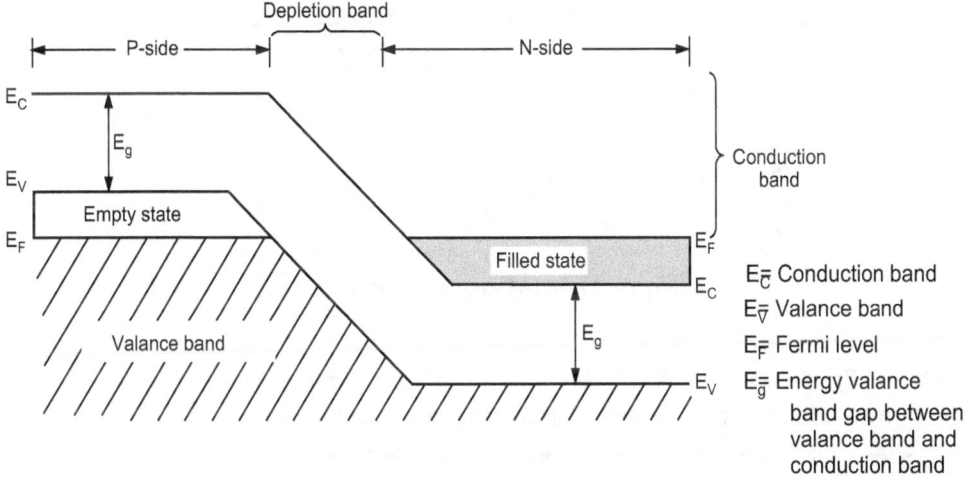

Fig. 6.9: Tunnel Diode at Open Circuit Condition

The operation of tunnel diode under the condition of open circuit is shown in Fig. 6.9.
The transfer for carriers (tunneling) takes place from n-side to the p-side if the filled state at one side is at the same energy level as the empty state at another side. Now, as shown in Fig. 6.9, the filled energy level at n-side is not at the same energy level as that of the empty state in the p-side so there is no tunneling of the carriers from one side to other. That means there is no flow of current in either direction across the junction.

In case of ordinary diode fermi levels is in the forbidden band. But in case of tunnel diode, both p and n regions are heavily doped regions. So at p side fermi-level is in the Valance Band and in n-side the fermi level is in the Conduction Band as shown in Fig. 6.9.

2. Forward Bias Condition:

When the forward bias is applied across the diode. Then at particular voltage the peak current is obtained, that peak current is I_p and corresponding voltage = V_p.

Consider that the forward voltage is applied to tunnel diode and the applied voltage is less than V_p ($0 < V < V_p$) then energy level of n-side is increased so some of the carrier present in the filled state of n-side comes at the same energy level as that of the empty state of p-side. Thus, electrons tunnel through the barrier from n-side to p-side.

Now, if the forward voltage is again increased then at one stage, the filled state and empty state appears at same energy level. So the maximum electrons tunnel through barrier from n-side to p-side. This is shown in Fig. 6.10.

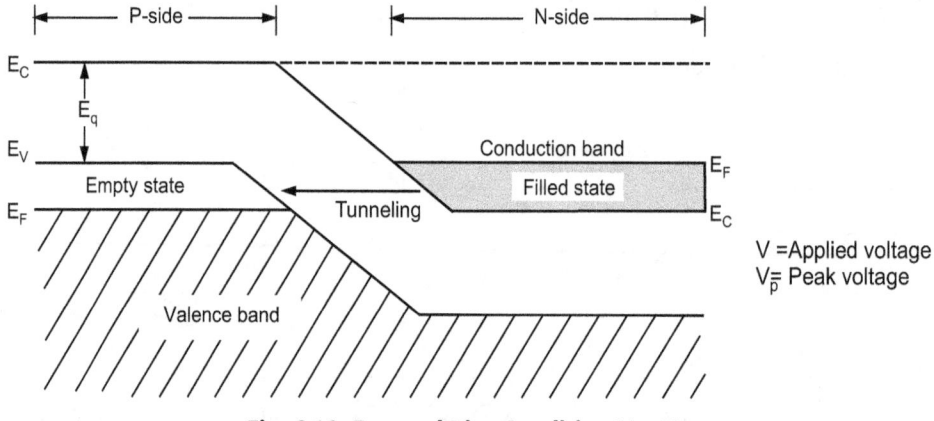

Fig. 6.10: Forward Bias Condition V = V_p

The maximum tunnel at the peak voltage V_p. At this stage peak at I_p is obtained. Now, if forward bias is again increased above V_p, this situation is shown in Fig. 6.11.

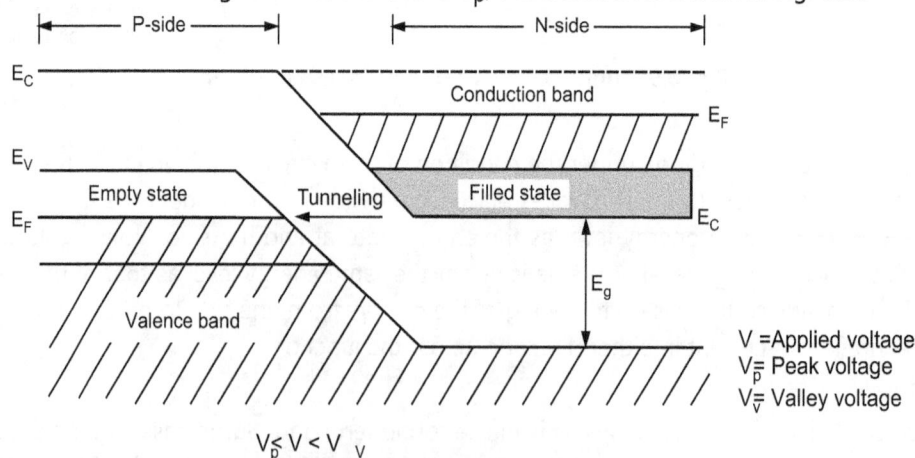

$V_p \leq V < V_v$

Fig. 6.11: Forward Bias Condition

When $V_p < V < V_v$ increases then very few can tunnel from n-side to p-side. This is because the energy level of n-side is again increased as compared to previous case.

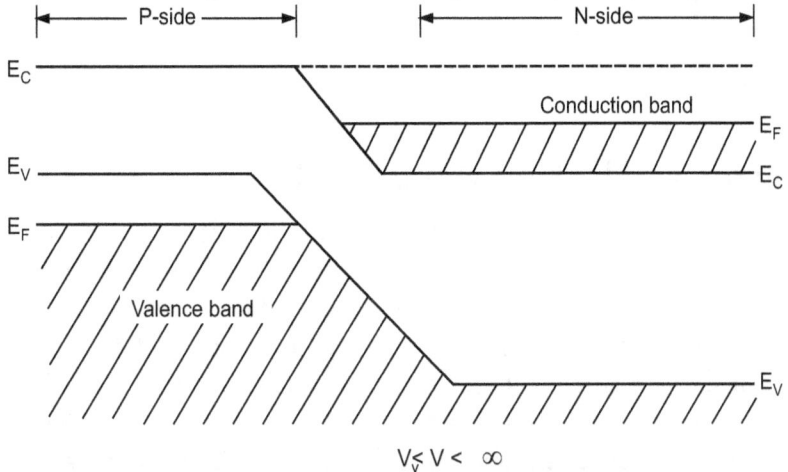

Fig. 6.12: Forward Bias Condition $V > V_p$

If again the bias voltage is increased, then the band structure is shown in Fig. 6.12 is obtained. Here, any portion of the filled state and energy state are not at the same energy level tunnel current stops.

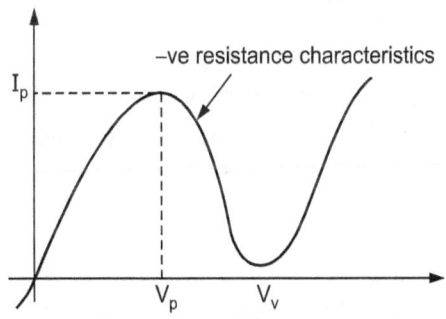

Fig. 6.13: V-I Characteristics

Now, when the forward voltage is increased further then injection carrier current flow total current flowing through tunnel diode is the sum of injection carrier current plus tunnel current as shown in Fig. 6.13.

6.5.2 Advantages of Tunnel Diode

The number of advantage of tunnel diode over other diodes are,
1. High speed.
2. Operates at low power.
3. Low noise generated.
4. Having high peak current to valley current ratio.
5. Low cost and light weight.

6.5.3 Applications of Tunnel Diode
1. Microwave application.
2. Microwave oscillation.
3. Binary memory.

6.6 Transferred Electron Devices (TED)

The common characteristics of all active two terminal solid state devices is their negative resistance. The real part of their impedance is negative over a range of frequencies. In a positive resistance, the current through the resistance and the voltage across it are in phase, the voltage drop across positive resistance is positive and a power of I^2R is dissipated in the resistor. In a negative resistance the current and voltage are out of phase by 180°, the voltage drop across it is negative and a power of (I^2R) is generated by the power supply associated with the negative resistance. In other word, positive resistance absorbs power (passive device) and negative resistance generate power (active devices).

TED's are bulk devices having no junction or gates compared to microwave transistor which operates with either junction or gates. TED's are fabricated from compound semiconductors such as GaAs and InP (Indium Phosphate).

TED's operate with hot electrons whose energy is very much greater than their thermal energy. Transistor operation with warm electrons whose energy is not much greater than their thermal energy. Gunn diode is example of TED's.

6.6.1 Gunn Effect Devices

In Gunn diode periodic fluctuations of current passing through the n-type GaAs specimen when the applied voltage exceeded a certain critical value. (2.4 kV/cms). Gunn effect can be explained on the basis of two valley theory or transferred electrons mechanism. Basic mechanism involved in the operation of bulk n-type GaAs device is transfer of electrons from lower condition valley i.e. L-valley to U-valley.

As shown in Fig. 6.14, there are two curvature in Conduction Band also called sub bands are different so that an electron in L-valley has a smaller effective mass (m_1) than in U-valley (m_2). The different effective masses mean different mobilities for the L-valley (μ_1) and the U-valley (μ_2) respect. The ratio of density of states in the U-valley to that in L-valley is about 60. Thus, the upper valley has a very high density, compared with k = 0 location.

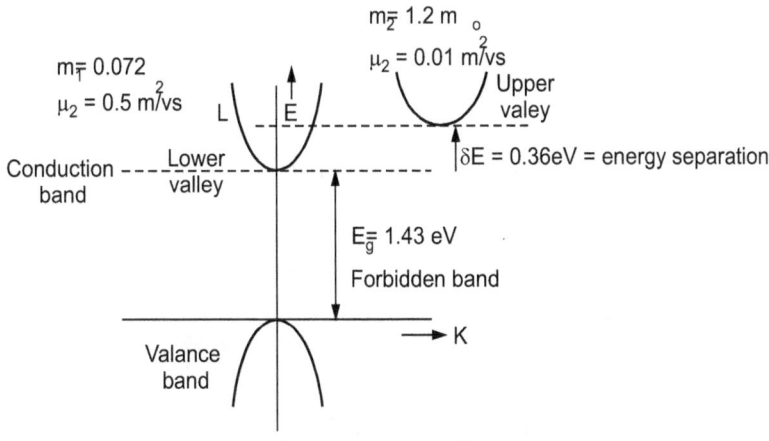

Fig. 6.14: Gunn Effect

At zero electric field conditions electrons are distributed in a manner determined by energy separation δE, lattice temperature T_0 and density of states. With typical values stated in Fig. 6.14, most of the electrons at low electric fields and at low lattice temperature will occupy states in the L-valley and carry ohmic current.

$$J = \sigma E$$

With $\sigma = \rho n_1 \mu_1 \approx \rho n_0 \mu_1$

where, n_1 = carrier concentration in L-valley and is assumed to be equal to the total carrier concentration n_0 and μ_1 = mobility of the L-valley.

As the applied field is increased, the electrons gain energy from applied field and move upward in the U-valley. Actually, this inter valley transfer of electrons is good as there are many available states in the U-valley. As electrons transfer to the U-valley, their mobility decreases and the effective mass is increased thus decreasing the current density 'J' and hence, the negative differential conductivity.

There is a certain threshold field, ≈ 3.3 kV/cm above which this inter valley transfer (also known as population inversion) of charges from L-valley to U-valley or the transfer electron effect takes place. As the transfer of electron is taking place, the current density should be given by,

$$J = \sigma E = \rho (n_1 + n_2) \overline{\mu} E = e n_0 \overline{\mu} E$$

where,

$$\overline{\mu} = \frac{n_1 \mu_1 + n_2 \mu_2}{n_0} = \text{The average mobility of electrons}$$

As the applied field is raised almost all the electrons in the L-valley are transfer to U-valley and the current density will be given as,

$$J = \sigma E = e n_2 \mu_2 E$$

where,

n_2 = Carrier concentration and

μ_2 = Mobility in U-valley

Thus, J-E curve is obtained which is similar to V-I characteristics of p-n junction diode.

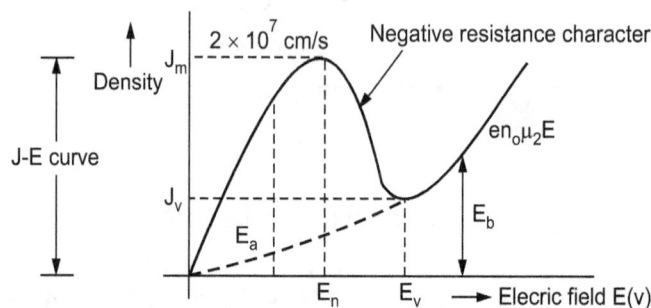

Fig. 6.15: J-E Curve of a Gunn diode

where,

J_m = Maximum current density

E_m = Maximum electric field required before start of negative conductance region

E_a = Maximum electric field for which

J = σE is valid

E_b = Electric field for which $J = en_2\mu_2 e$ holds

E_v = Electric field for corresponding to Jv

The region of the characteristics between E_m and E_v where current density decreases with increasing electric field is one of the negative differential resistivity (NDR).

6.6.2 Domain Formation

When a D.C. bias of greater than the threshold field is applied to n-type GaAs sample, the charge densities and electric field within the sample become non-uniform creating domains i.e. electrons in some region of the sample will be the first experience the inter valley transfer than the rest of the sample.

Depending on the material parameters and operating conditions, a gunn effect oscillator can be made to oscillate in any of four frequency modes.
1. Transit time domain mode.
2. Delayed or Inhibited domain mode.
3. Quenched domain mode.
4. Limited space charge. Accumulation LSA mode.

1. **Transit Time Domain Mode ($f_L = 10^7$ cm/sec.):**

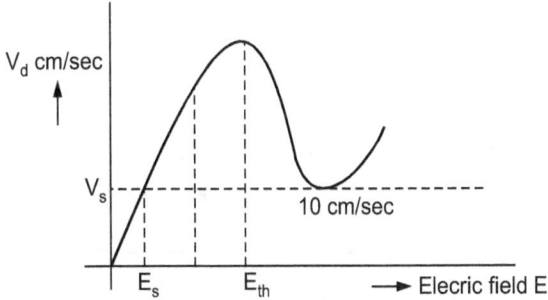

Fig. 6.16: Gunn Mode ($T_o = T_t$)

This is called as Gunn mode. Here, $f_L = 10^7$ cm/s = V_d, when $V_d = V_s$, the sustaining velocity, the high field domain is stable. In that case, oscillation period = Transit time i.e. $T_o = T_t$ as shown in Fig. 6.16.

Efficiency is below 10% because domain arrives at the anode at lower current level.

The operating frequency ($f = V_d/L$) in this mode is slightly sensitive to the applied voltage since the drift velocity V_d depends on the bias voltage. Bias voltage is normally maintained a little higher than E_{th}. As bias voltage increases V_d and hence operating frequency decreases.

This mode does not require any external circuit for its operation. It is a low power low efficiency mode and used for frequency less than 30 GHz.

- Efficiency (η) < 10%
- Frequency < 30 GHz
- Low power and low
- Frequency mode
- No external circuit required

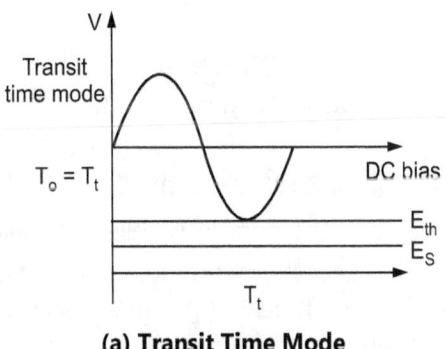

(a) Transit Time Mode

- Efficiency < 10%
- Frequency = 30 GHz

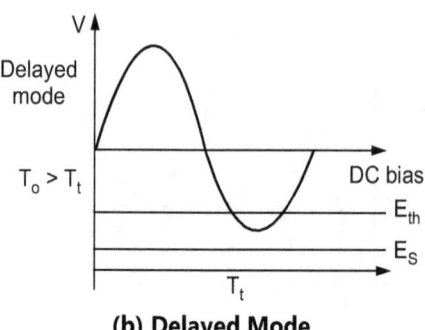

(b) Delayed Mode

- Efficiency = 13%

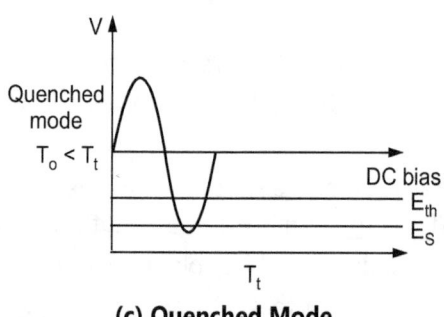

(c) Quenched Mode

- Efficiency is very high
- Operating frequency is upto 100 GHz

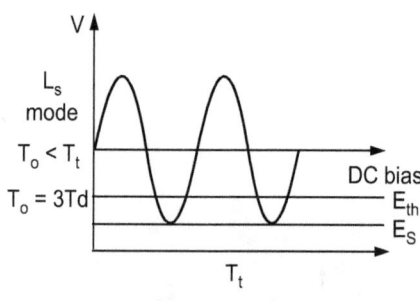

(d) LSA Mode

Fig. 6.17: Types of Modes

2. Delayed Domain Mode ($f_L > 2 \times 10^7$ cm/sec.):

When the T_E is selected such that the domain is collected while, $E < E_{th}$, a new domain cannot form until the field rises again above threshold, here the oscillation period is greater than the transit time period $T_o > T_b$. Efficiency (η) = 20%. Hence, operating frequency can be equal to or less than that in Gunn diode.

3. **Quenched Domain Mode ($f_L > 2 \times 10^7$ cm/sec.):**

If the bias field drops below sustaining fields E_s during the negative half cycle the domain collapses before it reaches the anode i.e. the domain disappears some where in the sample itself. Hence, the domain does not reach to anode and thereby the operating frequency will be higher than that of Gunn mode or delayed mode. When the bias field swings back above threshold value V_{th}, a new domain will be formed and the process repeats. Hence, in this mode domain is quenched before it reaches the anode, $(\eta) = 13\%$.

4. **LSA Mode ($f_L > 2 \times 10^7$ cm/sec.):**

This is the most important mode of operation for Gunn oscillator as this mode gives high power with high efficiency (η). In this mode, the domain is not allowed to formed at all. Operation is heavily dependent on external circuit. If domain is formed device gets destroyed.

6.7 Pin Diode

PIN diode consists of heavily doped narrow layer of p-type material and n-type of material, separated from each other by very lightly doped, high resistivity thicker intrinsic material as shown in Fig. 6.18.

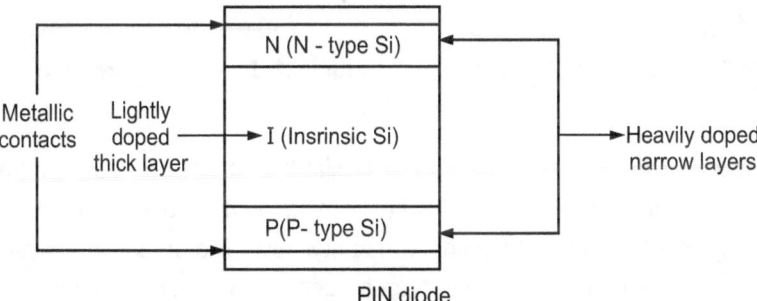

PIN diode

Fig. 6.18: PIN Diode

Silicon is widely used because of,
1. High power handling capacity,
2. High resistivity in intrinsic region and
3. Easy fabrication.

GaAs material can also be used for manufacturing same type of diode but without these advantages.

Electrical contacts are taken from two heavily doped regions. PIN diodes are widely used for microwave power switching, limiting and modulation.

PIN diode acts as a low frequency rectifier that could rectify more power than an ordinary p-n junction diode. Upto 100 MHz frequency the operation of PIN diode is similar to ordinary p-n junction diode. At higher frequencies PIN diode acts like a variable resistance. Rectification stops at higher frequencies due to carrier storage junction and the transit time across the large intrinsic region.

When PIN diode is reverse bias or zero bias, the diode has very high impedance at microwave frequencies and very low impedance when diode is forward bias i.e. as the biasing of PIN diode is changed from reverse bias to forward bias, its microwave resistance changes from 5-10 kΩ to 5 Ω as shown in Fig. 6.21. It means PIN diode behaves as a switch. Construction of PIN diode and its equivalent circuit is shown in Fig. 6.19 and Fig. 6.20.

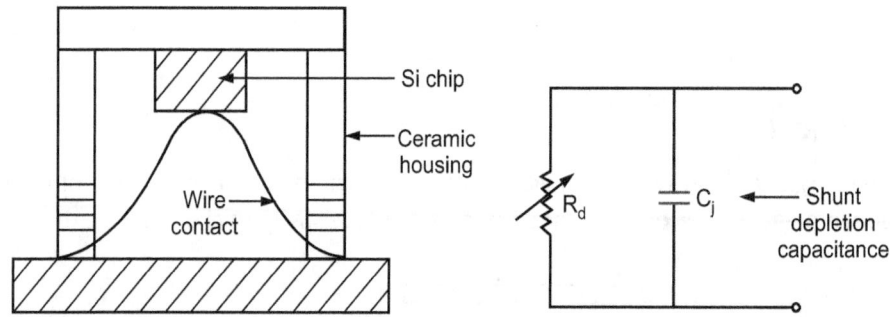

Fig. 6.19: Construction of PIN Diode   **Fig. 6.20: Equivalent Circuit of a PIN Diode**

When the diode is mounted across a 50 Ω co-axial line, it will not load the line under the reverse bias. When it is forward bias it reflects most of the power due to mismatch and loading. To improve the power handling capability, several diodes can be used in parallel and switching of more than 150 kW peak can be achieved. The shunt depletion capacitance C_j limits the upper frequency operation.

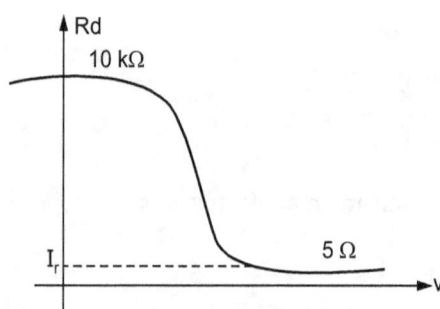

Fig. 6.21: Resistance Variation with Bias

Operation of PIN Diode:

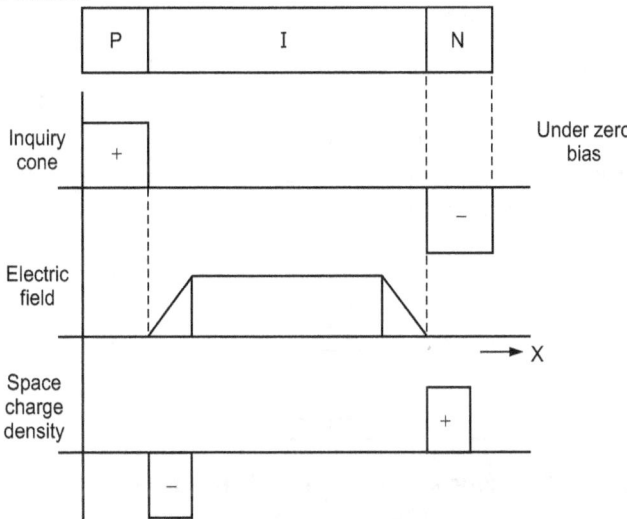

Fig. 6.22: Operation of PIN Diode

The operation can be explained by considering zero bias, reverse and forward bias conditions shown in Fig. 6.22.

1. **Zero bias:** At zero bias the diffusion of the holes and electrons across the junction causes space charge (density) region of thickness inversely proportional to the impurity concentration. As 'i' layer has no depletion region i.e. p-layer has a fixed negative charge and n-layer has a fixed positive charge under zero bias.

2. **Reverse bias:** As reverse bias is applied, the space charge regions in the p and n layer will become thicker as the carriers in p and n layer gets attracted towards battery. The reverse resistance will be very high and almost constant.

3. **Forward bias:** When positive terminal of supply is connected to the p-type of layer and n-type of layer is connected to the negative terminal of supply, then diode works in the forward bias. With forward bias carriers will be injected into the i-layer from p-side and n-side. This results in the carrier concentration in the 'i' layer becoming raised above equilibrium levels and the resistivity drops as forward bias is increased.

6.7.1 Applications of PIN Diode

1. **PIN diode as a switch:**

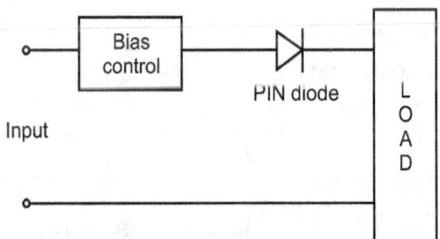

Fig. 6.23: PIN Diode as a Diode Connector Series

When PIN diode is used as a switch then it is connected either in series with load or in shunt with load. Suitable bias control is used to forward bias or reverse bias the PIN diode. In Fig. 6.23, PIN diode is connected in series with load. When the diode is reversed biased, switch is 'off' or open and when it is forward biased it is closed. In Fig. 6.24, when diode is forward biased, it offers a short circuit. Hence, energy is fully reflected back and no power flows to the load. Hence, switch is open. If reverse biased the diode is open. Hence, the load receives the power i.e. switch is closed.

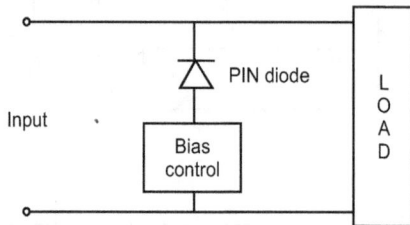

Fig. 6.24: PIN Diode as a Switch (Diode is connected in p-order)

2. PIN diode as an amplitude modulator:

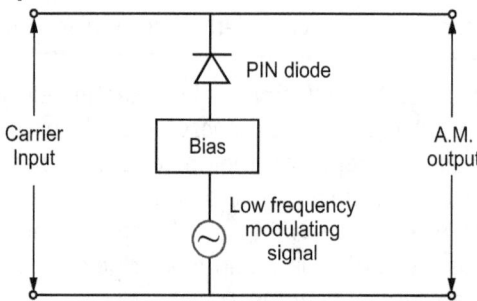

Fig. 6.25: Amplitude Modulator using PIN Diode

The diode is kept at low reverse bias and in series with the low frequency modulating signal. The modulating signal amplitude is kept smaller than the RF carrier signal. The modulating signal changes the RF resistances of diode so that varying amount of mismatch results. Hence, the amount of carrier power reflected back and hence the amount of carrier passed beyond diode circuit towards the output varies as the input value of modulating signal.

3. PIN diode as a limiter:

Fig. 6.26 shows input power (P_{in}) Versus Output load power (P_{out}) for a PIN diode. From this, it is seen that when input power is moderate, output follows input power and for larger input, the diode absorbs power and output will be limited i.e. will not vary much with the input power.

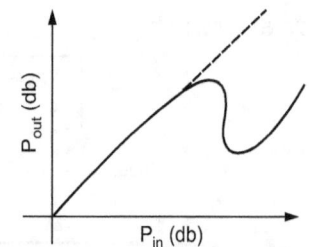

Fig. 6.26: Input Power (P_{in}) Vs. Output Load Pout for PIN Diode

6.8 Typical Characteristics of Gunn Diode

It typically uses a 10-12 V supply with typical bias current of 250 mA giving a continuous wave power of 25 mW in the transfer band (8.2 GHz to 12.4 GHz).

1. **CW power:** 25 mW to 250 mW X-band (5 to 15 GHz).
   100 mW at 18-26.5 GHz.
   40 mW at 26.5-40 GHz.
2. **Pulsed power:** 5 W (5-12 GHz).
3. Efficiency 2% to 12% (at 1.5 W CW to 50 mW CW) {CW = Continuous Wave}

1. **Gunn Diode Amplifier:**

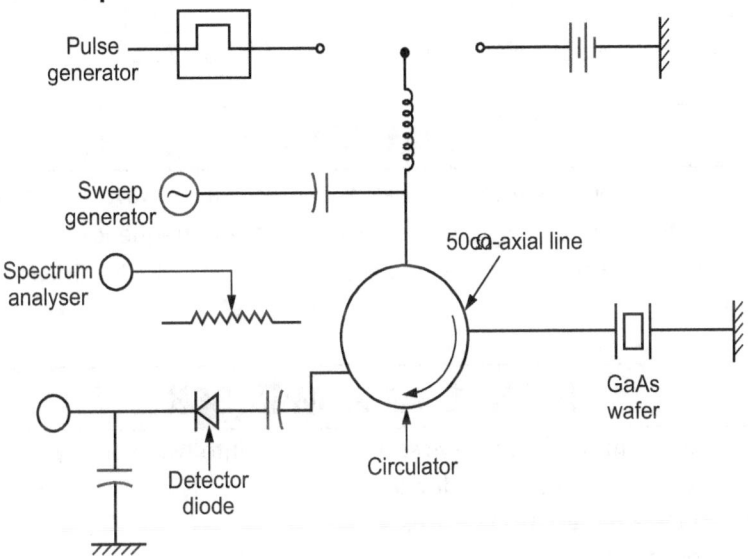

Fig. 6.27: Gunn Diode Amplifier

Similar to the tunnel diode, Gunn diode with negative resistance characteristic can be used as an amplifier, but less popular.

6.8.1 Performance Characteristics of Gunn Diode Amplifiers
1. Power: 1 W at frequencies between 4 to 16 GHz.
2. Gain bandwidth product: > 10 dB.
3. Average gain: 1-12 dB.
4. Noise figure: 15 dB.

6.8.2 Applications of Gunn Diode
1. In radar transmitters (Police Radar, CW Doppler Radar).
2. Pulsed Gunn Diode Oscillators used in Transponders for Air Traffic Control (ATC) and Industry Telemetry Systems.

3. Broadband linear amplifier.
4. Fast combinational and sequential logic circuits.
5. Low and medium power oscillator in microwave receivers.
6. As pump sources in parametric amplifiers.

6.8.3 Advantage of Gunn Diode
Gunn diode have lesser noise compared to IMPATT (Impact Avalanche Transit Time) diodes.

6.8.4 Disadvantage of Gunn Diode
Gunn diode is very temperature dependence 0.5-3 MHz/°C change.
Well designed devices have 50 kHz/°C for a range of –40°C to +70°C.

SUMMARY

- This unit leads to the classification of semiconductor microwave devices and also the limitations of the low frequency transistors at microwave frequencies. Construction and operation of microwave transistors, varactor diodes, PIN diode, GUNN diode is also discussed here.

POINTS TO REMEMBER

1. Microwave semiconductor devices are classified into two major types:
   (a) Avalanche transit-time devices.
   (b) Transferred electron devices.
2. **Varactor diode:**
   Varactor = Variable + Reactor
   These are specially made PN junction diodes designed to enhance the control of the PN junction capacitance with a reverse bias voltage.

EXERCISE

1. What causes the negative resistance in tunnel diode?
2. State the different types of losses in microstrip lines?
3. Can we use PIN diode as a modulator?
4. Why low power microwave solid state devices are preferred over conventional electron beam devices?
5. State different layers and their use in PIN diode.
6. State different regions in tunnel diode characteristics.

***

ORAL QUESTIONS

Section – I : Optical Communication

- What is the principle of OFC ?
Ans. Total internal reflection.
- What is a fiber optic system ?
Ans. Communication system that carry information through a guided fiber.
- What is the range of light frequencies in OFC system ?
Ans. 10^{14} Hz to 4×10^{14} Hz [1,00,000 to 4,00,000 GHz]
- What is the typical bandwidth of an OFC ?
Ans. 10% of 1,00,000 GHz 10,000 GHz.
- What are the advantages of fiber systems ?
Ans. Greater capacity, immune to cross talk and static interferences, resistive to environmental extremes, more secure and safer, easier to install and maintain.
- What are the different bands in the light frequency spectrum ?
Ans. Infrared, visible and ultraviolet.
- What are the primary building blocks of an OFC link ?
Ans. Transmitter, receiver and fiber guide.
- What are the blocks in the transmitter ?
Ans. Analog or digital interface, V to I converter light source and source-to-fiber coupler.
- What are the blocks in the receiver ?
Ans. Fiber to detector interface, photodetector, I to V converter, amplifier and analog or digital interface.
- What are the materials used for construction of optical fibers ?
Ans. glass, plastic or combination of glass and plastic.
- What are the varieties of fibers ?
Ans. (i) Plastic core and cladding (PCC).
(ii) Glass core with plastic cladding (PCS).
(iii) Glass core and glass cladding (SCS).
- What is the velocity of light in free space ?
Ans. 3×10^8 m/s
- What is refractive index ?
Ans. It is the ratio of velocity of light in free space to the velocity of light in given medium.

- What is critical angle?

Ans. It is the angle of incident light so as to produce the angle of refraction of 90°.

$$\left[\sin \theta_c = \sin^{-1}\left(\frac{n_2}{n_1}\right)\right]$$

- What is Snell's law?

Ans. $n_1 \sin \theta_1 = n_2 \sin \theta_2$.

- What is meant by modes?

Ans. The word mode simply means path. If there is only one path for light it is called single mode propagation.

- What is multimode propagation?

Ans. If the light takes more than one path for its propagation it is called multimode propagation, it is called multimode propagation.

- What is index profile?

Ans. It is a graphical representation of the value of the refractive index across the fiber.

- What are the basic types of refractive index?

Ans. (i) Step index : Where a central core has a uniform refractive index.

(ii) Graded index : Where the refractive index is uniform i.e. highest at centre and decreases gradually with distance outer edge.

- Draw the Single Mode Step Index (SMSI) multimode step index and multimode graded index fibers.

Ans. Refer the section "Optial Fiber Configurations".

- What are the advantages of SMSI fibers.

Ans. Minimum dispersion, larger bandwidth and higher information rates.

- What are the advantages of MMSI?

Ans. Inexpensive, simple to manufacture and easy to couple light in to and out of fibers.

- What are the advantages of MMGI fibers over MMSI fibers?

Ans. Easier to couple light, distortion due to multimodes is less.

- What is numerical aperture?

Ans. Light gathering ability of the fiber is called as NA

$$NA = \sqrt{n_1^2 - n_2^2}$$
$$= \sin \theta_{in} \quad \text{– for SI fiber}$$
$$= \sin \theta c \quad \text{– for GI fiber}$$

- What is acceptance angle ?

Ans. Acceptance angle, $\theta_c = \theta_{in} = \sin^{-1}\sqrt{n_1^2 - n_2^2}$

$= \sin^{-1} NA$

- What are the losses in OFC ?

Ans. Absorption losses, Rayleigh scattering losses, wavelength dispersion, radiation losses, model dispersion and coupling losses.

- What are the causes of absorption losses ?

Ans. Ultra violet absorption, Infrared absorption and ion resonance absorption.

- What is material or Rayleigh scattering losses ?

Ans. These are losses due to sub microscopic irregularities that are permanently formed in the fiber during the manufacturing process.

- What are the causes of radiation losses ?

Ans. It is due to microbends and constant radius bends.

- What is Model dispersion or pulse spreading ?

Ans. It is caused by the difference in propagation times of light rays that take different paths down or fiber.

- What is the effect of pulse spreading ?

Ans. It causes errors in digital transmission.

- Why the coupling losses occur ?

Ans. Due to lateral misalignment, gap misalignment angular misalignment or imperfect surface finish while coupling two fibers.

- A fiber with NA of 0.9 and NA of 0.6 is to be coupled. It is possible to couple ? Assume their core and cladding dimensions are same.

Ans. Possible to couple as the core and cladding dimensions are same. However, there will be loss due to change in numerical apertures.

- What are the light sources ?

Ans. LEDs and ILDs.

- What are the different light detectors ?

Ans. APD and PIN diode.

- What are advantages of LEDs ?

Ans. Omnidirectional, chromatic light power output, easy construction, low cost, low power, long life.

- What are major advantages of lasers ?

Ans. Unidirectional output with monochromatic or coherent light. Larger power.

- What are the types of lasers ?

Ans. Gas, liquid, solid and semiconductor lasers.

- List the characteristics of light detectors ?
Ans. Responsivity, dark current, transit time, spectral response.
- Whether the light will propagate in a step index fibers if they cladding is not there or not ?
Ans. All light power will not propagate as it may be refracted outside the fiber and also there is no total internal reflection in the absence of cladding.
- What is the principle of light emission in an LED ?
Ans. When the junction is forward biased, minority carriers are injected across the junction recombine with majority carriers and give up energy in the form of light.
- Why the normal p-n junction diode doesn't emit light when its junction is forward biased ?
Ans. In LEDs certain semiconductor materials and dopants are chosen such that the process is radioactive, a photon is produced.
- Attenuation is mainly a result of what three properties ?
Ans. (a) Light absorption losses
  (b) Scattering losses
  (c) Bending losses
- Define attenuation.
Ans. Attenuation is the loss of optical power as light travels along the fiber.
- What are the main causes of absorption in optical fiber ?
Ans. Intrinsic and extrinsic material properties.
- Extrinsic absorption peaks define three regions or windows of preferred operation. List the three windows of operation.
Ans. The first, second and third windows of operations are 850 nm, 1300 nm and 1550 nm respectively.
- What is the main loss mechanism between the ultraviolet and infrared absorption regions ?
Ans. Rayleigh scattering.
- Scattering losses are caused by the interaction of light with density fluctuation within a fiber. What are the two scattering mechanism called when the size of the density fluctuations is (a) greater than and (b) less than one tenth of the operating wavelength.
Ans. (a) Mie scattering, (b) Rayleigh scattering.
- Microbend loss is caused by microscopic bends of the fiber axis. List three sources of microbend loss.
Ans. Uneven coating applications, improper cabling procedures and external force.
- How is fiber sensitivity to bending losses reduced ?
Ans. Fiber sensitivity to bending losses can be reduced if the refractive index of the core is increased and/or if the overall diameter of the fiber increases.
- Name the two types of intramodal, or chromatic dispersion.
Ans. Material dispersion and waveguide dispersion.

- Which dispersion mechanism is a function of the size of the fiber's core relative to the wavelength of operation?

Ans. Waveguide dispersion.

- Modes of light pulse that enter the fiber at one time exist the fiber at different times. This condition causes the light pulse to spread. What is this condition called?

Ans. Modal dispersion.

- Which fiber optic component (splice, connector or coupler) makes a permanent connection in a distributed system?

Ans. Splice.

- What are the main causes of coupling loss?

Ans. Poor fiber end preparation of poor fiber alignment.

- Define the loss in optical power through a connection.

Ans. $Loss = 10 \cdot \log \dfrac{P_{in}}{P_{out}}$

- Fiber-to-fiber coupling loss is affected by intrinsic and extrinsic coupling loss. Can intrinsic coupling losses be limited by limiting fiber mismatches.

Ans. Yes.

- In fiber-to-fiber connections, Fresnel reflection is one source of coupling losses. Light is reflected back into the source fiber and is lost. What causes Fresenel reflection?

Ans. A step change in refractive index that occurs at fiber joints, caused by fiber separation.

- Reduction Fresenel reflection is possible by reducing the step change in the refractive index at the fiber interface. What material reduces the step change in refractive index at a fiber interface.

Ans. Index matching gel.

- List the three basic errors that occur during fiber alignment.

Ans. Fiber separation (longitudinal misalignment), lateral misalignment, and angular misalignment.

- How does index matching gel affect the amount of coupling loss caused by (a) Fiber separation, (b) Lateral misalignment and (c) Angular misalignment.

Ans. (a) Reduces coupling loss.
(b) Does not change coupling loss.
(c) Increases coupling loss.

- Which are more sensitive to alignment errors, single mode or multimode fiber?

Ans. Single mode

- Quality fiber end preparation is essential for proper system operation. What properties must an optical fiber end face have to ensure proper fiber connection.

Ans. Be flat, smooth and perpendicular to the fiber axis.

- What is the basic fiber cleaving technique for preparing optical fiber for coupling?

Ans. Score and break.

- List six types of fiber mismatches.

Ans. Core diameter mismatch, cladding diameter mismatch, core ellipticity, core and cladding concentricity differences, NA mismatch and refractive index profile differences.

- Define a fiber optic splice.

Ans. A permanent fiber joint whose purpose is to establish an optical connection between two individual optical fibers.

- What are the fiber splicing techniques?

Ans. Mechanical and fusion splicing.

- Describe a transparent adhesive.

Ans. An epoxy resin that seals mechanical splices and provides index matching between the connected fibers.

- What fiber property directly affects splice loss in fusion splicing?

Ans. The angles and quality of the two fiber end faces.

- What connection properties result in fiber optic connector coupling loss?

Ans. Poor fiber alignment and end preparation, fiber mismatches and Fresenel reflection.

- Which is the more critical parameter in maintaining total insertion loss below the required level, fiber alignment or fiber mismatch?

Ans. Fiber alignment.

- Fiber optic connectors can reduce system performance by increasing what two types of noise?

Ans. Modal and reflection noise.

- Which type of fiber optic connector brings the prepared ends of two optical fibers into close contact?

Ans. Butt jointed connectors.

- Is coupling loss from fiber separation and lateral misalignment more critical in expanded beam or butt jointed connectors?

Ans. Butt jointed connectors.

- Is coupling loss from angular misalignment more critical in expanded beam or butt-jointed connectors?

Ans. Butt beam connectors.

- An OTDR measures the fraction of light that is reflected from the fiber or link under test. What causes light to be reflected back into the OTDR?

Ans. Rayleigh scattering and Fresenel reflection.

- What is a temporary or permanent local deviation of the OTDR signal in the upward or downward direction called?

Ans. A point defect.

- What is an analog signal ?
Ans. A continuous signal that varies in a direct propagation to the instantaneous value of the physical variable.
- What type of modulation do most analog fiber optic communications system use ?
Ans. Intensity modulation.
- In NRZ code, does the presence of a high light level in the bit duration represents a binary 1 or a binary 0 ?
Ans. Binary 1.
- How can the loss of timing occur in NRZ line coding ?
Ans. If long strings of 1's and 0's are present causing a lack of level transition.
- How is a binary 1 encoded in RZ line coding ?
Ans. A half period optical pulse present in the first half of the bit duration.
- In manchester encoding, does a low to high light level transition occurring in the middle of the bit duration represent a binary 1 or a binary 0 ?
Ans. Binary 0
- Why is it generally only necessary to refer to point to point data links when discussing the process of fiber optic system design ?
Ans. Because fiber optic systems that incorporate complex architecture can be simplified into a collection of point to point data links before beginning the design process.
- List five system design parameters considered when system designers choose the system operational wavelength and link components.
Ans. Launch power, connection losses, bandwidth, cost and reliability.
- What two analyses are performed to determine if a link design is viable ?
Ans. Power budget and rise time budget.
- Which topology consists of equipments attached to one another in a closed loop ?
Ans. Ring topology.
- Which topology has a center hub interconnecting the equipments ?
Ans. Star topology.
- What are the three parts of a fiber optic transmitter ?
Ans. Interface circuit, source drive circuit and an optical source.
- Which part of a fiber optic transmitter converts the processed electrial signal to an optical signal ?
Ans. Optical source.
- What type of source is typically used in low data rate digital application ?
Ans. LED
- Why would a laser diode be used is a low data digital application ?
Ans. When extremely high transmitter output power and required.
- What type of source is generally used in high data rate digital applications ?
Ans. Laser diode.

Section – II : Microwave Communication

- The main advantage of microwave is that
Ans. Highly directive.
- Waveguide is which type of filter
Ans. High pass filter.
- Which wave does not exist in waveguide.
Ans. TEM waves.
- Which is the dominant mode in rectangular waveguide ?
Ans. TE_{10}.
- Which is the dominant mode in circular waveguide ?
Ans. TM_{11}.
- What is the relation of free space wavelength ?
Ans. Free space wavelength is less than guided wavelength.
- Which waveguide tuning component is not easily adjustable ?
Ans. Iris.
- Large microwave power can be measured by
Ans. Calorimeter wattmeter.
- Magic Tee is how many port network ?
Ans. Four port network.
- A matched load is which type of attenuator ?
Ans. Fixed attenuator.
- Attenuators always consists of
Ans. Only resistors.
- Microwave frequency can be measured with the help of
Ans. frequency meter.
- Scattering parameters can be measured with the help of
Ans. network analyzer.
- An isolator consists of how many ports ?
Ans. Two ports.
- What is a function of Reflex Klystron ?
Ans. Microwave oscillator.
- Which is operating principle of Klystron ?
Ans. Velocity modulation.
- The modes in reflex Klystron gives same frequency but different
Ans. transit time.

- The space between two cavities in a two cavity Klystron is called

Ans. Drift space.

- What is function of Klystron ?

Ans. Klystron can be used as both amplifier and oscillator.

- Frequency of oscillation of a Klystron depends on which factor ?

Ans. Repeller voltage.

- Klystron tube is which type of tube ?

Ans. 'O' type tube i.e. linear beam tube.

- Magnetron is which type of tube.

Ans. 'M' type tube i.e. crossfield tube.

- Magnetron is used as an

Ans. oscillator.

- What is the use of strapping in cavity magnetron ?

Ans. To prevent mode jumping.

- What is the use of magnetic field in cavity magnetron ?

Ans. To ensure that the electron beam will orbit around the cathode.

- (TWT) Travelling Wave Tube is basically used as

Ans. Wideband amplifier.

- What is the use of helix in TWT ?

Ans. To reduce the axial velocity of the R.F. field.

- What is the role of attenuator in a TWT ?

Ans. To prevent oscillations.

- Microwave components can be characterised by which parameters ?

Ans. s-parameters

- What is the use of permanent magnet focusing in TWT ?

Ans. Two avoid the spreading of electron.

- The characteristics impedance of a lossless transmission line is given by,

Ans. $Z = \sqrt{\dfrac{L}{C}}$

- Which microwave tube is used in microwave oven ?

Ans. Magnetron.

- A cavity is which type of filter ?

Ans. Band pass filter.

- What is the major advantage of TWT over a Klystron ?

Ans. Higher bandwidth.

- Name the two cavities used in two cavity Klystron ?

Ans. (1) Buncher cavity, (2) Catcher cavity.

- What is the most powerful solid state microwave device ?

Ans. IMPATT diode.

- Microwave semiconductor devices are basically which type of devices ?

Ans. Negative resistance device.

- GaAs is preferred to Si for use in Gunn diode because it has

Ans. suitable empty energy band which silicon does not have.

- Gunn diode can be operated in how many modes ?

Ans. 3 different modes.

- What is basic use of PIN diode ?

Ans. Use as a microwave switch.

- A microstrip is analogous to a

Ans. parallel wire line.

- A stripline is analogous to

Ans. co-axial line.

- What is the relation between Q of a microstrip resonator and waveguide resonator?

Ans. Q of a microstrip resonator is less than that of a waveguide resonator.

- What is the relation between the phase velocity and frequency in a hollow rectangular waveguide ?

Ans. The phase velocity decreases with increasing frequency.

- Which material is used for manufacturing of Gunn diode.

Ans. Silicon.

- The uplink and downlink frequencies of satellite communication are

Ans. 6 GHz, 6 GHz.

- In two hole directional coupler what is the distance between two holes ?

Ans. $\lambda/4$.

- What are the two applications of circulator ?

Ans. (1) For isolation of input and output.

(2) For isolation of transmitter and receiver.

- What are the advantages of dominant mode transmission ?

Ans. (1) Low loss.

(2) Low distortion transmission.

	let him just orbit on by. Here's our resident Space Bard, Furry Yuri Yankoff ...
YURI:	Buy my book!
HILERIO:	The whole team's here tonight — Yo Yo Gonzago, Bum Bum ("Chicken") Riselsky — I would introduce Yo Yo Kallustian, but he's off in space in a rolling balling ball all his own. The Press is here tonight — with so many lovers and dreamers and floaters around — even Charles Throat might be in the crowd.
HAPPY:	Prove it, Bubble Head!
HILERIO:	Happy Hamberger, the Space Heckler! Go organic, Happy! Eat it raw!

YO YO, BUM BUM, HAPPY, YURI, TWIXIE AND HILERIO FLOAT AROUND, SMOKING AND CHATTING FOR A FEW MINUTES BEFORE ANOTHER SONG CUE:

HILERIO:	And now, time to push a new song on the New World. The kickoff side for our new label — Round World Records. A break-out in Yalta, an uprising on Mars — so take a big hit (put that in your spacepipe and smoke it!), sit back, turn on your ears and listen as Dreamy Perry Slowfax, backed by Nick Danger and the Asphalt Arabs, do his original version of "The Communist Love Song!"

THE COMMUNIST LOVE SONG
WORDS AND MUSIC BY PHIL PROCTOR

The Bell was ringing
It was dark
The park was closing
Still she held onto my arm.
She was a peasant girl
A pleasant girl and yes —
She drove a tractor on a farm.
And as the summer night began

And as the trolleys sparked
That ran on silver tracks in circles
Round and round the park,
She squeezed my hand,
Manhattan hand,
And whispered low
Her five-year plan,
Then — we depart.

CHORUS:

Ah — Moscow memories!
You haunt me still!
Communist memories
Destroy my will!

The park was closed
The gate locked shut,
We walked the streets
The massive, empty streets alone —
And after walking all the night
I left at dawn.
I'd walked her home,
I'd kissed her once —
We said goodbye,
She had no phone.
And later on
So many years have passed
And now I sit on Wall Street
And recall
That in my youngest days
I kissed a Communist —
A red-haired Russian Lass.

CHORUS:

Ah — Moscow memories
You haunt me still!
Sweet Commie memories
Erode my will.

Now the Government has asked me
Please to sign my name to papers
Just to siphon off a little of my stash —
To fight a war, support a whore,
Or close a park or build an ark in space
Or give the President some cash.

| | And I can't do it!
| | I just can't do it!
| | For I remember — remember still

CHORUS: Those Moscow Memories,
Sweet Soviet Melodies,
Those Commie kisses
Destroyed my will!
Sweet whispered wishes —
Those Russian bitches!
Those Commie kisses
Destroyed . . .My . . . Will . . .

A WAVE OF APPLAUSE FOLLOWS YURI'S FINAL HIGH NOTE. HILERIO AND YURI TRADE QUIPS FOR A COUPLE OF MINUTES BEFORE . . .

HILERIO: Now, let's just turn the old Space Bubble over . . .

FROM THE AUDIENCE, SHOUTS OF "IT'S HIS BUBBLE" AND MOANS OF "IT'S MY LUNCH!" WHEN THE SPACE BUBBLE IS DONE SPINNING . . .

HILERIO: . . . and play the Other Side of our new single — a little space poem I wrote myself — done to music by the Asphalt Arabs and those sweet Firebelles! Here's "Affection No. 54."

AFFECTION NUMBER 54
(A Sweet Tomato Named Mary)
Words by David Ossman, Music by Phil Austin

Her gown was embroidered with a moon-faced lake
And when it thundered she wondered
How much she could take of it.
It hardly fit.
Her nanny-mammy dressed herself in gold and
　　yellow
While a solitary fellow
With one cold eye
Watched the marriage of the maiden
That he could not buy.

A sweet tomato named Mary
King Yi is her father
She's in such a hurry
That no one will bother.
She could take a Martian lover
But no one knows her story
No one knows her story.

Her face was reflected in the moon-fed lake
And the thunder
made her wonder
If she could make of it
Make a fake of it.
Her happy-pappy loved the sun all cold and yellow
But the solitary fellow with one gold eye
Married up with Mary
Whom he could not buy.

A soft tomato named Mary
Nothing could further
She's moving away now
And now she's much closer
She could take a Marian lover
But no one knows her story
But no one knows her story . . .

THE SONG COMES TO AN END AND THE SPACE BUBBLE ORBITS AWAY, LEAVING A MUSIC BREAK BY BIG JAY — "SOMETHING ON MY MIND."

WHEN WE RETURN, IT'S TO THE SURREALIST PARTY CONVENTION STAGE, WHERE SPEAKER FUDD IS CALLING OUT THE NAMES OF PAPOON SUPPORTERS . . .

SPEAKER: . . . National Association of Funny Names Clubs of America — National Spider Caucus — League of Wing-ed Voters — The March 8th Laughing Words Woman's Shock Team, American Friends of the Martian Space Party — The Morse Sugar Foundation — Pets for Papoon — Vets for Papoon — The Flies and Lizards New World Voter Registration Rippoff Band — Papillons pour Papoon, Parmesians para Papoon, Pillpoppers For Papoon . . .

AS THE ROLL CALL CONTINUES, WE RETURN TO THE CORRESPONDENTS.

WALTER (PP): As the Surrealist Convention approaches its climax, it does indeed seem as if there will be a landslide for Papoon. Isn't that right, Walter?

WALTER (PA): What? Oh, yes. When the Aphids and Puppydogs Coalition, released from their favorite son, Dr. Spot The Dog Doctor, went for Papoon, our computer gave up and agreed that there can be no doubts about the outcome of this Convention. When the Nomination begins, in just a few minutes, I think it's safe to say, we'll have one heck of a Demonstration.

ERIC (DO): Of course, Walter, where there's News, there's never enough. And I think they're demonstrating that right now on Monster Island. Charles, how bad does it really look now?

CHARLES (PB): Sorry, Walter, I wasn't listening.

ERIC: This is Eric, Charles.

CHARLES: Hello, Eric. How's Walter?

BOTH WALTERS: We're fine.

CHARLES: I wish I could say the same for the President. He's locked himself into a truly historic pose. His Presidency On Earth nearly over, his Residency on Mars nearly begun. He waits alone, strapped into the nose of the mighty rocket, The Spirit of '69.

ERIC: Do you think he'll get away, Charles.

CHARLES: Chances are 50-50 now, Walter. Eric. All of the Monsters have been lulled to sleep with drugs and loud music. Except for the great Glutamoto.

ERIC: The big guy.

CHARLES: Yes, the Old Fellow. What a Monster! But that's another story.

ERIC: Well, what's the story there?

CHARLES: This is no story, this is real. Glutamoto is on the loose, bigger than ever, and film crews have spotted him at the bottom of Lake Adams, near the Winner's Palace, and he is rumored determined to keep the President from getting off.

WALTER (PP): Thank you, Charles. We'll have you in our ear as we go now back to the Convention floor, where George Papoon's name is now being put into nomination . . .

BOB TACKLE (DO): . . . in the days when our Four Fathers were Men, and we foolishly thought that there were more of us than there are of you, they had an uplifting way of looking at the good side of things, without forgetting the bad. As so does the man whose name I'm about to pull out of a balloon and pop into the hat in the center of the ring!

THE SINGERS SING THE FIRST FOUR LINES OF AN OLD HYMN AND THEN HUM THE MELODY AS TACKLE MAKES THE NOMINATION.

SINGERS: Marching, marching to Shibboleth,
With the Eagle and the Sword,
We're Praising Zion 'til her death,
Until we eat our last reward —
The Flaming Ford . . .

TACKLE: You know his platform! Six inches off the ground, so no one falls off! The Guaranteed Annual Year! One Organism — One Vote! One Man — One Channel! Papoon! Papoon For President! There is no one to blame! Papoon for our Chief Resident! You know he's Not Insane!

AS THE AUDIENCE RESPONDS "NOT INSANE!" THE PROGRAM RETURNS TO THE CORRESPONDENTS AND A STATIC-FILLED STAND-UP.

WALTER:	Well, it's all over here but the shouting . . . what? I don't think there's much of a surprise here . . . what? . . . Well, there seems to be some word from Monster Island. Charles?
CHARLES:	. . . here and it seems, Gutamoto . . . 'isen from the lake, eating electricity as he goes . . . 'inal seconds now, before the final countdown. And boy, does he look angry! He's snapping off high tension towers like candy canes! He's really mad this time! His tail is lashing around and destroying what appear from here to be whole miniature villages! This is dangerous! There's a huge banner tied onto one of his tails, and I can read it from here, and Walter, believe it or not, it says "Not Insane!"

A QUICK RETURN TO THE CONVENTION CATCHES THE BEGINNING OF THE FINAL COUNTDOWN. THE AUDIENCE REPEATS EACH NUMBER, AND BETWEEN EACH NUMBER CHARLES REPORTS FROM MONSTER ISLAND.

TACKLE:	Not Insane! Let us launch the Papoon Balloon. Ten! Nine!
CHARLES:	Glutamoto breaks through the toy war machines as though they're toys!
TACKLE:	Eight!
CHARLES:	The scratches on the film don't seem to affect him at all!
TACKLE:	Seven!
CHARLES:	He's reached the Launch Pad itself — and . . . my God!
TACKLE:	Six!
CHARLES:	He's coiling himself around the rocket like a snake!
TACKLE:	Five!

CHARLES:	He is a snake!
TACKLE:	Four!
CHARLES:	They're going to blast off to Mars together, Walter!
TACKLE:	Three!
CHARLES:	The President and Glutamoto!
TACKLE:	Two!
CHARLES:	Locked in an Eternal Space Embrace!
TACKLE:	One! Liftoff!

THE AUDIENCE BREAKS INTO A FRENZIED DEMONSTRATION WHICH CONTINUES UNDER THE CLOSING BILLBOARD.

END OF THE MARTIAN SPACE PARTY

the FIRESIGN SUN DUCK

5 The Shoveler   2 The Smew

PAPOON NOMINATED

Surreal Platform

By Arnie Hovelich

Surrealist Candidate George Papoon, the sole Presidential hopeful who has publicly declared he is "Not Insane," outlined his campaign today for Papoon Cocoon volunteers from Channel City, Mixville and Duckberg.

His Platform, he explained, was re-cycled pine, about six inches off the ground, so no one can fall off and get hurt.

THREE PROMISES

His campaign promises are three in number. "Only three," he said. "I'm keeping the number of promises down, so I can keep them."

Papoon's Political Poop-Sheet reveals the following planks: <u>One Organism</u> - <u>One Vote</u>. (Voting not re-

(Cont. on p. 2)

'Prez' seen

Bomba City Observatory, P.I. (APE)

Janitors and other scientists reported the first sightings of The Presidents Martian-bound rocket, "The Spirit of '69," over this normally terrorized miniature village last night.

Owing to conditions of darkness,

(Cont. on p. 2)

Not Insane!?

By Hughie Gumbeaner

The 1st Grassroots Convention of The Nat'l Surrealist Light Peoples Party, held March 30, 1972 in the last resort city of San Clamaròn, unanimously nominated George Papoon their candidate for The Presidency.

Mr. Papoon did not appear at the Convention because, as Speaker Fudd quoted him, "That would be insane."

Papoon's name was put into nomination by the Rev. Bob Tackle of the Karate Bull Chapel in Freeway, Calif. It was seconded by General Blame, lately of the Veteran's Tap-Dance Administration.

CELEBS COME

Entertainment for the colorful event was provided by the noted Philipine character-actor, Mayor Sir Charles Gangabangalang, The Fire's-Sign Theater Group, and the casting of UTV's "Young Guy Motor Detective Show," including Hideo Gump, Harry Ames, Hideo Gump, Sr., and "Miki."

Providing music were such combos as Nick Danger with "The Asphalt Arabs," The Firebelles, and The New Dixie Space Choraleers. Celebrity hosts were raconteur Hilerio Spacepipe, poet Yuri Yankoff and "Mr. Monster" himself, Rocky Rocomoto.

(Cont. on p. 2)

FIRESIGN THEATRE IS A PLEASURE MACHINE

From an Interview with Proctor & Bergman by Gary McKeehan

PHIL PROCTOR: The Firesign Theatre has been called psychedelic in its effect on people because lots of people have heard our records under the influence of drugs. This is true. Many people have been conditioned to a response to our records by certain drugs. We create a psychedelic effect on the listener, and in that regard we tend to subjugate the true listener, the true participant in our records, to a kind of secondary position because he or she is forced to sit back and allow this flow of material to enter the mind through the years and through the stimulation.

PETER BERGMAN: Words — I can talk about words for hours. For example: I have often wondered why when you pun the audience goes awwww, or ssssss. I have figured it out. One of the bases for social security, I mean the security of social life, not Social Security itself, is that things are supposed to mean the same thing. A red light is supposed to mean stop at the first corner and the second corner. If you make a pun you are destroying security of the language and people are actually hurt, aww, sss, you're a villain. You are wielding a much stronger weapon than dealing in the various other forms of humor, and I've always loved to pun because it is like rhyming. Punning and rhyming are hallucinatory, when you figure that there are vibrations that form rhymes, and it gets you off. Lines pull toward the rhyme. They draw you like the moon draws water to that rhyme — when it comes, you release. Two things release you involuntarily if you can get free — orgasm and laughter. Both start with a perceived sensation, in other words orgasm with feeling, physical sensation, laughter with something you perceive, see or hear or mediated. But once you have mediated it goes into an involuntary convulsion which releases you. It is pleasurable. So the Firesign Theatre is a pleasure machine. Just like orgasm.

Peter Bergman 1939–2012